# Controlling
# CRIME

# Crime, Order and Social Control Course Team

**The Open University**

| | |
|---|---|
| Ann Boomer | *Discipline Secretary* |
| David Calderwood | *Project Control* |
| Hilary Canneaux | *Course Manager* |
| John Clarke | *Senior Lecturer in Social Policy* |
| Jonathan Davies | *Graphic Design Co-ordinator* |
| Margaret Dickens | *Print Buying Co-ordinator* |
| Nigel Draper | *Editor, Social Sciences* |
| Clive Emsley | *Professor of History, Arts* |
| Janis Gilbert | *Graphic Artist* |
| Peggotty Graham | *Sub-Dean (Courses and Teaching), Social Sciences* |
| Fiona Harris | *Editor, Social Sciences* |
| Frank Heathcote | *Staff Tutor, Social Sciences* |
| Jonathan Hunt | *Book Trade Department* |
| Sue Lacey | *Course Secretary* |
| Mary Langan | *Lecturer in Social Policy* |
| Patti Langton | *Producer, BBC/OUPC* |
| Eugene McLaughlin | *Senior Lecturer in Criminology and Social Policy* |
| John Muncie | *Senior Lecturer in Criminology and Social Policy (Course Team Chair)* |
| Lesley Passey | *Graphic Designer* |
| Doreen Pendlebury | *Secretary* |
| Lynda Preston | *Secretary* |
| Roger Sapsford | *Senior Lecturer in Research Methods* |
| Esther Saraga | *Staff Tutor, Social Sciences* |
| Richard Skellington | *Project Officer, Social Sciences* |
| Gill Smith | *Editor, Social Sciences* |
| Paul Smith | *Social Sciences Liaison Librarian* |
| Alison Tucker | *Producer, BBC/OUPC* |
| Liz Yeomans | *Freelance Graphic Designer* |

**Consultant Authors**

| | |
|---|---|
| Tom Burden | *Policy Research Unit, Leeds Metropolitan University* |
| Loraine Gelsthorpe | *Lecturer in Criminology, University of Cambridge* |
| Paul Gordon | *Academic Consultant, London* |
| Gordon Hughes | *Principal Lecturer in Sociology, Nene College, Northampton* |
| Victor Jupp | *Head of Sociology, University of Northumbria* |
| John Pitts | *Professor of Socio-Legal Studies, University of Luton* |
| Jim Sharpe | *Senior Lecturer in History, University of York* |
| Richard Sparks | *Professor of Criminology, University of Keele* |
| Sandra Walklate | *Reader in Criminology, University of Keele* |

**External Assessors**

| | |
|---|---|
| Pat Carlen | *Professor of Criminology, University of Keele (Course Assessor)* |
| Victor Jupp | *Head of Sociology, University of Northumbria* |

**Tutor Panel**

| | |
|---|---|
| Tom Burden | *Policy Research Unit, Leeds Metropolitan University* |
| Hilary Hiram | *School of Law, University of Glasgow* |
| Marilyn Woolfson | *Open University Tutor and Tutor Counsellor, London* |

# Controlling
# *CRIME*

*Edited by*

# Eugene McLaughlin
# and John Muncie

**SAGE Publications**
London • Thousand Oaks • New Delhi

in association with

The Open
University

This book is the second in a series published by Sage Publications in association with The Open University.

*The Problem of Crime*
edited by John Muncie and Eugene McLaughlin

*Controlling Crime*
edited by Eugene McLaughlin and John Muncie

*Criminological Perspectives: A Reader*
edited by John Muncie, Eugene McLaughlin and Mary Langan

The books are part of The Open University course D315 *Crime, Order and Social Control.*
Details of this and other Open University courses can be obtained from the Central Enquiry Service,
PO Box 200, The Open University, Milton Keynes MK7 6YZ. For availability of other course components,
including video- and audio-cassette materials, contact Open University Educational Enterprises Ltd,
12 Cofferidge Close, Stony Stratford, Milton Keynes MK11 1BY.

The Open University, Walton Hall, Milton Keynes MK7 6AA

The opinions expressed are not necessarily those of the Course Team or of The Open University.

SAGE Publications Ltd
6 Bonhill Street
London EC2A 4PU

SAGE Publications Inc
2455 Teller Road
Thousand Oaks
California 91320

SAGE Publications India Pvt Ltd
32, M-Block Market
Greater Kailash - I
New Delhi 110 048

**British Library Cataloguing in Publication data**

A catalogue record for this book is available from The British Library

ISBN 0 7619 5000-1
ISBN 0 7619 5001-X (pbk)

**Library of Congress catalog card number 95-071322**

Edited, designed and typeset by The Open University

Printed in Great Britain by Butler & Tanner Ltd, Frome and London

# Contents

# Preface

*Controlling Crime* is the second of three volumes in a new series of introductory criminology texts published by Sage in association with The Open University. The series, entitled *Crime, Order and Social Control*, explores key issues in the study of crime and criminal justice systems by examining the *diverse* nature of crime, the *varied* formal and informal means designed to effect its control, and the *multiplicity* of approaches and interpretations that criminologists have brought to bear on this study. Each volume, however, is free-standing and introduces readers to different aspects of the complex body of knowledge that makes up contemporary criminology. By emphasizing diversity – both in the nature of criminological knowledge and in its object of study – the series engages with taken-for-granted notions of the meaning, extent and causes of crime and of the role and function of criminal justice. Above all, we maintain that the study of crime cannot be divorced from the study of social order. Definitions of crime, and the ways in which it is understood and responded to, are not universal and unchanging. Crucially, the recognition of, and reaction to, crime are contingent on social, political and economic circumstances.

The main aim of these volumes is to chart and redraw the parameters of a contemporary criminological imagination. They provide an interdisciplinary overview of 'classic' and current scholarly work in crime, criminal justice and criminology by drawing on the approaches and modes of analysis found in such subjects as sociology, psychology, socio-legal studies, gender studies, social geography and political science. This again alerts us to the potentially disparate and diverse nature of our subject matter.

The three volumes are core components of an Open University course with the same title as that of the series. The first volume, *The Problem of Crime*, focuses on the shifting ways in which crime is defined. This volume, *Controlling Crime*, examines the changing and expanding parameters of criminal justice. The third, *Criminological Perspectives: A Reader*, explores the contested knowledges of criminology itself. Each is distinctive, not only in its chosen subject matter, but also because, unlike a majority of edited collections, it is primarily intended as a resource to aid teaching and student understanding.

To this end, this volume has been designed as an interactive teaching text. The chapters should be read sequentially, as each builds on those that have gone before, and each concludes with suggestions for further and more in-depth reading. The following features have also been built into the overall structure of the book:

- activities: these are exercises in which students are encouraged to take an active part whilst working through the text, in order to test understanding and develop critical thinking;

- comments: these provide feedback on activities and an opportunity for students to check their own responses;

- shorter questions: these are designed to encourage the reader to pause and reflect back on what has just been read;

- key concepts: concepts that are core to each chapter and central to the study of criminology are highlighted in the margins.

In addition, the majority of chapters include a number of short readings – newspaper articles, or extracts from academic books and articles – which are integral to the discussion as it develops and are designed both to encourage self-reflection and to aid in the application of central ideas and concepts to contemporary social developments and political ideologies. While each volume in the series is self-contained, there are also a number of references back and forward to the other volumes, and for those readers who wish to use the books for an integrated exploration of issues in crime, criminal justice and criminology, the references to chapters in the other volumes are printed in bold type. The aim of all these features is to help readers more readily to understand and examine critically the principal arguments not only of each chapter, but of each book and the series as a whole.

The production of this volume – and the series – has been made possible not simply through the work of its editors and chapter authors but through the collective endeavours of an entire Open University Course Team. Each chapter has gone through three drafts whereby content and teaching strategy have been modified and refined. In this respect, we are indebted to our consultants, tutor-testers and assessors who have given invaluable advice; a course manager who, against all odds, has ensured that all our efforts have been co-ordinated and that deadlines have been met; a course secretary who has suffered more than most from being asked to do the impossible; and a supportive team of production editors, designers, graphic artist and media librarian who have made sure the final product looks as good as it does. We thank them all.

*John Muncie*
*(on behalf of The Open University Course Team)*

# Introduction

No area of public policy is in such dire need of reform as crime ... Crime is the Passchendaele of Whitehall. The more money wasted on fighting it, the more is demanded by the generals for 'just one more push'.

(Simon Jenkins, *The Sunday Times*, 11 February 1989)

*I*n the UK in the period immediately following the Second World War, concerted efforts were made to remove the highly emotive question of what to do about crime from the formal political arena. In the wake of this depoliticization it was left to a group of professional experts to formulate what might be described as the social democratic welfarist 'canon' of effective crime control. This perspective proclaimed that the state should concentrate on tackling the societal 'fountain heads' and 'root drivers' of crime, most notably poverty, unemployment, poor housing, educational disadvantage and dysfunctional family and community formations. Diversion, decriminalization, welfare, treatment and rehabilitation, rather than criminalization, imprisonment and punishment, would be the 'domain assumptions' guiding the criminal justice system. This would apply particularly to juvenile offenders who were viewed, by and large, as victims of circumstances beyond their control. Despite the fact that the various agencies were encased in a 'spatchcock' of Victorian bureaucratic structures (see Chapters 1 and 4), radical *systemic* reform was ruled out. Rather, they would undergo a process of pragmatic, gradual and incremental modernization, rationalization and professionalization for three reasons. First, it was still believed that the British criminal justice system was the fairest in the world. Second, radical structural reform could upset all notions of operational autonomy and political impartiality. And, finally, the criminal justice agencies would have a limited role to play as the UK made the transition towards a projected 'golden age' of civic order, stability and pro-social behaviour.

With the unfolding of the 1970s – the 'decade of discontent' – the social democratic vision of a crime-free society turned into a quagmire of watered-down policies, uneasy compromises, professional disagreements, organizational rivalries, unintended consequences, trenchant critiques and disappointing outcomes. Radical criminology questioned the 'foundational truths' of the social democratic model by arguing that state interventions constituted more of a problem than a solution to the question of crime. Those promising effective crime control were raising false societal hopes and expectations that could never be fulfilled. First, the market for formal crime control is significantly determined by public reporting and police investigative and recording practices. These practices, in no small measure, *construct* and *maintain* the parameters of 'crime'. To the extent that such identification of crime is *partial* and highly *selective*, formal crime control reproduces the fiction that it is in the business of controlling all crime. Self-evidently, the energies and resources of the state's 'control system' constitute a narrowly focused spotlight on particular types of offence and offender. Furthermore, state interventions inevitably (if unintentionally) label and stigmatize, setting in process further deviance and criminality which justifies, in turn, the expansion of the boundaries and capacities of a multi-layered 'social control' apparatus.

During the 1970s 'crime', in a variety of guises, was repoliticized and increasingly came to occupy a central place in public consciousness and political discourse. For example, the recorded crime rate in England and Wales, driven by young offenders, increased from just over 790,000 in 1960 to 1.6 million in 1971. There was serious public disorder in the form of repeated clashes between the extra parliamentary right and left and the anarchistic actions of a confrontational counter-culture. 'Union barons' openly defied court rulings and caused turmoil by mounting unofficial wildcat strikes. Every major city developed racially torn 'wastelands' which it was argued were beyond the rule of law. The IRA's bombing campaign introduced new unpredictable risks to public safety. All of this fed into broader fears and concerns about a society whose citizenry was being repeatedly victimized by vandalism, incivilities, indiscipline, rowdiness and extremism. Public commentary began to link these disparate issues and to present a picture of a brutalized, forbidding society teetering on the verge of collapse with the state seemingly paralysed, incapable or unwilling to reimpose law and order and protect the rights and freedoms of law-abiding individuals.

The run-up to the 1979 general election witnessed the construction of an 'authoritarian populist' 'New Right' discourse which rested on cherished memories of a safer, more orderly society and a hard-hitting analysis on how to wrest society back from the criminals, terrorists, strikers, muggers and hooligans. The root causes of crime and disorder were located firmly with the criminal 'other' who had been aided and abetted by the 'sugar spin' storylines of the so-called experts and professionals. These 'social engineers' were blamed for promulgating irresponsible policies which had (a) not only denied but sought to erase all notions of human wickedness, right and wrong, self-discipline, personal responsibility and shame; and (b) undermined the core institutional arrangements and cultural precepts that were the essential sources of social order, discipline and shared moral meaning. The Conservative Party made crime control an ideological battle ground by promising that if elected they would, as a matter of priority:

- Restore the 'rule of law' to its rightful position in British society.

- Recentre individual free-will, guilt, just deserts, deterrence and punishment.

- Rebalance the interests and needs of victims of crime against the rights of offenders.

- Replace the welfarist 'culture of excuses', which positively encouraged criminality and violence, with a common-sense moral code which would condemn law-breaking plainly, consistently and without exception.

- Roll back the morass of moral relativism and re-establish the morally absolute boundary between right and wrong.

- Free the criminal justice agencies from the disempowering influences of welfare professionals and ideologies and provide them with the powers, resources and state patronage necessary to unleash a war against crime.

There is no doubt that the Conservatives' election pledge of 1979 was honoured in full. The New Right ideology that elsewhere stipulated that state intervention in the public sphere (for example, in housing, health and welfare) was misguided, because it acted to deny self-responsibility and violated individual rights, remained absent initially from *public* debates about criminal justice. There is considerable evidence to give substance to the claim that law and order was the hallowed no-go area for public expenditure cuts. In the first half of the 1980s total funding on the police increased by almost 40 per cent. An extra 14,000 personnel were recruited by police forces and individual officers were awarded pay rises of approximately 16 per cent in real terms. In the same time period there was an 85 per cent increase in prison expenditure; prison building was earmarked as a government growth area with the commitment to build 16 new penal institutions at a cost of £360 million.

Unprecedented systemic empowerment was also forthcoming under Conservative patronage. The police were equipped with contentious powers under the Police and Criminal Evidence Act 1984 and the Public Order Act 1986 (see Chapter 2). Magisterial powers, in determining type and length of custodial sentence (particularly for juveniles), were increased by the Criminal Justice Acts of 1982 and 1988 (see Chapters 3 and 6). The courts were encouraged to hand out longer sentences and the adult prison population in England and Wales first peaked at 50,000 in 1988: thus ensuring the highest rate of imprisonment per capita in Europe (see Chapter 5). It was because of such developments, and the promise that the strong state would erect a 'barrier of steel' to protect the honest citizen from the nefarious enemies within, that the 1980s have been characterized by radical and liberal criminologists as a period of increasing authoritarianism, coercion, repression and criminalization.

Despite the emphasis on law and order and the vigorous crusade to cut crime, it is difficult to regard the outcome of such hardline policies as a success. The rhetoric and policies of 'discipline and punishment' seemed to do little to halt a 'rising tide' of criminality and lawlessness. The recorded crime rate escalated to an unprecedented level during the 1980s, whilst the police clear-up rate fell from over 41 per cent to below 30 per cent. The inability of criminal justice policy to reduce the crime rate was also highlighted by failures in the 'deterrent' value of a punitive prison system. Despite tougher sentences – epitomized by the 'short, sharp shock' – just under a half of adult prisoners and two-thirds of young prisoners were reconvicted within two years of release (see Chapter 6). The first years of Conservative rule also witnessed nationwide inner-city riots and clashes between the police and trade unionists in various industrial disputes.

British society became painfully aware of the economic costs of crime. Legitimate businesses complained about the impact of a flourishing illegal economy in stolen goods. Hospitals, general practitioners and employers protested about the costs of supporting victims of crime. Local authorities had to divert scarce resources to combating vandalism on public housing estates. House and car owners were confronted with spiralling insurance premiums to cover escalating theft and burglary. Fear of crime and communal insecurity became just as important a public reality as crime itself.

There was a corresponding 'loss of faith' in the fairness and impartiality of the criminal justice system, particularly in the aftermath of the Guildford Four, Maguire Seven, Birmingham Six, Tottenham Three and Cardiff Three acquittals. Surveys reported that such cases had caused the public to lose confidence in the police and to believe that the judiciary was unrepresentative and out of touch with society and that it discriminated against defendants from minority ethnic backgrounds. At a more everyday level, concern was also expressed about the lack of sentencing consistency in the courts, with reports pointing out that the chance of immediate imprisonment depended not so much on the offence, but on the ethnic background and gender of the defendant and on where in the country the case was heard. By the beginning of the 1990s, with the appointment of a Royal Commission, it was the criminal justice system itself that was on trial (see Chapter 3).

The political reverberations of this 'failure to deliver' and downward spiral of falling support for the criminal justice system, compelled the government to rethink both its law and order policies and the uncritical public support it had traditionally given to the criminal justice system. As a result, a strategy was unveiled which attempted to redefine the *ownership* of the crime problem and promote managerialist solutions.

Part of the response to the failure of a tough law and order stance was a gradual withdrawal from wider philosophical and macro-level debates about the causes of crime and the purpose of criminal justice policies. Home Office officials informed the public at every opportunity that extreme caution was needed in 'reading' crime statistics because, despite media representations, most crime is petty in nature and the UK remains a relatively crime-free society. In addition, a certain level of crime was viewed as normal and inevitable and that it was therefore unrealistic to expect any set of policies to reduce the crime rate drastically. What governments could do, according to this new 'normalization of crime' orthodoxy, was to work with the community in order to lessen the opportunistic crime rate, and the fear of crime, to manageable and acceptable levels. As a consequence, the message was that the public and other social agencies would have to 'join up' in the war against preventable crime.

The public was told that it must recognize that the sources of crime and its control lie, first and foremost, in the actions of individual citizens and local communities. Shared responsibility and individual self-discipline and self-help were stressed through the 'target hardening' and fortification of homes and businesses and in the presumed greater security offered by membership of Neighbourhood Watch. With the coming of age of community safety, police community liaison and community punishment, responsibility for crime control was relocated to the realm of private citizenship. Primary blame was attached to 'careless' victims, especially repeat victims, who were lax in their efforts to prevent crime (whether it was a failure to protect their property adequately, or in learning to avoid dangerous situations) and to an anti-social 'underclass' who were failing to meet their moral obligations as parents and citizens. There was also the suggestion that the fight against the criminal 'other' could be the basis for the creation and maintenance of local social solidarity.

By the late 1980s private self-help efforts were also supplemented and augmented by inter-agency approaches to crime and prevention. The Home Office redoubled its efforts to devolve and disperse frontline obligation for the management of crime to other social agencies. Safer Cities and Crime Concern projects had as their common aim, for example, the creation of partnerships between local authorities, local businesses, voluntary organizations and statutory agencies, which would restructure institutional knowledge in order to identify patterns and trends and prepare effective policies and localized micro-level strategies to design out crime and reduce the fear of some crime (see Chapter 7). These shifts in rhetoric and practice reveal both a diminution of state responsibility for crime control matters and the attempted removal of questions of crime, criminality and punishment from the political and moral arena.

Given the nature of this strategy, it looked initially as if the criminal justice agencies would remain immune from public demands that they be held to account for their self-evident failures in preventing or controlling crime. However, by the late 1980s the seeming incapability or unwillingness of the various agencies to respond to increasing criticism and to put their own houses in order persuaded the Conservatives to open up the criminal justice system to the investigations of the Public Accounts Committee, the National Audit Office and the Audit Commission. As a consequence, law and order is no longer exempt from the processes of fiscal accountability, performance measurements and strict controls on expenditure (see Chapters 2, 3, 5 and 6).

A series of managerial, actuarial and legislative reviews and directives in the late 1980s and during the 1990s have signalled the government's commitment to this approach. By the mid 1990s numerous Audit Commission reports had been made on various aspects of police structure and practice, the probation service, the magistrates' courts, the Crown Prosecution Service, Legal Aid schemes and the Prison Service. The recommendations emanating from these sector-by-sector reviews have acted as a stimulus for further inquiries because they have uncovered the need for ever deeper change to resolve problems of chronic under-management. Reform and reinvention were to be achieved within an overall framework of *continuous* organizational and operational restructuring, fiscal accountability and rationalization. The different agencies have gradually come to justify their existence and re-imagine themselves in terms of quasi-market competitiveness, core competencies, rigorous resource control, customer responsiveness, quality of service and certifiable cost-effectiveness. As a consequence, certain activities and tasks have become centralized while others have been devolved. Since the requirement for market testing and innovation is ever present, some activities have been contracted out, 'disaggregated' or privatized (see Chapters 2 and 5). Such changes have had considerable implications for working practices and, perhaps more significantly, the conditions of service of the workforce, in core criminal justice agencies, because they necessitated the displacement of the old quasi-military models of public administration on which the criminal justice system was founded (see Chapters 1 and 4). Instead, 'transparent' management systems have been put in place internally and strenuous efforts made to *managerialize* the different agencies involved. This transformatory process has involved introducing new conceptions and strategies of control and disciplining of the workforce and new managerial ideas about how to produce and manage organizational and cultural change.

The overall purpose of this ongoing sea change in policy is to create a cost-effective, efficient and dove-tailed criminal justice system where strategic and operational roles, responsibilities and accountabilities are clarified and which will be suitably motivated to work with the community to manage the crime rate and reduce the fear of crime to acceptable levels. Within this overarching 'task environment' the professional remit of the agencies is to work together within nationally agreed sets of guidelines and standards to deliver a specific product – 'justice' – for their customers, whilst also ensuring that demands for the product are kept within economically manageable levels. Hence, the police, the Crown Prosecution Service and the courts have the role of ensuring the detection and conviction of the guilty by meeting strict procedural rules of evidence (see Chapters 2 and 3); the private and public Prison Service should treat prisoners with humanity and decency (see

Chapter 5); and the probation service and youth justice workers should deliver cheaper but tough and effective sentences in the community (see Chapters 3 and 6). Managerialism has been identified as the 'tailored, depoliticized pathway' to 'economy and justice'.

Taken collectively, these policy responses herald a series of potentially the most radical organizational reforms of the criminal justice system that have been witnessed since the early nineteenth century (see Chapters 1 and 4). It is increasingly apparent that sections of the New Right have a vision of a mixed economy of criminal justice which necessitates a hollowed-out state absolving itself of its traditional (many would argue, core) role. Ideally, it would become the purchaser of a multitude of law and order services and the provider of few. But the government's chosen pathway to reform has also resulted in a complex unravelling which has generated as many contradictions, tensions and dilemmas as it has resolved. The manner in which change has been implemented provoked considerable institutional opposition as criminal justice professionals and occupational groups (like their counterparts in the health service and education system) found their professional expertise and judgement excluded from the reform process. They and their 'special pleading' were seen as part of the problem rather than as part of the solution. The government faced particular difficulty in challenging and attempting to curb the discretion and autonomy of those professional groups that were empowered throughout this century and particularly during the 1980s.

The managerial reform process has also turned out to be extremely vulnerable because law and order remains a highly emotive political issue and potential vote winner. Survey after survey indicates that significant sections of the population believe that not enough is being done to crack this pressing problem. The media's saturation coverage of crime and victimization, and periodic storms of protest about criminals who have 'cheated' justice, continue to stoke public fears and demands for a more vigorous response. And politicians of all persuasions have moved sharply to prove to an insecure electorate that they are not soft on crime. Promises have been made to control crime by building more penal establishments, introducing stricter prison regimes, facilitating tougher sentencing, putting more bobbies on the beat, creating new national police agencies, extending 'hi-tech' surveillance systems and clamping down on the rights of suspects. Such promises have indeed raised public expectations, though are likely to create new stresses, fractures and potential crises for the criminal justice agencies as they are asked to do more but with closely scrutinized budgets. Broken or unfulfilled promises can only be expected to generate a further loss of faith in the formal criminal justice process and a loss of confidence in the capacities of the state. Just as significantly, as many of the chapters in this book suggest, such promises exclude the possibility of inaugurating a democratic, inclusive open debate that is necessary to examine honestly the 'quick fix' assumptions, myths and dogmas of the 'crime control' model. Moreover, any hastily conceived reform which is driven more by political expediency than by rational policy-making will tend to deny any constructive and imaginative discussion of how the state should redirect the £10 billion a year that it currently spends in order to find more 'locally appropriate' means of delivering criminal justice.

*Eugene McLaughlin and John Muncie*
*December 1995*

# Chapter 1
# The Origins and Development of the Police

*by Clive Emsley*

## Contents

# 1 Introduction

This chapter has straightforward aims. After working through it you should be able to make your own informed assessment of: first, the reasons behind the creation of police forces in Britain, particularly England and Wales; second, the role of these forces once created and the shifting patterns of local and central control; and third, the extent to which police development in Britain has been unique. You should note at the beginning of this discussion that using the generic term 'the police' can sometimes obscure the fact that there has never been a single police force in England, let alone Britain as a whole.

# 2 The origins of the police

## 2.1 Contrasting interpretations

There is no single school of police history; the divisions between the different interpretations of the origins and development of the police in Britain tend to reflect the way in which different individuals and competing theoretical positions regard the police and their role in society. The modern, bureaucratic police had their origins in political debates and discussions, which inevitably ended in some compromises. The police developed partly as a result of legislation, as well as through administrative decisions and the emergence of working practices and strategic policies. Many of the contemporary debates about police accountability and policework that you will encounter in Chapter 2 have their origins in these earlier compromises and decisions.

### ACTIVITY 1.1

Extract 1.1 shows how one of the earliest and most influential historians of the police in Britain accounts for their origins in terms of progress and advancement at the beginning of the nineteenth century. Extract 1.2, by contrast, adopts an alternative theoretical position that is more concerned with control and disciplinary aspects of the police role.

Read the two extracts now. As you do so, make notes on how Reith's interpretation of the origins of the police in Extract 1.1 differs from that of Storch in Extract 1.2.

## Extract 1.1 Reith: 'The police idea'

... authority [was] faced at the [beginning of the nineteenth century] with the menace of increase of crime, part of the problem of which, in London alone, was the army of the homeless children, estimated at eight thousand, who lived by stealing and begging. Worse still was the constant menace of mob disorder, and the knowledge that the 'thin red line' of the Guards was all that stood, from day to day, between order and chaos, and that the dangers of using it as a defence made it unable to save the dignity of Parliament and its members from one humiliation after another, whenever the mobs of the town found occasion to assemble in its neighbourhood. The reports [of parliamentary committees] confirmed emphatically and unhelpfully, the corruption, disunity, and utter uselessness of the rabble of beadles, watchmen, deputy-constables, and undisciplined police officers whose function was the maintenance of order, and rejected with strong and forceful language the controlled organization which was the obvious and only remedy. ...

Meanwhile, the state of affairs in London, serious as it was, had become only an item of the problem of crime and disorder which menaced authority from every part of the kingdom. The new town concentrations of population had become Londons of lesser size, with the same poverty and destitution, the same potential explosive properties, and the same deficiencies of power for the maintenance of order and the preservation of life and property. Both in towns and in the country-side the centuries-old organization of independent magistrate and parish constable was under pressure of the new phenomenon of vast mobs of desperate and starving men and women, springing up now here, now there, whenever a sudden jolt in the creaking and badly oiled new machinery of the Industrial Revolution deprived them of mass livelihood and drove them to mass despair.

(Reith, 1938, pp.188–9)

## Extract 1.2 Storch: 'The policeman as domestic missionary'

Historians of the police, public order, and the criminal law have understandably concentrated on the role of the police in the repression of crime, public disorder, and popular political movements or have studied the police from the point of view of social administration. The police had a broader mission in the nineteenth century, however – to act as an all-purpose lever of urban discipline. The imposition of the police brought the arm of municipal and state authority directly to bear upon key institutions of daily life in working-class neighbourhoods, touching off a running battle with local custom and popular culture which lasted at least until the end of the century. Riots and strikes are by definition ephemeral episodes, but the monitoring and control of the streets, pubs, racecourses, wakes, and popular fêtes was a daily function of the 'new police'. It was in some part on this terrain that the quality of police–community relations in the second half of the nineteenth century was determined. In northern industrial towns of England these police functions must be viewed as a direct complement to the attempts of urban middle-class elites – by means of sabbath, educational, temperance, and recreational reform – to mould a labouring class amenable to new disciplines of work and leisure. The other side of the coin of middle-class voluntaristic moral and social reform (even when sheathed) was the policeman's truncheon. In this respect the policeman was perhaps every bit as important a 'domestic missionary' as the earnest and often sympathetic men high-minded Unitarians dispatched into darkest Leeds or Manchester in the 1830s and 1840s.

(Storch, 1976, p.481)

# COMMENT

Reith was arguing the need for the establishment of an organized police force (namely the Metropolitan Police), though we might be tempted to suggest that 'mobs of desperate starving men and women' needed something rather different, and that menaces to 'authority' and threats to the 'dignity of Parliament' were less important than social problems such as poverty, destitution and unemployment. Reith's view of the origins of the police in Britain, though not that of a professional, academic historian, was in keeping with the **Whig historiography** of the period in which he was writing. Essentially this saw history as progressive, and for the Whig historians (and essentially this was a British school) the liberal British state and its institutions were at the forefront of progress. History was also largely concerned with 'great men'; in British history this meant those who were liberal, humanitarian, and farsighted enough to see how to develop progressive and necessary institutions. The nineteenth century was a particularly notable time for such men in the criminal justice system; they reformed the 'Bloody Code' of the eighteenth century, reformed the prisons, and established the police. Sir Robert Peel, the Tory Home Secretary for much of the 1820s and later prime minister, stood out among these 'great men' for his legal reforms and his creation of the Metropolitan Police in 1829.

*(margin note)* Whig historiography

There is no mention by Storch of any menace to authority or the dignity of parliament; the emphasis is on the need to control the new urban population – Reith's 'desperate and starving men and women' perhaps. While Reith sees the problem as one of crime and disorder, Storch describes the police as an institution established as another element in a broad strategy of 'control'.

Storch was the first of a generation of academic social historians to address the origins of the police and to develop a **revisionist** view. It might be argued against him that the parliamentary debates on policing in the first half of the century generally focused on the issues of public disorder and, above all, on the perception of increasing crime. Moreover, elites in several of the biggest industrial cities were, initially at least, strongly opposed to any suggestion from Westminster that they reorganize their policing systems along Metropolitan lines. Storch shows that the police played the role of 'domestic missionary' once they were on the streets, but it is not clear that this was a key reason for them being put on the streets in the first place.

*(margin note)* revisionism

Before the establishment of the police, policing depended on active magistrates, parish constables and night watchmen. These received a bad press from many nineteenth-century police reformers, and Reith, you will note from the paragraphs quoted above, accepted this criticism. Nor was Reith alone in this; for many years it was common for historians of the police to quote extracts from Shakespeare's comic constables – Dogberry and Verges in *Much Ado About Nothing* and Elbow in *Measure for Measure* – to imply, first, that Shakespeare was telling it how it was (rather than creating comic characters for dramatic effect) and, second, that nothing much changed, and rarely for the better, between 1600 and 1800. There were feeble magistrates, watchmen and constables in the seventeenth and eighteenth centuries, but there were also significant developments that took place over a longer time-scale than the old Whig school would have had us believe.

*Charles Rowe, a London watchman. Note the lantern, staff, cutlass and the rattle tucked into his cutlass strap. While Rowe is rather old in this picture, it must have been photographed some time after his retirement and the end of the watchmen in London – there were no photographs in 1829. Contrary to the declarations of the police reformers and Whig historians, some eighteenth- and early nineteenth-century vestries and parishes ensured that their watchmen were young and fit*

At the centre of these developments was London. It was a thriving capital and commercial city regarded with great pride, but also with increasing fear. Much of this fear was the result of London's size. This almost doubled during the eighteenth century, by the end of which it had a million inhabitants. This was almost a tenth of the English population and made London roughly twice as big as Paris, the capital of a country with almost 30 million people. There were teeming slums within London's sprawl, and it was these that provoked fears of crime and disorder. No crime statistics were collected for Britain as a whole or for London in particular before 1810, but there was a belief that crime was increasing and that the inhabitants of the poorer districts preferred idleness, with occasional expeditions for plunder to fulfil their desire for luxury, rather than an honest, frugal existence based on the proceeds of hard work.

In the middle of the eighteenth century Henry Fielding, the Bow Street magistrate perhaps better known as a novelist, differentiated between those who could not work and those who would not. At the end of the century Patrick Colquhoun, an active stipendiary magistrate lauded by the Whig historians of the police, fulminated against the 'extravagance, idleness and profligacy' of the poor, which they supported by 'gambling, cheating and thieving' (quoted in Emsley, 1987, p.53). Coincidental with the fear of crime, there seems to have been an increasing belief that a new level of order and decorum needed to be established. Such a belief was linked with the emergent political economy espoused by a significant section of the ruling elite, which refused any sympathy for the old moral economy of the crowd. Popular disorder in the shape of a demonstration over the high cost of food was no longer seen as community political action, with the crowd drawing their social superiors' attention to their plight and the elite responding with subscriptions to reduce prices and the prosecution of hoarders and profiteers. Political economy demanded that the market be allowed to work freely, and that disorder be suppressed and not be understood and met half way: this meant that community action, while not legal before, was increasingly stigmatized as criminal (see **Sharpe, 1996**). The week-long mayhem of the Gordon Riots in London in 1780 was exceptional, but it burned itself into the memory of the respectable classes of what crowd action could become, and this memory was aggravated in the decade following 1789 both by the lurid accounts of massacres in Paris during the French Revolution and the appearance of British Jacobins urging reform on the French model.

Legislation in the early eighteenth century allowed parishes to reorganize their night watch. Some took the opportunity to ensure that their watchmen were recruited from fit, relatively young men, and had them patrolling their beats in greater numbers than the 'new police' when they were introduced. The best known and most celebrated of eighteenth-century developments included the system established by Henry Fielding and his brother Sir John in Bow Street, with its thief-takers (the Bow Street Runners), patrols, information gathering and diffusion; there were also the police offices, stipendiary magistrates and their constables created for London in 1792 on the Bow Street model. However, it is wrong to assume, as the traditional Whig historians did, that the eighteenth-century developments led logically and inevitably to the Metropolitan Police. The Metropolitan Police's three thousand uniformed men, organized in a centralized, hierarchical and rigid body, were very different from the plain-clothes constables responsible to magistrates working out of the police offices, or the plain-clothes watchmen recruited by, answerable to, and paid for by local parishes. Parish watches in London were abolished with the creation of the 'new police', but the old police offices continued to function, and there was considerable friction throughout the 1830s between the stipendiaries and their constables on the one hand and Metropolitan policemen on the other.

## 2.2 Creating the Metropolitan Police

If the gradual changes in policing during the eighteenth century in London can be said to be the result of a new threshold for public order and increasing anxiety about the city's growth and its poorer inhabitants, there is still the need to explain the actual occasion of the creation of the very new style of police in 1829. Without subscribing to the 'great man' view of history, it can be argued that Peel's role was critical.

When Peel was appointed Home Secretary in 1822 he expressed his determination to rationalize and reform the criminal code. He already had experience of organizing a police system in the very different circumstances of Ireland, and he made it clear that he considered the creation of a preventive police force for England as central to any reform of the justice system. Key legal reforms were carried through by the middle of the 1820s, but police reform was delayed by suspicion of the idea of police. However, Peel persevered and limited to London what appear to have been original hopes for a national system. He created some uniformed constables for Bow Street in 1822, and in 1828 established a parliamentary select committee with men who shared his ideas. Not surprisingly the committee recommended in favour of a police force for London. Astute politician that he was, Peel adjusted the proposal by omitting the square mile of the City of London from the subsequent Bill – the powerful men of the commercial capital were jealous of their independence and might well have wielded enough political clout to defeat it. In his speech introducing the Bill, Peel argued that a preventive police was needed to stem the increase in crime, yet it is possible that the figures for committals which he cited (there were no figures for 'reported crime') showed an increase because his legal reforms were making prosecution easier and were consequently bringing more people before the courts. Nevertheless, parliament was convinced, the Bill became law, and the first Metropolitan constables began patrolling the streets in September 1829.

*'Sir Robert Peel: 'I want to teach people that liberty does not consist in having your house robbed by organized gangs of thieves and in leaving the principal streets of London in the nightly possession of drunken women and vagabonds'*

The new threshold of order was not something confined to the thinking of men in London: most government ministers responsible for fostering the new political economy had their country seats and sometimes served as county magistrates. But they also had a faith in the superiority of English institutions, and they rejected the notions of centralization to be found both in the France of the old regime, which had served as the model state for most of the absolutist monarchs of eighteenth-century Europe, and in the France of the Revolution and Napoleon, which provided a model for administrators even in those states of continental Europe which fought Napoleon. Large police organizations existed both under the old regime and under Napoleon, and these included significant political and military elements, both of which were anathema to the English ruling elite's perception of English liberty and constitutionalism. The concerns about spies and militarized *gendarmes* continued to underpin much hostility to the idea of police in England, and also influenced the way in which the English police developed.

*Cartoon from* The Political Drama, *no.11, June–July 1833. The original caption read: 'Reviewing the Blue Devils, alias the Raw Lobsters, alias the Bludgeon Men'*

## 2.3   Creating the provincial police

The Whig interpretation argues that the Metropolitan Police were such a success that the model was introduced into the incorporated boroughs by the Municipal Corporations Act of 1835 and into the counties by the Rural Constabulary Acts of 1839 and 1840. Certainly the Metropolitan Police did provide a model for provincial police reformers during the 1830s and 1840s, but it was only one model among several. These reformers were motivated by similar concerns to those in London, and there were experiments even before the creation of the Metropolitan Police.

An Act of parliament in 1829, predating the Metropolitan Police Act, established a system of professional constables for Cheshire designed to work under the county magistrates, to supervise the parish constables and to link with the police systems of the nearby industrial areas. Unemployment and disturbances among miners in Shropshire led the Quarter Sessions of that county to consider following Cheshire's lead in 1830 and 1831. Associations for the prosecution of felons and some small units of local government were also recruiting professional constables to carry out patrols and pursue offenders. It could be argued that the clauses of the Municipal Corporations Act which required the creation of watch committees to establish and supervise police forces were, like the rest of the Act, simply rationalizing the system of local government. Mayors and corporations had always had responsibility for policing their city or town; some had taken the responsibility more seriously than others and had already established police patrols under special legislation or general Acts. The Act of 1835 required that they all organize along the same lines.

The legislation of 1839 and 1840 followed on the heels of the Report of the Royal Commission on Constabulary (1836–39), which had recommended the creation of a national police. The traditional view has always been that the driving force behind police reform during the 1830s were the Benthamite reformers and, in particular, Edwin Chadwick, who was a key figure in both the inquiry into the Poor Law, which reported in 1834, and the Royal Commission on Constabulary. However, recent research shows that the government of Lord Grey, which came to power in 1830, went so far as to draw up a Bill for a national police system in 1832. The Bill eventually sank under the weight of events surrounding the Great Reform Act of that year, together with doubts about the ability of persuading parliament and local authorities to accept it, particularly the costs associated with a national system and the impact on local autonomy (Philips and Storch, 1994). The 1839 Act, and the amending Act of 1840, ignored both the national proposals of 1832 and those of the Royal Commission, and left matters to the magistrates who ran local government. It empowered county benches to create a constabulary if they so wished. Some did, but others did not, and during the 1840s there were continuing experiments to develop and improve the old parish constable system, most notably with the creation of professional superintendents to oversee and co-ordinate.

1839 was also a year of Chartist disorder. It is possible that this acted as a spur to the reforms overall, and it did have an influence in the development of policing systems in three burgeoning industrial urban areas which, since they were not incorporated boroughs, had been uninfluenced by the 1835 requirements. Three separate Acts of parliament established police in Birmingham, Bolton and Manchester, where Chartism appeared a powerful force and where local administrative rivalries had brought at worst friction and at best inertia. The police in the three towns were organized, initially, under government-appointed commissioners. They were passed on to local government control in the early 1840s when they were felt to be running efficiently and effectively.

*Manchester police on parade, 1845*

models of
police

By the middle of the nineteenth century there were several different models of police functioning in England, ranging from the Metropolitan Police in London to the revived parish constables in some counties who were now supervised by professional superintendents.

Further legislation was enacted in 1856 in the form of the County and Borough Police Act. This Act made it obligatory for all counties and boroughs to set up uniformed, bureaucratic, hierarchical police forces rather than reorganize the traditional parish system (a few of the smaller incorporated boroughs had still not complied with the 1835 legislation) and it established a national inspectorate to assess the efficiency of the forces once created.

Another forceful Home Secretary was behind the 1856 Act. Lord Palmerston served only briefly at the Home Office before becoming prime minister and handing over to Sir George Grey, but it was long enough for him to support the appointment of a select committee on police whose membership and witnesses appear, in general, to have been men sympathetic to the new models. It is perhaps significant that while the county of Kent had been the driving force behind the legislation reforming and reorganizing the old parish constable system, there were no witnesses called from Kent; however, the chair of the committee, the member for the Kentish port of Dover, was strongly in favour of the new police. Yet the reformers did not have it all their own way. The initial Bill brought forward by Palmerston in 1854 provoked massive hostility in the boroughs by proposing that henceforth the Home Secretary draw up their police regulations and that the smaller forces be amalgamated with the surrounding counties; the proposed amalgamation of the police of the five smallest counties with their larger neighbours also provoked fury. The offending clauses were dropped from the Bill introduced by Grey two years later. The second Bill also won support with its proposal that the central government would contribute one quarter of the cost of pay and clothing for forces deemed efficient by a new police inspectorate. It is probable that other events contributed to the Bill's success, though any precise assessment is, of course, impossible. For example, transportation had virtually ended in 1853, and there was concern about dangerous offenders who had once been shipped to the other side of the world now being released from prison into the community on a ticket-of-leave. The fall of Sebastopol in September 1855 meant the end of the Crimean War, with the return of much of the army to Britain, and while Victorians may have gloried in the feats of British redcoats overseas, they could be equally concerned about their habits at home, especially when demobilized.

## 2.4  Policing the Celts

Wales had been fully integrated with England since the Tudors, and the police legislation described above was equally applicable there. Police reform in Scotland followed a similar pattern, though there had been organized, military-style police in Edinburgh and Glasgow from the beginning of the nineteenth century, and Scottish law continued to maintain its separate identity.

Ireland, united with the British crown in 1801, was different. In England the magistracy prided itself on its independence, its ability to run local affairs and to cope in times of disorder. While as a last resort they might call in troops to suppress disorder, they were also known to meet and negotiate with rioters and to persuade them to return to their homes. The Irish gentry modelled themselves on their English counterparts, but their circumstances were very different. Often, though not always, they were divided from those who worked the land by both religion and language. They, like most of their English counterparts, regarded the Irish peasantry as a primitive race. But unlike the English rural magistracy, the Irish gentry showed themselves totally incapable of responding to, and coping with, disorder; and disorder in Ireland in the shape of occasional full-scale rebellion as well as continual agrarian unrest – sometimes manifesting itself in appalling violence – seemed endemic. The close of the eighteenth century saw a succession of policing experiments in both Dublin and the countryside. Disorder in the early part of the nineteenth century led Peel, as Chief Secretary for Ireland, to establish the Peace Preservation Force, which was gradually reshaped into the centralized, armed, *gendarmerie*-style Royal Irish Constabulary. Dublin was excluded from this system, but it too was given a centralized police. The concern here was not an ineffective gentry, but the influence of Catholic priests and 'demagogues' who, it was feared, might gain control of the police if Dublin were permitted the local government control allowed in the English and Scottish boroughs.

Do you think it was inevitable that a professional police force would be established in the early nineteenth century? What was the root cause for the creation of the police: crime; fear of disorder/revolution; or was it a logical development of the expanding role of the state?

The smug historian's response is that nothing is inevitable in history. Furthermore, it might be argued that there was no reason why police reform took the direction it did. Why wasn't there greater interest in, and reorganization of, the old parish constable system? Why wasn't there a determined decision to take the bull by the horns and create a national police?

Of course, we cannot measure any precise increase in crime or disorder, though fear that these were increasing probably fed into decisions to reform the police. So, too, did changing perceptions of what was acceptable behaviour on the streets. A case might also be made for state development (even allowing for the fact that the nineteenth-century British model was a very decentralized version). Increasingly, the state was involving itself in everyday life, introducing factory legislation, Poor Law reform and census enumeration, so we might well ask why it didn't also take a greater degree of responsibility for the maintenance of law and order?

Table 1.1 below summarizes the development of policing in England and Ireland in the latter half of the eighteenth and the first half of the nineteenth centuries.

## Table 1.1  The establishment of police forces in England and Ireland, 1750–1856

| England | | | Ireland | |
|---|---|---|---|---|
| Description of force | Location | Year | Location | Description of force |
| Bow Street Police Office. Magistrate and four thief takers. *C/D/N* | London | **1750** | | |
| Short-lived, eight-man Bow Street Horse Patrol. *C/S?/N* | London | **1763–64** | | |
| Small Bow Street Foot Patrol. Initial size unknown, 70 men by 1797. *C/S/N* | London | **1773** | Counties | Tiny, scattered baronial police. *L/D/N* |
| | | **1778** | Dublin | City-wide force, constables and watch, totalling 425 men. *L/D/N* |
| | | **1786** | Dublin | 450-man new police. *C/F/U* |
| | | **1787** | Counties | Originally in disturbed Cork, Kerry, Kilkenny, Tipperary; from 1795 in 11 counties. Lapses, c.1800. *C/F/U (motley)* |
| Seven Police Offices. Twenty-one magistrates and 42 constables. *C/D/N* | London | **1792** | Counties | Small forces in 15 counties other than those policed by the 1787 Act. *L/F/N* |
| | | **1795** | Dublin | Local force restored, 1786 police abolished. *L/D/U* |
| | | **1799** | Dublin | Centralized police replaces 1795 force. Fifty peace officers and 500 watchmen. *C/F & S/U* |
| Thames River Police. Three magistrates and a 60-man patrol. *C/S/N* | London | **1800** | | |
| Bow Street [Mounted] Horse Patrol re-established. Fifty men ('Redbreasts'). *C/F & S/U* | London | **1805** | | |
| | | **1808** | Dublin | Consolidation of 1799 police and addition of Horse Patrol (50 men) and Foot Patrol (100). *C/F & S/U* |
| | | **1814** | Counties | Peel's Peace Preservation Force. Initially in Tipperary; by 1822, 2,300 Peelers in 16 disturbed counties. *C/F & S/U (motley)* |
| 'Dismounted' Horse Patrol [foot patrol]. Ninety men. *C/F & S/U* | London | **1821** | | |
| | | **1822** | Counties | Irish constabulary. Compulsory in all counties. Mostly replaces, or in a few counties supplements, the Peelers. Initially 4,800 men; 7,500 by 1836. *C, L/F & S/U* |
| Peel's 3,200-man Metropolitan Police. Bow Street Patrols and Thames Police abolished, 1839. *C/D/U* | London | **1829** | | |
| Police forces begin to replace constables and watch in incorporated towns. *L/D/U* | Boroughs | **1835** | | |
| | | **1836** | Counties | Constabulary reformed and Peelers (1814 force) abolished. Force grows to 12,000 men by 1850. *C/F & S/U* |
| | | **1837** | Dublin | 1,100-man police replaces force established in 1808. *C/D/U* |
| *Optional* police forces; adopted in 15 whole counties by 1842 (a total of 1,900 men) and in 19 by 1856 (3,300 men): *L/D/U* | Counties | **1839** | | |
| Temporary government-controlled police. *C/D/U* | Manchester Birmingham Bolton | **1839-42** | | |
| *Compulsory* forces in all counties. *L, C/D/U* | Counties | **1856** | | |

Note: London = the metropolis, not the City of London.

Key:  *C* Central (i.e. government) control      *N* No uniform      *F* Armed with firearms
     *D* Disarmed: staff or truncheon only      *L* Local control      *S* Armed with short sword or cutlass      *U* Uniformed

Source: Palmer, 1988, p.32

# 3 Control and management

## 3.1 Accountability

Following the establishment of the new police, other individuals and groups continued to undertake 'policing' tasks. For example, the old parish constables were not automatically abolished – indeed, many continued to be appointed until well into the twentieth century. Gamekeepers and private watchmen continued to function on private property, and for much of the nineteenth century it was possible for landowners or businesses to pay for additional constables in their local police who would concentrate on guarding their property. Docks had their own police, though these were often speedily incorporated into new, local town forces. The railway companies continued to run their own police until their nationalization in 1948, which brought about the creation of a single British Transport Police, the only force authorized to act on both sides of the Anglo-Scottish border. The period since the Second World War has seen a considerable growth in private security companies for guarding premises and a variety of other tasks.

The number of police forces in England, Wales and Scotland varied throughout the nineteenth and twentieth centuries. A peak was reached towards the end of the 1850s, after which the numbers increasingly declined as the smaller forces either found it convenient, or were compelled, to amalgamate with their larger neighbours. In 1860 there were 226 forces in England and Wales; on the eve of the First World War there were still 188; and a series of amalgamations at the end of the Second World War brought the number down to 131.

These forces were of three different kinds – the London Metropolitan Police, borough or city police, and county police – and each kind had a different administrative and organizational structure. From the outset, the commissioners of the Metropolitan Police were directly accountable to the Home Secretary. This incensed many of the representatives of local government in London.

### ACTIVITY 1.2

The petition of the Parish of Marylebone to Viscount Melbourne, the Whig government's Home Secretary, in December 1832 was one of the more reasoned and restrained of such initial complaints. Part of this is reproduced in Extract 1.3 below. Read the extract and then answer the following questions:

1 What is the constitutional concern expressed in the petition?
2 What do you understand from this document to be the difference between the financing of the old Marylebone Watch and that of the new Metropolitan Police?

> ### Extract 1.3  'Petition of the Parish of Marylebone to the Home Secretary, 1832'
>
> Your Memorialists respectfully beg leave now to approach that part of the subject the most delicate ... , viz., whether the Force, as at present constituted and governed, is, or is not, accordant with the spirit of the Constitution and the Freedom of the Subject; a Force which will most likely, 'ere long, pervade the whole Kingdom, formed upon a Military System, regulated and directed by persons appointed by the Government, and altogether uncontrolled by those who pay for it, and the protection of whose persons and property is the presumed object of its formation.
>
> It will require no power of argument or deduction of reason to satisfy a mind, constituted like your Lordship's, that a Force such as this must be incompatible with the Liberty of the Subject. It differs from a Military Force only in the name, and ... [with] all the attributes and powers of any army, it may, at any moment of public excitement, be called out, at the will of the then existing government, in array against the people, from whom its members derive their daily pay ...
>
> Your Memorialists ... admit that so long as the Helm of the State is guided by those tried Friends of the People [the Whigs] who ... have for nearly half a century steadily pursued an undeviating course ... [toward] restoring to the People their long-usurped Rights, they have nothing to fear, but my Lord, ... it is not enough that the political integrity of the present Government is a guarantee to the people of the abuse of such a Force ...
>
> (quoted in Palmer, 1988, p.307)

## COMMENT

militarism    The petitioners are concerned that this is a **military-style** organization directly responsible to central government and with no local control. It could, therefore, be used against the people by an unscrupulous government. The old Marylebone Watch was financed and directed by the parish; the new Metropolitan Police continues to be financed by the London parishes, but they have no control over its operations.

These arguments were to flare up again and again during the nineteenth and twentieth centuries. In 1888, for example, when legislation was introduced to establish the London County Council, Liberals and Radicals urged that control of the police should be passed to the new body – after all, the constituent parts of London were paying for the police through their rates. The government's line, however, was that the Metropolitan Police had 'imperial' as well as 'local' tasks such as protecting the royal family and parliament. One government apologist warned: 'It is undeniable that if the London County Council held the control of the police, it would wield a weapon that might be handled with deadly effect against a weak Government, if the majority of the Council chose to make use of it for political purposes.' He went on to wonder whether 'any reasonable person [could] assert that there will never be a majority of extreme Radicals and Socialists on the County Council?' (Evans, 1889, p.449). The comment brought predictable outrage: 'This ... is the first time that I have ever heard the claim set up in England that the police are a body for the protection of the Government against the citizens.' It also brought the complaint that London was now the only place in Britain 'where a charge falls permanently on the rates ... and where those who manage the expenditure of that charge are not themselves responsible to the ratepayers' (Stuart, 1889, pp.629 and 626). But outrage and complaint did not sway the legislators or bring about any amendments. In the aftermath of the First World War the issue flared up again when the Labour majority on Poplar Council refused to pay their precepts for the Metropolitan Police, arguing that money was short and would be better spent on solving social distress and problems in the district; several council leaders were imprisoned as a result.

The Municipal Corporations Act of 1835 obliged incorporated boroughs to establish watch committees, which in turn were to appoint head constables and police forces. At the beginning these committees took a very serious interest in policing matters and gave precise operational details to their head constable on the deployment of his men; moreover the committees possessed the authority to hire, fire and discipline. Often, as the century progressed, an accommodation was reached between a committee and its head constable. Busy local politicians found less and less time to devote to police matters and were content to let their 'expert' get on with it. In some instances the small size of the police force – a few borough forces had less than two dozen men well into the twentieth century – and the consequent lowly origin of the head constable ensured that he remained very obviously the servant of the local politicians. But even the head constable of a very large urban force could find himself compelled to obey operational instructions from his watch committee which he regarded as ill-conceived. Liverpool, for example, had the largest provincial urban force in England during the 1890s. The watch committee became dominated by a group of moral reformers determined to stamp out prostitution, and the head constable was instructed to close down the city's brothels. Captain Nott-Bowyer, the head constable, advised against the policy, warning that it would not stamp out prostitution, merely move it, and that once the offence had moved it would take up a significant amount of police time pursuing it. His advice was ignored, and he was required to administer the policy, with precisely the results he had predicted. However, as will be explained in section 3.2 below, the authority of the watch committee was gradually undermined by Whitehall's growing professionalism, by the responses to a succession of emergencies, and by debatable legal rulings.

The chief constables of county police forces had much greater independence from the beginning. They were appointed by their police committees, but the Home Secretary approved the appointment. Generally during the nineteenth century they were drawn from the same social class as the county magistrates; in the second half of the century an increasing number were former military officers. Until the Act of 1888 which established county councils, they were in some measure answerable to the police committees of magistrates appointed by the county bench. The 1888 Act established standing joint committees made up of an equal number of magistrates and elected county councillors, although there were those who had argued that the police should be directly responsible to the new county councils. However, as with the London County Council, the government was wary and some of its supporters were outspoken in their fears of what might happen if trade unionists or socialists should gain control of a county and hence of its police.

## 3.2  Creeping centralization

centralization  There had been little in the way of centralization before the 1856 County and Borough Police Act, but this does not mean that the police forces did not have much in common. Indeed, as men moved from one force to another, especially as the new forces sought cadres of officers from those already in existence, particularly from London, they probably developed more and more similarities. The 1856 Act, by offering Treasury money to 'efficient' forces and by establishing inspectors who would assess that efficiency, gave the Home Office new and significant leverage over the development of the provincial police. A few proud boroughs maintained their independence and refused the Treasury grant, yet this was not the kind of policy to ensure a council's popularity with ratepayers at the polls, and even these few soon fell into line. In 1874 the Treasury grant was increased to one half the cost of pay and uniforms, and in the aftermath of the First World War this was raised to half the total cost of the force.

In addition to the leverage which the Home Office acquired through its financial involvement with the provincial police, there were other factors at work which served to undermine local control. Examinations for the Civil Service, introduced in the second half of the nineteenth century, led to an increasingly professional elite of bureaucrats in Whitehall. At the same time policemen were acquiring more knowledge of their trade and increasingly perceived themselves as the experts in matters of law and order, while new legislation dealing with, among other things, explosives and adulterated food gave direct executive power to the police with no reference to the local police committees. There was therefore no sudden change, but gradually senior police officers, particularly those of the larger forces, and Home Office bureaucrats began by-passing local government 'laymen'. This situation gathered pace at the turn of the century as the result of industrial disputes and spy scares; the First World War and the Russian Revolution accelerated the process. Government ministers and their advisers reasoned that big industrial disputes required a greater response than a single police force could often provide. A miners' strike in the West Riding in 1893 found the county police hopelessly stretched, not least because the dispute coincided with the policing demands of the Doncaster races. Troops were deployed, and at Ackton Hall Colliery, Featherstone, two miners were shot dead and fourteen others wounded. The Home Office urged police forces to enter into mutual aid agreements. At the close of the following decade the dynamic young Liberal Home Secretary, Winston Churchill, pushed the constitutional position to the limit, and probably legally exceeded his authority, by moving police and troops around the country as he saw fit. Churchill also urged the creation of police reserves to supplement the forces when stretched; some police committees took up the idea, but some boroughs refused, protesting that the Home Office was encroaching on their authority.

Immediately before the First World War there was a succession of spy scares, as a result of which chief and head constables were brought into contact with the embryonic secret service. The war itself strengthened such links, and again to the detriment of local control, since Labour and Independent Labour Party activists were often on the lists of anti-war suspects. The war emergency led to the creation of Authorized Competent Military Authorities – military officers responsible for the wartime management and supervision of their nominated regions; these officers liaised directly with senior police officers, again by-passing the lay police committees. The Authorized Competent Military Authorities were abolished at the end of the war, but, at the same time, closer links were forged between the police and the Home Office by a succession of conferences, circulars discussing how the police were to respond in future emergencies, and, finally, by the Emergency Powers Act of 1919. The latter authorized the executive to make 'regulations for the preservation of the public peace' and 'for any other purposes essential to the public safety and the life of the community'. The Act was untouched by the Labour government of 1924, and provided the basis for the management of the General Strike of 1926. Sir Arthur Dixon, one of the civil servants responsible for the Police Division of the Home Office during the 1920s, concluded that these developments and experiences 'established the [Police] Service in what was virtually a new, and certainly important, role as an executive Force, efficient, trustworthy and versatile, and ready at a call to guide, assist or restrain the civil population in a wide variety of ways' (quoted in Emsley, 1991, p.129).

The First World War exerted enormous pressures on those policemen who were not recruited into the military: the numbers of police declined, their average age increased, they were given a multitude of new, specifically wartime tasks, their leave and rest days were reduced, and their pay fell way behind with the impact of wartime inflation. Unionization of an *ad hoc* kind had emerged among different forces during the nineteenth century, and before the war a national police trade union had appeared. The experience of the war provided a considerable boost to membership, and in 1918 and again in 1919 the union brought its members out on strike – in the first instance essentially over pay and conditions, but on the second occasion for the very existence of the union. The second strike was a disaster for the union and for all those men who participated, some of whom had upwards of twenty years' service; the union was destroyed, and the strikers were dismissed and never reinstated. However, the strikes prompted the government to create a committee, chaired by Lord Desborough, whose recommendations with reference to conditions, pay and uniforms brought a much greater unity to the hundred or so forces then in existence. The recommendation that the smaller forces be amalgamated with their larger neighbours was viewed sympathetically by successive governments, by the Inspectors of Constabulary and by civil servants in the Home Office, but proposals for requiring such amalgamations brought the usual chorus of protest from the boroughs.

unionization

## 3.3 Twentieth-century redefinitions

Although the smaller boroughs, backed by the larger, were able to hang on to their own police forces, the relationship between them and their policemen was being redefined. During the nineteenth century borough policemen in particular were commonly regarded as the servants of local government. I have described above how the head constable of Liverpool gave way to the directives of his watch committee in 1890. Increasingly during the 1920s, however, official and semi-official voices began to deny that the relationship between policeman and police committee was one of master and servant. One of the clearest such statements was made by O.F. Dowson, a barrister and Assistant Legal Adviser to the Home Office, in a series of articles published in the journal *Justice of the Peace* in 1928.

... every police officer, irrespective of the authority under whom he is serving, possesses powers and is required to carry out duties at common law which seem at first sight, at any rate to be inconsistent with any theory that he is a mere servant of the police authority. Apart from the public character of his office he is clothed with functions and powers which, though exercisable locally only, are not dependent upon or under the complete control of the authority under whose management he is placed and at whose cost he is paid (apart from the Exchequer grant) ...

(*Justice of the Peace*, 13 October 1928, p.663)

The argument was given judicial force two years later with the ruling of Justice McCardie in *Fisher* v. *Oldham*. A man named Fisher was wrongly arrested by a policeman from the Borough of Oldham and, on his release, he brought an action for false imprisonment against the borough. The judge's ruling that a policeman 'is a Servant of the State, a ministerial officer of the central power, though subject in some respects to local supervision and local regulation' (quoted in Emsley, 1991, p.154) has been hotly debated and disputed, but it has become a crucial underpinning of the argument that the police have, and always have had, operational independence from local politicians.

operational independence

While it would be unwise to detect a conspiracy on the part of central government to forge greater links between itself, in the shape of the Home Office, and the police, it is true that during the inter-war period central government always backed chief constables in dispute with their police committees. Such disputes were not to be found in great numbers, but where they did occur the reason was invariably political. A few chief constables, particularly a trio in South Wales, insisted that they were upholding a non-political, British way of life against alien creeds; the police committees with whom they clashed had large numbers of Labour, and occasionally a few Communist, councillors.

The chief constables of counties had always had more freedom of action than those of boroughs; theoretically, if increasingly less in practice, the latter remained directly responsible to the local watch committee. But the 1920s also witnessed a serious conflict between a borough head constable and his watch committee which ultimately involved the Home Office. A.R. Ellerington, the head constable of St. Helens since 1905, had been given a virtual free hand in operational matters for twenty years, but friction developed in 1926 when he brought in police from Liverpool to assist his men during industrial trouble. Watch committee meetings became the scenes of ferocious arguments. The committee sought Ellerington's dismissal, but the Home Office ordered his reinstatement. Accusations were made about misconduct, but an inquiry found in Ellerington's favour and again the watch committee was instructed by the Home Office to reinstate him and maintain proper relations with him. Some thirty years later, in 1959, a similar conflict erupted in Nottingham after the chief constable, Captain Athelstan Popkess, launched an investigation into corruption in the city government. The Director of Public Prosecutions advised that no action should be taken, at which point the watch committee, hearing of the investigations for the first time, demanded a report from Popkess. He refused on the grounds that criminal investigation was his duty and no concern of the committee. The committee suspended him, but the Home Secretary insisted on his reinstatement. The Popkess affair was one of several incidents which led the government to establish a Royal Commission in January 1960. The principal question which the Royal Commission found itself having to confront was precisely where the ultimate control of the provincial police should reside.

In Scotland the increasing links between the police and central government, at the expense of local government, appear to have followed a pattern largely similar to that south of the border, though the history of Scottish policing is far less researched. In Ireland, as noted above, the bureaucratic police organizations developed during the nineteenth century, namely the Royal Irish Constabulary (RIC) and the Dublin Metropolitan Police, were always centrally directed. When, following partition in 1922, the RIC was replaced in the north by the Royal Ulster Constabulary and in the south by the *garda siochana* ('people's guard') the influence of the organization of the old force remained significant, especially on the former. Both of the new forces were made responsible, first and foremost, to government ministers. But in Northern Ireland, a fiercely Protestant state with a significant Catholic minority and a large Catholic neighbour, a major part of policing concerned the preservation of the border. This led to the creation of a Special Constabulary, heavily armed and quite unlike any other force in the United Kingdom.

Are the police in Britain 'political' or above politics; autonomous or subject to local/central control?

The official line has always been that the police in Britain are not political, yet, as Reiner has pointed out: 'This notion … rests on an entirely untenable narrow conception of "the political", restricting it to "the administrative apparatus of state and party organization" … In a broader sense all relationships which have a power dimension are political' (Reiner, 1985, pp.1–2). During the nineteenth century some borough police were political in an even narrower sense of obeying the directives of the political members of the watch committee. This position shifted, especially during the inter-war years, but it brought senior police officers much more within the supervision and direction of central government.

# 4 Police efficiency and effectiveness

## 4.1 The prevention of crime

The 'New Police Instructions' issued to the London Metropolitan Police in 1829 declared:

> It should be understood at the outset, that the object to be attained is 'the prevention of crime'. To this great end every effort of the police is to be directed. The security of person and property, the preservation of the public tranquillity, and all other objects of a police establishment, will thus be better effected than by the detection and punishment of the offender after he has succeeded in committing the crime. This should constantly be kept in mind by every member of the police force, as the guide for his own conduct. Officers and constables should endeavour to distinguish themselves by such vigilance and activity as may render it impossible for any one to commit a crime within that portion of the town under their charge.

> (*The Times*, 25 September 1829)

The instructions above were often used, word for word, by provincial forces established later in the century. What difficulties do you think might arise in assessing the effectiveness of this strategy of prevention?

If you take the absence of crime and disorder as the measure of success, how can you differentiate between general 'good' behaviour on the part of the public and good behaviour created by the presence of the police? What other bench-mark could be used to assess police effectiveness? The number of arrests? If you rely on the latter, could an increase in arrests (and convictions) mean (a) better policing; (b) more aggressive policing, which might not necessarily be better, but could be the targeting of 'easy' offences, and 'known offenders' picked up and even 'fitted up'; or (c) more crime and disorder? An increase in arrests and convictions might also be taken to imply a failure of 'prevention'.

prevention Prevention became an article of faith for the police, but the problems associated with it were soon apparent. There were certain kinds of offenders who could be picked up with relative ease. Drunks are an obvious example, though the stories are legion of drunks being moved by one constable to his neighbour's beat so that he could go to bed after a long night shift rather than having to take the offender back to his station, possibly having his uniform fouled on the way, and then having to hang around in the magistrates' court waiting for the case to be heard. Vagrants were another easy target. Statistics showing large numbers of vagrants thrown into borough or county gaols during the nineteenth century are a dubious guide to the incidence of vagrancy – more probably they were the result of orders to the police from a magistrates' police committee, a watch committee, or a head or chief constable to clamp down on itinerants. Catching thieves and burglars was rather more problematic; no-one produced any yardstick showing the extent to which their activities were, or could be, prevented by men in uniform.

In 1842 the belief that the new county police forces in particular were not achieving what they had promised in terms of efficiency and effectiveness, in spite of costing a considerable amount of money, led to campaigns by ratepayers across the country. Some demanded that the new police be reduced in size or even disbanded. The campaigns were cut short by a new wave of Chartist demonstrations, but not before the Lancashire Constabulary had been reduced from 502 to 355 men.

It is possible, of course, that the appearance of policemen on beats did reduce some opportunist crime. Furthermore, while on their beats, policemen were expected to check the preventive measures of shopkeepers and others. Constables checked for open windows and gates, and they 'shook hands with the doorknobs' to ensure that doors were properly closed and locked. Failure to report an open window, gate or door, especially if this led to 'failure' in 'preventing' a crime, could lead to a reprimand and punishment. Rewards often came as a result of arrests, and chances of promotion could be improved. Harry Daley, who joined the Metropolitan Police in 1925 and served for a quarter of a century, recalled how, in his first police station, the inspector approved of the 'snatchers' who arrested or summonsed any and everyone, since they made his district look active and important.

> He held up the snatchers as examples to others and threatened to delay promotion unless more work was done. When other detrimental factors were present, he occasionally carried out his threat. This pressure to make young

policemen work – to summons and arrest people – was always denied when questions were asked in Parliament ...

The Metropolitan Police Act entitles 'any constable to stop, search and detain any person reasonably suspected of being in possession of stolen property'. In my early days I made perfect use of this Act. As I stood in a doorway in the dead of night I heard hurrying footsteps and, peeping out, saw a man with a heavy bag which clinked with metal as he got closer. With heart in mouth I stopped a doctor carrying his instruments, returning from a nearby emergency call. Hearty laughter and a friendly parting, of course.

Snatchers ignored the words 'reasonably suspected' and by stopping everyone with a bag or parcel occasionally caught thieves carrying stolen property. They antagonised hundreds of innocent people and those almost innocent – such as workmen carrying home wood or paint which had been 'left over'. At night they interfered unnecessarily with happy drunks and made them drunk and disorderlies and assaults on police.

(Daley, 1986, pp.100–1)

## 4.2  Police strategies

Prevention arguably led to the targeting of 'criminal' areas and of particular individuals and social groups. The first commissioners of the Metropolitan Police spoke in terms of protecting the elegant, wealthy district of St. James by watching the slum of St. Giles. The St. Giles 'rookery' was demolished as one of a series of urban improvements in the middle of the nineteenth century, as much to remove the 'criminal class' from the centre of the city as to provide the wide new thoroughfare of New Oxford Street. Other rookeries met similar fates: in Manchester, for example, the building of the Central Railway Station and the widening of Deansgate provided the opportunity for demolishing part of one of the worst slums. The inhabitants of these districts then moved elsewhere, and the police maintained their surveillance of the new 'criminal' districts.

targeting

Of course, there were people living in the rookeries who did commit offences, but it is unlikely that everyone there could be labelled as a 'criminal'. Many of the inhabitants of these and other poor, stigmatized districts were casual labourers dependent on an uncertain job market. Parts of these districts were crammed with Irish immigrants who brought with them rural habits (such as keeping pigs) and the rough traditions of the faction fight. Irish districts in the Victorian city became notorious as 'criminal', yet it does not seem to have been property crime which singled out the Irish, but interpersonal violence, commonly committed among themselves, or else directed against the police. Paradoxically, while the police tended to equate 'Irishman' with 'criminal', a very high percentage of recruits to the police forces in those cities with large Irish populations were themselves Irish.

Another example of police 'labelling' during the nineteenth century was the way that a large number of women arrested for petty theft or as drunk and disorderly were listed by the police as 'prostitutes'. The situation was aggravated during the period when the Contagious Diseases Acts were in force (1864–83). These enabled the Metropolitan Police and the police of garrison towns to arrest women suspected of being prostitutes and have them medically examined. The Acts put any young working-class woman out alone, especially after dark, at risk from an over-zealous policeman. Even after their abolition the problem of such police officers apprehending young women on suspicion continued. This, together with the surveillance of the poor districts and the identification of certain districts as 'criminal', did not endear the police to the 'suspect' working class.

While crime statistics are notoriously difficult to use, those that we have for the nineteenth century suggest a general levelling out of most property crime (with the notable exception of burglary) and crimes against the person after about 1850. It is possible that the new police had some impact here; the spread of policing across the whole country, with the uniformed constables pounding their beats at the regulation two and a half miles an hour, may have deterred some of the opportunist crime. But it would be difficult to prove conclusively. Whatever their impact on crime statistics, the new police were probably only one of several reasons for this levelling out. Furthermore, changes in leisure habits, linked with developments in technology, presented a challenge to the strategies adopted by the new police.

For much of the nineteenth century the working classes, and particularly the poorer elements who were identified by the police as the objects for surveillance, took much of their leisure on the street. They would sit in the street, eat in the street, gamble in the street, argue and fight in the street. Organized sports – particularly with the development of football stadiums and dog tracks – provided new outlets. So too did the cinema. In addition to the leisure opportunities provided by new, specially designed public spaces, the twentieth century brought better housing provision for the working classes, together with new forms of home leisure provided by new technologies – the radio and the gramophone. But as the working classes gradually moved off the streets, so, again courtesy of the new technology, the traditionally respectable classes, who had never been the objects of police surveillance, moved on to the roads in their motor cars. The decade before the First World War witnessed nasty confrontations between motorists and the police, with a new pressure group, the Automobile Association, being founded to provide 'scouts', who would warn members of police speed traps, and legal assistance in court cases. By the middle of the inter-war period motoring offences were clogging the magistrates' courts, and concerns were being expressed about motoring legislation poisoning the hitherto good relations between the police and the public.

## 4.3  Crowd control

The statistics of riot and disorder are as difficult to assess, perhaps more so, as those of crime. However, most historians of popular disorder and riot suggest that there was a decline in the incidence of riot during the nineteenth century, together with a shift from the reactive riot inspired by legitimizing notions (food riots, recruiting riots, anti-enclosure riots, anti-Poor Law riots) to the proactive demonstrations organized by groups such as the new trade unions. The role of the police in this shift is difficult to estimate. As the century wore on police forces began more and more to replace the army in dealing with disorder. In part this was simply because there were more police available, and at times before 1856 the Home Office specifically instructed local authorities fearful of riot not to expect military support but to recruit a police force.

Policemen were less likely to kill people involved in disorder than soldiers, in as much as they were usually only armed with truncheons rather than the edged weapons and firearms of the military. Nevertheless it took the police some time to develop sensible crowd control techniques. Some of the techniques employed early in the century may have served to exacerbate violence rather than reduce it. For example, a political demonstration in Gray's Inn Road, London, in May 1833 saw the Metropolitan Police seal off streets to the sides of the crowds, thus cutting off lines of retreat and dispersal, while they charged the crowds with drawn batons from the front. The only fatality in this instance was a police constable who was stabbed in the chest; but the coroner's jury which sat on the case brought in a verdict of justifiable homicide on the following grounds:

crowd control

> that no Riot Act was read nor any proclamation advising the people to disperse; that the Government did not take proper precautions to prevent the meeting from assembling and that the conduct of the police was ferocious, brutal and unprovoked by the people. And we, moreover, express our anxious hope that the Government will, in future, take better precautions to prevent the recurrence of such disgraceful transactions in the Metropolis.

(Tobias, 1979, p.89)

While the authorities were outraged, the jury itself was celebrated in banners and medals, and the foreman was presented with a silver cup. Later in the century there were reports of policemen setting about crowds, including women and children, with their batons. The 1868 General Election was marred in Bromley, Kent, by the death of 78-year-old William Walter, trampled in a police baton charge. Questions remain about the incident: why were 200 Metropolitan Police brought in when there had been no violence or vandalism before the election day, and why were the local police sent home for the day? The Liberals, mounting a strong challenge to the local Conservatives who controlled the district, complained that the police were brought in by Tory JPs, but neither the police nor the magistrates admitted this. However, at the trials of twenty residents accused of assaulting the police, any witness giving testimony critical of the police was ordered from the court on the grounds that: 'The Bench was bound to believe the evidence of the police'. At the inquest on Walter, the solicitor who asked the local coroner if he might present evidence of police violence was informed that: 'You had better not say such things; because the police are a body whose duty it is to keep the peace, and when soldiers or police were brought into a town, they came to keep the peace and not to break it' (both quotations from Conley, 1991, p.39). Violent police behaviour during a strike at Silksworth Colliery in County Durham in 1891 was celebrated with a pastiche of Tennyson's 'The Charge of the Light Brigade':

> Down the hill, down the hill
> Fifty yards onward,
> All among the flying folk
> Ran the half hundred.
> 'Forward the 'Cop's' Brigade!
> Charge for the lot!' he said;
> Into the scattr'ing crowd
> Ran the half hundred.

Old men to the right of them,
Women to the left of them,
Bairns right in front of them,
Bolted and wonder'd;
Left free to have their way,
Nimbly their staves did play,
Into the fleeing crowd,
Into the roaring fun
Plunged the half hundred.

(*Sunderland Daily Echo*, 28 February 1891)

There are instances from the inter-war years when the police appear to have been the principal cause of violence in street demonstrations, either because of over-reaction or fear. The belief of some senior officers, and perhaps also some of their men, that they had a responsibility to protect the British way of life against alien creeds, and the identification of the National Association of Unemployed Workers with the Communist Party, may have contributed to some of the over-reaction. For example, in 1921 *The Police Chronicle*, a newspaper aimed at policemen, declared: 'There never was a time when public interests stood more in need of a police independent and uninfluenced by party politics ... The Bolshies in this country must be reckoned with and their defeat is assured only if we see to it' (quoted in Weinberger, 1987, pp.157–8).

One officer of the Metropolitan Police described ordering a crowd of hunger marchers to break up in the Edgware Road in November 1932, 'as it was about to become disorderly' (quoted in Stevenson and Cook, 1977, p.231). In September the same year police in Birkenhead appear to have got completely out of control in poor working-class districts of the town after a demonstration against the Means Test. There were no public inquiries into these events. As the chief constable of Liverpool put it to the Home Secretary after a baton charge – probably unnecessary – to disperse a meeting of the unemployed in September 1921:

> With regard to the advisability of holding any inquiry, I may say that we are at the present time passing through the most serious period of unrest in Liverpool. The unemployed trouble is being used by a gang of extreme Communists (all known to Sir Basil Thomson [the head of Special Branch]) for the purpose of a propaganda of violence. They are a self-selected committee acting as leaders of the unemployed and nothing but very firm measures in dealing with them can prevent serious trouble and disorder ... My considered opinion is that any inquiry into the question of whether the police used undue violence in quelling an unlawful assembly ... would seriously weaken the authority of the police at a time when it needs every possible support ... If the sworn evidence of ... experienced police superintendents ... is called into question how can they be expected to act with the necessary firmness when another occasion arises in which force may be necessary, and this may occur at any moment.

(quoted in Weinberger, 1987, p.160)

From the moment of their creation the police became involved in contests between labour and capital. The Master and Servant Act of 1824 made breach of contract by an employer a matter for civil law, while breach of contract by an employee could be pursued through the criminal courts. This meant that workers breaking a contract could be, and were, pursued by the police – another factor contributing to the potential for hostility between the working class and the police. The Master and Servant legislation was amended in the second half of the century, by which time organized labour and strike activity was becoming increasingly permissible within the framework of the law. But problems remained. How could the police appear neutral during a strike if called upon to protect bailiffs seeking to eject strikers from company housing (as was the case in the Silksworth Colliery disorder), or if called on to protect what employers called 'free labour' and what strikers called 'blacklegs' or 'scabs'? Legislation of 1875 and 1906 authorized 'peaceful picketing', but the definition of this remained obscure. It would appear that, following a Home Office circular issued in 1911 and again in 1913 which stated that a non-striker was only to be approached by one 'persuader' at a time, the Metropolitan Police decided not to allow more than one man as a picket. During the General Strike of 1926 some chief constables negotiated closely with strike committees to ensure the maintenance of the peace; others strongly resisted any such inclinations and regarded strikers with, at best, suspicion. The chief constable of Manchester complained that:

> In effect there is no such thing as 'peaceful picketing'. What is known as 'peaceful picketing' leads to more trouble than anything else the Police have to deal with in trade disputes, as pickets, when they see a favourable opportunity, will and do resort to means which certainly cannot be regarded as peaceful.

(quoted in Emsley, 1991, p.133, n.58)

*Special constables in London during the 1926 General Strike. More than 226,000 specials were recruited to help police the country, including 70,000 in the capital alone, although the majority were not uniformed*

Traditional histories of the police have put great stress on the football matches played by police and strikers: violent confrontation was probably the exception rather than the rule, and where it did occur it appears often to have been the work of undisciplined special constables sworn in for the duration of the emergency. However, there were violent incidents, as the police reward for 'little Kathleen Baggott' testifies (see the photograph overleaf).

*Illustration from* On and Off Duty, *July 1926, p.103. The original caption read: 'Little Kathleen Baggott, a twelve-year-old heroine of the general strike, receiving at Leigh, Lancashire, a gold wrist watch, given in recognition of her bravery in finding a means of escape from rioters for P.S. Cooper. She let him into her mother's house, and locked the door. The mob smashed the windows, but dispersed when police reinforcements arrived'*

## 4.4  Miscellaneous duties

While there is a common assumption that police duties are essentially crime fighting and the maintenance of public order, it is worth noting that during the nineteenth century the police acquired a variety of tasks often only loosely connected to these duties. In boroughs, particularly the smaller ones, policemen were required to assume a variety of petty responsibilities, from acting as mace-bearers on civic occasions to collecting market tolls. The town worthies reasoned that, if they were paying their police for one task, they might just as well perform another. The Education Act of 1870 resulted in constables being required to act as School Attendance Officers, pursuing parents who did not send their children to school. Policemen were appointed to act as inspectors of weights and measures, inspectors of lodging houses, and Poor Law relieving officers. Such duties may have brought them into contact with suspect individuals, but again it seems the reason for the acquisition of these duties was primarily that the policemen were already available and being paid, at least partly, out of local government coffers. In the early 1950s the Burrell Committee on Police Extraneous Duties issued a report listing a whole series of tasks which, it considered, the police should not be expected to perform; yet a decade later there were still forces where the men were required to change street signs, collect money due under maintenance orders, keep registers of domestic servants, license and inspect hackney carriages, and act as civic mace-bearers, court ushers, market inspectors, and mortuary attendants. It is, of course, impossible to assess the extent to which such tasks impeded the policeman's efficiency in the maintenance of order or as a crime-fighter. It is also worth considering the extent to which some of these duties may have provided part of the basis for police legitimacy.

# 5 Recruits, recruitment and police culture

## 5.1 Recruitment policies

It was Robert Peel's decision in 1829 that his Metropolitan policemen should come from the working class, and should be able to rise in rank through their own efforts. The commissioners of the new force were selected from 'gentlemen', but other ranks were to be open to ordinary working men who showed talent and merit. Similar policies were adopted by the provincial forces: the counties and the major cities generally chose their chief constables from gentlemen, at least until the Second World War, but all other ranks, including that of head constable in the smaller towns, were open to men who had first enlisted at the lowest grade of constable.

A cross-section of men generally from the unskilled and semi-skilled working class made up the bulk of recruits between 1840 and 1940. Large numbers were listed in the recruitment books simply as 'labourers'. This had been taken to mean agricultural labourer, and certainly there was a feeling among certain senior officers during the Victorian period that a man straight from the plough would be fit, tough and deferential to his superiors; but 'labourer' was a catch-all term, and recruits came from a much broader range of trades than simply those of the countryside. Furthermore, different forces had different recruitment policies. There were some large towns where chief constables refused to accept local men on the grounds that they would have difficulty carrying out some tasks if they found themselves having to deal with relatives and people with whom they had grown up. But there were other forces, particularly county ones, where the overwhelming majority of recruits were local men. Some chief constables in the Victorian period were reluctant to take former soldiers, suspecting that they might have become too fond of drink. But others had a predilection for former soldiers, considering them as disciplined and smart. In the economically difficult inter-war years some young men joined the army on three-year contracts with the specific aim of joining the police at the end of their service. It would appear also that, probably as a result of the economic depression during the inter-war years as well as improved educational opportunities, recruits were generally better educated and more likely to perceive the police as a career.

## 5.2 The recruit's aspirations

Many of the early recruits to the police joined to tide themselves over a period of unemployment, and they clearly had little idea of what the job would entail. Many men loathed it because of the ferocious discipline, the night-work (two-thirds of all nineteenth- and early twentieth-century beats were worked at night) and the exhausting and physically dangerous nature of the job. The turnover of recruits in the early years was enormous, but not just because of resignations by men who could not stand the life; a very large number were dismissed for disciplinary offences – particularly drinking or drunkenness on duty.

Until the Second World War men were required to ask permission to marry, and their prospective wives had their characters investigated to ensure that they were 'suitable' to be a policeman's wife. During the nineteenth century, and in some forces for part of the twentieth century, a policeman's wife was not allowed to take any form of paid employment. This had an obvious impact on the family budget since working-class wives commonly sought some kind of work. In police houses in the countryside the policeman's wife was expected to act as his auxiliary, taking messages when he was on patrol and, subsequently, answering the telephone; she was also expected to keep the police house in a high state of cleanliness. The policeman was held responsible for his wife's behaviour, and should she get into debt with local tradesmen, or commit any kind of offence (not necessarily 'criminal'), then her husband was called before his superior officers to explain.

However, there were some advantages to the job: a uniform was provided; some forces offered a degree of health care, even for a man's family; accommodation was found for some, though it was not free; and rent allowances were introduced at the beginning of the twentieth century. Most attractive, however, and a great rarity for working-class occupations in the nineteenth and early twentieth centuries, there was a pension. This pension was not guaranteed until 1890, but it provided a great incentive for a man who was in the job, and might also have been the prompt for some young men to join.

## 5.3 The culture of the job

The policeman's life was tough. Most patrolling was done at night, and it did not stop whatever the weather. In addition to the sickness brought on by exposure to the elements, policemen were commonly assaulted: during the 1890s, when assaults on police were on the decline, an annual average of some 12,000 individuals were brought before summary courts charged with assaulting policemen. The tough life appears to have contributed to a tough, masculine culture. Police autobiographies of the Victorian period and the early twentieth century commonly reveal the author taking a pride in his physical prowess and his ability to 'look after' himself in a fight. Victorian and Edwardian biographies are not the places to find discussions of sexual prowess, yet other evidence suggests that pride in vigorous heterosexual ability could be part and parcel of this tough masculinity.

police culture

There was an *esprit de corps*, which possibly had part of its origins in the police 'barracks' or section houses where the recruit constables to the London and other urban forces commonly began their careers; the horse-play and practical joking of the barrack was even known to spill over to the beat.

From early on policemen were known to back each other up when in trouble from attacks on the street, from complaints by the public, and from discipline charges by their superiors.

By the mid nineteenth century this *esprit de corps* was also linked with an emerging corporate consciousness and pride in the job. Individual forces petitioned, and even took industrial action, over pay and conditions. 'Trade' newspapers, *The Police Service Advertiser* (from 1866) and *The Police Review* (from 1893), fostered this consciousness. While the *Review* itself objected to a police union with the right to strike, this corporate consciousness contributed to the movement for a police trade union in the years before the First World War. The self-help ethos of the police newspapers, with their educational pages and their inspirational biographies of men who had made good in the service, was very similar to that of other self-consciously respectable working-class organizations, notably the trade unions.

Craft consciousness and pride instil the practitioners of a skill with the notion of being the 'experts' and the 'professionals' in that skill. Of course these practitioners are 'experts', and problems arise when this expertise is questioned by a layperson or when there appears a threat of dilution. While the evidence is sparse, it appears that some nineteenth-century bobbies, rather than maintaining an even temper whatever the provocation, even bridled at members of the middle class who dared to question their authority. The stigmatized slum-dweller doubtless reasoned that he stood more chance on the streets than in the courts if he challenged a 'crusher' (the costermonger's slang for policeman) and responded accordingly.

The exigencies of world war led to the rapid training of the unskilled for certain skilled trades; the dilution of their trade craft was more or less grudgingly accepted by the skilled, but only for the duration of the war. Gaps in police ranks created by wartime military demands led to men being kept on beyond retirement age and to the recruitment of special constables. But war also boosted the demand for women police – a demand articulated, from the closing years of the Victorian period, by different feminist groups. During the First World War large, temporary military camps were thought to attract prostitutes and were feared as potential corrupters of other young women, while at the same time munitions factories brought together large numbers of young female workers. Women police were employed primarily to patrol **women police** and protect women in these areas. Generally the recruits were from a different social class to the male police; they were socially privileged and often well-educated. A few had links with feminist and suffragette activists, but the early women police were much more concerned with social purity than political and social change. The women police had an ambiguous position and, significantly, while they were required to have a knowledge of the duties of a constable, they were denied his key prerogative – that of arrest. If a woman police officer witnessed a breach of the law, it was her duty to enlist the help of the nearest male constable in the vicinity.

Some chief constables were prepared to maintain small numbers of women constables after the war to deal with problems involving women and children only. Others could not wait to dispense with women police, convinced that policework was man's work. There has been no study of what the rank and file thought of the few women officers who served in the First World War and the inter-war period, and the rather larger number that began to be recruited during the Second World War. However, it is probably indicative that the Police Federation only agreed to accept women as full and equal members in 1949.

*A woman police officer chasing children caught bathing in the Serpentine in London's Hyde Park, c.1926*

Do you think that policing was just another working-class occupation? If not, in what respects was it different? Did a tough police culture develop as a result of the job, or did the recruits bring it with them?

Only very recently have such questions begun to be addressed by historians. Traditional historians of the police have tended to stress the developing professionalism of the police, while labour historians have rarely considered the police as anything other than the body deployed against strikers and the organized working class. There were obvious differences between the job of the policeman and most working-class jobs – the regimentation and strict discipline is the most obvious. Yet the aspirations of the policeman as a worker were not that different from those of other workers. A tough, masculine culture may have gained something from the job, but it also drew on the broader cultural context; plenty of other male jobs developed an aggressive, self-consciously tough masculine element in their workplace sociability. The recruitment of ex-soldiers (as well as the military-style discipline) probably contributed to the police culture. Perhaps, too, the Victorian and Edwardian police attracted a particular form of personality, but this would be extremely difficult to prove.

# 6 A comparative perspective

## 6.1 'The best police in the world'

Notwithstanding the fact that they do not do everything they should, I believe that the Metropolitan Police, after the City [of London] Police, are the best police force in the world.

(John Burns, Independent Radical MP, *Hansard*, 13 July 1900, col.1559)

[Captain Nott-Bower, Chief Constable of the City of London] remarked that on the testimony of foreign countries, England was, in police matters, *facile princeps* [easily the best].

(*The Times*, 19 May 1906)

'Robert's ... wonderful faculty for combining official integrity and detachment with the part of a man and a brother ... has made the English policeman the envy of the civilized world.'

(*Justice of the Peace*, 13 February 1926, p.112)

It was commonly stated by members of parliament, policemen, journalists and others, at least from the close of the nineteenth century, that the English (sometimes the 'British') police were the best in the world. The criteria for the boast, however, were not always apparent. Charles Reith attempted an explanation based on his Whiggish understanding of national development by identifying two forms of police: 'the kin police or Anglo-Saxon police system, and the ruler-appointed gendarmerie, or despotic totalitarian police system. The first represents, basically, force exercised indirectly, by the people, from below upwards. The other represents force exercised, by authority, from above, downwards' (Reith, 1952, p.20). During the inter-war years refugees from Europe boosted such notions by contrasting their experiences of police in their own countries with such meetings as they had with polite bobbies; while few American film stars seem to have met the British press without commenting, 'Gee, I think your police are wonderful!'. The strikers at Silksworth Colliery and men marching on a demonstration of the National Union of Unemployed Workers probably took a very different view. Perceptions of policemen often depend on personal experience: the experiences of the British MP, of the foreign victim of the *Gestapo* asking directions in London, of the demonstrator stigmatized as the supporter of an alien creed and baton charged as a result, were vastly different.

## ACTIVITY 1.3

Look at the following illustrations of the German *Schutzmann*, the French *gendarme*, and the English bobby c.1890–1910. Are there any apparent differences in uniform and equipment? Does this suggest anything different about them?

*German* Schutzmann *(left)*
*French* gendarme *(centre),*
*and*
*English bobby (right)*

## COMMENT

We could have chosen other illustrations here which might have given a rather different image: for example, some English police forces had spikes on their helmets similar to the German policeman's *Pickelhaube* (and similar to the parade uniform helmets of British infantry regiments at the end of the nineteenth and beginning of the twentieth centuries). Furthermore, some English policemen on particularly lonely or dangerous beats were authorized to carry revolvers on belts on the outside of their uniforms from the mid 1880s, and on occasions, in the middle of the century, cutlasses were issued for similar beats or for dealing with riots. Yet the non-military/military contrast between the bobby and his European counterparts remains valid in many respects.

## 6.2  The origins of continental police forces

During the eighteenth century, police forces were developing in continental Europe, and these generally were based on the systems established in France. The absolutist princes of eighteenth-century Europe admired most things French and sought to model themselves and their institutions on the monarchs at Versailles. French models were specifically rejected by the English as being inimical to the unique form of 'liberty' which, it was claimed, had been established by the Glorious Revolution of 1688. The roads of provincial France were patrolled by the *maréchaussée*, literally the men of the marshals of France. This force was never particularly large – it reached about 4,000 men on the eve of the French Revolution – but it increasingly acquired a good reputation and early on in the Revolution it was virtually doubled in size and renamed the *gendarmerie nationale*. What specifically led the English to reject the *maréchaussée*, and later the *gendarmerie*, as a model for police reform was the military nature of the force. The men were recruited from former soldiers, they were uniformed and equipped like soldiers, and they were ultimately responsible to the minister of war. The wars of the French Revolution and then Napoleon extended the impact of French models by bringing, often at bayonet point, the physical experience of French administration to many of the states of Europe; when Napoleon was finally defeated the general effectiveness of his administration remained in men's minds. *Gendarmes* followed the French armies to police the troops, and *gendarmeries* were established by the French in the Low Countries, in Italy and in parts of Germany. When the French left, some of their reforms were ripped up by the roots, but the new *gendarmeries* remained. In other states, some of which had been among Napoleon's most determined opponents, the *gendarmerie* model was adopted for rural districts either during the French wars or subsequently. The Kingdom of Prussia established its *gendarmerie* in 1812; Spain created the *gardia civil* in 1844; the Austrian Empire inherited a Napoleonic *gendarmerie* in part of its north Italian provinces and later established a force to cover all its territories. But the *gendarmes* were not simply policemen; they also had a role in state-building. The map of Europe that emerged at the Congress of Vienna in 1815, following the fall of Napoleon, was rather different from that which had existed two decades before at the outset of the wars. In 1815 there were fewer states and they were bigger. The populations of these states were largely peasants, for many of whom the state meant nothing; they did not even speak the national language. The small brigades of *gendarmes*, usually four to six men, in their village or small-town barracks over which flew the national flag, were one of the principal physical manifestations of the nation-state in the countryside. The *gendarmes* were there, the state maintained, to keep the peace and to protect the rural dwellers from bandits and brigands; but they were also there to ensure that the peasants paid their dues to the nation state in the form of taxes and the annual quota of military conscripts.

While notions of English liberty kept ideas of police reforms along the *gendarmerie* model at bay, it is also arguable that nineteenth-century England did not need a *gendarmerie* of the European variety. There were no bandits or brigands comparable with those of southern Europe. There was no conscription and no violent unrest over taxes. There was no independent peasant class like that of rural Europe. English was the common language, and even if the understanding of the British state was shaky among the working classes, it appears to have been firmer than similar perceptions in much of rural Europe. But this is not to deny that, on occasions, English policing came close to resembling that of the *gendarmerie*. Serious rioting in south-west Wales between 1839 and 1844 led to the deployment of Metropolitan Police and troops, who carried out joint, armed patrols in the disturbed districts. During the 1850s and 1860s a succession of chief constables proposed having their men armed and trained as an auxiliary military force in case of war with, and invasion by, France. The restraining influence throughout these years was the Home Office. In the 1880s Sir Charles Warren, a former army officer appointed to be Commissioner of the Metropolitan Police, completely revised the police training book on the lines of the infantry training manual. Warren sought to keep the Home Office at arm's length, and he responded to criticism of his militarization of the force with a counterblast to his critics, including politicians, in *Murray's Magazine*. The outcry which this provoked, together with the failure of his men to make any headway with the 'Jack the Ripper' murders in London's Whitechapel district, forced his resignation.

Across the Irish Sea the British government did create a *gendarmerie*. The rural detachments of the Royal Irish Constabulary (RIC) lived in small barracks and carried out armed patrols of their districts. Indeed, *gendarmerie*-style police were developed across the British Empire: in Canada the French title for the Royal Canadian Mounted Police is still today *La Gendarmerie Royale du Canada*, and when the force was first established in the 1870s to colonize the Canadian west, the only thing that can really be said to have differentiated it from a regiment of light cavalry was the name 'police'.

It has been commonly and popularly asserted that the RIC provided the model for Britain's imperial police, but, as ever, the reality is rather more complex. Certainly men destined to command imperial forces did attend the RIC training school, and many former members of the Irish force served in other imperial forces. But the men who governed the empire tended to be pragmatic in the way that they drew on policing strategies according to immediate circumstances. When England's rural constabularies were established in the 1840s the magistrates of some county benches looked to the Irish Constabulary for their officer cadres, reasoning that the Metropolitan Police had been created for a city and that the Irish model, designed for the countryside, was rather more relevant to their needs – though this did not lead to small barracks and armed patrols. Alongside the former army officers recruited to command county police forces in England after 1856, there were also men who had been officers in the British imperial *gendarmeries*. Moreover, RIC men patrolling in Irish urban districts were, by the end of the century, little different from their English counterparts, and did not regard themselves as different.

## 6.3  Urban police/political police

There is a popular misconception in contemporary Britain that all French policemen are *gendarmes*. This is not, and never has been, the case. *Gendarmes* patrolled the countryside, while in French towns there were, and are, different policemen. Although the *maréchaussée* was seen as a model by some European princes during the eighteenth century, even more effective in their eyes were the Paris police. In London around 1750 the Fieldings had their dozen or so Bow Street Runners, and the different parishes had their constables and watches of varying numbers and varying degrees of efficiency. In contrast, the Lieutenant Général de Police de Paris had some 3,000 men directly under his command. These men had a variety of tasks relating to the eighteenth-century European understanding of the word 'police' (*police* in French; *polizey*, in a variety of spellings, in German). During the seventeenth and eighteenth centuries 'police' was commonly used as a synonym for government, particularly the government and administration of a city. The model police of eighteenth-century Paris were thus not only responsible for the prevention and detection of crime and the basic maintenance of public order, but also for supervising everything from markets to street lighting, to wet-nurses and beyond. They maintained surveillance of beggars and vagabonds, and also of those higher up the social scale who were critical of the existing order. A belief in the existence of thousands of active police spies convinced many in England that a police force meant a spy force.

Political policing was given a further boost by the French Revolution. In France, as well as in countries numbered among its ideological enemies, spies were employed by governments to inform on those who were politically suspect. Even in Britain an internal spy network was developed within a section of the Home Office responsible for checking aliens.

political policing

The fall of Napoleon left a legacy of problems in continental Europe. There was the fear of liberalism, which menaced the restored monarchs with its ideas of the career open to talent. Nationalism threatened the independence of monarchs and princes in Italy and Germany – both of which were 'geographical expressions' rather than united national states; it also threatened the existence of the Austrian Empire which contained Czechs, Germans, Italians, Magyars, Poles, Slovaks and others. In France a variety of groups claimed the right to govern: royalists (and after 1830 there were two kinds of royalist), Bonapartists, and republicans of a variety of different hues. These problems ensured that governments maintained political police to keep a surveillance of both the ideas and the rivals. At times the police did rather more than this, employing *agents provocateurs*; the police chiefs in Paris during the 1820s acquired a particularly unenviable reputation in this respect. Revolutionary disorders in 1820–21, 1830 and 1848 convinced European governments of the necessity of political surveillance.

Britain stood aside from much of this. Of course, the police were expected to keep an eye on political radicals, notably the Chartists, but political surveillance was never developed in the way it was in continental Europe. British governments and political commentators noted smugly that while they might have experienced Chartism, unlike the rest of Europe, nineteenth-century Britain had not had to contend with revolution. Opponents of the new police had objected to the idea of police as spies, and it appears that successive governments, both Whig and Tory, were largely in sympathy with such objections. The revelation that a Metropolitan Police sergeant had exceeded his authority in investigating a radical group in the early 1830s led to a parliamentary inquiry and the man's dismissal. Forty years later, in the aftermath of the Paris commune, a permanent secretary at the Home Office could boast to a colleague in the Foreign Office that: 'We can safely rely on the good sense of the great bulk of our working-classes to check and defeat the wild and impracticable designs of the few' (quoted in Porter, 1987, p.10). Furthermore, when it was felt necessary to make some enquiries into the International Workingmen's Association, the Home Office decided that the best way was to write for information to that body's secretary – Karl Marx. This kind of innocence was not to continue.

The turning point in Britain came with the Fenian bombing campaign in the early 1880s. To meet the threat the Special Irish Branch was created within the Metropolitan Police. At the conclusion of the scare the new department was continued, and gradually the 'Irish' part of the title was dropped. Simultaneously the British government found itself under pressure from its continental neighbours to do something about the political refugees to whom it had opened its doors. Earlier in the century British governments had resisted such pressure, but anarchist bombings and murders in Europe, together with concerns that Britain was losing its industrial dominance and that the British 'race' was being undermined by an exceptionally high birth rate among the residuum in city slums, combined to make the government more prepared to develop a political police. It remained a relatively small-scale affair compared with most of its European counterparts. But even in continental Europe in the last quarter of the nineteenth century political policing was rather more restrained than it had been after the fall of Napoleon; the great exception was Russia, where the secret police (the *ochrana*) became a law unto itself and engaged in a savage war of terror and counter-terror against anarchists, nihilists, social revolutionaries and virtually anyone else to whom they took a dislike.

Shortly before the First World War it was still possible to find the British Home Secretary reacting furiously in parliament to the suggestion that the Special Branch was a 'political police', but the run-up to the war with its succession of spy scares had brought significant developments in links between provincial chief constables and the embryonic secret service. The war itself, and then the Russian Revolution, cemented these links and brought British political surveillance more in line with that in Europe. Of course, there was no *Gestapo* in Britain, but the traditional, popular image of *Gestapo* terror as all-pervading is itself fanciful. Recent research into surviving *Gestapo* files has demonstrated that this was a relatively small organization which put great reliance on support and information received from the general public (Gellately, 1990).

This discussion of political police has diverted me, as it diverted and obsessed many of the early opponents of the Metropolitan Police, from the subject of capital city police, though it remains closely linked. Political policing was not the only kind of policing regarded necessary in the capital cities of eighteenth- and nineteenth-century Europe. On 1 March 1828 a senior officer in the Prefecture of Police in Paris issued a circular:

> The essential object of our municipal police is the safety of the inhabitants of Paris ... Safety by day and night, free traffic movement, clean streets, the supervision of, and precaution against, accidents, the maintenance of order in public places, the seeking out of offences and their perpetrators ... The municipal police is a paternal police; that is the intention of the Prefect.

(quoted in Tulard, 1976, pp.436–7)

Napoleon had created the Prefect of Police to replace the Lieutenant-Général, who had disappeared along with the rest of the old regime's administrative structure during the Revolution. The description of this 'paternal police' might have fitted that of the Lieutenant-Général. Moreover, the year after this circular, in an attempt to improve the low standing of the Paris police following the employment of *agents provocateurs* and sensational revelations about the detective department, a new, reforming Prefect, Louis Debelleyme, created a new kind of uniformed patrolman – the *sergent de ville*. While far fewer in numbers than the constables of the Metropolitan Police, the *sergents* were lionized by their supporters in much the same way. 'The *sergent de ville* of Paris', according to one commentator in the early 1840s,

> is the guardian angel of the peaceable citizen, the terror of criminals. Without him your wives, your mothers, your sisters would, at every instant, be exposed to the coarseness of every lout. In the streets in your absence, to whom do they turn to bring an end to these vile insults? To the *sergent de ville* alone, *for this man is the law in uniform.*
>
> For these agents hard labours, weariness, unpleasantness; for us happiness and pleasure. When Paris enjoys the fine days of summer; when festivals and dances follow each other; when, in the public halls, carnival unravels its long chain of masks; when all Paris dances in the transports of feverish excitement, a single man remains impassive in the midst of turbulence. On his feet, immovable, throughout the long night he sees pleasure flit before him and laugh around him, without ever being able to take part himself.
>
> (Birroteau, 1840–42)

In the 1850s Napoleon III set out to improve the *sergents* by introducing various practices that he had witnessed at first hand among the London police, notably a regular beat system and numbers on the men's collars to make them instantly identifiable. Yet for all the praise heaped on the *sergents* (renamed, later in the century, *gardiens de la paix*), they never acquired the popularity of the London bobby among the respectable classes. At the end of the century Prefect Louis Lépine introduced another package of reforms to get rid of brutal and undesirable men and improve the public standing of the rest. The problem is how to explain the reasons for the different perceptions.

It would appear that, immediately before Lépine's appointment in 1893, discipline in the Paris police was poor, which may account for the brutality towards demonstrators and the cavalier treatment of bystanders, and that there was intense rivalry and hostility between different departments. Earlier I gave examples of brutal treatment meted out by London policemen during the nineteenth and early twentieth centuries; nevertheless, while there were criticisms and concerns expressed at times, the overall image of the Metropolitan Police does not appear to have reached the depths of that experienced by the *gardiens*. The only explanation I can offer is linked to the overtly political role of the Paris police and the differing attitudes held by articulate and influential members of society in Britain and France towards elements of constitutional government. Articulate and influential men in Victorian Britain rarely came into contact with policemen – remember, the police guarded St. James by watching St. Giles. In France, since such men could be Bonapartists, royalists or republicans, it was quite likely that they could find themselves, at some point in their lives, under police suspicion and surveillance. The French might have been proud to have given the world the idea of the rights of man, yet they recognized that this had not given them secure or stable government. In Victorian Britain, however, men took pride in a secure and stable government which had escaped the revolutionary upheavals of the continent; they criticized the political party to which they were opposed, but they did not criticize the constitutional and administrative system that was taken to be a model for others to follow. By the 1850s at the latest, the Metropolitan Police, and subsequently other police forces, appears to have been accepted as an integral part of the constitutional structure.

Outside of Paris the municipalities of France were policed by a mixture of state-appointed and locally appointed men. Legislation passed early in the French Revolution required every town with a population of 5,000 or more to have a *commissaire*. Under Napoleon the *commissaires* became central government appointees; larger towns acquired more than one, and in 1854 the post of chief *commissaire* was established in 23 major cities and towns with several such officers – Marseilles, for example, with a population of 198,000 in 1855 had one central and 18 other *commissaires*; Bordeaux, population 90,900, had one and 12 respectively. The *commissaires* had the usual police roles, but were also expected to keep in touch with, and pass information to, central government in Paris. However, the rank-and-file policemen who worked under the *commissaires* were appointed by the municipalities, and a complicated system of command and control could develop. When a local municipality was of a very different political complexion to the government in Paris, friction between the local mayor and the *commissaire* could become acute. The police of a few cities and towns were brought under the direct control of a departmental prefect. Lyon was the first of these in 1851; the city was notorious for its radical working class, which launched two full-scale insurrections (1831 and 1834) and was a constant worry throughout the revolution of 1848 and the short-lived (1848–52) Second Republic. It was believed that the Prefect of the Department of the Rhône – a government functionary with overall responsibility for the administration of the department – would have a better overall control of the police than the mayor. But more than fifty years were to elapse before another French city had its police taken over in such a manner (Marseilles in 1908), and the municipal police of France were not brought into a national organization until the Vichy regime in 1941.

I have largely stressed the Anglo-French comparisons in this discussion primarily because they provide significant models which others sought to follow. Liberals in nineteenth-century Europe looked to what they understood to be the Metropolitan Police model to develop a police system, but they generally lacked the political and social environment in which such a police could take root. Italian liberals, for example, were impressed by the English police, but equally their concerns for agrarian uprisings, anarchist bombs, socialist demonstrations and southern brigands ensured that they maintained their militarized *carabinieri* and developed a national civilian police in the shape of the *guardie di città* (or *guardie di pubblica sicurezza*). Yet, at the same time, many of the states which are generally assumed to have been far more centralized than nineteenth-century Britain continued to have urban police linked closely with the mayors and municipalities rather than central government. Towards the end of the nineteenth century in Italy, for example, there were about 10,000 *guardie municipali* responsible to local government. It was not until the 1890s that the Prussian state began seriously to contemplate taking over the municipal police in its various territories; this was partly because of concerns about democratized municipalities choosing left-wing mayors who were not considered the kinds of individual to be entrusted with the supervision of police forces.

Table 1.2 summarizes the development of policing and the establishment of police forces across Europe.

## Table 1.2  The establishment of modern police in Europe and the United States to 1860

| Urban police | Year | District or national police |
|---|---|---|
| | *1544* | France (*maréchaussée*) |
| Paris | *1667* | |
| Police Commissioners | | |
|   St. Petersburg | | |
|   Berlin | *1742* | |
|   Vienna | *1751* | |
| Dublin | *1786*[1] | |
| | *1787*[2] | Ireland (partial: disturbed counties) |
| | *1790* | France (*gendarmerie*): subsequently spreading throughout the Napoleonic Empire in Northern Italy, the Rhineland and the Low Countries |
| Glasgow | *1800* | |
| Edinburgh | *1805* | |
| | *1812* | Prussia; Bavaria |
| | *1814*[3] | Ireland (partial: disturbed counties) |
| | *1814* | Piedmont, Italy (forerunner of *carabinieri*; other Italian states followed suit) |
| | *1822* | Ireland (all counties: compulsory) |
| | *1826* | Russia |
| London | *1829* | |
| Scottish burghs (enabling Act; subsequent Acts 1847 and 1850) | *1833* | Greece |
| English boroughs (incorporated towns) | *1835* | |
| | *1836* | Ireland (reformed) |
| Dublin (reformed) | *1837* | |
| | *1839/40* | England and Scotland (partial) (enabling Acts for counties) |
| | *1844* | Spain |
| New York | *1845* | |
| Berlin | *1848* | |
| | *1849* | Austria |
| Turin, Italy | *1852* | |
| Paris (reformed) | *1854* | |
| Boston, Chicago, Philadelphia | *1855* | |
| | *1856* | England (all counties and boroughs: compulsory) |
| | *1857* | Scotland (all counties and burghs: compulsory) |

1 This centralized police was abolished in 1795, revived in 1799, and reformed in 1808.

2 Experiment lapsed *c.*1800.

3 This force was abolished in 1836.

Source: based on Palmer, 1988, p.17

# 6.4 The US alternative

A further, and final, comparison needs to be brought in here. The democratic nature of the United States kept police forces closely bound to the elected officials who ran urban government. Some police chiefs (in the shape of sheriffs) were themselves elected; elected mayors appointed others. In some nineteenth-century cities the bosses of electoral wards appointed police captains and even patrolmen. The system could ensure close links between the police and their communities: thus, there were occasions when local police refused to protect blackleg labour during strikes, especially if the employer was based out of town. But where the local mayor and corporation were employers, the police could find themselves deployed in an unashamedly partisan fashion against strikers, particularly when the latter were immigrants and could easily be labelled as un-American. The municipal police in the USA could be used in an equally blatant way at election time on the part of the faction in power. Yet the openness of US society meant also that the police were regularly under scrutiny in the courts and in the press. William McAdoo, a former chief of the New York Police, visited London in 1909 and was astonished by the difference between the police of the two cities:

> The internal workings of the machinery are not exposed to public view. Transfers of policemen and police officials are not noticed in the public prints …

> The press praises the police on every possible occasion. The press has no means of knowing of the daily volume of crime except through the courts or the reports of persons made directly to the newspapers, so the police are not held to the same direct accounting as in New York, where the statistics are inspected every hour, or, at least were under my administration …

> The [police] court treated the policeman as part of the machinery of the law, and as partners with it in the doing of substantial justice. Their intercourse is characterized by mutual respect and goodwill … Not a single policeman was reprimanded or criticized in any case, even when the court made prompt acquittals as against the charge of the constables.

> (McAdoo, 1909, pp.658–9 and 661)

From what you have read so far, in what respects are the British police different from police in other countries?

There is a problem establishing just what is meant by 'different' or 'unique'. In one sense every national police system is different or unique – there are clear organizational and structural differences between the British police and others. However, what they did and do on the ground is probably very similar – remember that the London Metropolitan Police system of beat patrols became a model for other states. What most commentators, politicians and policemen appear to be alluding to when they speak of 'difference' relates to the ethos of policing in Britain, with its alleged non-political nature and the fact that, as a general rule, officers have only rarely been armed. Of course, it can be argued that much, even most, of the difference is the result of contingency and good fortune, rather than design.

# **7** Conclusion

This brief history of the coming of the new police has highlighted the following issues. First, there was protracted resistance in England to the very *idea* of a police force on the grounds that such an instrument of government would invariably interfere with revered constitutional freedoms and liberties and disturb the peace of the country. Political opposition obliged the police reformers to drop all hopes of creating a national police force. Instead, a bewildering assortment of forces gradually took to the streets alongside a number of other individuals and groups who were performing local policing functions. While the differences must not be overemphasized, it nevertheless remains the case that three different types of police force gradually emerged in England and Wales, namely the Metropolitan Police, the borough constabularies and the county forces.

Second, during their formative period, numerous questions were raised about the precise purpose of the new forces. Questions of cost-effectiveness and efficiency surfaced repeatedly, particularly in relation to their crime prevention function, and eventually proactive strategies were developed in an attempt to curb crime. However, it was acknowledged by key sections of English society that a disciplined police *force* was manifestly useful when it came to industrial disputes, large-scale demonstrations and bringing some semblance of routine order to public thoroughfares.

Third, as the century wore on, discussion of the police centred on the vexed question of the precise nature of the political and legal relations governing policework and the constitutional implications of the claims by a growing number of chief police officers that they were operationally independent.

Finally, despite being strictly organized in a hierarchical bureaucracy, the English bobby on his beat enjoyed a considerable degree of legally mandated discretion in deciding how to respond to different offenders. How that discretion was exercised became a key question in the policing of different neighbourhoods and social groups.

As the next chapter makes clear, at the end of the twentieth century British society is still debating virtually all of the issues and controversies bequeathed by the creation of the new police.

# Further reading

The most recent thorough historical overview of the police in England is Emsley (1991). Palmer (1988) is an enormous, comprehensive study which compares the very different origins of modern police in England and Ireland. Carson and Idzikowska (1989) document and analyse the main structural processes underpinning the emergence and growth of the 'new police' in Scotland. The contributors to Anderson and Killingray (1991) examine how colonial policework was organized in various political, legal, administrative and anthropological contexts. Emsley and Weinberger (1991) detail how police forces in Western European states were constituted and how they worked within different political and legal mandates and developed distinctive policing styles and self-images. For a seminal analysis of the differences between the new urban police in England and the United States see Miller (1977).

# References

Anderson, D.M. and Killingray, D. (eds) (1991) *Policing the Empire: Government, Authority and Control, 1830–1940*, Manchester, Manchester University Press.

Birroteau, C. (1840–42) 'Le sergent de ville', in *Les français peints par eux-mêmes*, Paris.

Carson, K. and Idzikowska, H. (1989) 'The social production of Scottish policing, 1795–1900', in Hay, D. and Snyder, F. (eds) *Policing and Prosecution in Britain, 1750–1850*, Oxford, Clarendon Press.

Conley, C.A. (1991) *The Unwritten Law: Criminal Justice in Victorian Kent*, Oxford, Oxford University Press.

Daley, H. (1986) *This Small Cloud: A Personal Memoir*, London, Weidenfeld and Nicolson.

Emsley, C. (1987) *Crime and Society in England 1750–1900*, London, Longman.

Emsley, C. (1991) *The English Police: A Political and Social History*, Hemel Hempstead, Harvester-Wheatsheaf (second edn Longman, forthcoming).

Emsley, C. and Weinberger, B. (eds) (1991) *Policing Western Europe: Politics, Professionalism and Public Order, 1850–1940*, New York and London, Greenwood Press.

Evans, H. (1889) 'The London County Council and the police', *Contemporary Review*, vol.LV, March, pp.445–61.

Gellately, R. (1990) *The Gestapo and German Society: Enforcing Racial Policy, 1933–1945*, Oxford, Clarendon Press.

McAdoo, W. (1909) 'The London police from a New York point of view', *Century Magazine*, no.LXXVIII, September, pp.649–70.

Miller, W.R. (1977) *Cops and Bobbies: Police Authority in New York and London, 1830–1870*, Chicago, Chicago University Press.

Palmer, S.H. (1988) *Police and Protest in England and Ireland 1780–1850*, Cambridge, Cambridge University Press.

Philips, D. and Storch, R.D. (1994) 'Whigs and coppers: the Grey ministry's national police scheme, 1832', *Historical Research*, vol.LXVII, no.1, pp.75–90.

Porter, B. (1987) *The Origins of the Vigilant State: The London Metropolitan Police Special Branch before the First World War*, London, Weidenfeld and Nicolson.

Reiner, R. (1985) *The Politics of the Police*, Hemel Hempstead, Harvester-Wheatsheaf.

Reith, C. (1938) *The Police Idea*, Oxford, Oxford University Press.

Reith, C. (1952) *The Blind Eye of History*, London, Faber and Faber.

**Sharpe, J. (1996) 'Crime, order and historical change', in Muncie, J. and McLaughlin, E. (eds) *The Problem of Crime*, London, Sage in association with The Open University.**

Stevenson, J. and Cook, C. (1977) *The Slump: Society and Politics During the Depression*, London, Jonathan Cape.

Storch, R.D. (1976) 'The policeman as domestic missionary: urban discipline and popular culture in Northern England, 1850–1880', *Journal of Social History*, vol.9, no.4, pp.481–509.

Stuart, J. (1889) 'The Metropolitan Police', *Contemporary Review*, vol.LV, April, pp.622–36.

Tobias, J. J. (1979) *Crime and Police in England 1700–1900*, New York, St Martins Press.

Tulard, J. (1976) *Paris et son administration (1800–1830)*, Paris, Ville de Paris Commission des Travaux Historiques.

Weinberger, B. (1987) 'Police perceptions of labour in the inter-war period: the case of the unemployed and of miners on strike', in Snyder, F. and Hay, D. (eds) *Labour, Law and Crime: An Historical Perspective*, London, Tavistock.

# Chapter 2
# Police, Policing and Policework

*by Eugene McLaughlin*

## Contents

# 1 Introduction

**D**uring the last years of the twentieth century a significant reshaping of the structure, functioning and culture of the British police has been set in process. While some commentators perceive the shifts as just the latest of many 'patch and repair' attempts to improve the performance of the *police*, others argue that the changes are so profound and radical in implication that they amount to a paradigmatic revolution in *policing*. To evaluate these different viewpoints, this chapter provides an overview of the recurring debates about policing. It traces and analyses: the changing nature of local, national and international *policework*; re-dramatizations of the police 'self', including the re-imagining of the cultural identity of police officers; the debate about the use of police powers; and the changing structure of police governance.

Throughout the chapter a sense of perspective can be gained by keeping in mind the following points. First, there is no predetermined or indisputable reason why a society's need for social order requires the establishment or permanent maintenance of an organized police institution. Policing *may* be socially necessary, but bureaucratically constituted policework is not. The formation of a police bureaucracy in the UK, as discussed in Chapter 1, was not *inevitable* but *contingent* on a political élite's fear of the turbulent, volatile city and its vision of what an orderly, disciplined metropolis might look like.

Second, in many parts of the UK this vision of social order and authority was contested and strenuously resisted. From the outset, each new policing regime struggled to establish a legitimate licence to operate in the existing local framework of public, communal and private social controls. The new modality of policing was thus reworked and renegotiated with different audiences; multiple, relatively autonomous versions of policing were thus produced, each with particular *symbolic, communicative* and *instrumental* meanings for specific social groups.

Third, it is important to remember that none of these versions was necessarily permanent; societies have totally or partially reorganized or even discarded previously hegemonic police bureaucracies when they outlived their political usefulness or as a result of public disenchantment.

Fourth, the police institution is shaped or constrained not only by temporal, spatial and situational factors. Police organizations are able to exercise powerful pressure on society, actively influencing the context within which they operate and defining their own development.

Fifth, police officers as individuals have the autonomy necessary to transform and control to a degree their internal and external working environment. They are involved in a constant struggle to reconcile the policies and mission statements of the organization, legal procedures and public expectations with their idea of what meaningful policework is.

Finally, in the late twentieth century, fictional representations and media simulations structure and distort our perceptions of 'real' policing and policework by focusing on the crime control function.

Unless specified otherwise, the policing system of England and Wales is used as the key empirical point of reference throughout this chapter. However, the general conceptual issues raised are of relevance to debates about police, policing and policework in any democratic society.

# 2  The nature of public policework

As we have seen in Chapter 1, any serious consideration of public policing must ask the question: What role do the police perform in society?

### ACTIVITY 2.1

Examine Figure 2.1 to familiarize yourself with the nature of the modern police task. Do you think that these activities should be a police responsibility? Are they interrelated? Try to rank them on a scale of 1 to 5 according to what you think the core of modern policework should be. What factors influenced your ranking?

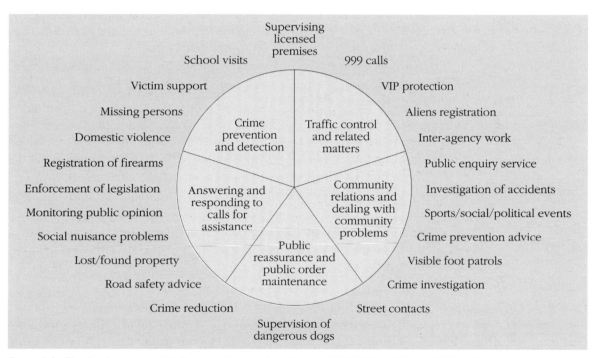

*Figure 2.1  The five key areas of policework (Source: Association of Chief Police Officers, 1993, p.2)*

## 2.1  Order maintenance or law enforcement?

Research suggests that the popular image of people making contact with the police to report serious violations of the criminal law is incorrect. The Association of Chief Police Officers (ACPO) estimates that over a full 24-hour period, typically only 18 per cent of calls for help are about crime, and they take up approximately 30 per cent of police time (Association of Chief Police Officers, 1993). The other 70 per cent of policework consists of reassuring the public; giving authoritative advice and assistance on a wide range of issues; taking control of and regulating problematic personal and interpersonal situations; dispute management; and dealing with miscellaneous social problems, the responsibility for which has been historically imposed on the police. Or as Bittner puts it, *reacting* to 'something-ought-not-to-be-happening-and-about-which-something-ought-to-be-done-NOW' calls (Bittner, 1974, p.30). This picture of policework lends support to those who argue that we must see the police, first and foremost, as a multipurpose 24-hour emergency order maintenance service (Punch and Naylor, 1973, p.358). The core question is why people think that calling the police will help. Bittner (1970) provides us with an important answer (see Extract 2.1); the arrival of the police creates the dramatic appearance of an authoritative, constraining, moral order. In this sense the police officer is the visible, symbolic representative of the state and of the rule and force of law.

### Extract 2.1   Bittner: 'Non-negotiable coercion'

Police intervention means above all making use of the capacity and authority to overpower resistance to an attempted solution in the native habitat of the problem. There can be no doubt that this feature of policework is uppermost in the minds of people who solicit police aid or direct the attention of the police to problems, that persons against whom the police proceed have this feature in mind and conduct themselves accordingly and that every conceivable police intervention projects the message that force may be, and may have to be, used to achieve a desired objective. It does not matter whether the persons who seek police help are private citizens or other government officials, nor does it matter whether the problem in hand involves some aspect of law enforcement or is totally unconnected with it.

It must be emphasized, however, that the conception of the centrality of the capacity to use force in the police role does not entail the conclusion that the ordinary occupational routines consist of the actual exercise of this capacity ... the actual use of physical coercion and restraint is rare for all policemen and ... many policemen are virtually never in the position of having to resort to it. What matters is that police procedure is defined by the feature that it may not be opposed in its course, and that force can be used if it is opposed. This is what the existence of the police makes available to society. Accordingly, the question, 'What are policemen supposed to do?' is almost completely identical with the question, 'What kinds of situations require remedies that are non-negotiably coercible?'

(Bittner, 1970, pp.40–1)

If we accept that the police are primarily involved in 'order maintenance' and that people call the police because of the nature of the 'force' that officers bring to bear on a situation, we are left with two intriguing questions:

*   What is the nature of the social order the police are maintaining?
*   In what situations and against which individuals will 'non-negotiable force' be employed?

## 2.2   Losing the fight against crime

When we think of the role of the British police in controlling crime, we immediately conjure up images of the bobby on the beat, acting as a deterrent and reassuring the public; of the police car rushing to the scene of crime and of detectives involved in the painstaking process of working out 'whodunnit'. However, if we examine the research that has been carried out on these classic forms of policework since the 1960s, we can see that their effectiveness has been increasingly called into question.

### 2.2.1 Patrol work

The constable on the beat, as Chapter 1 has indicated, has always been presented as the backbone of the British police and in most forces, the majority of officers are formally assigned to patrol work. However, Home Office research indicates that, because of specialization and factors including the shift system, holidays, training, sick leave, paper work, and time spent interviewing prisoners, uniformed constables spend between only one-half and two-thirds of their time outside the police station and approximately only one-third of that time actually patrolling (Morris and Heal, 1981). Moreover, routine *random* unsupervised patrol work, which has been inadequately briefed, appears to have minimal impact on local crime levels:

*PC George Dixon of Dock Green became the fictional embodiment of the English bobby on the beat and has come to represent a golden age of policing that lacks the uncertainties that plague present-day policework*

> Set in temporal and geographical contexts, crimes are rare events, and are committed stealthily – as often as not in places out of reach of patrols. The chances of patrols catching offenders red-handed are therefore small, and even if these are somewhat increased, law breakers may not notice or may not care. An average foot beat in a large British city covers a square half-mile, with 4–5 miles of public roadway and a population of about 4,000. Thus, given present burglary rates and evenly distributed patrol coverage, a patrolling policeman in London could expect to pass within 100 yards of a burglary in progress roughly once every eight years – but not necessarily to catch the burglar or even realise that the crime was taking place.
>
> (Clarke and Hough, 1984, pp.6–7)

According to Morris and Heal (1981), increasing the number of officers on the beat would not necessarily reduce the crime rate, nor would it constitute an effective use of resources in crime control teams. From this perspective, then, the constable on the beat is nothing more than an expensive public relations exercise.

Mobile patrols fare no better. According to available research, increasing the speed with which patrols respond to calls from the public ('fire-brigade' policing) is unlikely to achieve much:

'fire brigade' policing

> Police officers attending to calls from the victims of crime might travel fast and hopefully, but more often than not their arrival signals the beginning of a mundane, routinized and often frustrating course of activity. They usually arrive after the critical incident has occurred and so have to make do with a mere report of it. They must rely upon external sources to find an adequate 'trace' of what has happened, and so their active role is minimal beyond the routine checking of such sources. Furthermore, because they are now dealing with history, it is seldom critical for them to uncover quickly more evidence. The

officer attending the scene of an undisturbed and successfully accomplished midnight burglary the morning after will usually gain little more from interviewing the neighbours instantly rather than later. Neither his [nor her] own personal situation, nor that of the victim, nor in most cases that of the offender, will be much affected by instant action ... In most ... cases the role of the police, apart from giving advice and consolation would be little more than that of information processors, compilers of a formal record of what happened.

(Bradley *et al.*, 1986, p.174)

As became all too apparent in the 1970s, the decision to put officers in vehicles brought with it a whole series of damaging, unintended consequences. It effectively isolated the police by removing the need for officers to walk through neighbourhoods and cut out access to neighbourhood information and gossip:

What the patrol car officer sees is familiar buildings with unfamiliar people around them. What the public sees is a familiar police car with an unfamiliar officer in it. The public has little chance to tell the officer what is going on in the community: who is angry at whom about what, whose children are running wild, what threats have been made, and who is suddenly living above his apparent means. Stripped of this contextual knowledge, the patrol officer sees, but cannot truly observe.

(Sherman, 1983, p.149)

The old police skill of negotiating with thé public was also lost. Police officers finding themselves in a difficult public encounter could request immediate help ('back-up') from police vehicles cruising in the area. As a result, the potential for conflictual police–public encounters increased. Moreover, it encouraged adrenalin-driven policework as certain officers looked for thrilling chases and 'trouble'. In this version of policework, walking the beat was left to the most junior and inexperienced officers or became a punishment posting for those who ran foul of the organization.

### 2.2.2 Detective work: fact and fiction

In the period following the Second World War, detective work underwent significant developments with the establishment of specialist local, regional and national crime squads to deal with new forms of organized crime (see Hobbs, 1988; Maguire and Norris, 1992). It was also during this period that the detective became pre-eminent in media representations of policework. Two conceptions of detective work captured the public imagination. First, there was the image of the 'hard-boiled' detective called to the scene of the crime who, in the process of attempting to answer the question of 'whodunnit', used considerable organizational autonomy and professional skills to work out the logic and rationale of the criminal. The investigation unfolded: the results of forensic evidence were analysed; victims and witnesses questioned; the 'modus operandi' of particular criminals matched against the facts of the case; professional hunches followed; informants' hints and leads methodically inquired into and the usual suspects rounded up and questioned. The second image was even more dramatic, with élite squads of local detectives or Regional Crime Squads putting together sophisticated operations and 'stings' to catch professional criminal gangs in the act or to break multi-million pound crime rackets. Both images confirmed the idea that plain-clothes detectives were the direct heirs to the eighteenth-century 'thief-taker', spending a hectic working life putting dangerous criminals behind bars (see **Clarke, 1996**).

However, on several counts, such popular representations are hardly consistent with the reality of detective work. First, only 40–45 per cent of detective time is devoted to investigating crime. The rest of the time is spent on report writing, attending court, taking refreshments and miscellaneous duties (Burrows and Tarling, 1982). Second, detectives spend a considerable amount of time on 'relatively minor crime matters' which could have been handled by uniformed officers. Third, there is a low level of proactivity; that is, co-ordinated work aimed at identifying and apprehending offenders, especially the more serious or prolific criminals. Fourth, a significant number of offences are 'self-detecting' in

*In the mind's eye of Inspector Morse, crime analysis computer programmes, customers' charters, quality of service and performance league tables will take the romance and mystery out of detective work*

nature. The offender's identity is apparent from the outset; victims or witnesses know who did it, or the offender is caught red-handed or clearly implicated in some other way. As Hilliyard (1982) puts it, 'some crimes the police just can't help clearing up'.

Finally, in the course of the 1980s it became apparent that in certain forces detectives were continuing to manipulate the clear-up rates. To clear the books, they were depending heavily on criminals and convicted prisoners confessing to other offences. In 1986 a Kent police officer, PC Ron Walker, alleged that scores of his CID (Criminal Investigation Department) colleagues were involved in the routine fabrication of crime rates (*The Observer*, 24 September 1989). The detectives stood accused of persuading convicted criminals to 'cough' or confess to hundreds of crimes that they had not committed, or which had not even occurred, in order to improve the force clear-up rates. In some parts of Kent, such fabrications resulted in detection rates, for certain difficult categories of crime, which were almost twice the national average. This case demonstrated that there were serious problems with using the clear-up rate as an accurate indicator of police performance and success. At the very least, researchers argued, we needed to distinguish very carefully between *primary* clear-up rates, based on actual charges and cautions, and *secondary* ones, based on prison visits and offenders 'asking' for other offences to be taken into consideration (Walker, 1992; Audit Commission, 1990). The overall negative picture of this reactive policing is represented clearly in Figure 2.2.

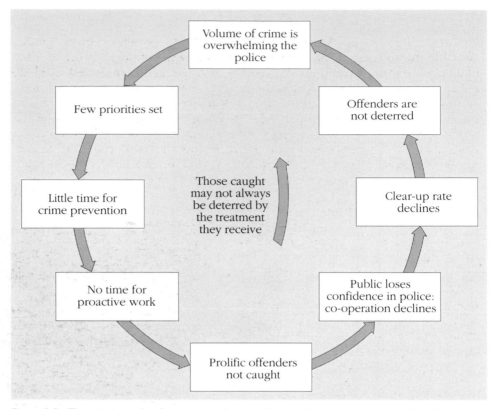

*Figure 2.2 The vicious circle of crime control: the police and the rest of the criminal justice system are caught in a vicious circle of reactive policing in which crime threatens to overwhelm them (Source: Audit Commission, 1993, p.40)*

### 2.2.3 Saturation policing: legal order or social order?

proactive policing

In the 1970s and early 1980s, certain police forces in England and Wales responded to the problem of the ineffectiveness of traditional methods by turning to labour-intensive pre-emptive tactics, or proactive policing. Rather than waiting for a call for assistance or reacting to yet another crime report, they launched high profile offensives against street crime, robbery and burglary. 'Lawless' inner-city neighbourhoods and 'troublespots' were, without warning, flooded with officers and special units who stopped, searched and questioned pedestrians, set up roadblocks, raided premises and engaged in intensive plain-clothes surveillance.

## ACTIVITY 2.2

Draw up a list of what you regard as the possible short-term advantages and disadvantages of this type of law-enforcement strategy. Try to assess how the various groups or audiences affected by the strategy might perceive it, and consider potential long-term outcomes for police–community relations.

## COMMENT

Senior police officers hoped that high visibility sweeps would: garner valuable information about the movements of local criminals; produce hard and fast evidence of criminal involvement by catching criminals 'red-handed'; deter potential criminals; boost the morale of officers; reassure potential victims; create a local image of police 'omnipresence'; and prove to the public that the police were capable of fighting crime. However, despite the proclaimed successes, the strategy generated serious problems for the police. First, it was perceived by those on the receiving end as a crude and heavy-handed exercise of power and authority which tended not to discriminate very effectively between the innocent and the guilty. Everyone in a given locale was treated as suspect, which caused widespread individual

resentment, distrust and estrangement, particularly among young people. Second, whole communities and neighbourhoods began to complain vociferously of civil rights violations, harassment, maltreatment, planting of evidence, provocation and *blanket criminalization* (**Keith, 1993**). Black communities, in particular, contrasted this over-policing with the lack of an adequate police response and 'under-protection' when they reported incidents of racial violence and harassment. Such actions also generated the first instances in the UK of 'neighbourhood watches' in which black communities watched and monitored the police, reported on their activities, collected testimonies of harassment and campaigned for independent inquiries (see McLaughlin, 1994). Finally, police–community relations in certain areas deteriorated to such a degree that both sides came to expect and prepare for conflictual contacts. Overall, it is no exaggeration to say that fighting the war against crime transformed these neighbourhoods into 'front-lines' where the police lost the 'hearts and minds' of people and were regarded as an army of occupation. The seemingly endless police pressure generated individual and collective protest, resistance and anti-police riots (see Extract 2.2).

*Operation Swamp began in Brixton on 6 April 1981. By 10 April police officers had made 943 stops which resulted in 93 people being charged with minor offences and one with robbery. On 11 April the neighbourhood was engulfed in anti-police riots*

## Extract 2.2   Lord Scarman: 'The Brixton disorders, 10–12 April 1981'

### 'Hard policing'

The view which I have reached is that Operation 'Swamp' was a serious mistake, given the tension which existed between the police and the local community ...

It was submitted, however, that if street crime was to be tackled, there was no alternative way of doing the job. Even if this be correct, it was still necessary to assess the risk to public order. The seriousness of the risk arose from the presence in Brixton of hostile and resentful young black people whose anger against the police had affected also the attitudes and beliefs of the older, more responsible, members of their community. The question for the police was, therefore: was it wise in the circumstances to mount the operation? Had policing attitudes and methods been adjusted to deal fully with the problems of policing a multi-racial society, there would have been a review in depth of the public order implications of the operation, which would have included local consultation. And, had this taken place, I believe, as I have already indicated, that a street 'saturation' operation would not have been launched when it was [in April 1981] ...

I would add two further comments. First, the evidence ... is not clear that a street saturation operation does diminish street crime: it may well only drive it elsewhere. And, after the operation is ended, street crime returns. If, therefore, such an operation is, in the short term, the only direct action possible against street crime, its efficacy is doubtful. But in the long term the development of a style of policing which is designed to secure public approval and respect is likely to be more effective. It is, therefore, remarkable that the opinion of the home beat officers, the importance of whose role is well understood by the senior command, was not sought on the wisdom of the operation.

For these reasons I conclude that attitudes and methods in the senior command of 'L' District had not become sufficiently adjusted to the problems of policing a multi-racial community. In the result, this failure became a factor not only in the loss of local confidence in the police but also in the causation of the April disorders.

(Scarman, 1981, p.68)

## 2.3   Managing crime effectively

The problem of developing effective crime control strategies has presented the police with a fundamental dilemma. On the one hand, Klockars warns senior officers that controlling crime will always be a highly problematic and indeed impossible mandate:

The fact is that the 'war on crime' is a war police not only cannot win, but cannot in any real sense fight. They cannot win it because it is simply not within their power to change those things – such as unemployment, the age distribution of the population, moral education, freedom, civil liberties, ambitions, and the social economic opportunities to realize them – that influence the amount of crime in any society. Moreover, any kind of real war on crime is something no democratic society would be prepared to let its police fight. We would simply be unwilling to tolerate the kind of abuses to the civil liberties of innocent citizens – to us – that fighting any real war on crime would inevitably involve.

(Klockars, 1988, p.241)

From this perspective the police should be careful not to represent themselves solely as professional crime busters or to make promises to politicians and the public on which they cannot deliver. On the other hand, the public, politicians, media and, indeed, rank-and-file officers *need* to believe that the police are or can become effective crime fighters. Thus the organization has been compelled to rethink, at a variety of levels, its entire approach to this core task.

### 2.3.1 The co-production of community policing

Lord Scarman's report into the 1981 'riots' stressed to senior officers that all aspects of policework should be premised upon *active* community *consent, trust* and *participation*. He argued that the police and society needed to recognize that the police working on their own could not make a significant impact on local crime problems. Effective crime prevention was the responsibility of the whole community. In the course of the 1980s, police forces underwent the painful process of moving towards 'community policing' by adjusting structurally to take account, through Scarman-supported consultation groups, of local people's perceptions, priorities and expectations. They began to forge proactive service-based policing styles and strategies which were sensitive to the needs of different audiences and which would, hopefully, break the circle of antagonism and alienation. Neighbourhood officers advised communities on how they could take front-line responsibility for their own safety and reduce the threat and fear of crime by setting up Neighbourhood Watch schemes, joining the re-vamped Special Constabulary, 'target hardening' their property and becoming more security conscious. The police also entered into multi-agency situational and social crime reduction partnerships with local authorities, public utilities and local businesses to tackle the immediate causes of specific local crime problems, and, hopefully in the long term, to reverse social disintegration and reactivate informal policing mechanisms (see **Clarke, 1980**; and Chapter 7 of this volume).

*[margin note: service-based policing]*

The approach to crime victims was overhauled generally and particular attention was paid to the impact of 'serial victimization' and the specific needs of victims of domestic and sexual violence and racial attacks. In these cases, the police conceded that the traditional 'neither assistance nor sympathy/do nothing' approach effectively 're-victimized' victims. Research had suggested a general lack of police interest in these serious crime areas, characterized by delayed responses; inadequate recording; aversion to investigation; refusal to arrest, charge and prosecute; unwillingness to afford adequate protection and, in certain instances, outright hostility to complainants. Critics drew a stark contrast between the lack of time devoted to these categories of serious crime and the considerable energy and resources expended on policing victimless crimes and harassing certain communities. They illustrated how the critical question of 'What is policed and what is not?' was gendered and racialized. Following pressure from community groups and the Home Office, forces overhauled their recording procedures, set up medical examination suites for rape victims and specialist units to deal with domestic violence and racial attacks, and moved from a 'mediation' to an 'interventionist' stance with more emphasis on arrest, charging and prosecuting offenders (see **Saraga, 1996**).

To improve clear-up rates and to try to ensure that fear was experienced not by the law-abiding citizen but by the criminal, forces also implemented high-profile crackdowns, such as the Metropolitan Police's Operation Bumblebee, launched against burglars in 1993 and Operation Eagle Eye, launched against muggers in 1995, and Operation Christmas Day, a national police operation launched against burglars in 1995. Such operations targeted resources against those they claimed were persistently involved in the planning and commission of specific repeat offences. Forces employed upgraded intelligence networks, paid informants, decoys, new surveillance technologies, crime analysis packages and forensic techniques in an effort to put the right people in court and ensure their conviction. This more proactive 'detect and arrest' approach is represented as the 'virtuous circle' (see Figure 2.3).

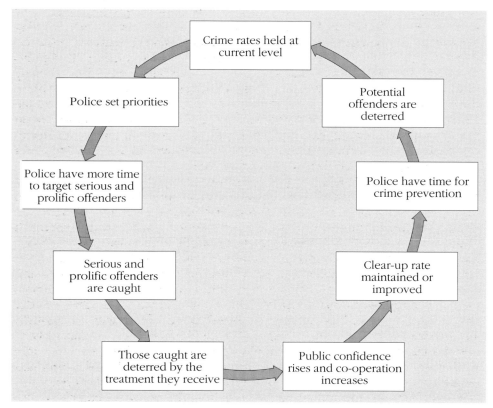

*Figure 2.3 The virtuous circle of crime control: clearer prioritization, emphasis on prevention and more resources moved into proactive work could produce a virtuous circle (Source: Audit Commission, 1993, p.49)*

Despite proactive shifts and initiatives, throughout the 1980s the crime rate continued to soar, the detection rate spiralled downwards and public confidence in the criminal justice system haemorrhaged as it became apparent that it was systemically incapable of controlling crime. Frightened, insecure and frustrated communities made clear and vociferous demands for an increased police presence to act as a visible 'scarecrow' deterrent. When senior officers explained that it was unrealistic to expect 24-hour police patrols, that constables on the beat were not an effective use of scarce resources because it was unlikely that they would be in the right place at the right time, and that crime was to some degree inevitable, some disillusioned private policing communities took their own direct concrete action to prevent crime. Private policing groups such as street patrols in the form of private security guards (charging householders a direct fee), local government community safety teams and constabularies, and 'have-a-go vigilantes' appeared in certain parts of the country. These unprecedented developments raised a fundamental question: Should the police have a monopoly over patrol work, especially if it was apparent that it could not deliver this service? Amid controversy, the Home Office set up a 'Review of Police Core and Ancillary Tasks' in 1994, to deliberate on which tasks were central to the work of the police and which could be farmed out to other statutory agencies, charities and private companies. Police Federation spokespersons emphasized that patrolling was the foundation stone for the entire edifice of public policework (order maintenance, law enforcement, intelligence gathering, instilling public confidence) and a potent source of legitimacy and authority (*The Observer*, 10 July 1994). Successful patrolling was one of the most difficult jobs officers were asked to undertake. Because of the variety of situations they were likely to encounter, officers underwent six months full-time training before being allowed to patrol. The Police Federation questioned the integrity of the ever-expanding private security industry; it warned the government that *de facto* privatization and commodification of policing services would be socially divisive and destabilizing because, if the experience of the USA was typical, the wealthy would benefit disproportionately. In the view of the Police Federation, the only solution was for central and local government to bear in mind that police constables are officers of the law, not employees, and to re-establish the borders and boundaries of public work by providing extra resources to put more police officers on the beat.

A Police Foundation/Policy Studies Institute report (1994) took the view that the public demand for an enhanced police presence was unlikely to disappear; and that there needed to be a critical reappraisal of how this demand could be met in a cost-effective manner which did not encroach unduly on the mandate and powers of the public police. The report argued that only fully trained sworn police officers should have the power to: arrest, detain and search citizens and to search and seize property; bear arms and exercise force; and have complete access to criminal records and criminal intelligence for operational purposes. But it also recommended that in order to halt what it viewed as the anarchic proliferation of unregulated self-help and private police agencies, an appropriately managed and regulated two-tiered adjunct policing system should be created. It offered two possible models: patrols of 'unsworn' police officers could be established, accredited by and under the control of the police or police authority, who could also take over burdensome administrative tasks from the police; or constabularies could create 'designated patrol officers' who, after proper training, would be authorized to use powers of stop and search and arrest in strictly defined situations.

This debate forced the police, politicians and academics to address the question whether the notion of a holistic public constabulary with a universalistic core mandate and monopoly market position was an anachronism in an increasingly pluralistic, diverse and fragmented society. If we refer back to Figure 2.1 and Activity 2.1, we might come to the conclusion that communities and a variety of public and private agencies could undertake, not just patrolling, but many of the routine tasks under the jurisdiction of the public police. Perhaps we need to think seriously about whether the UK will shift unevenly towards a US-style framework of 'grey policing' services:

grey policing

As crime rates have risen, and with them the public's fear and apprehension, the police monopoly on public safety has declined. Police have quietly been supplanted in shopping malls, stores, banks, office buildings, apartment houses, single-family residential communities, urban cul-de-sacs, schools and colleges, and factories. The police have been pushed out of what has been called 'private public space', that is, premises owned by private individuals but routinely accessible to the public with a reason to be there ... Although the police continue to have legal jurisdiction in such places, tangible protection is increasingly provided by private security guards, who have become the first line of practical defence against crime in much of modern life.

(Bayley, 1994, p.11)

### 2.3.2  National and transnational crime control

In the post-colonial period, public policing was spatially bounded by the nation-state and domestic concerns. But in the late 1980s, some senior police officers and politicians began to argue that the nationalization and transnationalization of certain policing functions was necessary to keep pace with the de-territorialization of serious organized crime. After considerable internal debate, the National Crime Intelligence Service (NCIS) commenced work in 1992, absorbing the national drugs and football intelligence units, the UK Interpol office and collecting, processing and distributing high-level intelligence relating to all aspects of serious crime across force boundaries. It was given no powers of arrest or surveillance and could not instruct either regional crime squads or local forces. Its supporters argued from the outset that if it was to develop into an effective FBI-style national police agency, Parliament would have to place NCIS on a statutory basis and chief police officers would have to allocate it full proactive operational capabilities.

transnationalization

In the late 1980s and early 1990s, police in the UK also became involved in politically sensitive discussions about how to develop and strengthen European police co-operation and whether a pan-European police force was feasible. Since the early 1970s, representatives of European police forces had been networking, both informally and through various multilateral and bilateral agreements instituted to facilitate extradition processes and foster cross-border collaboration against terrorism, espionage, drug trafficking, immigration and other threats to national security (see Bunyan, 1993; Hebenton and Thomas, 1994; Anderson and Boer, 1994). Concerted efforts were made by government and police representatives to co-ordinate, harmonize and institutionalize these largely piecemeal haphazard and overlapping initiatives. For example, after 10 years of discussion, in March 1994 the Schengen group of initially six European states created a core zone within the European Union which was free of internal frontier identity checks. To stop this open border policy becoming what was described as 'a criminals' charter', the states established the right of 'hot pursuit', stronger and stricter external border controls and the Schengen Information System (SIS), a data base of Euro-criminals and 'undesirables', which could be accessed by relevant police forces of the signatories to the agreement. In its first years of operation the British police were not allowed full access to the data bank because the British government refused to give up its border controls, arguing that they were essential to controlling illegal immigration, drug trafficking and terrorism.

However, the British police played a more central part in the establishment of Europol. Although in the early stages its remit was limited to collecting, processing, analysing and exchanging intelligence about major drug dealers and associated money launderers, its supporters successfully argued for a convention that would allow it to establish a database with permanent access to information on Europe's most menacing criminals. They also argued that eventually it should be given an operational wing which would have the right to cross national borders and, if necessary, override local forces.

The practical difficulties of establishing a fully operational Europol or meaningful compatible cross-border policing arrangements cannot be overstated. Each state has a different and shifting vision of what type of Euro-policing is needed, how it should be achieved and resourced, and what its priorities should be. Each has very different constitutional, police and legal frameworks and operational philosophies; delicate questions of sovereignty still abound and there remain very basic communication problems. It has also yet to be settled within each nation-state which police agencies will take the lead role in the rapidly expanding business of national and transnational policing. In the UK, for example, senior police officers have realized that they will face stiff competition from MI5 and MI6 – the state's traditional 'political policing' departments. With the end of the Cold War in the early 1990s, and the Ulster ceasefire of 1994, MI5 and MI6, together with the Metropolitan Special Branch, began to look for new areas of work. MI6, traditionally associated with combating external threats to the nation, reallocated approximately one-third of its resources to targeting organized crime; MI5, the internal security service, pressed for the law to be changed to allow it to play a more open and central role in anti-terrorism, drug trafficking, money laundering, computer hacking and commercial espionage (Dorril, 1994).

political policing

## ACTIVITY 2.3

Turn back to the beginning of section 2.3, and consider again the quotation from Klockars, bearing in mind the following questions:

1   Are those politicians and policing agencies who advocate a Europe-wide, and indeed global, war on organized crime and the other areas listed above, being realistic?

2   What are the implications of this blurring of boundaries between conventional police and political police? In responding to this question, you may want to consider aspects such as working practices and assumptions.

## 2.4   Maintaining public order

It has been argued that the *core* mandate of the police officer is to enforce dominant conceptions of public order. No matter what other roles officers adopt, if the status quo is challenged they will be called upon to defend it. Indeed radical critics such as Scraton (1985) maintain that the reason why police are unable to do anything to about crime is because crime fighting has never been their real function. Their usefulness to authorities has been as a standing army to deal with collective threats to political order (such as strikes, demonstrations, riots).

public order
policing

Public order policing is a particularly politically sensitive role which highlights the fundamental dilemma of how a democratic society can strike a balance between the right to peaceful assembly and public protest, and the right to public order and tranquillity. A police force which uses criminalization or excessive force to suppress popular dissent or discontent runs the real risk of being characterized as a state police rather than a public police; and, relying upon its monopoly of *force* and fear rather than *consent*, among an alienated populace, it risks losing legitimacy and public sympathy.

### 2.4.1 The golden age of tranquillity

Many commentators believed that maintaining public order in the post-war social democratic UK would not be a particularly significant or controversial aspect of policing for three reasons. First, serious public disorder would not be a feature of British life – the social democratic settlement ruled out the need to resort to violence to resolve political differences or achieve political goals; public protests and demonstrations would be orderly and peaceful. Second, on the rare occasion when the police would be called upon to maintain public order, they would do so in a manner that would not unnecessarily antagonize protesters, demonstrators or the wider public. Police officers would adhere, even if provoked, to the unique principles of British policing: policing by consent; maximum tolerance; policing by local officers; the exercise of legitimate authority; the use of 'minimum force'; minimum disruption; and steadfast neutrality. Finally, the community knew that the 'thin blue line' was unarmed and restrained and the police would ideologically 'win by appearing to lose'; if officers were attacked by demonstrators or strikers there would be a public outcry. The police would thus be able to control public order situations with minimum difficulty.

Of course this golden moment of social democratic consensus never materialized. The 1970s and 1980s were characterized by increasing industrial conflict, urban riots and political confrontations. Waddington has argued that during this period 'the police stopped "winning by appearing to lose" and started to actually "lose" and the response was to introduce changes designed to "win"' ( Waddington, 1991, p.129). In the aftermath of the miners' strikes of 1972 and 1974 and the inner city disturbances of the late 1970s and early 1980s, a reshaping and considerable strengthening of public order policing took place. As an alternative to the formation of a separate continental-style riot police, local forces established public order units. A national public order

mutual aid

policing capacity was established when mutual aid, the system whereby local police forces are authorized to provide support to other forces in need, was overhauled. The organizational capacity of the non-statutory National Reporting Centre (NRC) was enhanced, allowing it for the first time since its inception in 1972 to *deploy* (and some commentators would maintain *direct*) police from every constabulary in England and Wales – a capacity clearly utilized during the 1984–85 miners' strike to counter mass picketing and demonstrating a significant shift towards a *de facto* national police force. The Public Support Unit (PSU) system was also standardized to ensure that officers from different constabularies could work together when they were deployed in major public order situations. The PSU, many would argue, had been turned into a virtual 'third force' (Scraton, 1985).

New equipment, weaponry and surveillance technology were made available as the 1980s progressed and new public order powers were granted to the police, allowing them to exercise much tighter control over organizers, demonstrators and protestors. The final change manifested itself when these newly organized and equipped and legally empowered officers were deployed – it was apparent that they had been trained in new public order tactics, strategies and formations (Northam, 1988).

### 2.4.2 The case against paramilitarization

Commentators such as Jefferson (1990) reflected on the long-term consequences of these changes for British policing and argued that paramilitarization or 'Ulsterization' had taken place, a 'fatal attraction' because the coercive policing styles and cast of thinking that emanate from it fundamentally redefine the nature of police–community relations. Such approaches can seep insidiously into other policing styles. New tactics or strategies can move quickly from being exceptional, temporary, reactive measures to being the normal, institutionalized, offensive police response. Because public disorder is not a regular occurrence, 'flak happy' specialist units may be deployed on normal policing duties or be used to spearhead drives against certain forms of 'crime' and 'criminals'. And given the nature of their training for the 'worst case scenario' and their deployment as 'trouble-shooters', they are likely to have an adverse effect on police–community relations; the most vivid example of this is the deployment of the Special Patrol Group in black neighbourhoods in London in the late 1970s and early 1980s (see section 2.2). At a more general level, ordinary officers mobilized in riot control/public disorder situations may find it difficult to readjust to normal duty because they experience considerable role conflict.

paramilitarization

*'Senior officers privately conclude that once a baton charge is initiated, it is largely beyond their control to direct. The police are out of control'* (Waddington, 1991, p.177)

Once these systems are operational they can be deployed in situations where there is little real risk of serious disorder. Shows of overwhelming force can constitute an overreaction that provokes serious disturbances which prove that the initial deployment was necessary. The 1980s and 1990s are littered with examples where the 'new public order policing' led to various highly controversial 'battles' between the police and strikers, hippy convoys, peace protestors, students and poll tax demonstrators. During the 'Battle of the Beanfield' in 1985, for example, police officers in riot gear thought that they were facing a marauding group of dangerous drug addicts and anarchists who were prepared to use force to reach Stonehenge: 'Shortly before seven o' clock they went in to get them. They walked in with shields and helmets and sticks, the convoy started moving and the next thing, the entire operation had collapsed in confusion and violence' (Davies, 1995, p.22). Such incidents suggest that when riot police are sent in, unpredictable forces are released.

Finally, Jefferson argues, once the paramilitary pathway is taken, it is difficult to turn back. The 'mindset' of officers and forces becomes locked into these strategies, tactics and weaponry and new élite squads are created which are committed to developing public order policing from an art to a science. In addition, as Northern Ireland shows, there is every possibility that those in conflict with the police will develop aggressive counter-tactics to meet the anticipated police response. If this 'mirror dance' happens, front-line police officers will demand more public order powers and further paramilitarization. Critics argue for a general de-militarization of the police and a change in attitude. According to Jefferson, it should be drilled into senior officers that the real skill in public order policing is *avoiding* trouble and the use of force and deployment of riot squads (Jefferson, 1990, p.143).

### 2.4.3  The need for the strong arm of the law

Other writers, most notably Ascoli (1979) and Waddington (1991), argue that, whether we like it or not, we need the police to maintain a democratic social order; it is the police who furnish a sense of public security and facilitate free elections, freedom of speech, and freedom of movement and assembly. Ascoli and Waddington also ask us to keep the following points in mind. First, under the heading 'public order' are gathered very different situations – industrial disputes, football crowds, rallies, marches, meetings, communal riots and pop festivals. Second, the police tactics employed in any given situation are linked to the nature of the specific event and careful assessment of the risk of trouble. Third, the police spend a considerable amount of time informally negotiating with groups and offering advice to organizers rather than invoking public order legislation. Fourth, the vast majority of public order situations pass off peacefully, but the media and the critics prefer to focus on the disorder and violence. Fifth, police officers, at every level, try to avoid confrontation and trouble in public order situations because they know that media images of police violence will lead to calls for public inquiries and

A demonstrator spits beer over riot police during protests against the Criminal Justice Bill in October 1994

investigations. Finally, Ascoli and others maintain, we need to recognize that there are criminally minded groups in British society who hijack public events to 'have a go' at the police; society has a duty to provide its police with adequate protection from these extremist elements.

Waddington accepts that the creation of paramilitary units makes the police a more formidable force, but argues that such units and the rules governing their use improve discipline and control and make it more probable that the principles of 'graded response' and 'minimum force' will be maintained. Officers acting on their own in a disorganized manner are more liable to lose control and to lash out indiscriminately, whereas:

> More sophisticated tactics allow the police more options. If 'pushing and shoving' becomes too vigorous for the traditional cordon, the development of the 'chorus line' enables the cordon to be maintained and avoids the need for a more forceful police response. If serious disorder erupts and dispersal becomes necessary, then the use of CS smoke, in preference to the baton charge, eliminates the possibility of people in the crowd being arbitrarily struck. If a street is ablaze, with burning barricades obstructing movement and a hail of missiles preventing police intervention ... then arsonists can be stopped from committing possibly murderous actions by an incapacitating baton round, instead of the use of lethal force – gunfire.

(Waddington, 1991, p.216)

Waddington also maintains that the police cannot be held primarily responsible for any paramilitarization that has taken place: 'It was not the police who abandoned consent in favour of coercion. The acquisition of this technology has been, at every stage, a *reaction* to the violence with which the police have been faced (Waddington, 1991, p.217). He is convinced that the police and British society need to accept and acknowledge that police officers should be professionally trained to use 'force' in a disciplined manner. He also emphasizes that, in the final instance, facing the 'new public order police' is preferable to facing the army, as happens in many other countries.

The two approaches represented by Waddington and Jefferson disagree about the long-term implications of paramilitarization. Do you think there is any way of definitively resolving this debate?

It is very difficult to reach a definitive conclusion on this issue because in many respects it depends on where one stands politically, theoretically and, indeed, on which side of a public order situation. However, an important case study of some of the issues raised in this debate is provided by the policing of animal rights protesters who, during 1995, attempted to blockade ports used for the export of cattle and sheep. The police were faced with a complex public order situation. On the one side were the protesters, made up of a representative cross-section of local communities, who were requesting the police to recognize their right to demonstrate. On the other were the exporters demanding that the police protect their right to conduct their lawful trade and ensure unhindered passage on the Queen's highways. The police complained that they were being placed in a 'no win' situation and stressed that they would ensure that the 'game was played by the rules'. As we can see in the report from *The Guardian* (19 January 1995) reproduced overleaf, when the police decided that the protesters had overstepped the boundaries of lawful protest, an interesting scenario unfolded.

# Riot police thwart animal welfare protest

**James Erlichman on anger at operation**

POLICE were yesterday accused of brutality after animal rights protesters in Brightlingsea, Essex, were bundled aside to allow four lorry-loads of lambs to board a ferry bound for Belgium.

At least 250 police, some wearing riot gear, pulled around 500 people from the main street of the town where residents had successfully halted the first attempt to load lambs on Monday.

The scenes came as operators who had planned to fly calves from Swansea to the Continent pulled out after receiving death threats. Protesters had set up a round-the-clock vigil at the airport to prevent the exports.

Elsewhere, at Shoreham-by-Sea, West Sussex, and Plymouth, livestock ferries continued to operate.

At Brightlingsea, attempts to block a road with parked cars were thwarted as police moved vehicles. Some protesters dragged pub tables into the road, but they were brushed aside.

Assistant chief constable Geoffrey Markham described the operation as a success, with only two arrests and no serious injuries. But he added: 'I would have thought it would have been a frightening experience for young children to see that number of police officers deployed in that fashion.'

He also blamed sheep exporter Roger Mills for the size of the police action, which was the largest public order operation in Essex since the 1950s.

Mr Markham said: 'The exporter Mr Mills informed me that he intended to move his vehicles in Brightlingsea with or without police support. I considered that if he went on his own with those large vehicles, with the experience of Monday, that in the interests of public safety, that would have been an extraordinarily fraught situation.'

More disturbances are expected today. 'I am sure the exporters are intent through any means at their disposal to continue with the export of animals,' said Mr Markham. 'That is what they have said. I have absolutely no doubt people will continue to resist them.'

He added: 'I am sorry that we caused any upset to the people of Brightlingsea because that is the last thing we wanted to do.' He conceded that no more than 60 of the demonstrators were 'hardline outsiders'.

Rick Morgan, Brightlingsea mayor, praised the protesters and criticised the police, saying: 'I saw nothing but a peaceful protest and the level of police response in my opinion was over the top and completely unjustified.'

Clifford Brown, a retired carpenter, said: 'I have never before been in a demonstration and could not believe these police with truncheons and visors looking every bit like storm troopers.'

Heather Dewdney, a 16-year-old childminder, said: 'I was sitting in the road showing no violence when I was dragged across the road on my back. We then saw a man being beaten up by a policeman and when I asked for his number he punched me extremely hard between my breasts.'

Cambridge don John Meeres said: 'I have been pulled out of the crowd three or four times. It's an irony that this country says it doesn't support this trade yet police allow this to happen on our streets.'

Maria Wilby, of the pressure group Brightlingsea Against Live Exports, said she was shocked by police tactics and said dozens of people had been injured. 'There were mothers with toddlers here today and some were pulled out by their hair.

'People were petrified. We never expected a reaction like this.

'We didn't want people to be arrested. We know we can't stop them forever but we must make our protest. But the police have been so hostile I'm shocked.'

She claimed police had hit children with truncheons. 'It was disgusting that they were hurting them and then throwing them over the wall of the police station to get them out of the way.'

*(The Guardian, 19 January 1995)*

### 2.4.4 Deadly force

As we have seen, there are widely differing views on the changing nature of public order policing. One point *is* agreed upon, however: that the routine arming of the police would mark an irreversible transformation of British police and an irrevocable departure from their culture, custom and practice.

But there is evidence to suggest that this consensus might not last for much longer. In 1967 the Metropolitan Police established a specialist firearms unit after several police officers were murdered by armed criminals. During the 1970s, there was a significant nation-wide increase in firearms training for rank-and-file officers and the creation of specialist firearms support units. In the course of the 1980s, as a result of highly controversial police shootings, the police revised their policy and decided that a small number of officers should receive specialist training, to minimize the possibility of accidental shootings. Consequently, the number of officers authorized to carry guns was reduced, with the majority being attached to specialist protection squads. The remainder were either based in élite firearms teams, or patrolled in armed response vehicles (ARVs) which were introduced in the late 1980s. The rules of engagement, screening processes and training were also tightened up.

However, in the 1990s, after the murder of several police officers, further steps were taken towards the general arming of police officers. In 1994, for example, ACPO recommended that the decision to issue weapons to non-specialist officers would no longer have to be taken by a senior officer and that specialist firearms officers staffing ARVs would be overtly armed whilst on patrol. A more low-level form of rearming also took place to offer greater protection to police officers. The Police Federation successfully demanded that officers should be allowed to carry side-handled batons, gas canisters/sprays which would incapacitate aggressors in minutes, alarm radios and body armour.

At the time of writing it is not clear whether the British police will make the transition to being fully armed by the end of this century. The Police Federation carried out the largest ever survey of police officers on the issue and found that 79 per cent did not want to be routinely armed (*The Guardian*, 18 May 1995). However, there seems to be a feeling among many younger, urban police officers that they will be forced eventually to imagine the unimaginable because the UK is becoming a society in which people are more willing to carry and use firearms. These officers have posed an important question: If they are unable to protect themselves, how can police protect the general public?

Given his overall perspective on public order policing, it is interesting to note that Waddington cautioned these police officers against the dangers of campaigning for routine arming – see his article from *The Independent on Sunday,* 24 October 1993, reproduced overleaf.

*In 1989, three out of the 43 forces in England and Wales had mobile armed police squads. By 1995, the figure had risen to 38 out of 43. There was little public discussion about this because the decision to arm police officers is defined as an operational matter*

History has kept officers unarmed – to their benefit, says **Peter Waddington**

# Guns won't protect the police

… When Robert Peel started the 'New Police' in 1829, the idea faced profound and widespread hostility. Peel and his colleagues realised that the police could not defeat the mass of the population by force. Policing by consent was the only option, even if that consent was grudgingly offered by the lower social classes. That was why he consciously decided that the 'bobbies'', unlike the Bow Street Runners and other *ad hoc* groups of constables, should be unarmed. Even the truncheon was to be hidden away, lest it should appear offensive.

The doctrine of 'minimum force' came to mean that there was a ceiling on the weapons to which the police had access – and a low ceiling at that. When a serious threat presented itself, the military was called in.

The vulnerability of the police was turned to advantage. When PC Culley was stabbed to death during a riot in 1833, and the inquest jury returned a verdict of 'justifiable homicide', there was public outrage and the verdict was overturned on appeal. Periodically since then, the murder of police officers has aroused public sympathy; the more vulnerable the officer and the more callous the murder, the greater the public outcry.

The image of an unarmed police force has been nurtured throughout the past 160 years, even when the reality was very different. Following a spate of armed burglaries in the 1880s, the Metropolitan

Police allowed officers to carry a pistol on night duty if they wished. This policy was kept secret and officers were instructed to keep the gun hidden. Even today, uniformed armed officers on diplomatic protection keep their guns out of sight. When officers were allowed to carry carbines openly at Heathrow and other airports in 1987, much of the debate revolved around the effect this change would have on the public image of the police.

Rather than be accused of 'tooling up', the police made little attempt to train officers in the use of firearms, relying instead on officers who had received military training. It was only in the 1960s that such training began to be taken seriously. A few other countries have taken the same course. When Ireland became independent in the 1920s, the Garda Siochana – the police who replaced the Royal Irish Constabulary – were unarmed. This was intended to signal the change from a colonial to a post-colonial regime. New Zealand made a similar declaration by disarming the paramilitary police who had fought the Maori wars.

The colonial tradition has normally been less benign. Colonialism entails the suppression of the native population, who do not qualify as citizens. The relationship between them and the police tends to be that between an army and the 'enemy within' This relationship is reflected in the use of military tactics and weaponry designed to inflict maximum injury, or

death, not minimum force. Thus, the South African police still arm their officers with automatic rifles and train them in the use of hand grenades and mortars.

In countries where the police were armed, it was not because they faced greater dangers than the early Victorian British police, but because their origins lay in the military. On the Continent, civil policing evolved through paramilitary police, who had (and continue to have) a military and a police function. The French gendarmerie, for example, have light tanks and are expected to fight within France in time of war.

Do our police, facing gun-toting drug dealers, pay the price of a historical legacy of minimum force? Probably not: the vast majority of the world's police forces are armed and the murder of, and attacks on, the police vary enormously from one jurisdiction to another. It seems pretty clear that arming the police has little effect on their safety or on crime levels generally. The police are always vulnerable, no matter how heavily armed they are. The police must *react* to threat; the initiative, therefore, lies with the 'bad guys'. The FBI [Federal Bureau of Investigation] estimates that, in 50 per cent of police murders in the United States, the officer does not have time even to draw his gun.

Throughout the world, whatever the present level of arming, officers seek enhanced weaponry … In other countries, officers

demand 'quick draw' holsters and more powerful weapons and ammunition. In the US, the reliable six-shot revolver is being traded in for mechanically complex 'semi-automatics' that carry up to 18 rounds but are more difficult to use. This is despite evidence that, in most shootings involving the police, no more than three shots are fired. Recognising their vulnerability, police officers seek 'the edge', but they never have the edge, because they rarely have the initiative.

This is so even in a pre-planned armed operation. In 1984, PC Brian Bishop and his armed colleagues confronted an armed man in Frinton, Essex. PC Bishop called on the suspect to surrender, but the man fired two blasts from inside a bag he was carrying. Bishop was killed and a colleague seriously wounded. Fire was returned and the assailant seriously injured, but by then it was too late. Desperate, deranged and drugged adversaries are not necessarily deterred by armed police.

Nowhere in the developed world are armed police as well protected as their unarmed British counterparts. Genuine protection is not offered by weaponry, but by the conditions in which the police carry out their task. Instead of arming the police, we should attend to how order and justice can be maintained and enhanced.

*(The Independent on Sunday,* 24 October 1993)

# **3** Police culture and identity

It is frequently argued that police officers have a distinctive set of mutually reinforcing personality traits that set them apart from the public. There are two opposing perspectives on the origins of the 'police personality'. One view maintains that, because of the nature of the work, a police career attracts recruits of a particular psychological disposition or from a specific socio-economic background. The second, sociological perspective, which this chapter follows, stresses that it is group socialization, the task environment and complex of work and institutional routines that generate a particular working personality and a very strong occupational sub-culture (the 'canteen culture'). The concept is used to describe the traits (beliefs, perspectives, practices, rituals and discourses) which are handed down to recruits and probationers through subterranean socialization processes.

**canteen culture**

## ACTIVITY 2.4

Review and categorize the various aspects of policework that we have explored so far. What types of individual coping strategies and occupational culture might be engendered by working as a police officer ?

The process of becoming a police officer takes place inside a total institution and probationers have traditionally had to come to terms with being located at the bottom of a hierarchical, military-style rank structure. But, despite being part of a quasi-military bureaucracy which stresses command, discipline, regimentation and following orders, as 'sworn' police officers they also possess considerable autonomy and space from the organization for three reasons. First, the *office* of constable is *original* not *delegated* (see Chapter 1). Second, 'law enforcement' is a complicated activity. Many laws are general, logically ambiguous and permissive in texture; some are ludicrously antiquated. Officers will have to exercise their discretion as to whether in any given situation a criminal or disorderly act has taken or is taking place. In essence, they must transform 'written law' into 'law in action' and in so doing act as key decision-makers or gatekeepers to the criminal and juvenile justice systems:

**discretion**

> A superficial look at police work is enough to show that any patrolling police officer ignores a large number of offences or potential offences on every working day. In central London he walks past many illegally parked vehicles, drives behind speeding cars, walks past shops openly selling hard-core pornography, sees prostitutes soliciting, knows of many clubs selling liquor and providing gaming facilities without a licence, goes past unlicensed street traders, and so on, usually without taking any immediate action. Where he does take action over any one of these matters, this will usually occupy him for a considerable period, so that in the meantime he can do nothing about the others. This means that, far from 'enforcing the law' in a straightforward way, every police officer must constantly make decisions about which particular offences he should do something about.

> (Smith and Gray, 1985, p.14)

Third, much of their working life will be spent in situations of low visibility, with little direct supervision or monitoring by senior officers.

# Lonely cop who blew the whistle

**John McGhie** talks to the policeman who exposed corruption in the force and was ostracized by his colleagues

ON A CHILL November evening in 1983, PC Ron Walker of the Kent Constabulary faced a situation for which his 11 quiet years around the Medway towns had not prepared him. The crowd he saw coming round the corner was not one he had ever expected to witness on an English street, let alone a quiet suburb of Chatham.

Thirty men armed with swords, axes and meat cleavers were chanting 'Kill, Kill', and converging on a house where Walker and two young constables had just talked a chain-wielding maniac into laying down his weapon.

The question of what to do next was never in serious doubt. Marching out into the middle of the mob and brushing aside a sword thrust inches from his gullet, Walker picked out the ringleader and calmed him down long enough for assistance to arrive.

'In retrospect, of course, it was dangerous, but I suppose police training just took over. I did what any officer would have done. You are trained to make instant decisions and that's all I did.'

Walker's actions that night earned him a bravery citation from a judge, praise from the media and a commendation from his Chief Constable.

Six years later, that same policeman has been shunned by former colleagues, subjected to a smear campaign and threatened with disciplinary action.

His 'crime' was to blow the whistle on corruption among his own colleagues, thereby offending unwritten rules and tribal taboos. In a series of detailed allegations, given first to the Police Complaints Authority and then to *The Observer* in January 1986, Walker revealed that official statistics for crime clear-up rates in Kent were a sham.

According to Walker, police persuaded or cajoled criminals to have 'taken into consideration' hundreds of offences which they had never committed or, even worse, had never been committed by anyone. The creation of phantom crimes, which were then miraculously solved, was seen as an excellent way to fiddle the figures.

Middle-ranking and even some senior police officers were turning a blind eye to what was going on or were actively involved in this gigantic fraud on the Home Office and the public. Under this rogue system, honest detectives saw their careers suffer while some criminals who agreed to play the game were allowed to continue unmolested ...

After three years' investigation by two separate forces, a police disciplinary tribunal finally announced what measures would be taken. One detective sergeant was dismissed while 33 unnamed Kent officers were disciplined, either with fines and 'admonishments' or by being advised about their conduct. These officers are still secure in the jobs they have held since the inquiry began.

When Walker took his story to the authorities, he knew he might swiftly become a pariah. In this he has been proved sadly correct. He has been invited to return to work, after almost four years on sick leave ... but only if he agrees to perform routine police paperwork under the supervision of senior officers.

This has been too much for Walker to bear. He feels that after 'doing the right thing', and even being praised for it by his Chief Constable, he should be allowed to return to everyday 'hands on' police work.

But if Walker is to be believed – and the ostracism accorded to previous whistle-blowers certainly bears him out – he would not be able to go back to ordinary duties without attracting immense hostility from his former colleagues. While he considers what to do next, he has been warned that he could face disciplinary proceedings for refusing to work ... .

After it became apparent that his anonymity had been blown by those who had promised to protect him, he began to fear for the safety of his family. 'I could have stood the strain of suddenly being cut off from people I had worked closely with for years, but yes, I did worry constantly that one day I would come home and find that someone had poured petrol through my letterbox.

'After a while it became obvious they were not going to do anything physical, but even now I don't like to be away from the family too long because some of these bastards have got long memories, haven't they?'

It is the fear of that continuing hostility which prevents him returning to work and draws from him comparisons with *Serpico*, the true-life film of a New York cop whose career was savagely ended after he gave evidence about corruption. At the end of the film, which Walker has seen four times, Serpico is shot and badly wounded while his colleagues refuse to help.

'If I went back and faced the sort of situation I faced on that Chatham street, who knows, if I radioed in for help, maybe no one would turn up until it was all too late. It could happen and it would be all too easy.

'After all, Serpico made just one mistake, didn't he?' says Walker, jabbing a finger. 'He went back to work.'

(*The Observer*, 24 September 1989)

We have discussed some of the more general features of the occupational sub-culture and how it can influence policework. One point to make clear is that it is not static, unchanging or monolithic. What functions do we need to keep in mind if we are to produce a dynamic conception of occupational sub-culture?

We have always to keep in mind that there is not one police force but many, all with their own distinctive histories and cultural inflections. Within these forces different ranks have their own 'take' on the canteen culture. Various élite departments, different divisions, shifts or sectors develop their own distinctive sub-cultural orientations, which can include criminogenic tendencies. Each new generation of officers also brings with it new attitudes, values and concerns, some of which will be absorbed into or even refocus core aspects of the occupational culture. Finally, the culture has to adapt to new laws, rules and shifts in formal working practices and policing styles.

During the 1990s questions of gender, race and sexuality have threatened to make a serious and unprecedented attack on the traditional cultural outlook of police officers and the organization. These issues are explored in the following three sections.

## 3.1   Issues of gender

It is argued that the police organization as a whole, and the canteen culture in particular, 'represents' and projects a particular masculinity:

> in the emphasis on remaining dominant in any encounter and not losing face, the emphasis placed on masculine solidarity and on backing up other men in the group especially when they are in the wrong, the stress on drinking as a test of manliness and a basis for good fellowship, the importance given to physical courage and the glamour attached to violence. This set of attitudes and norms amounts to a 'cult of masculinity' which also has a strong influence on policemen's behaviour towards women, towards victims of sexual offences and towards sexual offenders.

(Smith and Gray, 1985, p.372)

In the post-war period, the police became one of the last occupations where the ideology of the full-time, single-occupation, male breadwinner, who worked outside the home providing for his family, had real meaning. This had considerable implications for women officers (see Figure 2.4).

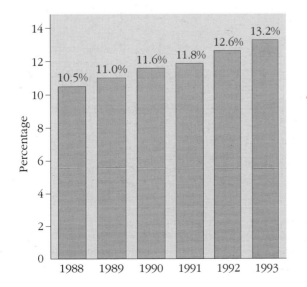

Figure 2.4   Police strength: female officers, England and Wales 1993 (Source: Her Majesty's Inspectorate, 1994, p.24)

The Sex Discrimination Act of 1975 compelled a deeply reluctant force to abolish separate policewomen's departments. Women found themselves in an institution that believed they would undermine the *essential* masculinity of the organization because:

- They did not have the necessary physical stamina needed to engage in routine policework.

- Their presence in violent situations would put their male colleagues at risk.

- They would not be an economic investment because marriage and family would inevitably come before careers and commitment.

- They would present a discipline problem. Supervisors would be less strict with female officers over deployment and shifts, and would have difficulty controlling male officers because of the unwanted sexual dynamic introduced into an intimate working environment.

Researchers agree that women suffered considerably as a result of integration into what Campbell has described as 'the most masculinized enclave in civil society' (Campbell, 1993, p.20). They endured stereotyping, derogatory banter, intrusive questioning about marital status or sexual orientation, unwanted sexual advances and outright harassment. They were excluded and side-lined from specialist departments which were crucial 'career fields' – for example, firearms, public order, drugs squads, CID. Without operational command experience it was virtually impossible to progress through the ranks (Heidensohn, 1992). They also stood outside all important 'old boy networks' and Freemason lodges. Women officers found themselves limited to administrative tasks because they had 'an instinct for tidiness' and/or looking after the victims of sexual offences, young offenders and children because of their supposedly compassionate nature (Brewer and Magee, 1991). There were also questions over whether the interests of women officers were adequately represented by the Police Federation, Superintendents' Association and ACPO (Jones, 1986).

Women fared badly when it came to promotion. Despite an overall doubling in the number of female officers, the number above the rank of constable fell from 11.2 per cent in 1971 to 5.8 per cent in 1988 (*The Independent*, 11 October 1990). And of course there were considerable regional variations – several forces had no women in senior positions. Hence, for decades there was no 'critical mass' of senior women officers to provide patronage or support to junior women officers or to push for cultural change within the organization. Just around the time forces received Home Office Circular 87/1989, which stressed the importance of implementing equal opportunity policies, the issue of sexism at all levels in the police finally surfaced as a public issue. In 1990, Alison Halford, the Assistant Chief Constable of Merseyside and the then most senior woman officer in the country, sensationally brought a sex discrimination case against the force on the grounds that she was being repeatedly turned down for promotion while male officers with less experience and qualifications were being appointed.

*Pauline Clare, appointed first woman chief constable in June 1995. Was her appointment largely tokenistic or will it give real encouragement to women officers with high aspirations in a male-dominated police force?*

Her decision to go public triggered a bitter dispute with her chief constable and the police authority (Halford, 1994). The senior officers of the force stood accused of intransigence, ingrained hostility to female officers, chaotic and capricious management, telephone tapping and operating a promotion system premised not on merit but on corrupt patronage and whim. She was, in turn, suspended from duty, and stood accused of being promoted way beyond her ability for reasons of political correctness, of lacking professional judgement, not being a team player, neglect of duty, discreditable conduct, irrational behaviour and falsehood.

In 1992, after it was decided that the authority had acted unfairly in opening disciplinary proceedings, and just before senior police officers were due to give evidence, the case was settled out of court. The police attempted to play down the significance of the Halford case by saying that her views and experiences were not representative. However, the issue did not go away. A Home Office study (1993) reported that nearly all the women officers surveyed had experienced some form of sexual harassment and this was at a significantly greater rate than that experienced by other women working within the police. A report by Her Majesty's Inspectorate in the same year concluded that breaches of equal opportunities policies were often instigated or defended by senior officers (*The Independent*, 26 March 1993). Both reports concluded that many female officers were suffering from routine low-level harassment; and that when they brought it to the attention of their senior officers, they were likely to meet with hostility, prevarication and pressure to drop the complaint. The reports agreed that women officers spent a considerable amount of their personal resources managing male colleagues instead of doing their job. The result, in certain cases, was stress, poor performance, absenteeism and demoralization (see Figure 2.5).

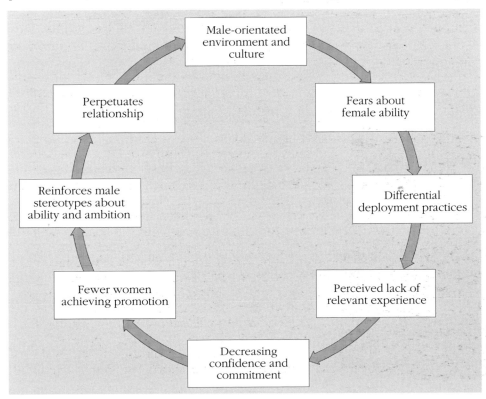

Figure 2.5 Causes and effects of discrimination (Source: adapted from Jones, 1986, p.109)

## 3.2 Issues of 'race'

Evidence has also surfaced in the media of the difficulties black police officers face in an overwhelmingly white ethnocultural organization. In the aftermath of the 1981 riots, the police were forced to consider once more the implications of predominantly white forces patrolling ethnically diverse neighbourhoods. Various reasons were put forward to explain the fact that in October 1981 black officers made up 0.5 per cent of the total strength of the Metropolitan Police and 0.3 per cent of the overall force. The police argued that there was no reason why people should be automatically interested in becoming a police officer; black applicants were failing to meet the entry requirements and many feared being alienated from their own community. It was also suggested that white people would not take orders from a black officer. Black organizations argued that no sensible black person would think of joining an overtly racist institution and that many young black people resented and feared the police (for reasons discussed earlier in section 2.2.3).

In the light of the findings and recommendations of the Scarman Report, efforts were made to recruit from minority ethnic communities. However, senior officers were forced to realize that tokenistic recruitment was not enough (see Figure 2.6). There was a high turnover among black officers and the main reason for this was the considerable racial prejudice and discrimination they encountered from certain of their colleagues.

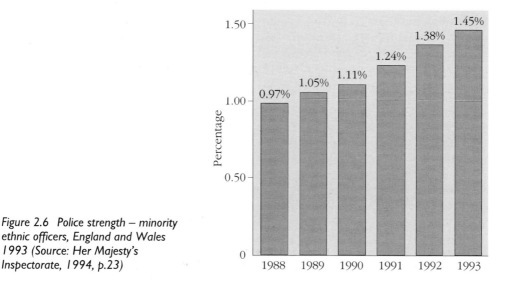

Figure 2.6   Police strength – minority ethnic officers, England and Wales 1993 (Source: Her Majesty's Inspectorate, 1994, p.23)

Smith and Gray (1985) found that black officers were isolated and extremely vulnerable and had to work in an environment where racist jokes, stereotyping and banter were the norm. A well-publicized industrial tribunal brought by Constable Surinder Singh in 1990 revealed a 'cancer of racism' at the heart of certain sections of the Nottinghamshire Constabulary. The tribunal found that PC Singh had been subjected to unlawful racial discrimination which led to his rejection when he took part in a scheme to test his suitability for the CID; it awarded him a record £20,000 in damages. In 1994 the Black and Asian Police Association was set up to act as a network group for its members and to provide support to those victimized by white colleagues (*The Guardian*, 12 August 1994).

## 3.3  Issues of sexuality

The final issue to emerge was sexuality. Many in the gay community viewed the police as an organization that: prosecuted men who 'trolled' in public parks; refused to respond effectively to 'queer bashing'; acted as *agents provocateurs* by loitering in public toilets known to be frequented by gay men; targeted and raided gay bars and clubs; and periodically orchestrated moral panics about the dangers of homosexuality. The police also stood accused of being openly hostile to the idea of gay police officers. Every time the question of anti-gay recruiting practices was raised, letters would appear in police publications claiming that gay men and lesbians should not be allowed to be police officers because they adversely affect the ability to:

- maintain discipline, good order, morale and authority on the streets;
- foster mutual trust and confidence;
- ensure the moral integrity of the system;
- facilitate the assignment and deployment of officers who must work in close proximity with minimal privacy;
- prevent blackmail and corruption;
- sanction same sex body searches (see Burke, 1993; Leinen, 1993).

However, in 1991 lesbian and gay police officers came 'out' and announced that a Lesbian and Gay Police Association covering every rank up to chief superintendent had been launched to campaign actively to make sexual orientation a mainstream issue within the force and to ensure there was no discrimination against lesbian and gay officers.

What impact do you think the issues discussed in sections 3.1, 3.2 and 3.3 might have on the police organization?

The issues of gender, 'race' and sexuality detonated powerful explosions under the foundations of the occupational culture and organization. For decades, the force leaders had ignored, denied or downplayed allegations of prejudicial attitudes and discriminatory behaviour in the public sphere; and so long as the ranks held together there was little possibility of addressing such complaints. However, once women, black and gay officers began to go public on their experience of the private world of the organization, one question above all others was bound to be posed: If this is how *colleagues* are discriminated against, what can the general public expect?

It was this uncomfortable reality that made equal opportunities an acknowledged organizational issue in the police in the 1990s. Various conferences and policy statements stressed that the police, like all progressive employers, would not tolerate a workplace ethos that was boorish, sexist and racist or harboured discriminatory working practices. The Metropolitan Police, for example, declared that it would work towards a police service that was genuinely representative at all levels of London's diverse communities. However, senior officers had to tread a delicate path because of the very real possibility of equal opportunities becoming a 'wedge issue' that could produce a rank-and-file backlash and new divisions. White, male, heterosexual officers of all ranks had to be reassured that there would be no preferential treatment, no political correctness, no quotas, no special pleading, no feminization of routine policework, no positive discrimination and no witch hunts. They were told that a balanced workforce could help to restore the tarnished image of police officers, improve community relations and rebuild public confidence. Moreover, it could foster a more effective approach to crime generally; it could enable an improved response to victims of crimes such as rape, domestic violence, child abuse, racial attacks and anti-gay violence; and it could transform the cultural outlook of the organization. Senior officers have had to take very seriously transatlantic evidence that women officers are especially effective in a number of areas (Heidensohn, 1992). They are skilled in defusing conflictual encounters, in toning the aggressivenenss of male colleagues, and in eliciting useful information from suspects, victims and witnesses; and they are more likely to receive public support. They are also more likely to understand the nature of disputes and seem to have a greater willingness to consider organizational transformations, new team models of management and sources of authority. They are also less likely to be involved in disciplinary proceedings.

# 4   Police powers and civil liberties

Baldwin and Kinsey (1982) have argued that there is an inherent tension in policework: how to strike a fair balance between ensuring that the police have the necessary powers to bring offenders to justice and ensuring that they use these laws impartially, responsibly and in a manner that is not an unwarranted infringement on civil liberties and human rights.

As it is not possible in this chapter to discuss every aspect of the debate about police powers, we will concentrate on facets of 'stop and search' on the street and interrogation in the police station as they operate in England and Wales.

## 4.1   The politics of law formulation

Any proposed review and change to the criminal law is likely to produce a predictable, often ritualistic exchange of charges and counter charges between the police and civil liberties groups. Police representatives tend towards a crime control/law and order stance, arguing that they are being forced to derogate from the rule of law and due process and that they need more powers and fewer restrictions to do their job properly (Pollard, 1995). Periodically they raise a hue and cry about collusion between members of the legal profession and the criminal fraternity; they argue that existing powers are antiquated and unworkable, that loopholes need to be closed to stop the acquittal of the guilty and they point out that law-abiding members of the public in a democratic society have nothing to fear from police empowerment.

Civil liberties groups take a due process/rule of law line, maintaining that extensions of police power will inevitably be at the expense of the rights of the individual and that so-called *technical loopholes* are in fact *rights and liberties* that guard against the conviction of the innocent. From this viewpoint, each act of police empowerment legitimizes pre-existing extra-legal police practices, becomes the basis for further extension of powers and erosion of civil rights and takes us one step further away from a *policed* state and towards a *police* state (Thornton, 1989). The civil liberties groups argue that legislators pay more attention to empowering the police than to providing a legal framework which manifestly safeguards the rights of the individual; they maintain, for example, that public order legislation never lays down statutory clauses which would place on a firm legal footing the right to participate in demonstrations, processions and assemblies. They believe that the police should have to prove, to an independent, democratically constituted review body, the contribution that a given power makes to the prevention and detection of crime. If proof is not forthcoming the power should be repealed or suspended. They also stress that the police have become a powerful and successful pressure group in the post-war period and accuse them since the 1970s of orchestrating a:

> very powerful public relations operation which disseminates [their] notions as an authorized, consensual view – an operation carried on out of our own taxes; which presses its spokesmen forward on every occasion upon the media; which lobbies inquiries and Royal Commissions, constantly pressing for larger powers; which bullies weak Home Secretaries (and boos them when they cross their wishes); which reproves magistrates for lenient sentencing; which announces unashamedly that the police are in the regular practice of breaking judges' rules when interrogating suspects; which slanders unnamed lawyers and lampoons libertarian organizations; which tells judges how they are to interpret the law; and which justifies the invasion of the citizens' privacy and the accumulation of prejudicial and inaccurate records ...
>
> What also is something new to a historian is the notion that we should be instructed as to what value we are to put on freedom and democracy, and be *instructed by the police*. And that the police are to be seen as, somehow, for themselves, rather than as servants to us, so that we are to be instructed by the police as to what is to be our place.

> (Thompson, 1980, pp.200–1)

## 4.2 Stop and search: controlling the streets

The use of police stop-and-search powers, which are premised on the notoriously loose concept of 'reasonable suspicion', has been the source of controversy between the police and certain communities for many years. The police argue that the powers are necessary to aid the detection of crime and arrest of offenders and allow for a crucial sifting or gatekeeping to take place prior to the decision to arrest.

reasonable suspicion

However, there have been persistent allegations that highly discretionary street policing powers are not used primarily to assist crime detection but to collect information on individuals, to target, control and criminalize communities and to discriminate against specific groups (Brogden, 1994). Critics point to research findings indicating that the vast majority of stops do not result in arrests and that no good reasons ('reasonable suspicion') for stops could be found in about one-third of cases. Smith and Gray (1985) found that officers:

> strongly tend to choose young males, especially young black males. Other groups that they tend to single out are people who look scruffy or poor ('slag'), people who have long hair or unconventional dress (who, they think, may use drugs) and homosexuals. We observed two cases where men were stopped purely because they appeared to be homosexual. In a few cases there appeared to be no criteria at all and the stop is completely random; this happens especially in the early hours of the morning when police officers tend to be bored.

> (Smith and Gray, 1985, p.496)

*In any street encounter the constable has the discretion to issue a stern warning or to invoke the full powers of the law*

They also noted the 'off the record' advice that one experienced officer was intending to pass on to a group of probationers about how to exercise their street powers: 'How does an experienced policeman decide who to stop? Well, the one that you stop is often wearing a woolly hat, he is dark in complexion, he has thick lips and he usually has fuzzy hair' (Smith and Gray, 1985, p.405).

The Police and Criminal Evidence Act 1984 (PACE) for the first time provided all police officers (from 1986) with a general power to stop and search a person in a public place, if they had reasonable grounds for suspecting that they would find stolen goods or prohibited articles. It also laid down strict procedural safeguards to ensure that the powers were not used in an arbitrary or capricious manner. Police officers would be required to state the purpose of a search and their grounds for undertaking it, before a search could be carried out. A record of the search had to be made (detailing purpose, grounds, date and time, place and outcome) and be made available to the suspect. Codes of Practice (which, like the Judge's Rules before them, do not have the force of law) accompanying the Act attempted to specify what constituted 'reasonable suspicion'. There had to be a firm basis for the officer's suspicion, not merely suspicion based on hunch, gut feeling or instinct:

> there must be some objective basis for it ... Reasonable suspicion can never be supported on the basis of personal factors alone. For example, a person's colour, age, hairstyle or manner of dress, or the fact that he is known to have a previous conviction for possession of an unlawful article, cannot be used along or in combination with each other as the sole basis on which to search that person. Nor may it be founded on the basis of stereotyped images of certain persons or groups as more likely to be committing offences.
>
> (Home Office, 1991, pp.13–14)

This was an attempt to modify the organizationally invisible behaviour of officers on the street by focusing their attention on the need for an objectively verifiable stop. It was argued that the new *inhibitory rules* would ensure that stops were used more sparingly and any that did take place would be on stronger grounds leading to more arrests. So what happened? When appraising Table 2.1, we need to keep in mind that in 1981 in London alone, approximately 700,000 stops took place with 67,275 resulting in an arrest (Willis, 1983).

Some commentators argue that these figures indicate that stop and search has been brought under control. Alderson (1993) goes as far as to argue that: 'the new comprehensive systems of recording are making intuitive stops and borderline suspicions not worth the bother which may accrue from their supervisors, or members of the public' (Alderson, 1993, p.16). However, other researchers (for example, Bottomley *et al.*, 1991) argue that the picture is more complex. First, there is only a requirement to record where searches

### Table 2.1  Stops and searches in England and Wales, 1986–94

| Year | Stops and searches | Arrests | Percentage leading to arrests |
|------|--------------------|---------|-------------------------------|
| 1986 | 109,800 | 18,900 | 17.2 |
| 1987 | 118,300 | 19,600 | 16.6 |
| 1988 | 149,600 | 23,700 | 15.8 |
| 1989 | 202,800 | 32,800 | 16.2 |
| 1990 | 256,900 | 39,200 | 15.3 |
| 1991 | 303,800 | 46,200 | 15.2 |
| 1992 | 351,700 | 48,700 | 13.8 |
| 1993 | 442,800 | 55,900 | 13.0 |
| 1994 | 576,000 | 70,300 | 12.0 |

Source: based on Home Office, 1995a

have taken place. Second, there is evidence to suggest that police officers have devised techniques and procedures that bypass or avoid the former safeguards (the 'ways and means' Act). One way round the rules, for example, is to negotiate 'consensual' encounters. A significant number, if not the majority, of stops and searches are not recorded because members of the public consent to being questioned and searched. In such cases, PACE, particularly the requirement of 'reasonable suspicion' and legal constraints, does not apply. Hence, Bottomley *et al.* argue that much street policework happens in the grey area between the clear exercise of coercive powers and the informed consent of citizens:

> The co-operation of citizens, many of whom do not know about their rights and police powers, is a valuable resource for every police officer, who has little incentive to establish whether that co-operation represents 'true' informed consent. If many searches are done without co-operation, and outside PACE procedures, who can say with certainty that suspects' rights are being consistently safeguarded under new legislation?
>
> (Bottomley *et al.*, 1991, p.40)

Third, there is considerable variation in the use of stop-and-search powers by different forces; whether the variations are due to differences in police policy or in recording practices is difficult to establish. Fourth, the arrest rates indicate that the 'hit rate' has not changed appreciably. Fifth, there is little meaningful monitoring of the stop-and-search records by supervising officers. There is no way of knowing, for example, whether the reason stated in the record is in fact the same as the original reason that led to the stop and search (Sanders and Young, 1994). As Smith (1986) has argued:

> a policy like stop and search *cannot be effectively regulated through the law* and its embodiment in the criminal justice system. A law on stop and search is essentially permissive; like the law against obstructing a police officer it represents a resource that the police may use. We can argue about whether the police exceed their statutory power – I say they do – but this is ultimately irrelevant since there is no conceivable way in which such a vague (and necessarily vague) criterion as 'reasonable suspicion' can be made to constitute an effective constraint. In this field, the law is just a source of *presentational rules* which exist to put an acceptable face on practices we prefer not to look at squarely.
>
> (Smith, 1986, p.93)

It seems likely that the debate about the police use of stop-and-search powers will intensify as a result of the Criminal Justice and Public Order Act 1994. This Act gave superintendents or higher officer grades the power to authorize uniformed officers to stop and search pedestrians and vehicles and their occupants, within a specified area, for offensive weapons, if there were reasonable grounds for believing that violence might occur in the area. In exercise of these powers, a constable is able to stop and search 'whether or not he has grounds for suspecting' that the person is carrying weapons or articles of that kind.

## 4.3  Police powers in the station: the interrogation process

Obtaining a confession is one of the most cost-effective ways to clear up crimes because it 'enables the police to avoid gathering other kinds of evidence ... and also avoids unnecessary delays ... Besides a confession recognizes the righteousness of the investigating officer's case, the soundness of the judgement and serves to reinforce perceptions of his skill and credibility amongst his colleagues' (Evans, 1993, p.1). A signed confession, *even if uncorroborated*, makes a guilty plea more probable, simplifies proceedings and avoids the over-reliance on witnesses. Interrogation sessions may also serve other important purposes, such as helping to clear up other crimes, recovering stolen goods and establishing new flows of information. It is because of the crucial role played by interrogation and confessions that one of the traditional organizing principles of the English criminal justice system was that the prosecution must prove the guilt of the accused. Until this had been accomplished to the satisfaction of the judge and jury or magistrates, the accused had to be considered innocent.

Hence, although a suspect was required to submit to police detention and repeat interrogation sessions, police officers, until 1994 when the wording was revised, had to caution her or him with the famed: 'You do not have to say anything unless you wish to do so, but what you say may be given in evidence'. This right to silence meant that no-one, including suspects, could be required to give information to the police in the course of a criminal investigation. A suspect under interrogation could refuse to answer questions altogether, or decline to answer particular questions or not address particular issues in her or his answers to questions. Moreover, a person charged with a criminal offence could not be required to give evidence in court at any stage of criminal proceedings. Suspects who chose to exercise the right to remain silent suffered no automatic legal sanction during any subsequent trial. Juries could not be asked by prosecuting counsel or the judge to treat refusal to answer police questions as an indication of guilt.

Why do you think the right to silence has been deemed to be important?

The right to silence recognized that citizens were extremely vulnerable situationally and psychologically when in custody. Police officers could use a variety of pressure techniques to gain a confession, such as oppressive questioning, abuse, threats, bullying tactics, bargaining, inducements, and playing co-defendants off against each other; they could 'exploit the timidity, ignorance, lack of foresight and stupidity of the suspect in order to obtain a confession' (Evans, 1993, p.2).

McBarnet (1983) argued that suspects could be 'persuaded' and 'convinced' that they had committed an offence even when the legal components of the offence had not been established or the suspects did not understand the significance of what they were saying. In addition, officers could 'gild the lily' by altering the words of suspects to create a particular impression, by not recording what was said in full or by complete fabrication.

PACE laid down new rules and procedural requirements both to govern the questioning of suspects by investigating officers and to enhance the rights of suspects. One of the primary aims of the Act was to promote the use of formal settings and uniform frameworks for discourse between investigating officers and suspects, thus improving the reliability of evidence. PACE stated that a custody officer, who is independent of investigations, is responsible for ensuring adherence to the rules, and thus the welfare of those in their custody. This includes authorizing the release of a suspect for interview, informing suspects of their rights of access to legal advice and detailing all actions or decisions regarding suspects in a custody record. The custody record is designed to act as a control by guarding against 'informal chats'. In addition, PACE required interrogations to be contemporaneously recorded, with increasing emphasis upon tape recording, and the accused to be invited to verify the accuracy of the record. Any confession made during interrogation must be excluded if it was or may have been obtained by 'oppression' or as a result of any conduct likely to render the confession unreliable.

In the late 1980s and early 1990s, police behaviour during interrogations came under intense scrutiny as a result of a string of high profile miscarriages of justice, quashed convictions and successful appeals. Police officers and their allies argued that such occurrences were 'historical legacies' of an unmonitored and exceptional period of 'noble cause corruption' (see McConville and Bridges, 1994). 'Middle England' was assured that such miscarriages of justice could not happen under PACE.

However, research into the operation of the current system indicates that there is still considerable cause for concern about the interrogation process. McConville *et al.* (1991) found that many custody officers were not strictly adhering to PACE. They appeared to ignore breaches of the Codes of Practice, actively colluded in such infringements or were coerced into breaches by forceful detectives. 'Off-the-record' interviews were still taking place with officers visiting cells for a 'quick word' or because the suspect had 'requested' to speak to a particular officer. Furthermore, certain custody officers were authorizing a suspect's release to the interview room without a record being made on the custody sheet. Research by Reiner reached similar conclusions: 'the idea of the custody officer as an independent check ... has proved chimerical' (Reiner, 1992a, p.1).

It is also claimed that those officers who prefer to stick to the letter of the law rather than its spirit have 'informal' chats at the scene of the crime or take the scenic route to the police station before suspects reach the protection of the custody officer or their legal representatives: 'In most cases there is no record of the content of the exchanges and even when records are ostensibly kept, they are typically inadequate' (Moston and Stephenson, 1993, p.46). Researchers are agreed that the police–suspect conversations outside of the formal interview are crucial for understanding why suspects subsequently make admissions. It is during these unseen têtes-à-têtes that the real bargaining, negotiation and threats take place. The 'final' statements made by suspects on tape are, in certain cases, the outcome of a series of conversations. The formal interview, therefore, is only the closing part of the process.

The Codes of Practice were revised in 1991 in an attempt to eliminate outside interviews except in certain specified circumstances. Any interview taking place outside the station had to be recorded contemporaneously. The Code also made a distinction between (i) interviewing; (ii) the questioning of a person regarding her or his involvement or suspected involvement in a criminal offence; and (iii) questioning, obtaining information or an explanation of the facts in the ordinary course of the officer's duty. This last activity was not prescribed but it was permitted. Hence Moston and Stephenson argue that: 'there will *always* be scope for officers to have a quiet word "off the record" ... In reality, there is simply no practicable way to record or monitor every possible occasion in which a police officer has an opportunity to speak with a suspect' (Moston and Stephenson, 1993, p.46).

Other researchers continue to argue that the overall *character* of the formal interview process remains deeply problematic and that unreliable confessions premised on fatally flawed evidence and injustice remain predictable outcomes, given the organizational and public pressure to clear up crime. McConville *et al.* argue that the overarching purpose of interrogation is 'to elicit *from the suspect* those facts which are relevant to resolution of the case, at least so far as the suspect is concerned. The accused is seen as the repository of information which can confirm or dispel police suspicion, and it is the task of the police to uncover this hidden data bank' (McConville *et al.*, 1991, p.65). As long as 'the search for the cough' remains of paramount importance, police officers will utilize forms of questioning which are premised upon confirming the guilt of the suspect rather than inquiring after the 'truth'. McConville *et al.* detail how certain types of questions – leading questions, statement-type questions, legal closure questions, imperfect syllogistic questions – manipulate the suspect's decision-making capacities so that the likelihood develops of a confession consistent with the police version of reality:

> 'Facts' are not elicited, they are *created*. The 'facts' generated during interrogation are the product of a complex process of interaction between suspect and officer, much of which is directly traceable to the style and manner of police questions. The creation of such facts is not an unusual or aberrant feature but absolutely endemic to police interrogation. Nor are such 'facts' accidentally created: they are precisely what the process sets out to achieve.
>
> (McConville *et al.*, 1991, p.67)

From this critical socio-legal perspective, it is not surprising that, despite all the assurances about PACE, in the first half of the 1990s miscarriages of justice were still coming to light as can be seen in the report from *The Guardian,* 17 December 1992, reproduced opposite.

However, the police believe that the pendulum has swung too far towards the protection of the accused and regard PACE as an overly bureaucratic and demoralizing code which works to conceal the truth, hampers the collection of evidence and protects a hard core of professional criminals. They complain that the rule tightening introduced after the miscarriages of justice have made cases impossible to investigate: Table 2.2 provides examples of the type of paperwork involved in modern policing. Police called for a fresh look at plea-bargaining; pre-trial reviews; compulsory disclosure of defence evidence; the right to trial by jury; and modification of the right to remain silent. The Criminal Justice and Public

'Menace' of police interview horrified appeal judges

# Wrongful conviction due to 'human error'

**Duncan Campbell**
**Crime Correspondent**

HUMAN error was blamed yesterday by the Lord Chief Justice for the wrongful conviction of three men jailed for life in 1990 for the murder of a prostitute in Cardiff.

Lord Taylor urged police, solicitors and prosecuting authorities to learn the lessons of a police interviewing technique which had 'horrified' the Court of Appeal and effectively brainwashed a suspect into confessing.

In a 45-minute, 24-page judgement on the conviction of the Cardiff Three – Stephen Miller, Tony Paris and Yusuf Abdullahi – Lord Taylor was highly critical of two South Wales detectives who had 'oppressively' interviewed Mr Miller.

The interviews had clearly led to his conviction and assisted in the convictions of the other two. All three had been found guilty at Swansea crown court of murdering Lynette White, aged 21, who had suffered more than 50 stab wounds. The three were released from life sentences last week when the appeal was allowed.

'Miller was bullied and hectored,' said the Lord Chief Justice, sitting with Mr Justice Popplewell and Mr Justice Laws. 'The officers, particularly Detective [Constable Peter] Greenwood, were not so much questioning him as shouting at him what they wanted him to say.' The court had been horrified by the tape recording of the interview.

'It is hard to conceive of a more hostile or intimidating approach by officers to a suspect,' he said. 'It is impossible to convey on the printed page the pace, force and menace of the officer's delivery.'

The Lord Chief Justice said that he was referring copies of the tape to the Chief Inspector of Constabulary, the Director of Public Prosecutions and the chairman of the Royal Commission on Criminal Justice.

But he stressed that he was doing so to lay down guide-lines and not to provoke a prosecution. The case did not indicate flaws in the Police and Criminal Evidence Act of 1984, but 'a combination of human errors'.

He said: 'The object is not to instigate a witch-hunt against those involved but to provide those authorities with an example of what we hope never to hear again in this court.'

The seventh of the tape-recorded interviews conducted with Mr Miller by DC Greenwood and DC John Seaford was oppressive and thus in contravention of the act, the Lord Chief Justice said. Mr Miller was said to be on the borders of mental handicap, with a mental age of 11, an IQ of 75, and a reading age of eight.

The interviews ought not to have been admitted in evidence. One pair of officers had been tough and confrontational and the next pair had been milder in manner. Mr Miller had denied involvement more than 300 times.

'It is perfectly legitimate for officers to pursue the interrogation of a suspect with a view to eliciting his account, or gaining admissions,' said the Lord Chief Justice. 'They are not required to give up after the first denial or even a number of denials.' But the officers had made it clear to Mr Miller that they would go on interviewing him until he agreed with the version of events they required ...

(*The Guardian*, 17 December 1992)

Order Act 1994 controversially narrowed defendants' rights to silence and courts were given more freedom to draw unfavourable inferences from a suspect's refusal to answer police questions. The inferences extended to a failure to account for objects or substances in the suspect's possession or marks on her or his person; and failure to account for her or his presence in a particular place. In future, suspects would be informed that: 'You do not have to say anything. But it may harm your defence if you do not mention when questioned something which you later rely on in court. Anything you do say may be given in evidence'.

## Table 2.2  The bureaucratic nightmare

### After an arrest

| | |
|---|---|
| MG1 | File front sheet |
| MG2 | File content check list |
| MG3 | Defendant details |
| MG4 | Copy of charge or summons |
| MG5 | Summary of evidence |
| MG6/a/b | Confidential background information |
| MG6c | Unused material disclosure schedule |
| MG6d | Sensitive material (Informants or surveillance) |
| MG7 | Initial remand application |
| MG8 | Breach of bail conditions |
| MG9 | Witness list |
| MG10 | Witness non-availability |
| MG11 | Witness statement(s) |
| MG12 | Exhibit list |
| MG13 | Interview notes |
| MG14 | Voluntary statement |
| MG15 | Record of taped interview |
| MG16 | Previous convictions |
| MG17 | List of cautions |
| MG18 | Other offences to be taken into consideration |
| MG19 | Compensation claims |
| MG20 | Further evidence/information |
| NIB74D | Records update |

Note: MG – manual of guidance. Most arrests require the completion of the majority of the above forms. Additionally, custody records are also maintained by station custody sergeants.

### On patrol

Three incident or arrest booklets
Notebooks
Three accident report books
Three process books (motoring offences)
HRT1 (for motorists without documents)
Stop slip pad (for stops/searches)
Fixed penalty notices (motoring)
Premises search booklets
Metropolitan Police calling cards
Witness statement forms
Crime report sheets
Missing person forms

Source: based on Kirby, 1993

Opponents insisted that this unwarranted empowerment of the police would only encourage senior officers to ask for more. In 1995 their worst fears were confirmed when police representatives declared that they were losing all faith in the law, warned that officers were bending the rules in the public interest and stepped up their campaign for further changes to the criminal justice system to make convictions easier to obtain. They also contrasted the success that the police had with their empowerment 'shopping list' with the abject failure of those campaigning for the new powers to be accompanied by enhanced structures and processes of accountability.

# 5 Controlling policework

### ACTIVITY 2.5

To what extent and to whom do you think the British police should be accountable? In addressing these questions, you will need to consider:

1   What 'accountability' means.
2   Different modes and levels of accountability.
3   The difference between accountability and control.
4   Who should determine policing needs and priorities (for example, should it be the community? the organization? politicians?).
5   From your reading of the first two chapters in this book, what do you think are the issues which might cause the notion of accountability to be a sensitive and complicated concept in policework?

Brogden *et al.* argue:

> police accountability becomes an issue when there is public concern that the arrangements for ensuring the police perform satisfactorily any part of their role are not working. Such concern may arise through dissatisfaction with … the biased use of powers and the wasteful deployment of resources to practices unacceptable to any section of the public: with anything, in short, which threatens to undermine any of their central obligations.

(Brogden *et al.*, 1988, p.153)

Senior police officers assert that the police is one of the most accountable organizations in the country. Constables, it is argued, are accountable to the courts; to the Crown Prosecution Service which scrutinizes all prosecution cases; and to an organizational disciplinary code governed by an act of parliament, with complaints investigated by an independent Police Complaints Authority. Chief constables are constrained by the law and are accountable to police authorities and, ultimately, the Home Secretary for the running of their forces. Police representatives also argue that they are accountable to the community through community liaison panels, Neighbourhood Watch and victim support schemes, and through the investigations of a highly critical media. Critics of the present system stress, however, that we must distinguish between formal, paper modes of accountability and substantive meaningful ones.

## 5.1 Controlling the constable

### 5.1.1 Legal accountability

Being accountable to the courts can be regarded as the *ultimate* form of accountability because both statute and common law specify the powers available to the constable and establish the legal ground rules of policework. As we have noted earlier, a court can exclude a confession where there was oppression or if anything has occurred to make it possibly unreliable. It also has the discretion to exclude evidence that might influence the fairness of the trial (Section 78 of PACE allows judges to exclude evidence if they feel it is prejudicial to the fairness of the trial). Police officers are also constrained by a panoply of pre-trial checks, such as the custody record, the tape recording of the interrogations and the Crown Prosecution Service's demand for transparently credible and well-prepared cases. But questions remain about the capability of the legal system to police the police. Critics argue that the legal mode of accountability is *retrospective* and selective in that it tends to turn on technical points of law rather than critically scrutinizing the principles and processes of routine policework. And as the above account of the Cardiff Three appeal indicates, judges tend to work with a human error or 'rotten apple' theory of police malpractice rather than countenancing the idea of institutional or systematic rule-breaking. Furthermore, as Sanders and Young (1994) argue, judicial control only applies to those cases that are brought to trial and the vast majority of defendants plead guilty. Thus, the legal gaze can be remarkably short-sighted.

### 5.1.2 The complaints process

The Police Complaints Authority (PCA) was set up under PACE to supervise the investigation of serious complaints against police officers and also of cases not based on complaints but voluntarily referred to the PCA by a police force because they raise grave or exceptional issues. It also reviews completed investigations, whether supervised or not, to decide whether police officers, below a certain rank, should face disciplinary charges. Supervision consists of a PCA member approving the appointment of the investigating officers and then overseeing the conduct of the inquiry and examining the evidence as the inquiry takes shape. Once the investigation has been concluded, the PCA issues a formal statement as to whether it has been satisfactory or not. If the final report suggests that a police officer may have committed a criminal offence, it is passed to the Crown Prosecution Service which evaluates the evidence and decides whether to prosecute. If there is no criminal prosecution, the chief officer of the force involved must decide whether a disciplinary charge would be appropriate.

From its inception, the PCA has been embroiled in considerable controversy. Police officers denounced it as a body that had too many powers, touted unscrupulously for business and victimized good people doing a messy job (Kirby, 1989). Civil liberties campaigners condemned it because it depended on serving police officers to carry out the actual investigations and had few real powers. Because of their socialization and orientation, civil liberties groups maintained, police officers were incapable of viewing other police officers critically or of truth-seeking and would by design or default continue to brush complaints against other officers under the carpet. (Less than 8 per cent of the 150,000 formal complaints lodged between 1985 and 94 resulted in an officer being disciplined; see also Figure 2.7.) Both the civil libertarians and rank-and-file police officers are united in their demands for it to be replaced by a fully independent and impartial complaints investigation body.

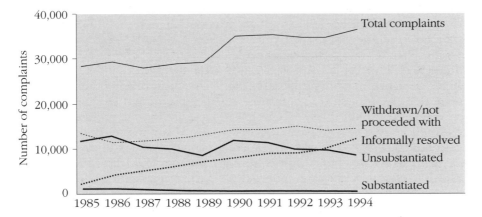

Figure 2.7  Number and outcome of completed complaints received by police, 1985–94
(Source: Home Office, 1995b, p.5)

The PCA acknowledges that it faces a number of problems in carrying out its work effectively (see Police Complaints Authority, 1995). For example, because most stops and searches or arrests are one-to-one, complainants have considerable difficulty in producing corroborative evidence, unless exceptional violence has been used by officers. Moreover, the PCA has found in many important cases that very few officers are willing to give evidence against each other.

Finally, many officers exercise their right of silence when questioned over alleged improprieties. Hence the Crown Prosecution Service has been forwarded cases where there is not enough evidence to proceed any further.

Internal disciplinary proceedings are difficult to pursue because, as a result of rank-and-file campaigning, the standard of proof in police discipline cases is uniquely the same as that of a criminal trial; that is, proof beyond reasonable doubt, as opposed to that of a civil trial, the balance of probabilities. Additionally, criminal lawyers may be engaged by officers to refute disciplinary allegations, though not to substantiate them.

Furthermore, the PCA has found that officers under investigation can undermine the inquiry by leaving the force on medical grounds with full pension rights. This leaves a significant number of cases unresolved and pre-empts the outcome of disciplinary proceedings. Not surprisingly, given the obstacles that investigators face, there have been serious delays in bringing cases to court and important cases have been thrown out by the courts.

The PCA has also complained about undue restrictions on the release of information about the progress of cases. Section 98 of PACE makes it a criminal offence for a member or officer of the PCA to disclose information about its work except 'in a summary or other general statement made by the authority which does not identify the person from whom the information was received or any person to whom it relates'. This means that its work is shrouded in secrecy.

But perhaps the most fundamental problem remains the reluctance of many people with grievances to activate the formal complaints procedure because of distrust of police officers, the potent threat of their evidence being subsequently used against them if their complaint fails or intimidation and harassment by colleagues of the police officers concerned. And, of course, the PCA's manifest lack of success in bringing officers to justice and lack of adequate explanation confirms to many the pointlessness of using the formal complaints machinery. It is in this context that certain solicitors have continued to advise clients that private prosecutions and civil proceedings are more effective ways of seeking redress and justice. 'The consequence of winning a civil action is compensation in money whereas if a complaint is upheld, you receive nothing beyond the satisfaction of knowing there is a chance that the officer(s) in question will be disciplined or, just possibly, prosecuted' (Thornhill, 1989, p.345). In 1994 the Metropolitan Police paid out £1.76 million in settled actions following claims for wrongful arrest, false imprisonment and assault. However, critics argue that this is unsatisfactory because in such cases police forces do not have to admit liability or guilt, do not have to apologize and are under no obligation to take further disciplinary action against the officers involved.

## 5.2   Democratic accountability

The 1964 Police Act, for the first time in the history of the public police, constitutionally established a tripartite structure of police governance which attempted to achieve the impossible by answering the following questions: What degree and forms of control should a police authority exercise over a chief constable? And what degree and forms of control should a Home Secretary exercise over a chief constable and a police authority?

Police authorities, composed of two-thirds local councillors and one-third magistrates, were given the responsibility to secure and maintain adequate and efficient local forces. They had the powers to appoint chief constables and could require their retirement on efficiency grounds. However, all major decisions made by the authorities were subject to the final approval of the Home Secretary who was also given the important fiscal responsibility for allocating a central grant, representing half of each force's annual budget. Police forces were placed under the direction and control of the chief constables. To ensure political impartiality, the Act enshrined the 'operational independence' of the chief constables from the police authorities and the Home Secretary, reiterating that they were not civil servants or local government employees and that they should be free from conventional processes of democratic accountability. Chief constables could be required to submit *ex post facto* reports on local policing matters, but could exercise discretion and refuse to do so if they considered the information not to be in the public interest or outside the authorities' remit. They could also appeal to the Home Secretary against such demands. Chief constables were also given responsibility for all appointments and promotions below assistant chief constable and the disciplinary authority for these ranks. The Home Secretary's supervisory powers spanned pay and regulations, the monitoring of force performance through an inspectorate of constabulary and, controversially, continuing to act as the police authority for the Metropolitan Police.

During the deliberations on this Act there were angry protests from local government representatives that the powers of both the Home Secretary and the chief constables were being clarified and enhanced at the expense of the local government police authorities. The Act, it was claimed, was not sustaining a tripartite but creating a bipartite structure of police governance. The police authorities would in any conflict be squeezed between the Home Secretary who had the power of veto and the chief constables who were constitutionally entitled to ignore them. Lord Denning put a final seal on the legal position of the chief constables, *vis-à-vis* the Home Secretary and the police authorities, when he proclaimed:

> I hold it to be the duty of the Commissioner of Police, as it is of every chief constable, to enforce the law of the land. He must take steps so to post his men that crimes may be detected, and that honest citizens may go about their affairs in peace. He must decide whether or not suspected persons are to be prosecuted, and, if need be, bring the prosecution or see that it is brought; but in all these things he is not the servant of anyone, save of the law itself. No Minister of the Crown can tell him that he must or must not prosecute this man or that one. Nor can any police authority tell him so. The responsibility for law enforcement lies on him. He is answerable to the law and to the law alone.

> (Lord Denning *R V Commissioner of Police for the Metropolis, ex parte Blackburn*, 1968, 2 QB 118, p.136)

As Jefferson noted, chief constables were no longer constrained by police authorities, their operational independence was constitutionally guaranteed, and their professional status and power enhanced as the result of the creation of fewer and larger police bureaucracies in the latter half of the 1960s. They 'could debate with the Home Office as equals, with each "side" supported by its own army of professional advisers. Thus, professionalization not only penetrated deeply into the reshaped structure but augmented the power granted to both the Home Office and the chief constables under the 1964 Act' (Jefferson, 1987, p.18).

However, in the 1970s and 1980s, in response to increasing complaints and unease about police racism, violence and corruption, and controversial public order policing strategies, certain community groups campaigned for: police powers to be limited to those which were strictly necessary; discretionary powers to be curbed; a general tightening of policework rules and procedures; and the establishment of effective independent institutions to investigate police malpractice. This community concern manifested itself in the same time period as certain chief police officers and staff associations ideologically pledged themselves to authoritarian law and order policies that, to a considerable degree, mirrored those of the Conservative Party. As a result, the image of the British police as non-political was seriously eroded (**Hall, 1980**).

Communities also asked their elected representatives on local police authorities to explain how and why a particular course of police action had been decided on. Why had fascists been allowed to march through a black neighbourhood when two weeks previously an anti-fascist march had been banned? Why was 'cottaging' a force priority rather than domestic, racial or anti-gay violence? Why was the force pressing for a state-of-the-art riot training centre when neighbourhood police stations were being closed? Why were armed police officers being deployed routinely in the city? How much was the mutual aid operation costing the taxpayer? Did the police authority approve of the drive against street crime? Why had the residents of 'Jonesville' not seen a constable on the beat in two weeks when it had just been announced that the force was putting more officers back on the streets? Why was the policing style of the Greater Manchester Police so different to that of Devon and Cornwall? Authority members had to declare that they had no say in the decisions, but would attempt to elicit answers from the chief constable. And on many occasions, the reply from force headquarters was that these were operational questions which were not open to deliberation or negotiation. As Councillor Gray of the Northumbria police authority argued in 1982, the defining point of power between the chief constable and the police authority was information. One side had it, the other did not:

> They should see some of the reports we get from chief constables. Five page exercises in how to say absolutely nothing. ... half of ours this year was devoted to full page photographs of our chief constable with the Queen. Is that being answerable to the police authority? We have a perfectly amicable relationship with him as long as we do not ask him any questions. He can tell us how many police dogs he is retiring this year and so on, he will not tell us how he runs his force. When we push and push he says: 'Ask the Home Secretary but I can tell you now he is on my side.' He is right. It is a waste of time going to the Home Secretary. If we took every question that our chief constable will not answer to the Home Secretary he would have time for absolutely nothing at all. This is practically worse than nothing because it's a facade; it pretends that it is doing something and it gives the police something to hide behind. I am sick of people standing up and saying: 'Well, speak to your police authority; your elected representatives are responsible.' But it is not up to us because your elected representatives on police authorities can do nothing in the face of an absolutely intransigent chief constable ... Police authorities are worse than a waste of time because I think they take away the initiative for doing something positive.

> (Gray, quoted in Armstrong, 1982, p.30)

The fact that virtually every question seemed to be covered by the term 'operational' generated campaigns of democratic renewal to move the 43 police authorities away from a *subordinate and passive* relationship with their chief constables to a more equal and proactive one. Some argued that police authorities should be legally able to require chief constables to *account retrospectively* for their decisions by explaining and justifying particular policies and actions. Others argued for democratically reconstituted police committees which would have *prospective control* of the formulation of policing policies, patterns and priorities. They would also have responsibility for all appointments, disciplinary proceedings and promotions and be able to *require* reports and to inspect files and records. In this division of duties, chief constables would be public servants, responsible for operationalizing and enforcing, in accordance with the rule of law, these democratically agreed policies and decisions. Democratization and the re-empowerment of police authorities would also make it clear to the community that answering the previously posed questions was *political* as well as *legal* in nature. Campaigners also pointed out that few democracies allowed police forces such organizational autonomy. Chief officers in the USA are subject to the formal electoral process whilst in Europe they are servants of Internal Ministers of Justice or municipal authorities, who are themselves democratically accountable.

Senior police officers and the Conservative government made it clear that they would oppose any moves towards the political control of policing because this would undermine the sacred principles of operational independence and impartiality. The campaign for democratic accountability was fatally undermined by:

- The policing of the miners' strike (1984–85) when police committees were forced to realize that they had no control over the financial costs of the massive mutual aid operation; and that two non-statutory authorities, ACPO and the National Reporting Centre, were working in tandem to co-ordinate with the Home Office a *national* policing operation which paid little attention to *local* policing needs.

- The failure of the Merseyside and Greater Manchester police authorities to remove very controversial chief constables with whom they could not work.

- The abolition of the radical Metropolitan police authorities in 1985 and their replacement with more conservative and deferential bodies.

- The Northumbria police authority case in which the appeal court ruled that chief constables could be furnished with plastic bullets from a Home Office depot if their authorities refused to purchase them.

- Home Office circulars which were much more mandatory and directive in nature and content and aimed at the minutiae of policing policy.

- The lack of an effective means to discipline, and indeed remove, chief constables who made overtly political statements.

- Lord Scarman's refusal to recommend a democratically elected police authority for London or extra powers for the provincial police authorities. Instead, he championed police–community consultative groups which critics argued were powerless and would not be able to deliver local determination of policing needs.

## 5.3 Managerial accountability

In the late 1980s and early 1990s, the question of police accountability resurfaced. This time, however, it was what Reiner (1993) describes as 'calculative and contractual', rather than democratic, accountability that was foregrounded. A series of unprecedented official investigations into police effectiveness and efficiency evaluated, assessed, measured and quantified virtually every aspect of the organization. They started from the premise that the police constituted an enterprise with a total workforce of approximately 180,000, a budget which rose by almost 90 per cent in real terms between 1979 and the early 1990s to £6 billion per year and a clear-up rate which had collapsed from 41 per cent to approximately 25 per cent in the same time period. They wanted to know whether the taxpayer was getting value for money and how the organization was managed.

Suddenly, senior police officers found themselves facing a set of seemingly non-political managerial questions:                                         managerialism

- Why has the force so many middle managers?

- Why is a rank structure needed?

- Why are the lines of financial management blurred?

- How should effectiveness be measured?
- How is performance evaluated?
- How can being a monopoly provider be justified?
- What is the core task?
- Why have support tasks not been market tested?
- How is customer satisfaction with the level of service evaluated?
- Why are staffing levels fixed according to national rather than local needs?
- Why does the organization emphasize rank rather than role?
- Why has the organization not developed work performance indicators?

The problem for the police was that the Audit Commission, the National Audit Office and the Sheehy Inquiry had quietly managed to sidestep the question of 'operational independence', to get inside the organization, and to establish that it was *administered* rather than *managed* and was a 'mock bureaucracy' where the glossy image of managerialism, rather than its structures and processes, was maintained. The old organizational model was deemed to be no longer able to cope with the demands of a drastically different, constantly changing task environment. They recommended a fundamental shake-up of the managerial and financial configuration, personnel policies, motivational rationales and working practices of the organization to promote sound management and cost-effectiveness.

After heated debate, high-profile media campaigns and many significant political compromises and climbs down, the 1994 Police and Magistrates' Courts Act was passed, bringing with it yet another reorganization of the tripartite structure (see Figure 2.8). From April 1995, free-standing, more business-like police authorities, with drastically reduced memberships, were given responsibility for producing, in conjunction with the chief constable, an annual local policing plan which detailed crime control targets, objectives and expenditure. The police authorities would also set a lawful budget for the year and be responsible for raising approximately 17 per cent of the funding from the council tax. The Home Secretary's role would be to lay down key national objectives and publish league tables overviewing the performance of all forces and police authorities. She or he could also determine a variety of policy matters by issuing codes of practice and would have enhanced sanctions to give directions to police authorities in the case of an adverse report from the upgraded inspectorate of constabulary. The Home Secretary was also given the power to 'fast-track' force amalgamations. Finally, because police budgets were cash limited, detailed central government controls over police expenditure were relaxed and chief constables, who retained overall charge of operational matters, were given the freedom to manage their budgets, personnel and resources. To facilitate personal accountability, senior police officers were also placed on fixed-term contracts and moved towards performance-related remuneration (Audit Commission, 1995).

This set of changes sparked a furious debate. On one side were those who argued that a final centralization of power was taking place which would lead eventually to a nationalized police organization. The battery of powers and levers allocated to the Home Secretary would enable her or him to determine local police practices which would constitute a direct

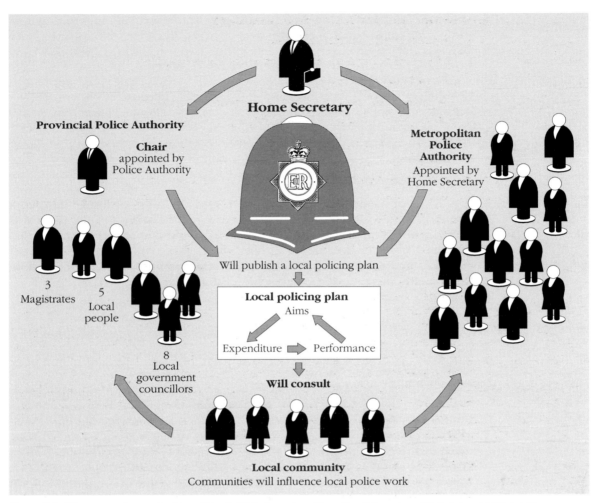

Figure 2.8 The new police authorities of April 1995 (based on Guardian Education, 12 October 1993, p.11)

infringement on the operational independence of chief officers. The new
police committees were being given awesome responsibilities and would be
directly accountable to central government. Because of their size and
composition, these quango-like committees could not be said to represent
local interests in a democratically accountable manner. The foregrounding of
crude, over-simplistic, quantitative plans and targets, which highlighted crime
control as being the core police task, would be counter-productive and have
an adverse effect on the overall quality of policing and police–community
relationships. Forces would concentrate on those activities that could be
easily identified and quantified and deliver immediate results. Officers would
be forced to cut corners, bend the rules and twist the statistics to deliver their
targets, resulting in a high level of wrongful convictions (see Reiner, 1995).
Chief officers on fixed-term contracts and financial incentives would be
forced to collude to protect their jobs. Overall, the 'calculative and
contractual' mode of accountability would corrupt the unique ethos and deep
structures of British policing by transforming the police from a local public
service into a state-run 'crime control' business.

Others argued that it would be necessary to study carefully the workings of the new quasi-purchaser/provider regime because a complex and paradoxical unravelling was likely to happen. The reforms would undoubtedly generate new organizational pressure points, divisions, conflicts, contradictions and strategic alliances. Decentralization and devolution as well as centralization could happen, because in order to deliver on the local policing plan, responsibility for operational policework would have to be located as near as possible to the point of service delivery. Performance targets, league tables and customer charters may be a crude starting-point, but as benchmarks they compel police authorities and police forces to account publicly for differences in effectiveness in clearing up crime, efficiency, priorities and resourcing. There was no reason why more sophisticated quantitative and qualitative measurements of local policework could not be constructed which foiled easy manipulation. Finally, there was no rational reason for asserting that a managerial mode of accountability was incompatible with democracy. Indeed, it could be argued that the proper stewardship of public finances was a crucial dimension of the modern lexicon of democratic accountability (McLaughlin and Murji, 1995).

At the time of writing, it remains to be seen how the new modes and cultures of accountability work out in practice. However, it is important to note that in the various debates and disputes there were some significant omissions. From your reading of the earlier sections in this chapter, can you identify any areas of policework which were not considered in the debates surrounding accountability?

You may have noted that there was little mention of the national policing bodies which are locking into formal and informal transnational and multi-national police networks and coalitions. Because these agencies are capable of operating above and beyond the narrow confines of the traditional nation-state, it seems that questions of democratic accountability and scrutiny no longer apply. There was also very little discussion of the accountability of the booming private policing sector. And finally, there was little discussion of the role communities might play in securing greater accountability of local officers, particularly communities in which there has been a history of poor relations between local people and the police.

# 6 Conclusion

In the 1980s it became apparent that police policies and practices were failing to deliver on core symbolic and instrumental tasks. Senior officers had always asserted that if they were given the requisite powers and resources they could not only control but defeat crime. Both were forthcoming in the 1980s and yet the crime rate, the fear of crime and public disorder escalated and the clear-up rates dropped. It was these realities and the accompanying fiscal crisis, the political fall-out and public loss of faith that induced the Conservative government to unveil a radical reform agenda. The stated aim was to remake the public police for the twenty-first century and to refashion its culture, style and methods. The old administrative police force, which worked to the principle that effective crime control was dependent on the amount of public money spent on policy, was to be transformed into a new, professional, managerialized police service based on principles of flexibility, diversity, consumer sovereignty and cost-effectiveness. In doing so, it would have to unlearn the habits of decades.

However, as we have seen in this chapter, there are special difficulties in reforming this particular public bureaucracy. It has shown itself to be inherently resistant to changes which threaten or infringe upon its professional autonomy or bind it into radical modernization projects. The workforce has traditionally been sceptical of any changes that fundamentally interfere with working patterns, practices and conditions of service. Senior officers have dreaded changes which require them to take major managerial decisions for which they can be personally held to account. Moreover, because this public bureaucracy operates in such multi-faceted task environments it has been difficult to devise meaningful structures, processes and cultures of accountability. It is this resistance to change that may eventually force serious reflection on the questions of monopoly provision and market competition.

There are as yet no formal proposals to subject the police to the free rein of market forces, but it could be argued that the unravelling logic of the reform process and the quasi-market approach mean that communities or police authorities ought to be able as of right to purchase the policing service they want from among a range of competitive providers. The edges are beginning to blur because of the scale of involvement of the private sector, the *ad hoc* hiving off of certain police tasks to other agencies and the increase in direct community self-policing. If this process is allowed to continue, the public police may find that national and transnational crime control and public order are their core responsibilities. Some police officers would argue that this is as it should be.

What are the long-term implications of such a shift? Insecure and unsafe communities, neighbourhoods, businesses and individuals in the next century might be forced to purchase their own specialist policing requirements. This could underpin the development of a truly global market in certain police and security services where multi-national police corporations compete for local policing franchises. A shift of responsibility to the community might also occur if neighbourhoods opt or are forced to take total responsibility for the co-production of their own policing arrangements or if the boundaries between the local police and local government services collapse completely and multi-purpose co-operative community safety teams are formed and regulated by local authorities. All these scenarios might begin to play out at the same time, generating new hybrid modalities of policing, community safety and systems of law enforcement and risk management; and constituting both a dispersal and intensification of policing and social control. Even if none of them come to pass, the fact that we can discuss and imagine them is an indication of how the old certainties about the British police collapsed in the course of the 1980s and 1990s.

# Further reading

The most accessible overview of the British police remains Reiner (1992b), while South (1988) and Johnson (1992) discusses the origins, nature and future of private policing. The Audit Commission Reports on policing provide an important insight into the 'new managerialist' perspective on the organization and core tasks of the public police, while Anderson and Boer (1994) provide an overview of European policing initiatives. *Policing the Crisis* by Hall *et al.* (1978) remains the most important Marxist text on the relationship between the police and the state and the processes underpinning the tense relationship between the police and black communities. Hanmer *et al.* (1989) analyses the key issues in women's relationship to policing. Jefferson and Grimshaw (1984) presents the most sophisticated analysis of the police accountability issue. For a comprehensive socio-legal analysis of the debate around police powers, see Sanders and Young (1994). A valuable set of comparative papers discussing policing beyond the state is presented in Findlay and Zvekic (1993). *Modern Policing* by Tonry and Morris (1992) is an important volume which gives an overview of future developments in policing, focusing primarily on the USA.

# References

Alderson, J. (1993) 'The police', in Stockdale, E. and Casape, S. (eds) *Criminal Justice Under Stress*, London, Blackstone.

Anderson, M. and Boer, M. (eds) (1994) *Policing Across National Boundaries*, New York and London, Pinter.

Armstrong, D. (ed.) (1982) *Changing Policing*, Department of Extra Mural Studies, University of London.

Ascoli, D. (1979) *The Queen's Peace*, London, Hamish Hamilton.

Association of Chief Police Officers (1993) *Your Police: The Facts*, London, ACPO.

Audit Commission (1990) *Effective Policing: Performance Review of Provincial Police Forces*, London, HMSO.

Audit Commission (1993) *Helping with Enquiries: Tackling Crime Effectively*, London, Audit Commission.

Audit Commission (1995) *Cheques and Balances: A Framework for Improving Police Accountability*, London, Audit Commission.

Baldwin, R. and Kinsey, R. (1982) *Police Powers and Politics*, London, Quartet Books.

Bayley, D. (1994) *Police for the Future*, New York, Oxford University Press.

Bittner, E. (1970) *The Functions of the Police in Modern Society: A Review of Background Factors, Current Practices, and Possible Role Models*, Rockville, MD, National Institute of Mental Health.

Bittner, E. (1974) 'Florence Nightingale in pursuit of Willie Sutton: a theory of the police', in Jacob, H. (ed.) *The Potential for Reform of Criminal Justice*, Beverley Hills, CA, Sage.

Bottomley, K., Coleman, C., Dixon, D., Gill, M. and Wall, D. (1991) *The Impact of PACE: Policing in a Northern Force*, University of Hull.

Bradley, D., Walker, N. and Wilkie, R. (1986) *Managing the Police: Law, Organisation and Democracy*, Brighton, Harvester.

Brewer, J.D. and Magee, K. (1991) *Inside the RUC: Routine Policing in a Divided Society*, Oxford, Oxford University Press.

Brogden, M. (1994) 'Gatekeeping and the seamless criminal justice system', in McConville and Bridges (1994).

Brogden, M., Jefferson, T. and Walklate, S. (1988) *Introducing Policework*, London, Unwin Hyman.

Bunyan, T. (ed.) (1993) *Statewatching the New Europe: A Handbook on the European State*, London, Statewatch Publications.

Burke, M. (1993) *Coming Out of the Blue: British Police Officers Talk about their Lives in "The Job" as Lesbians, Gays and Bisexuals*, London, Cassell.

Burrows, J. and Tarling, R. (1982) *Clearing Up Crime*, London, HMSO.

Cain, M. (1973) *Society and the Policeman's Role*, London, Routledge and Kegan Paul.

Campbell, B. (1993) 'Too much of a woman for the boys in blue', *The Independent*, 1 June, p.20.

**Clarke, J. (1996) 'Crime and social order: interrogating the detective story', in Muncie and McLaughlin (1996).**

Clarke, R. and Hough, M. (1984) *Crime and Police Effectiveness*, London, Home Office.

**Clarke, R.V.G. (1980) '"Situational" crime prevention: theory and practice', *British Journal of Criminology*, vol.20, no.2, pp.136–47. (Extract reprinted in Muncie *et al.*, 1996.)**

Davies, N. (1995) 'Shields, helmets, sticks and gas', *The Guardian*, 31 May, p.22.

Dorril, S. (1994) *The Silent Conspiracy: Inside the Intelligence Services in the 1990s*, London, Mandarin.

Evans, R. (1993) *The Conduct of Police Interviews with Juveniles*, London, HMSO.

Findlay, M. and Zvekic, U. (eds) (1993) *Alternative Policing Styles*, Deventer, Kluwer.

Graef, R. (1989) *Talking Blues: The Police in their Own Word*, London, Collins Harvill.

Halford, A. (1994) *No Way Up the Greasy Pole*, London, Constable.

**Hall, S. (1980) *Drifting into a Law and Order Society*, London, Cobden Trust. (Extract reprinted in Muncie *et al.*, 1996.)**

Hall, S., Critcher, C., Jefferson, T., Clarke, J. and Roberts, B. (1978) *Policing the Crisis: Mugging, the State and Law and Order*, London, Macmillan.

Hanmer, J., Radford, J. and Stanko, E. (1989) *Women, Policing and Male Violence*, London, Routledge.

Hebenton, B. and Thomas, T. (1994) *Policing Europe*, London, Macmillan.

Heidensohn, F. (1992) *Women in Control: The Role of Women in Law Enforcement*, Oxford, Clarendon.

Her Majesty's Inspectorate (1994) *Report of Her Majesty's Chief Inspector of Constabulary for the year 1993*, London, HMSO.

Hilliyard, B. (1982) 'Why they fail: an ex-policeman on the facts behind the figures', *The Sunday Times*, 26 September.

Hobbs, D. (1988) *Doing the Business*, Oxford, Clarendon.

Home Office (1991) *Police and Criminal Evidence Act 1984 (s.66) Codes of Practice* (2nd edn), London, HMSO.

Home Office (1993) *Sex Discrimination in the Police Service in England and Wales*, London, HMSO.

Home Office (1995a) *Operation of Certain Police Powers Under PACE*, Home Office Statistical Bulletin, Issue 15/95, London, Government Statistical Service.

Home Office (1995b) *Police Complaints and Discipline*, Home Office Statistical Bulletin, Issue 13/95, London, Government Statistical Service.

Jefferson, T. (1987) 'The police', in The Open University, D310 *Crime, Justice and Society*, Block 3, *Delivering Justice* Part 1A, Milton Keynes, The Open University.

Jefferson, T. (1990) *The Case Against Paramilitary Policing*, Buckingham, Open University Press.

Jefferson, T. and Grimshaw, R. (1984) *Controlling the Constable*, London, Muller.

Johnson, L. (1992) *The Rebirth of Private Policing*, London, Routledge.

Jones, S. (1986) *Policewomen and Equality: Formal Policy versus Informal Practice*, London, Macmillan.

**Keith, M. (1993) *Race, Riots and Policing*, London, UCL Press. (Extract reprinted as 'Criminalization and racialization' in Muncie *et al.*, 1996.)**

Kirby, T. (1989) 'Complaints body attacked', *The Independent*, 18 May, p.3.

Kirby, T. (1993) 'Five hours of paperwork after a simple arrest', *The Independent*, 25 September.

Klockars, C.B. (1988) 'The rhetoric of community policing', in Green, J.R. and Mastrofski, S.D. (eds) *Community Policing: Rhetoric or Reality?*, New York, Praeger.

Leinen, S. (1993) *Gay Cops*, New Brunswick, NJ, Rutgers University Press.

McBarnet, D.J. (1983) *Conviction: Law, the State and the Construction of Justice*, London, Macmillan.

McConville, M. and Bridges, L. (eds) (1994) *Criminal Justice in Crisis*, Aldershot, Edward Elgar Publishing.

McConville, M., Sanders, A. and Leng, R. (1991) *The Case for the Prosecution: Police Suspects and the Construction of Criminality*, London, Routledge.

McLaughlin, E. (1994) *Community, Policing and Accountability*, Aldershot, Avebury.

McLaughlin, E. and Murji, K. (1995) 'The end of public policing? Police reform and the "new managerialism"', in Noaks, L., Levi, M. and Maguire, M. (eds) *Contemporary Issues in Criminology*, Cardiff, University of Wales.

Maguire, M. and Norris, C. (1992) *The Conduct and Supervision of Criminal Investigations*, London, HMSO.

Morris P. and Heal, K. (1981) *Crime Control and the Police,* London, HMSO.

Moston, S. and Stephenson, G.M. (1993) *The Questioning and Interviewing of Suspects Outside the Police Station*, London, HMSO.

**Muncie, J. and McLaughlin, E. (eds) (1996) *The Problem of Crime*, London, Sage in association with The Open University.**

**Muncie, J., McLaughlin, E. and Langan, M. (eds) (1996) *Criminological Perspectives: A Reader,* London, Sage in association with The Open University.**

Neiderhoffer, A. (1967) *Behind the Shield*, New York, Doubleday.

Police Complaints Authority (1995) *Annual Report*, London, Police Complaints Authority.

Northam, G. (1988) *Shooting in the Dark,* London, Faber and Faber.

Police Foundation/Policy Studies Institute (1994) *Independent Committee of Inquiry into Role and Responsibilities of the Police*, London, Police Foundation.

Pollard, C. (1995) *Criminal Justice?*, BBC2 Television Programme, 12 March.

Punch, M. (1979) *Policing the Inner City: A Study of Amsterdam's Warmoesstraal,* London, Macmillan.

Punch, M. and Naylor, T. (1973) 'The police: a social service', *New Society*, 17 May, pp.358–60.

Reiner, R. (1992a) 'Codes, courts and constables: police powers since 1984', *Public Money and Management*, January–March, pp.1–10.

Reiner, R. (1992b) *The Politics of the Police,* Brighton, Harvester Wheatsheaf.

Reiner, R. (1993) 'Police accountability: principles, patterns and practices', in Reiner, R. and Spencer, S. (eds) *Accountable Policing*, London, IPPR.

Reiner, R. (1995) 'The perfidy of the paramour: how the police fell out of love with the Conservatives', *The Times Literary Supplement,* 1 September.

Sanders, A. and Young, R. (1994) *Criminal Justice,* London, Butterworth.

**Saraga, E. (1996) 'Dangerous places: the family as a site of crime', in Muncie and McLaughlin (1996).**

Scarman, Lord (1981) *The Brixton Disorders 10–12 April 1981: Report of an Inquiry*, Cmnd 8427, London, HMSO.

Scraton, P. (1985) *The State of the Police*, London, Pluto.

Sherman, L. (1983) 'Patrol strategies for police', in Wilson, J.Q. (ed.) *Crime and Public Policy*, San Francisco, CA, ICS Press.

Smith, D.J. (1986) 'The framework of law and police practice', in Benyon, J. and Bourn, C. (eds) *The Police: Powers, Procedures and Proprieties*, Oxford, Pergamon.

Smith, D.J. and Gray, J. (1985) *Police and People in London: The PSI Report,* London, Gower.

South, N. (1988) *Policing For Profit: The Private Security Sector,* London, Sage.

Thompson, E.P. (1980) *The Secret State*, London, IRP.

Thornhill, T. (1989) 'Police accountability', in Dunhill, C. (ed.) *The Boys in Blue: Women's Challenge to the Police*, London, Virago.

Thornton, P. (1989) *Decade of Decline: Civil Liberties in the Thatcher Years,* London, Liberty.

Tonry, M. and Morris, N. (eds) (1992) *Modern Policing,* Chicago, IL, Chicago University Press.

Waddington, P.A.J. (1991) *The Strong Arm of the Law: Armed and Public Order Policing,* Oxford, Oxford University Press.

Walker, M.A. (1992) 'Do we need a clear up rate?', *Policing and Society*, vol.2, pp.293–306.

Willis, C. (1983) *The Use, Effectiveness and Impact of Police Stop and Search Powers,* London, HMSO.

Young, M. (1991) *An Inside Job: Policing and Police Culture in Britain,* Oxford, Oxford University Press.

Young, M. (1993) *In the Sticks,* Oxford, Oxford University Press.

# Chapter 3
# Critical Decisions and Processes in the Criminal Courts

*By Loraine Gelsthorpe*

## Contents

# 1 Introduction

*T*he criminal justice system is always in some degree of flux and any particular account of it is conditioned by its state at that time. Public concerns about criminal justice are relatively constant, but in the late 1980s the justice system provoked an unusual level of anxiety, particularly with respect to miscarriages of justice and instances of police malpractice which culminated in the creation of a Royal Commission on Criminal Justice in the early 1990s. Nonetheless, it must be remembered that the basic structures of the criminal courts are medieval (and therefore pre-democratic) in origin and may thus be resistant to change.

The aim of this chapter is twofold: first, to set out some theoretical considerations in trying to establish what precisely is meant by 'criminal justice'; second, and more crucially, to examine some of the major issues which arise out of the operation of the criminal justice system. These include:

- Whether the judiciary and magistracy can truly be said to be impartial and how far their discretionary powers affect procedural justice.
- Whether the courts discriminate against particular social groups.
- Whether there is equality of access to justice.

Whilst the chapter considers numerous empirical research findings on these issues, the broader aim is to encourage critical reflection on the processes through which 'justice' is delivered and, indeed, on whether either 'impartiality' or 'discrimination' can ever be empirically 'proved'. The chapter concludes with a brief discussion of possible alternatives to formal and adversarial systems of justice. Throughout, the criminal justice system of England and Wales is used as a key point of reference, but the general issues raised are of relevance to all formal systems that attempt to deliver 'justice'.

# 2 Questions of justice

### ACTIVITY 3.1

What do you think are the main elements of 'justice'? Can these be realized in criminal justice systems?

Look at the picture of the statue of Justicia (reproduced opposite) who stands blindfold on top of the Old Bailey in London with the scales of justice in one hand and a sword in the other. What do you think she symbolizes? What message does she give?

### COMMENT

The blindfold, the scales and the sword usually conjure up notions of *impartiality*, the thoroughness of a *fair* trial and the *sureness of punishment* for wrongdoing. Justicia is an icon that symbolizes objectivity, neutrality and fairness. But 'justice' is a term which is debated time and time again in the history of ideas. It is a term which is easy to picture, but hard to grasp. The dimensions of the question 'What is justice?' are enormous. Is it fairness? Is it

*Justicia: the figure of Justice surmounts the dome of the 1906 'Old Bailey' sessions-house in London*

equal treatment? Is it just deserts? Is it getting one's due? And does any concept of justice depend on a particular social and political setting, a particular set of social goals and conventions, or is it something bigger and more universal than that – something which we can readily and instinctively divine? Indeed, we could ask, 'Is there some natural or divine law from which our criminal and civil laws derive?'

A starting point for some people trying to answer the question 'What is justice?' would be the familiar passage from Exodus in the Bible: 'an eye for an eye, a tooth for a tooth'. There is perhaps a basic urge for retribution: 'measure for measure'. The moral philosopher Immanuel Kant (1724–1804) argued uncompromisingly that retribution and retribution alone necessitates and justifies punishment (see Kant, 1796–97). In fact, Kant argued that, even if there were no point in deterring future crime or curing the criminal or if there were no practical purpose to expressing the authority of the state, it would still be necessary to punish offenders – to repay crime with punishment.

justice

In contrast, John Stuart Mill (1806–73) took social utility to be the only justification for punishment (see Mill, 1859). He speculated on a natural 'outgrowth' of two sentiments: self-defence and sympathy. Mill argued that we are not only capable but find it necessary as rational creatures to generalize from our own good to the good of all; in matters of punishment we realize that 'any conduct that threatens the security of society generally is

109

threatening to our own'. The sentiment of justice is thus the 'natural feeling of retaliation or vengeance'. The problem with the natural feeling of vengeance, of course, is that it is indiscriminate, but, as Mill recognizes, when we think through the implications of this, we can see that it is best to think in terms of resenting a hurt to society, not just to oneself. In this way vengeance becomes constrained by the overarching principle that defines all moral action: the public interest, or 'the greatest good of the greatest number' (see also **Beccaria, 1764**).

More recent philosophical debates about justice revolve around the widely acclaimed book *A Theory of Justice* (1971) by John Rawls. We imagine that our courts give *fair* and *just* punishment. Rawls' contribution has been to argue that the concepts of justice and fairness are essentially the same. He tells a fairy story in which a group of men and women, who do not belong to any particular society, have come together in a kind of constitutional convention to choose fundamental rules for a new society. There is nothing particularly distinctive about these people; they have specific identities, specific weaknesses, specific strengths, and specific interests. But they suffer from amnesia; they have no idea who they are, whether they are young or old, black or white, talented or stupid. In particular (and crucial to Rawls' argument), they do not know what their own beliefs are regarding what is valuable in life. Each person has some sort of conception as to what he or she wants life to be like, but no-one else knows. Indeed, they are separated from their own personalities by what Rawls calls a 'veil of ignorance'. Nevertheless, they must agree upon a political constitution and rules for governing social life. In this situation, Rawls argues, the construction of rules would very much reflect what people believed would be best for them – as individuals. Each person would be interested to establish the fairest rules possible because they would not be protected by social or any other advantages.

Rawls suggests that people would very likely agree on two main principles. First, everyone would have basic liberties – such as equal liberty to speak, freedom of conscience, freedom to hold personal property, to be protected in your person, not to be arrested suddenly and without due cause, and so on. Indeed, these are what we might call the conventional liberal liberties. Rawls' second principle relates to wealth. He argues that no difference in wealth should be tolerated unless that difference works for the benefit of the worst-off group in the society. The first principle is of more relevance to us here because we can see that punishment might be used to protect liberties. It is likely that we would all look at the system from the standpoint of the least advantaged representative man or woman, in which case inequalities are only permissible when they maximize, or at least contribute to, the long-term expectations of the least fortunate group in society.

Subsequently Rawls' theory has come under attack, not least from those who believe that the idea of a rational agent situated behind 'the veil of ignorance' is faulty. There are also those who suggest that it is one thing to establish rules for a 'desert island' society, where wealth has somehow fallen from the sky and has to be divided out, but quite another in situations where there are differential entitlements. Nozick (1974), for instance, dismisses Rawls' interest in equality by stressing the importance of 'liberty'. Whilst Rawls is perhaps trying to tie the two principles together, Nozick argues that they are fundamentally incompatible and that if there is a choice to be made, it must be for liberty – an inalienable right in his view, and the only right which the state can legitimately defend without interfering too much in people's lives. An obvious implication of this view would be that punishment, as such, has to be restricted to those who have broken the law – it cannot extend to those who *might* break the law.

Where do these debates take us, and what have these broad perspectives on justice got to do with criminal justice and the operation of contemporary criminal justice systems? Such abstract discussions perhaps have limited utility in trying to understand the behaviour of the courts. As Foucault (1980) and others would argue, the pursuit of abstract ideas of justice is perhaps futile; it is more interesting to ask how the discourse of justice functions in society and whose interests it serves to perpetuate. They *are* important debates, of course, but not ones which are easily resolved; indeed, the rhetorical and controversial nature of the debates reminds us that 'justice' is a *social and political issue*. To some extent it could be argued that the broad questions should provide a theoretical backcloth to all that takes place under the cloak of criminal justice, though it is hard to imagine politicians and policy-makers sitting round discussing such grand conceptions of justice. However, the criminal justice system cannot be separated from broader issues about the rules which govern society – indeed, the system gives the appearance of serving to defend the righteous, protect the innocent and punish offenders. Philosophical debates about justice remind us that we need to think about the social and political *choices* involved in establishing legal rules. If the criminal justice system is concerned with those who break the rules, we need to question not only whether they are the 'right' rules (whose values and aims do such rules reflect?), but also the procedures of criminal justice through which it is assumed such rules are upheld and maintained.

# **3** Questions of criminal justice

When we begin to examine criminal justice in our society, we need to ask: What shapes and 'drives' the criminal justice system? And what kinds of values and debates inform its operation? A common-sense view might be that what 'drives' the criminal justice system is simply a desire to catch criminals, take them to court, judge them and, if they are found guilty, punish them. But things are not quite this simple. It is helpful to consider such questions from the following series of perspectives (derived from Packer, 1969; King, 1981). Imagine these perspectives as 'windows' through which you can view criminal justice and its processes. Each window provides a particular (though partial) view of what is 'driving' the criminal justice system.

A due process perspective emphasizes the need to administer justice according to legal rules and procedures which are publicly known, fair and seen to be just. The main function of the criminal courts is to act as an impartial arbitrator of conflicts arising between the state and its citizens. Central to this perspective are the presumption of innocence, the restraints of arbitrary power and the inviolability of legal rules and procedures. Such procedures do not weight the process against the accused or in favour of those in power, but rather seek to guarantee a measure of judicial equality to all parties: hence the absolute need to abide by strict and formal procedures, to ensure that adherence to 'due process' results in a smooth-running, fair and impartial system (see **von Hirsch, 1976**).

due process

crime control    A crime control perspective stresses that the primary function of the criminal courts is to punish offenders and, by so doing, to control crime. The aim of criminal justice is, first and foremost, to repress criminal conduct. The courts are thus more guardians of law and order than upholders of impartial justice. While 'due process' values prioritize civil liberties in order to ensure that the innocent are acquitted (even at the risk of acquitting some who are guilty), 'crime control' values stress the goal of convicting the guilty (even at the risk of convicting some who are innocent and of infringing some civil liberties). In a due process perspective, the actions of criminal justice agencies are tightly regulated; in a crime control perspective, formal rules of procedure are often seen as obstacles standing in the way of securing a defendant's conviction. As the ultimate aim is to punish offenders and to deter future crime, the criminal justice system cannot afford a high acquittal rate: 'In order to operate successfully the process must produce a high rate of apprehension and conviction … there must be a feeling of speed and finality' (Packer, 1969, p.159).

In England, the due process approach is often associated with the attitudes of the legal profession, particularly those involved in defence work, and with the aims of such organizations as Liberty. The crime control approach is more reflective of traditional conservative views of the proper function of the courts. The tension between these opposing perspectives is often viewed as the single most important source of conflict and contradiction in the operation of contemporary justice systems. It is the interplay between their respective goals which gives criminal justice its most clear and defining characteristics.

welfare    A welfare (and rehabilitative) perspective, on the other hand, stresses that the aim of criminal justice is not to deter or punish, but to restore defendants to a state of social health whereby their 'threat' to society may be diminished. Working from positivist assumptions regarding the individual and social causes of crime, this perspective maintains that the courts' objectives should be to diagnose, treat and cure, on the basis of information gathered from a defendant's family background, work record, education, medical history, and so on. Each case is thus individualized and a greater degree of discretion is afforded to decision-makers (judges and magistrates but also probation officers and social workers). Strict adherence to inflexible rules and principles is seen as misguided and inappropriate.

power    A power (and domination) perspective views criminal justice as a means of legitimating and maintaining class and other forms of domination and of preserving existing patterns of social, economic and political power in society through repression. In this perspective, 'due process', 'crime control' or 'welfare and rehabilitation' are all ways of meeting the same goal of giving legal and judicial justification to coercive and repressive social orders (Quinney, 1974). Much of this approach has dwelt on the social, economic and ideological origins of criminal law and criminal justice in the late eighteenth and early nineteenth centuries (Hay *et al.*, 1975; Thompson, 1975), noting in particular how the development of the nation-state depended on the law to regulate social relationships, to coerce and to protect, and to bind society to the dominance of private property and market relations.

managerialism    A managerial (and bureaucratic) perspective views the criminal justice system precisely 'as a system' – a set of bureaucracies, governed by rules, roles and routines which control the way in which criminal justice is delivered. Criminal justice practice is dominated by 'what happens next in the process', rather than by grander goals and philosophical desires. Thus increasing emphasis is placed on what might be termed 'formal justice' as opposed to 'substantive justice', an approach derived from Max Weber's analyses of types of legal thought (Weber, 1954). According to Weber, law can be irrational or rational and it can be formal or substantive in orientation. Law is rational to the extent that its operation is guided by general rules rather than by substantive reaction to individual cases, or by irrational formal means, such as oracles or ordeals. *Substantively rational law* is determined by general rules derived from extra-legal ideologies (such as a system of morality, a religion or a political ideology). *Formally rational law* is guided by general rules so that in both substantive and procedural matters only unambiguous general characteristics of the case are taken into account. There is, then, a close relationship between due process ideals and the bureaucratic perspective. However, whilst due process is designed to protect the individual against arbitrary power, the bureaucratic objective is simply to ensure that the system follows standard procedures and is operated as efficiently and effectively as possible, irrespective of any wider goals.

A closely related perspective concerns the apparent dominance of 'managerial values'. The management model has been described in the following way:

> The management model ... is based on the insight that some crime is inevitable in any society and conceives the task as being to manage, reduce or prevent the amount of crime so as to make its occurrence as little damaging to society as possible. On this model the responsibility for devising ways of 'dealing' with crime falls largely to central administration, which has to measure the efficacy of any particular means of 'dealing' carried out by any of the agencies involved, and to extend or replace it according to its utilitarian value in reducing or preventing the kind of crime which damages society.

> (Tuck, 1991, pp.23–4)

Commenting on shifts in criminal justice in the 1980s and 1990s, McLaughlin and Muncie (1994) refer to the development of a mixed economy of criminal justice in which the state absolves itself of its traditional role as the natural provider of law and order – through the privatization of various functions of the criminal justice system (for example, the prisons); the increasing role of the public (with expectations that they will in some way 'police' and 'protect' themselves); and an enlarged role for voluntary organizations (for example, in the realm of community sentences and secure training orders for children). Again the key concern is with matters of efficiency, but tempered by an overriding interest in cost-effectiveness and in establishing new boundaries of state responsibility and new modes of regulation.

These five perspectives on the criminal justice system are not exhaustive. But they should serve to remind us that there are competing models of criminal justice (just as there are competing models of justice and social order) which impact on how the system is (or should be) run. Similarly, we should not expect any *one* model to operate in isolation. Criminal justice systems are more an uneasy compromise or a contradictory adoption of elements of each approach. There are no simple 'facts' about criminal justice; it is a social, political and legal process, a contested and negotiated arena. This points *back* to the broader questions of what justice is and how society should be governed: Who defines the rules by which people live? What is the nature of legalized power and what constrains it? But it also points *forward* to the domain of controversies: How is injustice generated from justice systems? How does ideology penetrate the workings and operation of criminal justice?

It is to some of these controversies that we now turn.

# 4  The delivery of justice and injustices

## ACTIVITY 3.2

From a range of newspapers (preferably both tabloid and broadsheet) from the past week, locate any articles which focus on criminal justice system practices (courts, prisons, probation, the legal profession):

1   Make a list of any general issues underlying these articles. (You might identify issues such as perceptions of 'justice' and 'injustice', the efficiency and costs of the system, public confidence in the system.) Are the articles critical of the system? Do they point forward to the need for reform?

2   Do the five perspectives discussed earlier shed any light on such debates and controversies?

## COMMENT

When an activity such as this was completed in 1995, a number of critical issues were raised:

- The notion of disparity and discrimination in sentencing.

- The possible erosion of the privilege against self-incrimination through the loss of the right to silence.

- The possible unreliability of scientific evidence presented to the courts.

- The failure to provide adequately for mentally disordered offenders.

- The seeming reluctance to create access to justice in the court room for non-English speakers.

- The fact that the concept of legal aid was under extreme threat which might have meant that some people would be disadvantaged in the court room.

- The neglect of victims in the delivery of criminal justice.

Many of these issues can be seen to stem from the contradictions between 'due process', 'crime control' and 'managerial' perspectives. The abandonment of defendants' 'right to silence', for example, is reflective of a crime control approach, whilst the restriction on access to legal aid, because of its increasing costs, may suggest the primacy of 'managerial' objectives. The failure to provide for mentally disordered offenders may suggest a need for the injection of more overtly 'welfare and rehabilitative' ideals. Similarly, commenting on the unreliability of some scientific evidence may be a means of arguing that, for the purposes of 'due process', only reliable and sustainable 'evidence' should be entertained.

The remainder of this chapter focuses on four general issues as illustrative of the controversies we have so far discussed. These are suggestions that:

- Magistrates' discretion in sentencing should be more tightly controlled.

- The judiciary are not the impartial body they are supposed to be.

- The jury system (which is a key feature of the English system) is under threat.

- The criminal justice system (particularly the courts) is imbued with discriminatory attitudes and practices. In other words, sentencing appears to be arbitrary or even whimsical, and is often based on inadequate information.

If 'criminal justice' is difficult to define, then it may help to examine perceived 'injustices'. All four of the issues listed here suggest that there is a perceived, and very often real, injustice; an examination of these issues may lead us closer to a sense of what we mean by 'criminal justice'.

*Thames Magistrates' Court*

## 4.1   Disparities in sentencing

Ever since the reforms of the criminal justice system at the end of the eighteenth century, there have been attempts to establish some rational relationship between the seriousness of the offence and the severity of the punishment. This is known as the principle of proportionality; in essence, this means that the perceived seriousness of the offence should be dealt with by way of an appropriate penalty, one which is neither too lenient nor too severe, but is in proportion to the offence. It is this principle which is the reason why it is not usually considered appropriate to give custodial sentences to petty property offenders.

Generally speaking, however, judicial discretion has prevailed and sentencing powers have been untrammelled; at best, the system could be described as individualistic and pragmatic. The judiciary and Magistrates' Association have celebrated the use of discretion and *individual sentencing*. This is not to suggest that sentencers have been totally unfettered; indeed, various attempts have been made to confine the use of discretion and to structure it (regulating its use in advance). It has also been checked in various other ways. For example, under the 1982 Criminal Justice Act, the courts were directed to avoid passing custodial sentences on young offenders unless it appeared that no other sentence was available, and were required to check the case against three specific criteria. Thomas's (1979) *Principles of Sentencing* also facilitated the checking of discretion by providing an accessible digest of general sentencing principles. This handbook, first produced in 1970, became a sentencers' bible and is informally referred to as such. The Court of Appeal, of course, has also served as a valuable check on

sentencing

judicial discretion, though some have argued that there has always remained a serious weakness in the self-regulatory capacity of this court (Cavadino and Dignan, 1992; Rozenberg, 1994; Zander, 1989).

discretion While there has been a certain degree of self-regulation practised by sentencers, wide discretion has been the hall-mark of the system. Various attempts to change patterns of sentencing and, in particular, to reduce the use of custody (where the government thought that this was inappropriate, or where continuing penal crises dictated that the prison population should be reduced), have been circumvented by sentencers. For example, when community service orders were introduced (largely as an alternative to custody, though the aim was perhaps never entirely clear), research revealed a strong element of 'up-tariffing' (Pease, 1980); that is, their use replaced the use of penalties lower down on the scale rather than custodial penalties. As a second example, though the introduction of partly suspended sentences in 1977 was intended to reduce the use of custody, in practice offenders were often taken 'from below'; that is, those who would not normally have warranted a custodial sentence were given a 'taste of imprisonment' through the introduction of the partly suspended sentence (Bottoms, 1981; Harris, 1992). In essence, new sentences conceived as alternatives to imprisonment were simply used as additions and had no impact on the use of custody at all.

Not surprisingly, the English system has occasionally been ridiculed, with sentencing practices described as a 'smorgasbord' or 'cafeteria' approach, where sentencers can 'pick and choose' or 'pick and mix' different sentences, with no apparent reason for their decisions. The very range of underlying theoretical precepts at play (deterrence and incapacitation, rehabilitation and just deserts for instance) underlines this (see von Hirsch and Ashworth, 1992; and Chapter 5 of this volume). In practice, the regional variations in sentencing (particularly in the resort to custody) are notable. In 1990, for example, a male adult offender appeared to be more than two and a half times more likely to be sent straight to prison by magistrates in the south west of England than in the south west of Wales (Liberty, 1992, p.2). Ashworth (1983), for one, has described the system as a disgrace to the common law tradition.

In 1990, the government finally responded to these and similar criticisms by publishing a White Paper, *Crime, Justice and Protecting the Public* (Home Office, 1990a). This formed the basis of an important step to limit the exercise of discretion and to institute clear principles and rules in sentencing which were to be included in the Criminal Justice Act 1991 (see Extract 3.1).

Cavadino and Dignan (1992, pp.107–8) discerned four key themes in the White Paper.

1 A reinterpretation of the doctrine of judicial independence, which reasserted government responsibility for formulating sentencing policy while affirming the principle of non-interference in individual cases.

2 The theme of 'just deserts' essentially meant that the sentence imposed for a given offence must match, or be in proportion to, the seriousness of the offence.

3 The retention of a twin-track (or bifurcatory) approach to sentencing (which at its crudest, means that those who can be diverted from custody should be, and that those who have committed the most serious offences deserve the most severe punishment.

## Extract 3.1 The Home Office: 'Punishment in the community'

2.1 The Government's aim is to ensure that convicted criminals in England and Wales are punished justly and suitably according to the seriousness of their offences; in other words that they get their just deserts. No Government should try to influence the decisions of the courts in individual cases. The independence of the judiciary is rightly regarded as a cornerstone of our liberties. But sentencing principles and sentencing practice are matters of legitimate concern to Government, and Parliament provides the funds necessary to give effect to the courts' decisions.

2.2 The sentence of the court prescribes the punishment for criminal behaviour. Punishment in proportion to the seriousness of the crime has long been accepted as one of many objectives in sentencing. It should be the principal focus for sentencing decisions. This is consistent with the Government's view that those who commit very serious crimes, particularly crimes of violence, should receive long custodial sentences; but that many other crimes can be punished in the community, with greater emphasis on bringing home to the criminal the consequences of his actions, compensation to the victim and reparation to the community. ...

2.6 Reforming offenders is always best if it can be achieved. It is better that people should exercise self-control than have controls imposed upon them. This needs self discipline and motivation. Many offenders have little understanding of the effect of their actions on others. Compensation and community service can bring home to offenders the effect of their behaviours on other people. The probation service tries to make offenders face up to what they have done, to give them a greater sense of responsibility and to help them resist pressure from others to take part in crime. Voluntary organisations have a long tradition of helping offenders to turn away from crime.

2.7 It was once believed that prison, properly used, could encourage a high proportion of offenders to start an honest life on their release. Nobody now regards imprisonment, in itself, as an effective means of reform for most prisoners. If there is continued progress against overcrowding in prisons, the recent reforms should enable better regimes to be developed, with more opportunities for education, and work, and so a greater chance of turning the lives of some inmates in a positive direction. But however much prison staff try to inject a positive purpose into the regime, as they do, prison is a society which requires virtually no sense of personal responsibility from prisoners. Normal social or working habits do not fit. The opportunity to learn from other criminals is pervasive. For most offenders, imprisonment has to be justified in terms of public protection, denunciation and retribution. Otherwise it can be an expensive way of making bad people worse. The prospects of reforming offenders are usually much better if they stay in the community, provided the public is properly protected ...

4.3 The Government believes a new approach is needed if the use of custody is to be reduced. Punishment in the community should be an effective way of dealing with many offenders, particularly those convicted of property crimes and less serious offences of violence, when financial penalties are insufficient. The punishment should be in the restrictions on liberty and in the enforcement of the orders. All community service orders place some restrictions on an offender's liberty and so may probation orders when, for example, they require an offender to attend a day centre for a lengthy period. The discipline exerted by these orders on offenders may extend over many months. These orders intrude on normal freedom, and the court should be satisfied that this is justified ...

4.5 Restrictions on liberty would become the connecting thread in a range of community penalties as well as custody. By matching the severity of the restrictions on liberty to the seriousness of the offence, the courts should find it easier to achieve consistency of approach in sentencing. The more serious the offence is, the greater the restrictions on liberty which would be justified as a punishment.

(Home Office, 1990a, pp.5–6, 18–19)

4  A partnership between the legislature and the judiciary – with parliament establishing a framework consisting of general principles, and the courts (including the Appeal Courts) being left to decide how these principles should apply in any given instance.

The new framework also reflected an intention to focus on the *offence*, and not so much on the *offender* (Ashworth, 1992a). By curtailing judicial discretion, the 1991 Act gave primacy to some elements of 'due process', but by stressing the punitive nature of all sentences it was also reflective of some 'crime control' concerns.

The Criminal Justice Act 1991 directly encouraged sentencers to pass fewer custodial sentences by introducing statutory criteria to limit their use. It also encouraged the use of community penalties, not least by changing the name from 'non-custodial penalties' to 'community penalties'. Other aspects of this shift included attempts to make pre-sentence reports more informative and the content of community penalties better known; the increased involvement of the courts in enforcing community orders; the removal of the somewhat 'artificial' concept of alternatives to custody; and the bifurcation of crimes into those serious enough to justify imprisonment and those which can be dealt with by punishment in the community. Harris (1992) added to this list by suggesting that private sector involvement in community punishment might be an encouragement to sentencers to use community penalties more and imprisonment less. (The use of electronic monitoring – promoted by private companies – can be seen as a way of buttressing community penalties in this respect by adding to the 'controlling' and 'punitive' content of community penalties so that they are not seen by sentencers nor, indeed, by the public, as a soft option.)

It was thought that private sector involvement with the Probation Service (who organize and enforce community penalties), through management inspection and through inter-agency work, might also improve the credibility of community penalties and serve as an encouragement to sentencers to use them more. Further, it might be seen to increase or improve the accountability of the Probation Service. This reflects a government notion that 'private sector' management expertise is of use to 'public service' organizations; here the key concerns are more clearly bureaucratic or managerial in intent.

It was also hoped that the introduction of 'national standards', in the production of pre-sentence reports and in the operation of community penalties, might increase respect for, and thus use of, community penalties (Ashworth *et al.*, 1992). Additionally, an attempt to make the system of fining fairer (and thus perhaps to increase confidence in the use of fines) was made by introducing a 'unit fine system' based on calculations of disposable weekly income and ability to pay.

However, in subsequent years, many of the Act's aims were undermined through magisterial, public and political pressure. Initial assessments of the impact of the Act suggested that community penalties were no more credible to magistrates than they were before the Act. The 'Unit Fine System' was met with resistance from sentencers from the outset and was repealed in the 1993 Criminal Justice Act (Rex, 1992; Gibson, 1990; Moxon *et al.*, 1990). Amidst furore about the future role of the Probation Service (and attempts to denude its rehabilitative or 'social work' orientations), the Home Secretary was adamant that such community penalties did *not* work and that penalties had to be made even tougher.

Thus, the attempt to implement a *rational* criminal justice system, formulated over the previous five years, was immediately subverted by political expediency and magisterial demands for more powers.

While there may have been some acceptance of the general pragmatic aims of the 1991 Act (for example, to reduce the use of imprisonment), there appeared to be a limited recognition of its conceptual objectives – proportionality, denunciation, retribution, public protection, reparation and reform) (Crow *et al.*, 1993). However, even when *legislative* change fails, pressure on financial costs and resources may gradually constrain or erode judicial prerogative in sentencing (Home Office, 1992; Bottoms, 1995). Is this then a case of managerial (cost-effectiveness) goals superseding all others?

An alternative to the Criminal Justice Act 1991, and the philosophical and political changes that it signified, would have been to adopt sentencing guidelines for the courts – in much the same way as in Australia and some states in the USA. Such guidelines essentially prescribe in advance the appropriate penalty for a whole range of offender/offence combinations (Pease and Wasik, 1987). However, as Cavadino and Dignan point out, 'By providing sentencers with one set of criteria relating to the circumstances of the offence in question, and a different range of criteria taking into account relevant characteristics of the offender, the guidelines operate rather in the manner of a road mileage chart, enabling the appropriate, or 'presumptive', penalty to be simply 'read off' from the matrix supplied' (Cavadino and Dignan, 1992, pp.104–5). This suggests fixed and unchangeable sentencing, though closer reading of the guidelines would suggest that they are intended as a starting point and sentencers are free to depart from the 'grid' if they can justify reasons for doing so. (The most famous of these guidelines are those in Minnesota – Ashworth, 1992b – but there are many variations.) It remains extremely unlikely that English sentencers would contemplate the use of such guidelines. However, some critics of the English and Welsh system *would* countenance the setting up of an independent Sentencing Council (Ashworth, 1983), in which it is assumed that wide representation of sentencers, from all levels of court and from other criminal justice professionals, would automatically lend itself to the development of some realistic guidance acceptable to all (see Cavadino and Dignan, 1992).

## ACTIVITY 3.3

Consider the implications of curtailing or allowing sentencers too much discretion. What would count as 'too much' discretion? Does discretion provide a means to offer individualized justice or will it automatically lead to a series of injustices? Would sentencing guidelines or a sentencing council make any difference?

# 4.2 The neutrality of the judiciary and magistracy

impartiality The concept of impartiality is arguably the foundation stone and guiding philosophy of the English legal system upon which the credibility and legitimacy of the criminal justice system depends; a judicial system which is partial cannot command universal consent or respect. 'The social service which the judge renders to the community is the removal of a sense of injustice', wrote Lord Devlin (1979).

It is a common claim that *judges* are elderly, male and white. However, there is a maximum retiring age of 75 for the most senior judges (70 for others) and in the 1980s the average age for circuit and High Court judges was 60 years and nine months. Senior judges, though, still come from a social and educational élite. Of the new appointments to the judiciary from 1989 to 1991, 84 per cent had attended public school and 77 per cent were graduates of either Oxford or Cambridge. According to Padfield, in 1994 there were 487 circuit judges (28 women), 795 Recorders (42 women) and 496 Assistant Recorders (51 women) (Padfield, 1995). She further cites that there were no black or Asian High Court judges and that there were only four circuit judges from minority ethnic groups.

Although *magistrates* are no longer predominantly male, successive studies have shown them to be overwhelmingly white, middle-aged and middle class. In the 12 months ending June 1993, 5 per cent (85) were from minority ethnic groups. They also tend to be 'middle-minded', partly, but not exclusively, because of the selective (and until the 1990s highly secretive) 'puff of smoke' recruitment procedures by which they are appointed. They are socialized and imbued with a particular self-perception about their role in a way that comes close to producing a consistent ideology. Indeed, Parker *et al.* (1989) have shown that the chief formative influence on sentencing practice in magistrates' courts is not the law or the advice received from other professionals in court, nor even the way in which similar cases have been decided by that particular court in the past. Instead, the principal influence is the 'sentencing culture' of a particular bench, into which new recruits are gradually socialized by watching their more experienced colleagues at work.

Judges appointed in the High Court or above must have been former barristers. In 1995, solicitors were not eligible, though this was under review. circuit judges, Recorders and assistant judges can be either solicitors or barristers – though a good proportion in each category are still barristers. It is sometimes alleged that most judges have been to public school and 'Oxbridge' (Griffith, 1991, pp.30–5); it could be argued that entrants to the legal profession in general, and barristers in particular, are largely middle class and university educated (see *Daily Mail*, 10 April 1993, reproduced opposite).

Few people would subscribe to the view that there is a crude relationship between judges and politics, but the social origins and political views of judges can, of course, have a subtler influence. According to Griffith (1991), judges interpret the 'public interest' from the point of view of their own class. Moreover, he argues that their main role is to be seen as upholders of law and order, of the established distribution of power and of the conventional view (see Extract 3.2).

# New silks from same top drawer

**By ANTHONY DORAN**

THEY are the embodiment of the rich professional.

Well-connected, white, male and with the right school ties.

The very word 'silk' says it all, suggesting the sleek image of the QC emerging from an elite background to snatch the best briefs and end up very rich and, perhaps, a judge.

Some 70 QCs were celebrating their new status yesterday. One was hunting in the Rhone Valley, another was touring Spain. Most were heading for the shires. By and large, the traditional, upper-class image was reinforced.

The Daily Mail social profile of the QC in 'classless' Britain, 1993, is based on sparse information culled from a secretive appointments system.

Most of the new Queen's Counsel are in their forties, almost half went to Oxbridge and the independent schools, and one was a former equerry to Prince Philip.

*Eton, Harrow, Charterhouse, St Paul's, Ampleforth, Winchester* ... the names in the list from the Lord Chancellor's department echo self-confidence and the right to rule.

Being a QC is a passport to more lucrative and interesting legal work and even higher social circles. From now on the new ones will be rubbing shoulders with fellow QCs, with Who's Who entries listing clubs such as The Garrick, Guards, Cavalry and Hurlingham.

There were 471 applications to become QCs from working barristers. Of the 70 appointed, six are women and one is from an ethnic background.

Judge Mota Singh, one of only two Asian judges on the bench, says there are simply not enough ethnic minorities coming through. 'The pool of experienced people needs to be much larger. It is only after seven to ten years' experience as a barrister that you can apply, so it is going to take a long time before the picture changes.'

But QC Harry Wolton, head of a leading Birmingham chambers, says the system is changing fast. We don't go in for anybody because of school, university or parental background. We go for individual character, talent and personality. Background doesn't carry the weight it used to. It will gradually disappear as a stepping stone.' ...

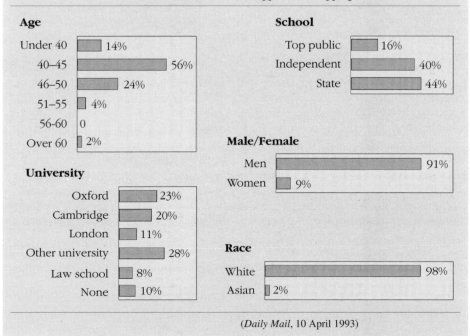

**Age**

| | |
|---|---|
| Under 40 | 14% |
| 40–45 | 56% |
| 46–50 | 24% |
| 51–55 | 4% |
| 56-60 | 0 |
| Over 60 | 2% |

**School**

| | |
|---|---|
| Top public | 16% |
| Independent | 40% |
| State | 44% |

**University**

| | |
|---|---|
| Oxford | 23% |
| Cambridge | 20% |
| London | 11% |
| Other university | 28% |
| Law school | 8% |
| None | 10% |

**Male/Female**

| | |
|---|---|
| Men | 91% |
| Women | 9% |

**Race**

| | |
|---|---|
| White | 98% |
| Asian | 2% |

(*Daily Mail*, 10 April 1993)

## Extract 3.2   Griffith: 'The political role of the judiciary'

Many regard the values of the bench and Bar in Britain as wholly admirable and the spirit of the common law (as presently expressed) to be a national adornment. The incorruptibility of the English bench and its independence of the government are great virtues. All this is not in issue. When I argue that they regard the interests of the State or the public interest as pre-eminent and that they interpret those interests as meaning that, with very few exceptions, established authority must be upheld and that those exceptions are made only when a more conservative position can be adopted, this does not mean that the judges are acting with impropriety. It means that we live in a highly authoritarian society, fortunate only that we do not live in other societies which are even more authoritarian. We must expect judges, as part of that authority, to act in the interests, as they see them, of the social order.

The judges define the public interest, inevitably, from the viewpoint of their own class. And the public interest, so defined, is by a natural, not an artificial, coincidence, the interest of others in authority, whether in government, in the City or in the church. It includes the maintenance of order, the protection of private property, the promotion of certain general economic aims, the containment of the trade union movement, and the continuance of governments which conduct their business largely in private and on the

advice of other members of what I have called the governing group ...

Judges are concerned to preserve and to protect the existing order. This does not mean that no judges are capable of moving with the times, of adjusting to changed circumstances. But their function in our society is to do so belatedly. Law and order, the established distribution of power both public and private, the conventional and agreed view amongst those who exercise political and economic power, the fears and prejudices of the middle and upper classes, these are the forces which the judges are expected to uphold and do uphold.

In the societies of our world today judges do not stand out as protectors of liberty, of the rights of man, of the unprivileged, nor have they insisted that holders of great economic power, private or public, should use it with moderation. Their view of the public interest, when it has gone beyond the interest of governments, has not been wide enough to embrace the interests of political, ethnic, social or other minorities. Only occasionally has the power of the supreme judiciary been exercised in the positive assertion of fundamental values. In both democratic and totalitarian societies, the judiciary has naturally served the prevailing political and economic forces. Politically, judges are parasitic.

(Griffith, 1991, pp.327–8)

The distinguished former Law Lord, Lord Devlin, objected to Griffith's argument largely on the grounds that he glosses over important differences between judges and their pronouncements (indeed, 'many of them refuse to toe the party line'), but there is a telling clue in his response that 'the oligarchs who rise to the top in a democratic society are usually mature, safe and orthodox men' (Devlin, 1979). Devlin stresses both the real impartiality of judges and the importance of the 'appearance of impartiality': justice must be seen to be done. This is a further telling clue, for it seems that just as it is important for judges to be impartial for justice to be done, the *appearance* of impartiality can perform the critical function of maintaining the consent of the governed to the rule of law, thereby underpinning the legitimacy and stability of the whole social order (see Extract 3.3).

While this suggests an active process – where law is negotiated – Griffith argues that there is an underlying conservatism in all this and that the judges favour the Establishment. But it would have to be admitted that comprehensive surveys of decisions do not support the strong claims of Griffith that *all* decisions reflect the fact that judges are biased against the common man (*sic*). Zander provides useful evidence to suggest that at least

## Extract 3.3   Devlin: 'The appearance of impartiality'

In theory the judiciary is the neutral force between government and the governed. The judge interprets and applies the law without favour to either and its application in a particular case is embodied in an order which is passed to the executive to enforce. It is not the judge's personal order; it is substantially the product of the law and only marginally of the judicial mind. If its enforcement is resisted or evaded, the judge is no more concerned than if he were an arbitrator.

British judges have never practised such detachment. The reason may lie in their origin as servants of the Crown or perhaps in the fact that for a long time the law they administered was what they had made themselves. A mixture of the two has left the High Court with the power to enforce its order in civil cases by treating disobedience as contempt itself.

In the criminal law the judges regard themselves as at least as much concerned as the executive with the preservation of law and order. Then there is what can best be described as the expatiatory power. Whereas under most systems the judgment is formal, brief and to the legal point, the British judge may expatiate on what he is doing and why he is doing it and its consequences; and because of his prestige he is listened to.

These high powers make the British judiciary more than just a neutral arbitral force. On the whole their wise and cautious deployment has enabled the judiciary to use its reputation for impartiality and independence for the public good. But it is imperative that the high powers should not be used except in support of consensus law. If the judges are to do more than decide what the law means, if they are also to speak for it, their voice must be the voice of the community; it must never be taken for the voice of the government or the voice of the majority.

(Lord Devlin, 1972, quoted in Griffith, 1991, pp.272–3)

*some* legal decisions go in favour of the 'common man' (in cases involving disputes between workers and employers) and he reminds us that in a number of cases Conservative government ministers have been called to task (Zander, 1989, p.122).

What about impartiality in criminal cases? There is some evidence to suggest that the relationship between judicial authorities and politicians is rather too cosy; in the cases of the Guildford Four and the Maguire family, for example, whose predicaments were put forward to the Home Secretary (alongside the predicament of the Birmingham Six) in an all-party delegation of MPs and peers in January 1987, the Home Secretary refused to intervene. Correspondence in *The Guardian* of 23, 24, 27 and 30 January 1987 involving the then junior Home Office Minister, Mr David Mellor, and his predecessor Mr Alex Lyon, reveals that, until Lyon put a stop to the practice, the Home Office had been in the habit of asking the Lord Chief Justice for his view as to whether a case should be referred back to the Court of Appeal, and not re-opening it if he thought that it should not be (Zander, 1989, p.207). Moreover, the courts have been more than reluctant to admit that occasionally they get things very wrong.

One of the underlying issues in this debate is whether or not judges should be involved in the formulation of justice or in its mere delivery. While there are those who presume that the function of the judge is simply to apply disinterestedly the known law (procedural justice) there are arguments that the process of applying the law is inevitably political. Griffith (1991) is persuasive in his argument that the judiciary serves as an 'essential part of the system of government in underpinning the stability of that system and as protecting the system from attack by resisting attempts to change it'. In other

procedural justice

words, judges act as a 'tool' of government, reflecting its most conservative policies in order to preserve the status quo. Devlin's (1979) position, as we have indicated, is that judges should act according to what they perceive to be the consensus in order to give the appearance of impartiality – this position goes some way to recognizing that judges are not free from the pressures of society, whilst it preferences the role of judges as deliverers of justice rather than law-makers or formulators of justice.

Griffith's claims have been qualified in light of suggestions by Roshier and Teff (1980), amongst others. In response to Griffith's first edition (1977) of *The Politics of the Judiciary,* they suggest that we can describe the politics of the judiciary as reflecting a plurality of different factors, since, they argue, the outcomes, directions and tendencies of judicial policy do not appear to conform to any one pattern. Indeed, they remind us of tensions between the different courts (especially the Court of Appeal and the House of Lords). (We can also see in studies of magistrates' courts that there are clear differences in the way they operate: those involved in the legal process do not behave in a uniform way – see Parker *et al.,* 1989). But Roshier and Teff are equally prepared to admit that judges are attached to formal rules – a *formal legalism* – which is fundamentally conservative and which reflects the structure and strictures of a politically designed 'justice'.

It is arguable, however, that political interference in the so-called independent judiciary is sometimes necessary – witness the introduction of the Criminal Justice Act 1991 and its attempt to structure the discretion of sentencers in order to achieve a more equitable system of justice. At least some parts of that Act remain progressive – especially the attempt to encourage sentencers to reflect before sentencing offenders to imprisonment and to reduce the scale of penal responses to crime.

*The Lord Chancellor heads the procession of judges and QCs for the start of the legal year in Westminster, 3 October 1994*

What is at issue is perhaps more a question of judges' and magistrates' world view, sensibility and values, than their party politics. Discretion may be a good thing, but unfettered discretion is clearly not, for it will reflect a particular world view. How far do you think that procedural justice and the exercise of discretion should be (or can be) balanced?

## 4.3    Fair trial by jury?

Trial by jury is one of the oldest and most venerated aspects of the English legal process. It has long been associated with the preservation of individual liberties and the distinctive spirit of English law, because trial by one's 'peers' (as ordinary lay citizens) is seen to impose justice in a context of a hierarchical, adversarial, confusing and often perplexing legal drama in which the defendant sometimes has only a 'walk-on part'. It is also true that trial by jury in the higher courts can lead to a higher rate of acquittal than in magistrates' courts (Vennard, 1985). Interestingly, whilst defendants may be aware of the higher acquittal rates in the Crown Courts, research reveals that many defendants who elect for trial in the Crown Court are unaware of large differences in sentence severity between the Crown Court and the magistrates' courts (Hedderman and Moxon, 1992).

The basic rules governing juries are found in the Juries Act of 1974. The minimum age to serve on a jury is 18, though the maximum age of jury members was raised from 65 to 70 in the Criminal Justice Act of 1988 (jury service is voluntary after the age of 65). A jury does not necessarily reflect the community as a whole; the initial selection is from names on the electoral roll and many people may not be registered. Some people are not eligible to serve on a jury, because of the jobs they do (judges and those concerned with the administration of justice are ineligible, along with the clergy) or because they are mentally disordered. Some people are disqualified from jury service because they have been sentenced to more than five years' imprisonment; those who have served any period of imprisonment or who have been given a suspended sentence are also disqualified for specified periods. Those on bail are disqualified from jury service. The composition of juries has been a cause for concern. The Commission for Racial Equality (1991) has raised questions about the selection of jurors and the need for juries to reflect a multicultural society. A black defendant confronted with an all-white jury may not feel that he or she is receiving a fair trial.

However, Zander and Henderson's Crown Court study (1993) rather contentiously suggested that neither women nor people from minority ethnic groups were badly under-represented. Women made up 47 per cent of jurors (but only 22 per cent of jury foremen and women – that is, spokespersons for the jury as a whole) and 5 per cent of the jurors were from minority ethnic groups (as compared with 5.9 per cent of the population when the research was carried out). As Padfield (1995, p.280) has described, what is of chief concern is perhaps the distribution of jurors in individual cases. In 65 per cent of cases there were no people from minority ethnic groups on the jury and in one case, there were no white jurors. The Court of Appeal held, in *R* v. *Ford* [1989] QB 868, that there is no right to a multiracial jury. However, the Royal Commission on Criminal Justice (1993), prompted by the concerns of the Commission for Racial Equality, has indicated that, in some cases, 'race' should be taken into account. The suggestion is that, before trial, the prosecution or defence should be able to apply to the judge for a multiracial jury (including up to three members from minority ethnic groups), though the judge would only grant this if the applicant's case was reasonable because of some special feature. One important question is whether the background of jury members makes any difference to the verdict. Early research found that it was very difficult to predict verdicts on the basis of general characteristics such as age, sex, 'race' or social class (Sealy and Cornish, 1973). More recent research on the Crown Court, carried out by Zander and Henderson (1993), looked specifically at the influence of age and found that it had little or no effect on jury verdicts. Indeed, despite some expressed anxiety that the qualifying jury service age of 18 was too young (and that jury members of this age would be too inexperienced), the researchers found that, if anything, older juries were more likely to acquit than the younger. This research was limited to the influence of age, however, and should not be taken as a guide to the influence of 'race', class and gender. In the absence of up-to-date detailed research, we simply do not know what the influence of such factors might be; and, in any case, bias may well intrude into the court room in more subtle ways than by overt discrimination (for example, through jury members' reaction to a defendant's demeanour).

We should also note criticisms that perhaps juries are 'rigged' to favour the prosecution or, at the very least, that the random selection of jurors is avoided (Baldwin and McConville, 1979; Roshier and Teff, 1980). At the same time, they can be seen more positively by the public as a defence against the oppressive use of state power, as in the case of Clive Ponting, for example, the civil servant who was acquitted by a jury in relation to the allegation that he had disclosed 'official information' concerning the sinking of the Belgrano in May 1982 to an unauthorized person (in this case Tam Dalyell, MP). The jury – representing the public – believed Ponting's defence that he had disclosed official information because he felt it to be 'in the interest of the state'. Though the acquittal could not have been predicted, what is established beyond doubt from this case is that juries cannot be relied upon to convict under the Official Secrets Act a defendant who is seen to act in the public interest. At the same time, there are plenty of cases in which the jury has initially given 'unsafe' verdicts (for example, in the cases of the Guildford Four, when four men found guilty of pub bombings which killed five people in October 1974 were sentenced in 1975 to life imprisonment, yet had their sentences quashed in October 1989; and of the Birmingham Six, in which six men, found guilty of 21 murders arising from the bombing of two Birmingham pubs in 1974 and sentenced to life imprisonment, had their convictions quashed in 1991). Juries can and do make 'unsafe' and apparently 'unfounded' decisions.

*Acquitted members of the Birmingham Six, sent to prison in 1975 for the IRA's bombing of two pubs, gather with their Member of Parliament (centre) after they walk from court as free men, 14 March 1991*

Defendants do have some say in the matter of selection of jury members, though, arguably, their powers to 'choose' the jury members are extremely limited. Those summoned for jury service constitute the jury panel. From the jury panel (of 20) the jury is selected randomly in open court, by the clerk reading out the names. Each juror may be challenged by the prosecution or the defence. The defence used to have the right of peremptory challenge – that is, the right to challenge prospective jurors without having to give reasons – but this was reduced from seven to three challenges for each defendant in the Criminal Law Act of 1977 and abolished altogether in the Criminal Justice Act 1988. The government felt that peremptory challenges interfered with the random selection of the jury, were being abused by defence counsel (particularly in multi-defendant cases) and were leading to unmerited acquittals (a case here of 'due process' being subverted by 'crime control', perhaps?). Research provided no foundation for the government's move, however. Vennard and Riley (1988), for example, found no link between the use of the peremptory challenge and acquittal rates.

What such challenges did allow for was the right of defendants or their counsel to exclude prospective jury members whom they perceived to be unlikely to reach a fair verdict. At the time of writing in 1995, the defence only has the right to 'challenge for cause' (that is, they have to give reasons); the prosecution has a similar right and in addition can, in very exceptional circumstances, require a juror to 'stand-by for the Crown' (which is rather like a peremptory challenge). Criminal records and other security records can be checked to see whether or not prospective jurors are 'dubious', but this practice remains controversial because it is seen by some as interference in the random selection of juries and thus in the administration and delivery of justice.

Debates about the role of the jury have been given fresh impetus over cases involving serious fraud which are notoriously long, difficult, expensive and arguably beyond the limits of the jurors' comprehension, and certainly beyond their powers of endurance. The Law Society has suggested certain reforms to the process in such cases to limit the time that they take (Law Society, 1992).

Other issues concern the exalted position of the 'plain common sense' of the jury over a panoply of legal and professional judgement. Former Metropolitan Police Chief Commissioner, Sir Robert Mark, once exclaimed that juries 'know little of the law, are occasionally stupid, prejudiced, barely literate, and are not applying the law as public opinion is led to suppose they do' (*The Observer*, 16 March 1975). Simulated jury exercises (McCabe and Purves, 1972; Baldwin and McConville, 1979), provide *some* reassurance that 'real' juries and 'mock' juries concord, but this does not mean that their decisions are appropriate or rational.

The centrality of the jury trial to the English criminal justice system is undeniably slowly being eroded, not least because only a very small percentage of cases are dealt with in the Crown Court (about 5 per cent in 1994). But it seems that in an increasingly technical, managerial, government and Treasury-led criminal justice system (Bottoms, 1995), their very role is being questioned (see *The Independent* 8 October 1994, reproduced overleaf).

# Howard wants to curtail right to elect trial by jury

COLIN BROWN AND
JASON BENNETTO

MICHAEL HOWARD is considering ending the right to trial by jury for theft and other categories of crime in order to stop criminals dodging tougher sentences.

Millions of pounds could be saved by abolishing the right to elect for trial by jury, according to the Royal Commission on Criminal Justice. It would also relieve pressure on the High Court allowing it to concentrate on more serious cases.

The commission, chaired by Lord Runciman, warned that the present courts system 'does not work as it is intended'. Research showed that in 70 per cent of the cases where defendants had opted for jury trials they pleaded guilty.

The Runciman report said one of the three main objectives for opting for trial by jury was to put off the trial. This was sometimes to enable defendants to have part of their sentence counted while they were on remand in a softer prison regime, including the right to wear their own clothes.

The Home Secretary is expected to announce tougher prison regimes at the Conservative Party conference next week to head off criticism from 'rank-and-file' Tories over lax discipline in jails.

Mr Howard promised an 'austere' regime in prisons at last year's Conservative Party conference in his list of 27 measures to combat crime. There were calls for his resignation last month after the discovery of Semtex among IRA prisoners' belongings at Whitemoor jail, Cambridgeshire.

The Home Secretary will use his set-piece platform speech in an attempt to shore-up his reputation, which has been damaged by the defeats in the House of Lords on the Criminal Justice Bill. The package included the removal of the 'right to silence', against the advice of the majority report by the Royal Commission.

Sources close to the Home Secretary confirmed that Mr Howard was studying the proposal to limit the option for jury trial. The commission said 35,000 cases went to trial.

It cost £13,500 to hold a trial compared with £1,500 in a magistrates' court.

It found that many defendants thought they would stand a better chance of acquittal by a jury. They also thought they would get lighter sentences from judges, which was shown to be untrue.

Charles Elly, president of the Law Society, representing 76,000 solicitors in England and Wales, said yesterday that he would only support the abolition of the right for a jury trial in a limited number of cases. 'I would not think it is right to reduce the right for a defendant to be tried by a jury where dishonesty is an issue ...'

However, he argued that in cases involving alleged motoring offences, such as dangerous driving, a jury was unnecessary.

The Law Society is also keenly awaiting his response to the commission's suggestion that the right to refer cases to the Court of Appeal, following a spate of miscarriages of justice, should be taken out of the hands of the Home Secretary and given to a new body.

(*The Independent*, 8 October 1994)

## 5  Discriminatory practices?

discrimination

One of the chief concerns about sentencing in recent years has been the possibility of discrimination, particularly in terms of 'race' or gender. Of course, 'discrimination' is a legally defined concept but its interpretation lies well beyond the law. There are indeed a number of problems when it comes to defining and measuring discrimination. For example, what is conceived of as 'racial' may vary according to its external determinants/other factors (Fitzgerald, 1993). In other words, the disadvantages experienced by minority ethnic groups (housing, education, harassment) may also be experienced by others; therefore not all disadvantages can be attributed to racial discrimination, even if experienced disproportionately by minority ethnic groups. Second, it is important to recognize that there are differences in the experiences of minority ethnic groups, and that there may be no 'common' experience. What is racial may be multi-faceted; it may arise and manifest itself differently in different places at different times for different groups. *Moreover, it is extremely unlikely that any one research method can conclusively pin down the chimera of 'pure' discrimination which seems to be required to recognize that discrimination exists* (Reiner, 1993). Similarly, one of the arguments in debates about discrimination is that some people receive 'worse' treatment than others. This is not easy to define. For example, is cautioning 'better' or 'worse' than a recommendation for prosecution, which has some chance of resulting in an acquittal? Similarly, is a probation order 'better' or 'worse' than some other penalty?

The ideal of justice is abstract and, as we have mentioned, there is an assumption that all are equal before the law. However, there is room for discussion about what is equal treatment. At one extreme, it means the impartial application of existing rules and principles, regardless of the outcome (procedural justice). At the other, there is the view that any policies or procedures that have the effect of punishing a higher proportion of one social group than another are unjust, and that law and policy should be adjusted so as to achieve equal outcomes (substantive justice).

Some rules or procedures may work to the disadvantage of a particular social group (for example, Afro-Caribbeans may be remanded in custody rather than bailed because their family circumstances do not directly fit the criteria used in such decisions). Ensuring that equal proportions of different social groups are punished cannot be a valid aim of the criminal justice system, since we generally believe that the verdict in individual cases depends on the evidence and the punishment on the offence and previous record of the offender. These two extreme views parallel models of justice implied in anti-discrimination law. McCrudden *et al.* (1991) describe them as, respectively, the *individual justice model* and the *group justice model* of legislation against 'race' and sex discrimination. With regard to *individual justice*, the aim is to secure fairness by eliminating illegitimate considerations in the process of dealing with individuals. With regard to *group justice*, the aim is to improve the relative economic position of certain social groups (minority ethnic groups, for example). This

*The waiting room outside Highbury Magistrates' Court, London*

becomes relevant when we learn that a high proportion of people in minority ethnic groups are unemployed and there may be links between this factor and crime rates.

Much of the research evidence on discrimination, in relation to both 'race' and gender issues, is statistical in nature with obvious limitations. First, there is an assumption that discrimination can be proved or dismissed through sophisticated statistical analysis (and perhaps even manipulation). Clearly this is not the case. Second, it ignores the more dynamic aspects of decision-making – the significance of the defendant's appearance and

demeanour, agents' prejudices revealed in attitude rather than in specific decisions, and the interaction between defendants and officials. Third, it assumes that discrimination is something that can be considered in an ahistorical, atheoretical and apolitical context – which is not the case (Jefferson, 1993; Modood, 1994; Brittan and Maynard, 1984). Fourth, it is rather myopic to assume that the snapshot images of sentencing, produced through research, give a complete picture; it is more useful perhaps to think of discrimination in terms of the cumulative and interactive effects of disadvantage. Research often focuses on a single process or moment of decision-making, and on a single factor (for example, 'race' *or* gender *or* class), when a number of factors may be relevant *in combination*. Despite these limitations, it is worth considering some of the issues and evidence in more detail. (The terminology used in the following sub-sections tends to reflect that used in the research studies under discussion.)

## 5.1 'Race' issues in the court room

The starting-point for any discussion about the possibility of racial discrimination in sentencing has to be the over-representation in prisons of minority ethnic groups. The minority ethnic population of Great Britain is 5.5 per cent (according to the 1991 Census; Labour Force Surveys put the figure at around 2.7 million of the total population). The minority ethnic population of the national prison population, however, runs at about 16 per cent. The over-representation is greatest among prisoners classified as West Indian and African – or Afro-Caribbean; it is especially pronounced among remand prisoners and among women. Some of the disproportion may be accounted for by the imprisonment of foreign nationals – but not all of it by any means. Afro-Caribbean males provide some 10 per cent and Afro-Caribbean females 29 per cent of the total, figures which grossly exceed the Afro-Caribbean 1 per cent presence in the general population. Asians, in general, have incarceration rates more nearly in line with their presence in the population (see Chapter 5).

How would you explain the over-representation? Is it a simple issue of racial discrimination or can the disparity between representation in the general population and representation in the prison population be explained some other way?

### 5.1.1 Differential crime patterns

What is the involvement in crime of minority ethnic groups? The prison figures suggest that crime rates amongst Afro-Caribbeans are much higher than those for whites. The gulf is larger for women than for men but this would appear primarily to be explained by the presence of a relatively large number of foreign nationals (mainly from West Africa) sentenced for drug smuggling and due for deportation at the end of their sentences. That is, Afro-Caribbean females who are normally resident in the UK may be over-represented in British prisons, but only to the same degree as their male counterparts.

Setting aside questions of the exact degree of over-representation, there are good reasons to expect that crime rates for whites and Afro-Caribbeans will differ. The Afro-Caribbean population is, on average, younger than the white and therefore a higher proportion of this group falls within the 'peak age' for offending (the peak age for offending is 18 for males and 14 for females; see *Criminal Statistics: England and Wales, 1994* – Home Office, 1995). In particular, Afro-Caribbean males are strongly characterized by socio-economic factors associated with high offender rates (high levels of unemployment, low educational attainment and residence in high crime areas). However, no attempt has been made to see whether apparent ethnic differences in offending rates would diminish if unemployment, education and residence were taken into account.

It is also important to note that there are few studies of self-reported offending (which involve surveys of people and their self-confessed or reported involvement in crime) which can demonstrate ethnic differences in *actual* offending levels. It is difficult to establish whether there *are* higher rates of offending amongst ethnic minority groups or whether it is a matter of perception, but at least one self-report study found that Asian youth 'have significantly lower rates of offending than whites and Afro-Caribbeans who have very similar rates of offending' (Graham and Bowling, 1995, p.2).

Whatever the differences in actual offending rates, research suggests that there are also important differences in the trajectory of whites and Afro-Caribbeans through the criminal justice system. It cannot be assumed that these differences are evidence of a simple racial prejudice; rather, the available research findings suggest that many are explained by a mixture of legal *and* social factors *and* prejudice. Indeed, it may be the *interaction* of these points which determines how people are treated. We need to look at the research and statistical data more closely to help us understand how this might occur and to help us recognize that disparity in the treatment of different groups does not necessarily mean discrimination. Because of the apparent differences, it is important to examine the different stages of decision-making throughout the criminal justice system. The first step however, is to identify the key stages of decision-making in the court room, since this will help us understand whether there is discrimination.

### 5.1.2 Court of trial and bail and remand decisions

Studies which touch on the issue of court of trial find that Afro-Caribbeans are more likely than whites to be tried at Crown Court. There are two broad explanations for this: (a) Afro-Caribbeans are tried for more serious crimes; (b) a higher proportion of Afro-Caribbeans facing triable-either-way charges go to Crown Court (an offence which is triable-either-way can be dealt with either in the magistrates' court or in the Crown Court, depending on the seriousness of the offence).

There is some conflict in the studies over the extent to which this is due to defendants electing trial by jury or to magistrates declining jurisdiction in cases involving Afro-Caribbean defendants. Shallice and Gordon, in their study of four London magistrates' courts in 1985, suggest that it was defendants' choice to go to Crown Court (Shallice and Gordon, 1990), whereas Brown and Hullin, in their study of magistrates' courts in Leeds in 1988, suggest that a much higher proportion of cases going to Crown Court result from committal by magistrates (Brown and Hullin, 1992).

Differences in plea may have important consequences for outcome in that they may be related to the court of trial. Thus it appears that Afro-Caribbeans are more likely to plead not guilty and, partly for this reason, are more likely to be tried at Crown Court. Once tried, they are more likely to be acquitted (apparently vindicating their plea). (It should be noted, though, that in the study in Leeds by Jefferson *et al.*, Asians who were also likely to plead not guilty were less likely than whites to be acquitted – Jefferson *et al.*, 1992.) On the other hand, if they are found guilty, they may incur heavier penalties; defendants who plead 'not guilty' are more likely to be sentenced at Crown Court and do not benefit from the 'discount' associated with a 'guilty' plea.

The published statistics *consistently* show even greater over-representation of Afro-Caribbeans in the remand population than amongst sentenced prisoners. Hood, who constructed a 'custody remand score' to take account of legally relevant variables (that is, to determine risk of custody), found that whites in his sample were slightly less likely to be remanded than expected (taking into account such factors as the seriousness of the offence and previous offences, for example), but that Afro-Caribbeans were very significantly more likely to be remanded rather than released on bail (Hood, 1992).

### 5.1.3 Sentencing

pre-sentence
reports

Prior to the 1991 Criminal Justice Act, social inquiry reports were used to provide the courts with essential social background information on offenders (including reference to education, family circumstances, remorse, employment status and likelihood of responding to a particular penalty in a positive way so as to avoid further offending). The change in name from social inquiry to pre-sentence reports, which took place in the 1991 Act, signified a new focus on the *current* offence and circumstances of the offender (the seriousness of the offence, for example). In the Criminal Justice Act of 1991 the government decided that reports should be mandatory whenever sentencers were considering a custodial sentence but later, in the Criminal Justice and Public Order Act of 1994, it reverted to previous policy allowing sentencers to request reports where and when they think necessary. (Such controversies highlight the tensions between judicial discretion and procedural justice and between due process and crime control initiatives.)

The absence of a report can disadvantage a person because it may lessen their chance of receiving a community penalty where they are found guilty after a trial. Studies by Moxon (1988) and Voakes and Fowler (1989) found that the relative absence of pre-sentence reports on Afro-Caribbean (compared with white) offenders could be linked to their greater likelihood of pleading not guilty. Reports are not usually prepared on those who plead not guilty.

In cases where offenders plead guilty, sentencers are more likely to call for pre-sentence reports on black offenders than on whites. Where this occurs, there are two key considerations: whether probation officers' recommendations are similar (taking all relevant factors into account) for different groups and whether the courts are equally disposed to follow probation officers' recommendations.

The research evidence with regard to bias in reports seems to be difficult to interpret. Some studies suggest that reports are biased in the sense of using inappropriate language or assumptions, for example:

> Since about the 2nd or 3rd of this month he has not shown any particular signs or symptoms of true mental illness. Admittedly there is about him a mild paranoid attitude which I believe to be part of cultural mores associated with his ethnic propensities … as far as I am able to ascertain, his personality is that of a normally developed person considering his background and origins.

(quoted in Whitehouse, 1983, p.44)

Others argue that overt racism is no longer the issue and that, instead of simply analysing reports to detect racism, we should look at the processes of production – for example, how cases are allocated to officers to prepare reports, the home visits in order to prepare reports, gate-keeping and monitoring (which often involve peer groups or managers checking reports). There may be discrimination in these parts of the production process which are not captured in the 'polished' report presented to the court (Gelsthorpe, 1992).

There is clear evidence of differential sentencing between blacks and whites when it comes to non-custodial/community disposals, although there is no overall pattern to the types of non-custodial/community disposal given to those from minority ethnic groups. This tends to differ from one study to another (possibly reflecting general differences between courts in patterns of non-custodial disposal). There does tend to be agreement, however, that Afro-Caribbeans are less likely than whites to receive probation (Brown and Hullin, 1992; Moxon, 1988; Mair, 1986; Walker, 1989).

Nevertheless, commentators have usually come to diametrically opposite conclusions from the research data, suggesting, on the one hand, that they provide evidence of 'up-tariffing' of Afro-Caribbean offenders (where Afro-Caribbeans are given higher penalties than others) and, on the other, that there is no significant difference in the court disposal of offenders from minority ethnic groups once relevant variables are taken into account (for example, age of defendant, court of trial, charge, plea, previous convictions and pre-sentence report suggestions).

### 5.1.4  A cumulation of factors

Few studies have attempted a comprehensive analysis of all the relevant variables. McConville and Baldwin (1982), in their analysis of four random samples of Crown Court trials in London and Birmingham in 1975 and 1979, and Mair (1986), in his analysis of cases in two magistrates' courts in Leeds and Bradford in 1983, attempted to match white offenders with those from minority ethnic groups on a range of variables before making comparisons. Both studies, however, are characterized by methodological problems: McConville and Baldwin grouped Afro-Caribbeans and Asians together and the size of Mair's sample was perhaps too small to draw any firm conclusions.

Hood (1992) has shed considerable light on the interaction of factors. His study, with a sample of 6,000 individuals sentenced at five Crown Courts in the West Midlands in 1989, found that black males had a 17 per cent greater chance of imprisonment than whites (see the article from *The Guardian*, 10 December 1992, reproduced overleaf). Hood found a 5 per cent greater risk of custody for black males than for whites with the same characteristics. Moreover, he points out that the disparity would have been greater still if Afro-Caribbeans had not already been disproportionately remanded in custody. A remand in custody itself is a strong predictor that a custodial sentence is likely to be imposed, so discrimination is often cumulative. In this case a greater number of black than white males had been remanded in custody and at least part of the apparent discrimination can be attributed to this, rather than to discriminatory attitudes towards black males at the sentencing stage. On the other hand, Hood found that there were no significant differences for women; that the overall custody rate for Asians was rather lower than the score predicted; and that the differences seemed to be confined to men over 21. The study also confirmed Mair's finding that, relative to whites, black defendants with social inquiry reports were disadvantaged not by the recommendations of the reports (given their case characteristics), but by the greater extent to which the courts sentencing a higher proportion of black defendants to custody ignored these recommendations. The fault thus lay with the courts, not the probation officers.

# Blacks' jail risk 'increased by biased judges'

**Clare Dyer**
**Legal Correspondent**

BLACKS have a significantly higher chance than whites of going to prison from crown courts, according to the first study of racial bias in sentencing, published yesterday by the Commission for Racial Equality.

The study of 3,300 cases at five West Midlands courts in 1989, carried out by Dr Roger Hood, director of the Centre for Criminological Research at Oxford University, shows evidence of racial discrimination by some crown court judges.

Black males had a 17 per cent greater chance of going to jail than whites, while Asians were 18 per cent less likely to be imprisoned.

After adjusting for 15 key factors including seriousness of the crime, blacks still had a 5 to 8 per cent greater chance of a custodial sentence. But the overall figures mask much more significant discrimination in some of the five courts.

While blacks and whites got similar sentences at Birmingham crown court, blacks sentenced at Dudley crown court in the West Midlands had a 23 per cent greater chance of a prison sentence than whites.

A black offender sentenced at Dudley had a 29 per cent greater chance of going to prison than if he had been dealt with at Birmingham.

Of the 18 judges who passed sentences at Birmingham, Dudley, Stafford, Warwick and Coventry crown courts, three sentenced fewer blacks than whites to custody, eight were even-handed, and seven sent a much higher percentage of blacks than whites to prison.

The disparity was greatest for less serious offences, where judges have the most discretion. The Race Relations Act, which forbids racial discrimination, does not apply to judges. The commission's chairman, Sir Michael Day, said: 'This research reveals a pattern of racial discrimination in certain crown courts. This is a matter of serious concern.

'All parts of the criminal justice system have a responsibility to act with conspicuous fairness, even if they are not covered by the Race Relations Act. We look for appropriate action to be taken.'

The report, A Question of Judgement, found that blacks suffered additional indirect discrimination because they were more likely to plead not guilty and lost the unofficial sentence 'discount' – one-third in the

West Midlands – that judges give for a guilty plea.

Sir Michael called for a review of the practice of sentence discounts for a guilty plea and more pre-sentence reports by probation officers.

The study urges a system of monitoring defendants' ethnic origins, with information on sentences analysed by ethnic group made available to all judges and to the court.

The Lord Chancellor, Lord Mackay, who supported the research, and the Lord Chief Justice, Lord Taylor, said in a joint statement that they recognised the importance of the matters dealt with in the report. Ministers were considering how to collect ethnic data from the courts, they added.

Peter Herbert, chairman of the Society of Black Lawyers, said the organisation would seek an urgent meeting with the Lord Chancellor and Lord Chief Justice to discuss what steps should be taken.

He called for the identification and suspension of the seven 'clearly racist' judges until they completed a course on good sentencing practice.

(*The Guardian*, 10 December 1992)

From Hood's study there emerges evidence of both direct and indirect discrimination at the Crown Court and of the influence of social criteria:

- Direct discrimination is implied by the findings of unexplained ethnic differences for men (when all relevant explanations were taken into account) in the bail/remand decision, in the rate at which black people were sentenced to custody, and in the length of the custodial sentences imposed on those who pleaded not guilty.

- Hood also points out that defendants from minority ethnic groups were inadvertently subjected to a form of *indirect discrimination* at the point of sentence, because they more often chose to contest the case than others (and were thus ineligible for the usual discount on guilty plea), and because there were therefore no reports from probation officers (probation officers tend not to prepare reports on those who contest cases). Hood maintains that black people put themselves at risk of custody and longer sentences in these ways.

- Importantly, Hood suggests that the use of *social criteria* such as employment and family circumstances may put members of certain groups at a particular disadvantage. One obvious example concerns the effect of unemployment on the bail/remand decision since a very high number of black people are unemployed. Interestingly, whereas the probability of black offenders receiving a custodial sentence is between 5 and 8 per cent higher than for white offenders, the probability of their having been remanded in custody is at least double that (16 per cent higher). There are thus 'knock-on' or cumulative effects.

Hood's research is not without flaw: there are possibly some definitional problems with his terminology regarding the categories of 'white', 'black' and 'Asian', problems with his sampling and problems of generalizability, given the exclusive focus on Crown Courts (Halevy, 1995). However, his research is significant in that first, it adds to available evidence that racial discrimination can and does occur in the criminal justice system, and second, it demonstrates the complexity of the problem. Discrimination occurs neither systematically nor universally, which suggests that there is a need for more sophisticated understandings of how (and where) it occurs and how it can be dealt with (see *The Guardian,* 31 January 1994 and *The Guardian*, 18 February 1994, reproduced on the following pages).

Above all, recognition should be given to the way in which the decisions of criminal justice agencies (and other relevant bodies, including the legal profession and forensic experts) interact with and compound each other. None can be viewed in isolation; even if there are small ethnic differences in the key decisions taken by each, their cumulative impact may be very large indeed (Reiner, 1993).

# Judges take course in how to remove race bias in court

**Clare Dyer**
**Legal Correspondent**

JUDGES are to be reminded this week that black people dislike being called 'coloured' and that non-Christians may be offended if their first names are described as Christian names.

The warning comes in background papers distributed to judges taking part in a pilot race awareness seminar in London. They will be involved for the first time in practical exercises designed to combat racial stereotyping and prejudice following research showing that some judges sentenced blacks more harshly.

'It is, perhaps, surprising how one may still hear from time to time the unwitting use of phrases such as "working like a black" or "the nigger in the woodpile"' says the paper on cross-cultural communication.

Judges are warned against more subtle ways of unintentionally causing offence, such as speaking of all Nigerians or Chinese as if they were the same.

Another is conveying a patronising attitude by using a phrase such as 'you people must realise', or referring to 'the way we do things in this country".

A third is by seeming to imply that certain ethnic groups have particular criminal characteristics, as through use of popular stereotyping phraseology such as 'black muggers' and 'black crime'.

The seminar will be launched on Thursday night with a reception and dinner attended by 'a number of very interesting people from ethnic minority communities in London', according to the judges' briefing pack.

Each guest will be assigned to a particular host judge for drinks and dinner at a London hotel.

Guests will be asked to 'share their experience and understanding of the issues' with the judges. Before the next day's session, judges have been told they should reflect on what they have learned from the previous night's conversation.

The seminar, run by the Judicial Studies Board, is the brainchild of Mr Justice Brooke, chairman of the board's ethnic minority advisory committee.

It follows findings by a leading criminologist, Dr Roger Hood, of Oxford University, that black male defendants received heavier sentences in some courts.

As well as full-time circuit judges, barristers, and solicitors who sit part-time as judges in the crown courts will take part in seminars around the country. A key aim is to help judges identify how and why blacks are treated less favourably in court.

The judges have been given background papers on Dr Hood's research, ethnic minorities in England and Wales, names, how people should be addressed, oath-taking, body language, and cross-cultural communication.

The warning on the use of the term 'coloured' follows several cases where judges have used similar expressions.

The late Sir James Miskin, when the senior judge at the Old Bailey, spoke of 'nig nogs' and 'murderous Sikhs' in an after-dinner speech.

The Society of Black Lawyers complained to the Lord Chancellor, Lord Mackay, after a part-time judge, dealing with a credit card fraud, said: 'This is the type of offence which is all too prevalent in the Nigerian community.'

(*The Guardian*, 31 January 1994)

## 5.2 Gender issues in the court room

### ACTIVITY 3.4

How do you think women are treated in the courts compared with men? Do you think there are differences in the way they are treated? Justify your responses with examples, if possible.

# Judges 'are resisting race training'

**Clare Dyer**
**Legal Correspondent**

SOME judges are resisting moves to train the judiciary in race awareness, a leading black barrister and part-time judge claims today.

Resistance to the programme, which started this month, comes from both High Court and circuit judges, according to Lincoln Crawford, a Bar Council member and former commissioner of the Commission for Racial Equality.

The training scheme, which follows research showing that some judges sentenced black defendants more harshly, covers circuit judges and part-timers – recorders and assistant recorders – but not High Court judges.

Writing in the Bar journal, Counsel, Mr Crawford, aged 47, cites four reasons for judges' opposition.

'First, the belief held by judges that they apply the law fairly and do not need to be trained in race awareness because they are not racist.

'Secondly, the feeling that it is an affront to their judgment to be asked by anyone to try to understand the cultures or way of life of those black and Asian members of society who appear before them.

'Thirdly, a measure of bloody-mindedness arising out of a feeling that, since race awareness training for judges is advocated by the blacks and their liberal spokesmen, it cannot be accepted – either because this is the thin end of a thick wedge or because black and Asian members of society should take the British legal system as they find it.

'Fourthly, there is a misplaced fear that race awareness training smacks of interference and is bad for the judiciary.'

Mr Crawford, who was born in Trinidad, says: 'A judiciary which fears and feels nervous about plurality and diversity runs the danger of becoming closed, narrow and brittle.'

He says Britain's judges are products of an education system which 'produced people who were self-confident, rightly proud of their heritage and history and deeply grounded in their society's basic values, but without any knowledge of the ethnic minority communities, their cultures, sensitivity and sentiments.'

He endorses racial awareness training for judges, and calls for more black and Asian judges, magistrates and industrial tribunal chairmen.

(*The Guardian*, 18 February 1994)

A common assumption is that women are treated more leniently than men in the criminal justice system. They are thought to be less likely than men to be arrested, prosecuted, convicted or imprisoned. This is often referred to as the 'chivalry' hypothesis, since the majority of decision-makers are male (the magistrates' court is an exception to this, with nearly as many women as men) and it is believed that they respond to female offenders in much the same way that they respond to their wives, daughters and mothers. Some writers,

chivalry

however, describe the process in quite a different way. They see the criminal justice system's treatment of women as discriminatory and sexist, and believe that women are punished for breaching not only the criminal law, but also traditional sex role expectations.

Criminal statistics seem at first glance to support the 'chivalry' hypothesis, since they have repeatedly shown that a far greater proportion of women than men are cautioned by the police, rather than prosecuted (Home Office, 1995). They also show that a smaller proportion of women than men (21 years and over) receive custodial penalties (the figures for 1994 were 8 per cent and 20 per cent respectively) and a greater proportion of women than men receive probation or discharges (the figures for 1994 were 19 per cent and 32 per cent for women compared with 11 per cent and 16 per cent for men). This picture is similar for both Crown Courts and magistrates' courts and for offences for which women are commonly sentenced (for example, theft from shops) and for offences for which women are rarely sentenced (for example, assaults). Compared with men, women are also generally given shorter sentences of imprisonment for all offences (except drugs).

These statistics do not necessarily show that women are dealt with *more leniently* than men; they show that women are being dealt with *differently* from men, but they do not tell us why this occurs. Before accepting the 'chivalry' hypothesis, therefore, we need to know whether these differences arise simply because of the sex of the offender or for some other reason. We would perhaps expect those with either no or very few previous convictions to stand a greater chance of being cautioned (instead of prosecuted) than those with many previous convictions. If they were prosecuted, we would perhaps expect them to be less likely to receive custodial penalties. We thus need to examine whether there is any evidence that women are 'less serious' offenders and less criminally sophisticated than men, which alone might account for the differences in cautioning and sentencing outcomes.

Overwhelmingly, recorded crime is a male activity. In 1994, about 81 per cent of those found guilty, or cautioned for indictable offences, were men, while only 18 per cent were women – with 1 per cent of offences committed by others, for example, companies (Home Office, 1995). Furthermore, if we consider the likelihood of conviction, on the basis of data from the 1977 Criminal Statistics, Farrington calculated that almost half of all men (44 per cent) but only 15 per cent of women are likely to be convicted of offences (excluding motoring) at some time in their lives (Farrington, 1981). An analysis of 1982 data showed some change (Farrington, 1992). The comparable figures were 40 per cent for men and 12 per cent for women.

What type of offences do you think men and women commit? Can you identify any differences between them?

Table 3.1 shows that two-thirds of women's offences are theft-related (primarily theft from shops) compared with 40 per cent of men's. The other main disparity in offending occurs in relation to burglary, with 2 per cent of women compared with 11 per cent of the men being found guilty or cautioned for this offence. Overall, it is accepted that women generally commit less serious offences than men. *Within* offence categories (since legal categories cover a multitude of sins), research also suggests that women again commit the less serious offences: for example, research into theft from shops suggests that women steal fewer items, and of less value, than men (Farrington and Buckle, 1984).

This would indicate that women are both less serious and less frequent offenders than men. It may be these differential crime patterns which explain the differing police cautioning and court sentencing patterns, not the mere sex difference.

**Table 3.1  Percentage of offenders found guilty or cautioned by type of offence, age group and sex, England and Wales 1994**

|  | All ages | | 18 and under 21[1] | | 21 and over | |
|---|---|---|---|---|---|---|
|  | Male | Female | Male | Female | Male | Female |
| Violence against the person | 12 | 10 | 10 | 9 | 13 | 9 |
| Sexual offences | 2 | 0 | 1 | 0 | 2 | 0 |
| Burglary | 11 | 2 | 13 | 2 | 8 | 1 |
| Robbery | 1 | 0 | 1 | 0 | 1 | 0 |
| Theft and handling stolen goods | 40 | 66 | 36 | 62 | 37 | 61 |
| Fraud and forgery | 4 | 7 | 3 | 8 | 6 | 10 |
| Criminal damage | 3 | 1 | 3 | 1 | 3 | 1 |
| Drug offences | 15 | 7 | 22 | 11 | 16 | 9 |
| Other (excluding motoring) | 9 | 5 | 10 | 6 | 11 | 6 |
| Motoring | 3 | 1 | 2 | 0 | 4 | 1 |
| TOTAL | 100 | 100 | 100 | 100 | 100 | 100 |

1 Until Criminal Justice Act 1991, offenders aged 17 and under 21.

All figures have been rounded.

Source: Home Office, 1995, p.117, Table 5.12

### 5.2.1  The sentencing of women in the court room

Whilst evidence for the preferential treatment of women by the police, because they are women, is weak (Carey, 1979), research findings with respect to sentencing have produced contradictory findings. Kapardis and Farrington (1981) adopted an experimental approach in which magistrates were presented with a description of a hypothetical theft offence and were asked to say which sentence they would regard as appropriate. Only the value of the goods and the sex of the offender were varied in order to test the effect of both sex and the seriousness of the offence on sentencing. They found that there was *no difference* in the sentencing of women and men involved in the *less serious* offences but that women were treated *more leniently* than men for the *more serious* offences.

Farrington and Morris (1983) abstracted information from court records on just over 100 women and almost 300 men and found that women appeared to be dealt with more leniently than men. However, when the nature of the offence and previous convictions were taken into account , they found that the two sexes were dealt with in the same way. Sex was not related to sentencing severity independently of other factors. Women only received more lenient sentences because they committed less serious offences and were less likely to have been previously convicted. Type of offence, current problems and previous convictions were the main influences in the sentencing decisions.

Mair and Brockington (1988), on the other hand, using a different methodology (matching male and female defendants on certain characteristics, such as offence) did not produce such clear-cut results. They collected data on 225 women and 950 men who appeared in two magistrates' courts and were sentenced for indictable or triable-either-way offences. On the basis of unmatched data, female defendants received fewer community service orders and more probation orders than male defendants. Though the situation changed when matched groups were compared, women, even when matched, were more likely to be conditionally discharged and less likely to be fined than men. Disparities in sentences of imprisonment, however, were reduced by matching. Overall, no firm conclusions were drawn.

Moxon (1988) suggested more conclusively that women were dealt with more leniently than men. He examined sentencing practice in the Crown Courts and found that women were significantly more likely than men to receive non-custodial sentences even after allowing for the nature of the offence and criminal record.

Dominelli (1984), however, claimed that women were dealt with more harshly than men. From an examination of all community service orders made in one area between 1976 and 1981, she suggested that women given community service orders had often been convicted of less serious offences and had fewer previous convictions than their male counterparts. However, if sentencing is based on a clear 'just deserts' approach, it can be argued that it might be expected that women who are first and less serious offenders should be concentrated in the lower tariff options. Dominelli did not, however, examine sentencing practice *generally* in the areas she studied, and her claim that women were dealt with more harshly than men is thus of doubtful validity.

In contrast, in a study of women who kill their children (Wilczynski and Morris, 1993) which involved the analysis of 474 cases recorded between 1982 and 1989, there was evidence of lenient treatment towards women: mothers were less likely than fathers to be convicted of murder (they were convicted of lesser charges such as manslaughter – often on the grounds of diminished responsibility); they were also less likely to be sentenced to imprisonment and more likely to be given probation and psychiatric disposals (though psychiatric disposals are not always lenient and are open to different interpretation).

## ACTIVITY 3.5

In light of the preceding discussion, study the reports from *The Guardian*, 20 May 1994 and *The Sunday Times*, 9 April 1995, reproduced on the following pages. How can we make sense of such diverse research findings? Make a list of possible explanations and the factors involved in interpreting the data.

## COMMENT

The very different findings may simply mean that different research methodologies (experimental, matching, multivariate analysis) tend to produce different results. Or it may be that different courts in different areas operate in quite different ways (the magistrates' courts covered in the projects mentioned above were in Cambridge and West Yorkshire). Or it might be that we need to consider the importance of *gender* rather than *sex* to explain the apparent disparities in sentencing.

# Courts 'lenient toward women'

**Alan Travis**
**Home Affairs Editor**

**H**OME OFFICE research published yesterday challenges the widely held assumption that the courts and criminal justice discriminate against women.

Academics and pressure groups have long argued that women are treated much more severely by the courts than men, a claim based on statistics showing that 38 per cent of women in jail are there for their first offence compared with 10 per cent of men.

A Home Office research study, by Carol Hedderman and Mike Hough, now claims that when it comes to men and women with similar criminal backgrounds charged with similar crimes, women receive more lenient sentences.

The research into court treatment shows that girls are much less likely to commit the sort of crimes carried out by young boys, such as burglary or breaking into cars. 'Although there has been a rise in the proportion of females dealt with for violence and drug offences in the last 10 years, 71 per cent of their offences in 1992 were theft and handling – in contrast to only 43 per cent of males.'

Three-fifths of women convicted of offences were cautioned, compared with only a third of men. At court women were far less likely to receive a prison sentence, except in drug cases where there appeared little difference.

Women are also far less likely to go to crown court, and so receive on average 17 months for women over 21 – compared with 21 months for men.

(*The Guardian*, 20 May 1994)

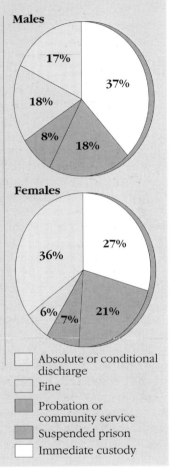

Males

17%
37%
18%
8%
18%

Females

36%
27%
6% 7%
21%

☐ Absolute or conditional discharge
☐ Fine
▨ Probation or community service
▨ Suspended prison
☐ Immediate custody

*Sentencing adults: Percentage of males and females sentenced for offences – 1992 (figures rounded to the nearest whole number)*

Gender-related behaviour is that social behaviour we associate with each of the sexes; masculinity is a characteristic we normally associate with men, whilst femininity is a social characteristic we normally associate with women. Gender considerations denote the assumptions we have about appropriate and inappropriate sex-role behaviour which are socially and not biologically constructed. Thus, traditionally, women were expected to be passive, dependent, wives and mothers; men, on the other hand, were expected to be active, independent, breadwinners. These are, of course, stereotypical conceptions, but nonetheless they appear to remain influential today, and thus the woman who enters the court room is expected to behave in certain ways.

# Courts condemn women to tougher sentences than men

### Liz Lightfoot and Andrew Anderson

WOMEN are consistently receiving harsher sentences than men. Many are being jailed by courts that allow men who have committed virtually identical offences to walk free.

Probation officers, academics and prison support groups blame the discrimination on judges and magistrates, who they say are less tolerant of women who commit crimes, particularly if the offence is seen as 'setting a bad example' if they are also mothers.

Government policies to target persistent serious offenders are also penalising women, particularly those who return before courts because they are too poor to pay fines.

Last year the number of women imprisoned rose by nearly a quarter to almost 3,000, causing an overcrowding crisis in jails. The growing concern over the sentencing of women is to be addressed by the Magistrates' Association at a meeting next month.

The trend, which challenges the notion that women are treated more sympathetically by courts, is typified by Sheila Kent, 48, who gets out this week after a four-month sentence imposed by magistrates in Boston, Lincolnshire.

Kent, who has two children, was jailed after failing to keep up with her £10-a-month fine for motoring offences and not having a television licence. Although she had met her payments for 11 months, she was able to pay only part of the fine for two months because of a delay in receiving child benefit.

Yet the day after Kent was jailed in February, the same magistrate sitting at the same court gave Michael Hardstaff, 28, a 28-day suspended prison sentence after he admitted he had not made any payment of his £20-a-week fine, imposed for burglary and motoring offences, for 17 months.

Hardstaff, who had been told

by Sheila Bannister, the magistrate, that the court took a 'very dim view' of his non-payment, admitted this weekend that he had been leniently treated compared with Kent. 'I was expecting to be sent down for a lot more than 28 days but they let me go,' he said.

Women offenders and their families are not alone in their concern about discrimination in sentencing. Prison support groups say a growing number of women inmates – including those on remand – are there unnecessarily and to the detriment of their families.

Although women make up less than 4 per cent of the total prison population, the number of women receiving 'immediate' custodial sentences in England and Wales (as opposed to fine defaulters) rose by 24 per cent last year to 2,952.

Many are in jail for 'minor' offences. Last year more than 300 women were imprisoned for non-payment of fines for not having a television licence, according to research by Leeds and York universities. 'The imprisonment of women for non-payment of television fees is one of the great scandals of our time,' said Professor Jonathan Bradshaw, of York.

The upsurge in the number of women jailed has led to crisis measures in women's prisons. Internal prison service documents reveal governors are being forced to find places in high-security jails for women whose offences mean they should serve their sentence in low-security prisons.

Even for women who escape jail, punishments are still tougher than for men. A *Sunday Times* survey of more than a third of the 54 probation areas in England, Wales and Northern Ireland has shown that

women are twice as likely as men to receive probation for first offences.

Rosemary Thomson, chairman of the Magistrates' Association, said government changes to toughen up probation had reduced sentencing options. 'It appears probation is still being used for women who have not committed serious offences but need help with their lives. It is wrong, but it is understandable.'

Women are also being jailed because the alternative – community service orders – are not felt suitable. Magistrates and probation officers believe the work is too physical or is not suitable for mothers with family commitments.

For Rebecca Gillon, 26, the findings come as no surprise. She was seven months pregnant when she was jailed for 21 days last year for her first offence of 'borrowing' £380 from her bank employers. Gillon, from Lesbury, Northumberland, was jailed for stealing from Barclays, even though she paid the money back before an audit showed it was missing. She was given a conditional discharge after an appeal.

•Lord Mackay, the lord chancellor, called yesterday for more women to apply for top jobs in the judiciary and promised 'affirmative action' to ensure all applicants were treated fairly on their merits. Fewer than a tenth of the applicants for the bar are women.

His concerns were echoed by Cherie Booth, the barrister wife of Tony Blair, the Labour leader. She said the lack of women high court judges – only six out of 95 – was a result of few women coming to the bar.

*Additional reporting by Ciaran Byrne, Rajeev Syal and Michael Greenwood*

(*The Sunday Times*, 9 April 1995)

Broadly speaking, a large body of research has identified three main themes which are particularly relevant for the sentencing of women – pathology, domesticity and respectability. We can, however, add one further theme, sexuality, which is particularly relevant for girls.

First, a women who enters the criminal justice system has been described as 'incongruous', 'out of place', 'invisible' (Worrall, 1990). Explanations for her presence are sought within the discourse of the 'pathological' and the 'irrational': menstruation, mental illness, poor socialization, broken homes, for example. Men are not viewed as so out of place in the court room and so their offending is explained in different ways, within the discourse of 'normality' and 'rationality'. Their behaviour is more likely to be viewed as the product of such factors as boredom, greed and peer group pressure. These different types of explanations for women's and men's behaviour may then influence subsequent processing through the criminal justice system.

In addition, certain factors seem to influence the sentencing of women but not that of men. Farrington and Morris (1983) found that distinctions were made in court between women (see Table 3.2). The main distinguishing factors were: the involvement of other offenders, marital status, family background and the sexual composition of the bench. Women convicted with one or more other offenders were more likely to receive more severe sentences than those convicted on their own. Divorced and separated women received relatively more severe sentences than married women, as did women coming from a 'deviant' rather than a stable background. Women appearing before a bench made up of two women and a man were dealt with more severely than women appearing before benches of two men and a woman.

### Table 3.2 Factors influencing sentence severity in order of importance

| Total sample | Men | Women |
| --- | --- | --- |
| Type of offence | Type of offence | Current problems |
| Current problems | Current problems | Convicted in the previous 2 years |
| Number of previous convictions | Number of previous convictions | Other offenders involved |
| Legal representation[1] | Legal representation | Number of Theft Act offences |
| Convicted in the previous 2 years | Number of Theft Act offences | Marital status[3] |
| Age | Age | Family background |
| Plea[2] | Plea | Sexual composition of the bench[4] |

1  Those represented received the more severe sentences.

2  Pleading guilty led to more severe sentences.

3  Divorced and separated women were given more severe sentences.

4  Women appearing before a bench containing two female magistrates were sentenced more severely than those appearing before a bench containing two male magistrates.

Source: Farrington and Morris, 1983, p.244

Simple statistical analyses such as these, however, are not able to answer the question of why differences in sentencing might occur; rather, they enable researchers only to speculate about why these differences might appear. Most of the researchers, for example, neither observed magistrates nor judges at work, nor interviewed them. Nor did they pay much regard to those processes which might shape sentencing outcomes (pleas in mitigation or the provision of social inquiry or pre-sentence reports). A few researchers did do this, however, and it is to their research that we now turn.

Pearson (1976) conducted a small-scale observational study of the magistrates' court in Cardiff. She focused only on women (which restricts the general applicability of her research), but basically argued that the sentencing of women was highly individualized and that women were not seen to be fully responsible for their offences: 'quasi-juvenile status' is how she describes it. Edwards (1984) also studied only female offenders. She observed cases in Manchester City Magistrates' Court and in some Crown Courts. Her conclusion was that women were 'on trial both for their legal infraction and for their inappropriate femininity and gender roles'. So women's respectability was at issue. This was particularly noticeable when women appeared before the Crown Court for violent offences. However, Edwards' conclusion is based on the observation of only a small number of cases and must be treated with caution.

The theme of punishment for the breach of traditional sex role expectations is reiterated in Carlen's (1983) interviews with male sheriffs in Scotland. The most significant finding was that the women who were sent to prison were those who, in the eyes of the sheriffs, had 'failed' as mothers. Thus sheriffs wanted to know not only whether the woman was a mother but also whether or not she was, in their view, a 'good' mother:

> If she's a good mother, we don't want to take her away. If she's not a good mother, it doesn't matter …
>
> If a woman has no children then it clears the way to send her to prison. If they are in care, I treat her as a single woman …

(Carlen, 1983, p.67)

Here domesticity is the key issue. Worrall cites a prison governor who once echoed these sentiments: 'Women should come here for at least 6 months, then we can train them to be good mothers and they're grateful' (Worrall, 1990, p.61). Eaton, on the other hand, argued (on the basis of observation of over 100 cases involving women and over 200 involving men and interviews with magistrates) that family circumstances are considered important in deciding sentences for *both* sexes, along with the nature of the offence and the offender's previous record (Eaton, 1986). The family was central to pleas in mitigation offered by counsel and to social inquiry reports prepared on behalf of both women and men. Magistrates commented that they would be influenced by the presence of children if the defendant was responsible for child care, whether that defendant was male or female. However, responsibility for children was more likely to arise in cases involving women and, because of this, women and men were presented differently to the court – 'women as dependent and domestic' and 'men as breadwinners'. This model reinforced 'traditional' gender roles. The result, according to Eaton, was that women who were negatively assessed *as women* were dealt with more severely.

Allen (1987) reached the opposite conclusion. She argued that the psychiatric and social inquiry reports which she examined (100 on women and 100 on men) drew on sex stereotypes which systematically placed women 'at a moral advantage and men at a moral disadvantage'. She found other striking differences. Reports on female offenders almost invariably addressed the woman's mental state. This was in sharp contrast to reports on male offenders which tended to focus on the more external aspects of the offender's behaviour and life-style. According to Allen, such differences occurred independently of the material facts of their behaviour.

If report writers, advocates and decision-makers view women in a particular way, it is hardly surprising that certain dispositions (probation and hospital orders, for example) are 'naturally' recommended for and given to women whilst others (community service, for example) are not. The Probation Inspectorate (1991) found that all the community service schemes they visited during their inspection had at least some child-minding provision; but they also found, four years after research on the issue by Jackson and Smith, that social inquiry reports on female prisoners continued to refer to the unsuitability of a mother for community service:

The ages of her children mean she is not suitable for community service …

As a single woman with two small children she is not suitable for community service …

Community service, regrettably, is not a viable option in view of her responsibilities as a mother …

(Jackson and Smith, 1987, quoted in Probation Inspectorate, 1991, p.47)

Paradoxically, all of these women (and other women in the six prisons where the Inspectorate examined social inquiry reports) had been sent to prison and yet, as stated by the Inspectorate, at least some of the women came from probation areas known to have child-minding facilities (Barker, 1993). It is also important to note that requests for a social inquiry report are more commonly asked for on women (Mair and Brockington, 1988) despite the increasing emphasis that probation is meant to be a high tariff option. This confirms the suggestion that women in court are 'out of place' and hence their presence requires explanation. The content of the reports frequently focuses on the social and sexual behaviour of the women, suggesting that women are sentenced for who they are and not what they have done.

Mair and Brockington (1988) also argue that the mere existence of a social inquiry (pre-sentence) report tends to lead to a move up the tariff: towards probation and away from discharges and small fines. They also stress that it seems that probation is being used differently for women (low tariff and for welfare/need reasons) and for men (high tariff and for punitive/offence reasons).

## ACTIVITY 3.6

What are the main lessons of this review of the research findings with regard to gender discrimination in the courts? Imagine that you have been asked by a newspaper editor to provide a very short statement about the sentencing of women in the courts. What would you say?

## COMMENT

In summary, there is *some* evidence that *some* women are dealt with in a discriminatory way. Essentially, it is argued that those who fit stereotypical conceptions of 'ladies' or 'nice girls' seem to receive different (and more lenient) sentences from those who breach these expectations. This issue is more complex, however, since gender interacts with both ethnicity and class. It is inappropriate to present women's experiences in the criminal justice system as a unitary experience. Black women, for example, are over-represented in our prisons. We need to be able to account for this. To assume that men are dealt with in non-sexist and non-discriminatory ways is patently also incorrect. Men and male defendants are socially 'constructed' (though in different ways from women and girls), and clearly, certain men are punished more harshly than others. For example, black men are over-represented in our prisons and, as suggested earlier, this is not fully accounted for by differences in offence gravity or previous record. Distinctions are drawn between different women. There is perhaps no crime other than women killing their own children in which there is such a direct confrontation with our notions of 'femininity' and 'motherhood'. Wilczynski (1991) examined 22 infanticide cases in her research, 14 of whom were clearly identified as essentially 'good' women and mothers for whom something had gone tragically wrong. They were given probation or hospital orders. Eight women, however, were given prison sentences. These women tended to be viewed as having acted in ways inconsistent with traditional stereotypical conceptions of women's appropriate behaviour. That is to say, they were viewed as 'bad' women – selfish, cold, neglectful, uncaring and sexual. According to Wilczynski, these were not 'real' or 'objective' categorizations, but they are examples of the types of distinctions which can be drawn between women who have committed the same serious act.

### 5.2.2  A 'sex-neutral' criminal justice system?

A key question that arises is whether there can there be a 'sex-neutral' criminal justice system. Taken overall, these research findings do raise the question of whether or not we could, or should, aim to have a sex- (and 'race'- and class-) neutral criminal justice system.

The White Paper *Crime, Justice and Protecting the Public* (Home Office, 1990a) stated that: 'there must be no discrimination because of a defendant's race, nationality, standing in the community or any other reason' (sex is implicitly rather than explicitly included). Discrimination is not always conscious, direct or overt, however; it may be argued that it is very often unconscious, indirect and covert. How can we ensure, then, that stereotypical conceptions of 'women' and 'men', of female and male offenders, or of defendants' 'needs' and 'responsibilities' do not affect assessments of, for example, a defendant's 'just deserts'?

There is also a much broader, theoretical point relating to the concept of equality. MacKinnon (1987) has written that any approach which focuses on equality assumes that the sentencing of men is somehow 'right' and sets the standard against which women should be judged. This led Allen (1987) to argue that women should be dealt with more punitively in order to further women's equality. She described leniency as a 'tactic of patriarchal oppression' and argued that women should be 'exposed to the full rigour of penal sanctions'. An alternative approach would be to deal with men less punitively. Furthermore, this focus on equality assumes that the law operates in a gender- or sex-neutral way; but the law, in its construction and its practices, is already gendered (Kingdom, 1981). To ask for one practice – discrimination – to cease to be gendered may be meaningless **(Smart, 1990)**.

A further question is whether equal treatment is the correct objective. There may be differences between women and men which justify differential dispositions. Walker (1981) drew a distinction between paper and real justice. 'Paper justice' would involve giving like penalties to women and men for like offences; 'real justice', on the other hand, would involve taking into account the consequences of a penalty: for example, it is a fact that, at least in this culture and at this time, child-rearing is primarily the responsibility of women; real justice would involve taking account of the likelihood that children suffer much more from their mother's imprisonment than their father's. This distinction once more highlights the fact that we cannot take the concept of justice for granted and that criminal justice is not necessarily synonymous with social justice.

'Paper justice' and 'real justice'

Carlen (1990) has advocated what she calls 'a women-wise penology'. It has two fundamental aims: to ensure that penal policy for women does not further increase their oppression as women and that penal policy for men does not brutalize them to the extent that they become more oppressive to women. In practical terms, she identifies the danger that pre-sentence reports for women may push women further up the tariff in order to help them with their 'problems', rather than offer such help in a non-statutory context.

Heidensohn (1986) also raised the question of whether there is a 'female' or 'feminist' conception of justice which would be more appropriate for women than the system of justice we have at the moment. In attempting to answer this, she distinguished two models which she called Portia and Persephone. Portia, the woman in Shakespeare's *The Merchant of Venice* who tricks Shylock out of his pound of flesh, represents what can broadly be called the due process model and stresses rights, fairness, formality and equality. It is said to be a model unresponsive to the needs of women and to be a 'masculine' approach. Persephone, the goddess of harvest exemplifying the cycle of fertility, represents what can broadly be called the welfare and rehabilitation model and stresses reformation, co-operation, informality and reparation. Heidensohn sees the latter as more appropriate for women since it represents 'feminine' values, but, it can be argued, does little more than replicate traditional welfare approaches which have been criticized for stereotyping women.

The difficulty is how to find ways to challenge stereotypical pictures of women (and men) and at the same time to meet women's (and men's) real needs and responsibilities. While these needs and responsibilities might in theory be best met outside of the criminal justice system, in practice it seems unlikely that this will happen. However, it can be argued that factors such as child-care and child-rearing responsibilities should be irrelevant at the sentencing stage (because otherwise discriminatory practices may be perpetuated), but should be relevant in the determination of penal policy: for example, in the provision of crèches for women doing community service, in changes in the nature of mother and baby units in prisons and in increased contact with children during a prison sentence.

## 5.3   Other forms of discrimination and 'injustice'

When focusing on 'race' and gender issues, it is important also not to lose sight of the notion of a class-based justice. Whilst Sanders (1985) confines his attention to differential rates of prosecution between different agencies, Messerschmidt (1986) more directly discusses the ideology of the law and suggests that it is a tool of the middle/upper class and that it reflects and protects their interests by criminalizing the behaviour of others. Criminal acts and anti-social behaviour may certainly be interpreted in different ways.

### ACTIVITY 3.7

Consider the following cases:

1    the theft of goods from a shop (to the value of £500)
2    a solicitor embezzling £500 from clients' funds
3    a fight outside a pub
4    a doctor sexually touching a patient
5    a fight inside a pub
6    a factory owner not adequately fencing factory machinery, which leads to an injury to a worker

What is likely to happen in each of these cases? Do you think that prosecution will result in each case?

### COMMENT

In practice it is likely that the shop theft will be prosecuted, but the embezzlement dealt with by the Law Society (which could involve severe sanctions but not necessarily prosecution). Those involved in the fight outside the pub may be prosecuted, but the offence inside the doctor's surgery may be dealt with by the General Medical Council (again, there may be severe sanctions, but sanctions which will fall short of prosecution). Those involved in the fight inside the pub may or may not be prosecuted (the managers of the pub could decide to take action themselves and simply throw the offenders out), whilst the factory offence might be dealt with by the Factory Inspectorate, or a private prosecution could be initiated.

We thus need to be aware that different anti-social acts can be seen as subject to the criminal law and/or other regulatory bodies and that there can be different methods of enforcement (Sanders, 1985; Cook, 1989; Lidstone *et al.*, 1980; McBarnet, 1981). We also need to be aware that differences in socio-economic circumstances can lead to or inhibit a criminal lifestyle (Farrington *et al.*, 1986a). Traditional criminological texts provide some support for the links between social class, lifestyle and crime (Elliott and Huizinga, 1983; Cohen, 1955; Merton, 1968; Cloward and Ohlin, 1960). In a recent survey of known offenders in England almost three-quarters were below the poverty line and showed very poor educational attainment (Home Office, 1990b). But some criminologists would argue that any links between social class and crime result from systematic bias. Tittle *et al.* (1978) suggest that a 'lower-class' person is more likely to be observed and detected than those from other classes and that a lower-class person is more likely to be arrested if discovered).

The variable of social class is too crude to explore direct discrimination and a consideration of a cluster of factors, which are themselves linked to low social class, is likely to be of more use. Indeed, Farrington *et al.* (1986b) suggest that, although socio-economic deprivation is an important risk factor for offending, low family income, poor housing and large family size are better measures and produce more reliable results than low occupational prestige. But does any of this affect decision-making in the court room? It is probably of more direct relevance to consider the possible influence of unemployment:

> One often has to think of the reasons why people commit offences. Often it's because they are basically criminal people, professional criminals, but in my experience of magistrates' courts, that tends to be only a small minority of people. The vast majority of defendants who come before the magistrates' court are the disadvantaged, the inarticulate, and almost by definition, therefore, the people with little or no income, often the unemployed. So I don't think it's tunnel vision at all to regard that as a prime feature of any research.

> (solicitor quoted in Crow and Simon, 1987)

Crow and Simon (1987) suggest that unemployment has a limited direct impact on sentencing. However, it is important to remember that sentencing is a social process that takes place within a social context. Whilst they suggest that sentencers have some awareness of changing circumstances, with regard to the prospects of long and continued employment in a harsh economic climate and recession, they also found evidence of more traditional attitudes, such as 'anyone who seriously wants a job will get a job,' and the belief that some unemployed people are lacking in motivation and self-discipline. An employment record is often seen to reflect stability and character, reinforcing traditional attitudes towards work, its meaning and the way in which these attitudes are reflected in the court room. It is possible that the courts need to develop a broader concept of the purpose of sentencing in so far as it relates to the circumstances of the offender, placing rather more emphasis on the merits of the individual as a whole and less on his or her employment status and history.

# 6 Conclusion: beyond formal justice

The idea of alternative courts is not a new one. It is generally based on a critique of the existing system that maintains that: it is too expensive and too slow; there are problems of access; there is a legitimation crisis; and it is too centralized and too coercive, reflecting a formalism (Harrington, 1985). Critics have also suggested that the system is anonymous and that neither defendants nor victims feel involved in the judicial process. There are further claims that the system can no longer ignore the fact that we live in a multicultural society and that it should adapt accordingly.

There are, of course, a number of forms of non-judicial settlement. Corporate and public agency regulatory practices often focus on the informal rather than the formal (Marshall, 1985). There are also forms of non-judicial settlement in the community: for example, dispute settlement, community mediation and reparation, community courts and neighbourhood justice. Indeed, many critics of the existing system argue for greater involvement of the 'community' (Tuck, 1991) or express opposition to the shift towards 'the

non-judicial settlement

market' ethos of public institutions (with increasing emphasis on economy and efficiency as opposed to ideals and values) by promoting what is called 'relational justice' (Schluter, 1994). 'Relational justice', according to Schluter, would be 'to regard crime primarily as a breakdown in relationships; even in those cases where the offender does not personally know the victim, a relationship can be said to exist by virtue of their being citizens bound together by rules governing social behaviour' (Schluter, 1994, p.24). In some sense, then, 'relational justice' would be a 'healing process', with each agency involved in the criminal justice system recognizing that it has a 'caring' function in dealing with offenders. The concept thus includes promotion of mediation and reparation schemes. It also reflects some of **Braithwaite's (1989)** thinking on the importance of 'shaming and reintegration' in responding to offenders. Braithwaite argues that punishment (shaming) is most effective when it is tied to the reintegration of offenders in the community, and it is counter-productive when it results in stigmatization. It could be argued that sentences of imprisonment exacerbate the isolation of the offender from both his or her family and the locality, reducing any prospect of reintegrative shaming. There is obviously implicit support for *community penalties* here, whether meted out by a judicial system or some other informal system.

formalism

Other non-judicial forms of settlement include informal policing, police cautioning, fixed penalties and fines, community diversion schemes, police vehicle rectification schemes and preventative arrest, for example (though these practices are more closely tied to the formal system than are more imaginative community mediation and reparation schemes). The common 'enemy' – if we can put it this way – is formalism (and its concomitant heavy bureaucracy, inflexibility and considerable use of professionals). All non-judicial approaches reject (to varying degrees) formal legal institutions and processes. The intellectual critique of formalism, however, has not given way to a trouble-free and pure concept of 'informalism'; informal approaches to criminal justice have also developed an administrative apparatus, lines of authority and a 'professional role'. In many cases, informal mechanisms have developed alongside formal mechanisms, thus aggravating the very system they were intended to supplant (Abel, 1982). It is also suggested that some informal approaches to criminal justice lead to an expanded state control (Scull, 1977; Cohen, 1988).

Advocates of informalism have portrayed community justice as less coercive and oppressive than the state system, but this may not always be so. For example, whilst the Family Group Conference system in Maori New Zealand is heralded as a major break with the formal system, and one which reflects cultural differences and sensitivities, it is also clear that 'community-designed penalties' can sometimes be just as harsh as those meted out by the state (Maxwell and Morris, 1993). Thus while the formal criminal justice system is beset with problems, the informalism of community-based justice will probably not provide a complete and readily accessible alternative.

Think back to the 'windows' on criminal justice discussed in section 3. To what extent can any of the ideals or models of informal justice outlined above be incorporated into existing models? To what extent would their adoption or promotion mean complete abandonment of existing models of criminal justice?

Some fundamental questions about criminal justice have been raised in this chapter. Perhaps the most searching and over-arching question, however, is how far formal (or any other) systems deliver 'justice' or 'injustice'? We encourage you to reflect on the meaning of 'justice' as it is currently construed and practised in the criminal courts, and to identify strengths and weaknesses in the system. The controversies and debates surrounding the criminal courts cannot be easily resolved. There will remain the need for continuous review and reflection as particular systems grapple with their own contradictions and are forced to meet changing circumstances.

# Further reading

A useful introduction to criminal justice processes can be found in King (1981), not least because he is one of a few who attempt to give the debates and issues some theoretical underpinning. It is also worth looking at Rozenberg (1994). Bottoms (1995) discusses the philosophy and politics of sentencing in general (along with other contributors to Clarkson and Morgan, 1995). The impact of differential treatment in the courts is explored by Hood (1992), Fitzgerald (1993) and Reiner (1993) in regard to 'race', and by Eaton (1986), Worrall (1990) and Kennedy (1992) in regard to gender. Both Carlen (1976) and Parker *et al.* (1989) provide fascinating accounts of the ideologies and practices which govern the production of 'justice' in the court room. **Braithwaite (1989)** and Schluter (1994) present stimulating accounts of how we can re-imagine the pursuit of justice without recourse to formal and inflexible systems.

# References

Abel, R. (ed.) (1982) *The Politics of Informal Justice,* vols I and II, New York, Academic Press.

Allen, H. (1987) *Justice Unbalanced: Gender, Psychiatry and Judicial Decisions,* Milton Keynes, Open University Press.

Ashworth, A. (1983) *Sentencing and Penal Policy,* London, Weidenfeld and Nicolson.

Ashworth, A. (1992a) *Sentencing and Criminal Justice,* London, Weidenfeld and Nicolson.

Ashworth, A. (1992b) 'Sentencing reform structures' in Tonry, M. (ed.) *Crime and Justice: A Review of Research,* vol.16, Chicago, University of Chicago Press.

Ashworth, A., Cavadino, P., Gibson, B., Harding, J. and Rutherford, A. (1992) *Materials on the Criminal Justice Act 1991,* Winchester, Waterside.

Baldwin, J. and McConville, M. (1979) *Jury Trials,* Oxford, Clarendon.

Barker, M. (1993) *Community Service and Women Offenders,* London, Association of Chief Probation Officers.

**Beccaria, C. (1963) *On Crimes and Punishments,* New York, Bobbs-Merrill (first published in 1764). (Extract reprinted in Muncie *et al.,* 1996.)**

Bottoms, A.E. (1981) 'The suspended sentence', *British Journal of Criminology,* vol.21, pp.1–26.

Bottoms, A.E. (1995) 'The philosophy and politics of sentencing', in Clarkson, C. and Morgan, R. (eds) *The Politics of Sentencing Reform,* Oxford, Clarendon.

**Braithwaite, J. (1989) *Crime, Shame and Reintegration*, Cambridge and New York, Cambridge University Press. (Extract reprinted as 'Reintegrative shaming' in Muncie *et al.*, 1996.)**

Brittan, A. and Maynard, M. (1984) *Sexism, Racism and Oppression,* Oxford, Blackwell.

Brown, I. and Hullin, R. (1992) 'A study of sentencing in the Leeds Magistrates' Courts: the treatment of ethnic minority and white offenders', *British Journal of Criminology,* vol.32, no.1, pp.41–53.

Carey, K. (1979) 'Police policy and the prosecution of women', unpublished paper.

Carlen, P. (1976) *Magistrates' Justice,* London, Martin Robertson.

Carlen, P. (1983) *Women's Imprisonment: A Study in Social Control,* London, Routledge and Kegan Paul.

Carlen, P. (1990) *Alternatives to Women's Imprisonment,* Milton Keynes, Open University Press.

Cavadino, M. and Dignan, J. (1992) *The Penal System: An Introduction,* London, Sage.

Clarkson, C. and Morgan, R. (eds) (1995) *The Politics of Sentencing Reform,* Oxford, Clarendon.

Cloward, R. and Ohlin, L. (1960) *Delinquency and Opportunity: A Theory of Delinquent Gangs,* New York, The Free Press.

Cohen, A. (1955) *Delinquent Boys: The Culture of the Gang,* New York, The Free Press.

Cohen, S. (1988) *Against Criminology,* New Brunswick, NJ, Transaction.

Commission for Racial Equality (1991) *Evidence to the Royal Commission on Criminal Justice,* London, Commission for Racial Equality.

Cook, D. (1989) *Rich Law, Poor Law: Different Responses to Tax and Supplementary Benefit Fraud,* Milton Keynes, Open University Press.

Crow, I. and Simon, F. (1987) *Unemployment and Magistrates' Courts,* London, NACRO.

Crow, I., Cavadino, M., Dignan, J., Johnston, V., Moore, J. and Walker, M. (1993) 'Evaluating the Criminal Justice Act 1991: some early indications of how agencies are responding', British Criminology Conference Paper (July) (unpublished).

Devlin, P.D., Baron (1979) *The Judge ,* Oxford, Oxford University Press.

Dominelli, L. (1984) 'Differential justice: domestic labour, community service and female offenders', *Probation Journal,* 31, pp.100–3.

Eaton, M. (1986) *Justice for Women? Family Court and Social Control,* Milton Keynes, Open University Press.

Edwards, S. (1984) *Women On Trial,* Manchester, Manchester University Press.

Elliott, D.S. and Huizinga, D. (1983) 'Social class and delinquent behaviour in a national youth panel', *Criminology,* 21, pp.149–77.

Farrington, D. (1981) 'The prevalence of convictions', *British Journal of Criminology*, vol.21, no.2, pp.173–5.

Farrington, D. (1992) 'Criminal career research in the United Kingdom', *British Journal of Criminology,* vol.32, no.4, pp.521–36.

Farrington, D. and Morris, A. (1983) 'Sex, sentencing and reconviction', *British Journal of Criminology*, vol.23, no.3, pp.229–48.

Farrington, D. and Buckle, A. (1984) 'An observational study of shoplifting', *British Journal of Criminology*, vol.24, no.1, pp.63–73.

Farrington, D., Gallagher, B., Morley, L., St Ledger, R. and West D. (1986a) 'Unemployment, school leaving and crime', *British Journal of Criminology*, vol.26, pp.335–56.

Farrington, D., Ohlin, L. and Wilson, J.Q. (1986b) *Understanding and Controlling Crime,* New York, Springer-Verlag.

Fitzgerald, M. (1993) *Ethnic Minorities and the Criminal Justice System*, Royal Commission on Criminal Justice Research Study No. 20, London, HMSO.

Foucault, M. (1980) *Power /Knowledge*, Brighton, Harvester.

Gelsthorpe, L. (1992) *Social Inquiry Reports: Race and Gender Considerations*, Home Office Research Bulletin No.32, pp.17–22.

Gibson, B. (1990) *Unit Fines*, Winchester, Waterside.

Graham, J. and Bowling, B. (1995) *Young People and Crime,* Research Findings No.24, Home Office Research and Statistics Department, London, HMSO.

Griffith, J.A.G. (1991) *The Politics of the Judiciary* (4th edn), London, Fontana.

Halevy, T. (1995) 'Racial discrimination in sentencing? A study into dubious conclusions', *Criminal Law Review*, April, pp.267–71.

Harrington, C. (1985) *Shadow Justice: The Ideology and Institutionalization of Alternatives to Court*, Westport, CT, Greenwood.

Harris, R. (1992) *Crime, Criminal Justice and the Probation Service*, London, Routledge.

Hay, D., Linebaugh, P., Rule, J.G., Thompson, E.P. and Winslow, C. (eds) (1975) *Albion's Fatal Tree: Crime and Society in Eighteenth-Century England*, London, Allen Lane.

Hedderman, C. and Moxon, D. (1992) *Magistrates' Court or Crown Court? Mode of Trial Decisions and Sentencing*, Home Office Research Study No.125, London, HMSO.

Heidensohn, F. (1986) 'Models of justice: Portia or Persephone?', *International Journal of the Sociology of Law*, vol.14, no.3–4, pp.287–98.

Home Office (1990a) *Crime, Justice and Protecting the Public* (White Paper), Cm 965, London, HMSO.

Home Office (1990b) *National Prison Survey,* London, HMSO.

Home Office (1992) *The Costs of Criminal Justice*, London, HMSO.

Home Office (1995) *Criminal Statistics: England and Wales*, London, HMSO.

Hood, R. (1992) *Race and Sentencing,* Oxford, Clarendon.

Jefferson, T. (1993) 'The racism of criminalisation: police and the reproduction of the criminal other', in Gelsthorpe, L. ( ed.) *Minority Ethnic Groups in the Criminal Justice System*, Cropwood Conference Series, No.21, University of Cambridge, Institute of Criminology.

Jefferson, T., Walker, M. and Seneviratne, M. (1992) 'Ethnic minorities: crime and criminal justice: a study in a provincial city', in Downes, D. (ed.) *Unravelling Criminal Justice*, London, Macmillan.

Kant, I. (1796–97) *Rechtslere*, (trans. T.M. Knox, 1942, as *Philosophy of Right*, Oxford, Oxford University Press).

Kapardis, A. and Farrington, D. (1981) 'An experimental study of sentencing by magistrates', *Law and Human Behaviour*, 5, pp.107–21.

Kennedy, H. (1992) *Eve Was Framed: Women and British Justice*, London, Chatto and Windus.

King, M. (1981) *The Framework of Criminal Justice*, London, Croom Helm.

Kingdom, E. (1981) 'Sexist bias and law', in *Politics and Power vol.3: Sexual Politics, Feminism and Socialism*, London, Routledge and Kegan Paul.

Law Society (1992) *Evidence of the Law Society to the Royal Commission on Criminal Justice*, London, Law Society.

Liberty (1992) *Unequal Before the Law*, London, Liberty.

Lidstone, K., Hogg, R. and Sutcliffe, F. (1980) *Prosecution by Private Individuals and Non-Police Agencies*, London, HMSO.

MacKinnon, C. (1987) *Feminism Unmodified*, Cambridge, MA, Harvard University Press.

Mair, G. (1986) 'Ethnic minorities, police and magistrates' courts', *British Journal of Criminology*, vol.26, no.2, pp.147–55.

Mair, G. and Brockington, N. (1988) 'Female offenders and the probation service', *Howard Journal of Criminal Justice*, vol.27, no.2, pp.117–26.

Marshall, T. (1985) *Alternatives to Criminal Courts*, Aldershot, Gower.

Maxwell, G. and Morris, A. (1993) *Family, Victims and Culture: Youth Justice in New Zealand*, Social Policy Agency and Institute of Criminology, Victoria University of Wellington.

McBarnet, D. (1981) *Conviction*, London, Macmillan.

McCabe, S. and Purves, R. (1972) *The Jury At Work*, Oxford University Penal Research Unit Occasional Paper 3, Oxford, Blackwell.

McConville, M. and Baldwin, J. (1982) 'The influence of race on sentencing in England', *Criminal Law Review*, vol.29, pp.652–8.

McCrudden, C., Smith, D. and Brown, C. (1991) *Racial Justice at Work: The Enforcement of the 1976 Race Relations Act in Employment*, London, Policy Studies Institute.

McLaughlin, E. and Muncie, J. (1994) 'Managing the criminal justice system', in Clarke, J., Cochrane, A. and McLaughlin, E. (eds) *Managing Social Policy*, London, Sage.

Merton, R. (1968) *Social Theory and Social Structure*, New York, The Free Press. (First published in 1949.)

Messerschmidt, J. (1986) *Capitalism, Patriarchy, and Crime: Toward a Socialist Feminist Criminology*, Totowa, NJ, Rowman and Littlefield.

Mill, J.S. (1859) *On Liberty*, London, Parker.

Modood, T. (1994) *Racial Equality: Colour, Culture and Justice*, London, Institute for Public Policy Research, Commission on Social Justice.

Moxon, D. (1988) *Sentencing Practice in the Crown Court*, Home Office Research Study No.103, London, HMSO.

Moxon, D., Sutton, M. and Hedderman, C. (1990) *Unit Fines – Experiments in Four Courts*, Home Office Research and Planning Unit Paper No.59, London, HMSO.

**Muncie, J., McLaughlin, E. and Langan, M. (eds) (1996) *Criminological Perspectives: A Reader*, London, Sage in association with The Open University.**

Nozick, R. (1974) *Anarchy, State and Utopia*, New York, Basic Books.

Packer, H. (1969) *The Limits of the Criminal Sanction*, Stanford, CA, Stanford University Press.

Padfield, N. (1995) *Text and Materials on the Criminal Justice Process*, London, Butterworth.

Parker, H., Sumner, M. and Jarvis, G. (1989) *Unmasking The Magistrates*, Milton Keynes, Open University Press.

Pearson, R. (1976) 'Women defendants in magistrates' courts', *British Journal of Law and Society*, 3, pp.265–73.

Pease, K. (1980) 'Community service and prison: are they alternatives?', in Pease, K. and McWilliams, W. (eds) *Community Service By Order*, Edinburgh, Scottish Academic Press.

Pease, K. and Wasik, M. (1987) *Sentencing Reform: Guidance Or Guidelines?* Manchester, Manchester University Press.

Probation Inspectorate (1991) *Report on Women Offenders and Probation Service Provision*, London, Home Office.

Quinney, R. (1974) *Critique of Legal Order*, Boston, MA, Little, Brown and Co.

Rawls, J. (1971) *A Theory of Justice,* Cambridge, MA, The Belknap Press of Harvard University Press.

Reiner, R. (1993) 'Race, crime and justice: models of interpretation', in Gelsthorpe, L. (ed.) *Minority Ethnic Groups in the Criminal Justice System*, Cropwood Conference Series, No.21, University of Cambridge, Institute of Criminology.

Rex, S. (1992) 'Unit Fines – twenty questions', in Ashworth, A. *et al.* (eds) (1992).

Roshier, B. and Teff, H. (1980) *Law and Society in England*, London, Tavistock.

Royal Commission on Criminal Justice (1993) *Report,* Cm 2263, London, HMSO.

Rozenberg, J. (1994) *The Search For Justice*, London, Hodder and Stoughton.

Sanders, A. (1985) 'Class bias in prosecutions', *Howard Journal of Criminal Justice*, 24, pp.176–99.

Schluter, M. (1994) 'What is relational justice?', in Burnside, J. and Baker, N. (eds) *Relational Justice: Repairing the Breach*, Winchester, Waterside.

Scull, A. (1977) *Decarceration: Community Treatment and the Deviant – A Radical View*, Englewood Cliffs, NJ, Prentice Hall.

Sealy, A. and Cornish, W. (1973) 'Jurors and their verdicts', *Modern Law Review*, 36, pp.496–508.

Shallice, A. and Gordon, P. (1990) *Black People, White Justice? Race and the Criminal Justice System*, London, Runnymede Trust.

**Smart, C. (1990) 'Feminist approaches to criminology or postmodern woman meets atavistic man', in Morris, A. and Gelsthorpe, L. (eds) *Feminist Perspectives in Criminology*, Milton Keynes, Open University Press. (Extract reprinted in Muncie *et al.*, 1996).**

Thomas, D. (1979) *Principles of Sentencing* (second edn), London, Heinemann.

Thompson, E.P. (1975) *Whigs and Hunters*, London, Allen Lane.

Tittle, C., Villemez, W. and Smith, D. (1978) 'The myth of social class and criminality', *American Sociological Review*, 43, pp.643–56.

Tuck, M. (1991) 'Community and the criminal justice system', *Policy Studies*, vol.12, no.3 pp.22–37.

Vennard, J. (1985) 'The outcome of contested trials', in Moxon, D. (ed.) *Managing Criminal Justice*, London, HMSO.

Vennard, J. and Riley, D. (1988) 'The use of peremptory challenge and stand by jurors and their relationship to trial outcome', *Criminal Law Review*, pp.731–8.

Voakes, R. and Fowler, Q. (1989) *Sentencing, Race and Social Enquiry Reports*, West Yorkshire Probation Service.

**von Hirsch, A. (1976) 'Giving criminals their just deserts', *Civil Liberties Review*, no.3, pp.23–35. (Extract reprinted in Muncie *et al.*, 1996.)**

von Hirsch, A. and Ashworth, A. (1992) *Principled Sentencing*, Boston, MA, Northeastern University Press.

Walker, M. (1989) 'The court disposal and remands of White, Afro-Caribbean and Asian Men (London 1983)', *British Journal of Criminology*, vol.29, no.4, pp.353–67.

Walker, N. (1981) 'Feminists' extravaganzas', *Criminal Law Review*, pp.379–86.

Weber, M. (1954) *On Law in Economy and Society* (trans. E. Shils and M. Rheinstein), Cambridge, MA, Harvard University Press.

Whitehouse, P. (1983) 'Race, bias and social enquiry reports', *Probation Journal*, vol.30, no.2, pp.30–2, 43–9.

Wilczynski, A. (1991) 'Images of women who kill their infants: the mad and the bad', *Women and Criminal Justice*, 2, pp.71–88.

Wilczynski, A. and Morris, A. (1993) 'Parents who kill their children', *Criminal Law Review*, pp.31-6.

Worrall, A. (1990) *Offending Women: Female Law Breakers and the Criminal Justice System*, London, Routledge.

Zander, M. (1989) *A Matter of Justice: The Legal System in Ferment*, Oxford, Oxford University Press.

Zander, M. and Henderson, P.F. (1993) *The Crown Court Study*, Royal Commission on Criminal Justice Study No.19, London, HMSO.

# Chapter 4
# Prison Histories: Reform, Repression and Rehabilitation

*by John Muncie*

## Contents

# 1  Introduction

*T*his chapter traces the origins and development of the prison in British society. The discussion is restricted, in the main, to three key moments of transformation and their associated discursive rationales: namely, the *reform* of prisons and prisoners towards the end of the eighteenth century; the *repressive* practices of the mid nineteenth century; and, at the beginning of the twentieth century, the emergence of notions of prisoner *rehabilitation*. Prior to this, we provide some idea of the scale and role of incarceration in feudal or pre-capitalist societies. Throughout, it is our intention to recall, and account for, the shifting role of, and claims made for, the imposition of imprisonment.

It is important to note from the outset that there is no *one* history of prisons and imprisonment. Whilst legislative and organizational landmarks can be placed quite accurately, the role and purpose of the prison is the subject of dispute and controversy. Following the lead taken in Chapter 1 (on the history of the police), throughout this chapter *competing* histories of penal transformation will be presented and analysed. Broadly speaking, a basic distinction between Whig histories and revisionist histories will be drawn upon in order to illustrate the issue of historical interpretation. For example, until the 1970s historians relied more or less solely on documentary material that frequently provided only one side of the historical story. Characteristically, interest was focused on the reforming zeal of powerful and/or key individuals. History was thus usually constructed 'from above', with little or no attention paid to the voices of those on the receiving end of penal practices and policy. It was not until after 1970 that more detached historical approaches were formulated. Recent oral histories and criminal biographies have attempted to open up the area, and the work of revisionist historians, such as **Foucault (1977)**, Ignatieff (1978) and Garland (1985), marked a radical departure from those traditional Whig accounts of penal reform which have tended to celebrate reform as progress or improvement. In short, revisionism was intent on retelling the story of reform in the context of economic interests, power relations and the diversification and strengthening of state power. Reform was analysed not so much as benevolent progress, but as a more insidious extension of structures of centralized power and control. However, by the late 1980s the limitations of such a polarized debate came increasingly to be recognized by many sociologists and historians alike, such that an integration of the two positions has been proposed (for example, Garland, 1990; Weiner, 1990). Nevertheless, the distinction remains important in alerting us to the issue of historical interpretation and serves as a fruitful starting-point for any student of penal reform.

The key point to stress about historical research is that, contrary to superficial impressions, it is neither atheoretical nor untainted by ideological and political concerns. As Thomas remarks: 'History is a profoundly political subject and the way in which it is written deeply affects our perception of the present' (Thomas, 1988, p.2). Similarly, Pisciotta concludes that: 'historians would be more honest in their search for "truth" if they wrestled with their own assumptions and made them explicit in their writings' (Pisciotta, 1981, pp.122–3). The unveiling of assumptions and the demystification of rhetoric in social history research are two of the key issues addressed by this chapter.

# 2 Gaols and houses of correction

Before beginning any exploration into the origins of the prison we would be well advised to heed Harding *et al*.'s (1985) warning that the task is doomed to failure if we look specifically for a precise statutory enactment. As they remark, some form of detention becomes necessary as soon as disputes are settled in any but the most brutal fashion.

The holding of defendants prior to trial was probably the earliest use of imprisonment. According to Pugh (1968), in England this practice dates from the ninth century. At that time, the use of custody pending trial was reserved for the foreigner or for those who could not stand their own surety. Some of the gaols in which they were held were purpose-built (such as the Tower and the Fleet), but the majority were within existing castles or walled towns. Their use was rare and haphazard. An early attempt to establish a gaol in every English county was made by Henry II in 1166, and by the thirteenth century the first national network of prisons – the county gaols – was in place. Pugh argues that, in medieval England, imprisonment came to serve three main purposes:

1   Custodial – to provide for the custody of those awaiting trial or execution of sentence.

2   Coercive – to provide for the coercion of fine defaulters, debtors and those contemptuous of the court.

3   Punitive – as a punishment in its own right.

This three-fold conceptual distinction clearly remains pertinent today. However, the main purposes of the medieval prison were custodial and coercive. Fox argues that the penal law of Europe at the time was dominated by the 'idea of the illegality of imprisonment as a punishment' (Fox, 1952, p.20). Imprisonment was not considered a proper punishment. The primary role of the prison was to detain rather than punish. A majority of inmates were indeed incarcerated for failure to pay fines and released only when such civil debt was met: it would thus be the poor who were the more likely to be subjected to such detention. As we will see, the punitive function of gaols – custody as punishment – whilst present in medieval society and on the increase from the thirteenth century, did not attain prominence until the late eighteenth century.

The county gaols of the thirteenth century were supplemented by 'franchise' and 'municipal' prisons, privately owned by local lords or ecclesiastics. It is likely that most private courts had access to a private prison. Although standing in conflict with the wish of successive monarchs to centralize justice, such prisons survived until the end of the eighteenth century. They differed in vital respects from their modern counterparts in that they were small, of widely different design and were not always intended to be used solely as prisons. Their population was also generally small – each holding about 30 inmates at any one time. They were almost exclusively commercial undertakings: gaolers charged prisoners for accommodation, food and all other services (including the hammering on and the knocking off of leg-irons!). Prisoners were also hired out to local contractors. Thomas (1988, p.9) argues that these privatized, commercial and profit-making activities remained a part of penal organization until centralization in 1878 (only to re-emerge in the 1990s: see Chapter 5). Fortunately for the poor prisoner, the practice of alms-giving was regarded as a Christian duty, especially in Catholic England. Without such relief, survival in, or release from, prison would have been impossible for many.

A prison sentence for those without resources was virtually a death sentence. Unsanitary conditions, risk of disease and starvation were forever present. Prison conditions were generally regarded as deplorable, despite attempts to ensure regular inspections and to discipline prison staff who broke regulations. Above all, imprisonment in medieval society, whether imposed for custodial, coercive or punitive reasons, was largely retributive and deterrent. Expense, exposure to disease and bodily hardship were viewed as necessary corollaries of imprisonment. The success of a prison was measured not by the reform of offenders, but by its ability 'quite simply to prevent escapes; to hold suspects until the courts required them; to hold debtors until they paid up; and those under punishment until the sentence of the court expired' (McConville, 1981, p.5). To this end, the use of irons and stocks (being cheaper than the provision of secure buildings) was widespread.

During the fifteenth and sixteenth centuries the use of imprisonment, whatever its purpose, was to decline. Until then the death penalty and mutilation had been used only in extreme cases to supplement fines and imprisonment; now they were to become the most common measures. Draconian penal codes were developed throughout Europe to combat a perceived increase in crime from vagrants, 'vagabonds', beggars, robbers and the unemployed. Clearly, such groups were considered to pose a threat, not only in criminal terms, but as a danger to the social order. Execution, banishment, mutilation, branding and flogging became commonplace public spectacles. Practically every crime was punishable by death; judicial discretion remained only in deciding the manner in which death should be inflicted.

Towards the end of the sixteenth century, however, methods of punishment began to undergo a gradual change. The possibility of exploiting the labour of prisoners now received increasing attention. Galley slavery, transportation to the colonies and penal servitude with hard labour were introduced. By the middle of the seventeenth century transportation to America (and subsequently to Australia in the eighteenth century) became one of the principal ways of dealing with petty, serious and political offenders alike. Those escaping such measures found themselves facing a new philosophy of imprisonment in the county gaols and in houses of correction.

Houses of correction combined the principles of individual reformation and punishment. The key rationale behind their establishment was the counteraction of idleness (Spierenburg, 1991, p.12): their aim was to make the labour power of unwilling people socially useful. By being forced to work, it was hoped that prisoners would form industrious habits to facilitate their return to the labour market. It was through these means, outside the

correction · penal system, that the function of correction was to be introduced into penal philosophy. Initially, such institutions were created for the specific purpose of ridding the towns of beggars and vagrants. The earliest house of correction was probably the Bridewell in London, established in 1555. England thus led the way in the development of houses of correction, but it reached its peak in Holland at the end of the century. The reasons for this appear to lie in the fact that, at the time, Holland was the most developed capitalist society in Europe, but it did not have the reserve of labour power that existed in

England after the breakdown of the manorial system and the onset of the first enclosure movement. In Holland, therefore, such innovations in reducing production costs and drawing on all available labour reserves were enthusiastically welcomed.

This use of imprisonment for 'reformatory' purposes was a radical departure from existing practice, where custodial and coercive principles were paramount. As a result, Mannheim (1939) and McConville (1981) both cite the house of correction as the first example of modern imprisonment: a point underlined by Spierenburg's (1991) preference to call such institutions 'prison workhouses'. The usual inmates were able-bodied beggars, vagrants, prostitutes and thieves. However, as the reputation of the institutions became established, more serious offenders, as well as the poor, the needy and spendthrift dependants, were interned. Their labour power was utilized either for the economic advantage of the institution itself or for the benefit of external private employers. Men were usually engaged in rasping hardwoods to be used by dyers (the Rasp Huis first introduced in Amsterdam) and women prepared textiles. This example was studied and followed throughout Europe, particularly in the Hôpitaux Généraux in France and the Spinnhaus in Germany. The function of the houses of correction was, however, not only to enforce the discipline of labour, but also to encourage religious observance. Reformation was couched as much in moral as in economic terms.

Austin van der Slice (1937) attributes the rise of the houses of correction to the increasing numbers of 'vagabonds' and vagrants resulting from changes in land tenure and enclosure. He argues that their use was progressive in that they provided a more humane alternative to the county gaols and offered the possibility of reformation rather than simply detention. Rusche and Kirchheimer (1939), however, provide a rather different interpretation of their function. They argue that, far from being motivated by humanitarianism, the establishment of houses of correction reflected a growing demand for a regulated and disciplined labour force in the days of emerging agrarian capitalist and mercantile societies. In reviewing changes in forms of punishment from the late Middle Ages to the 1930s, they contend that:

> transformation in penal systems cannot be explained only from changing needs of the war against crime. Every system of production tends to discover punishments which correspond to its productive relationships ... the origin and fate of penal systems ... are determined by social forces, above all by economic and then fiscal forces.

(Rusche and Kirchheimer, 1939, p.5)

The rationale for the houses of correction, it is argued, lies in the fact that they were primarily factories turning out commodities at a particularly low cost due to their cheap labour. Their use burgeoned in Holland because the relative labour shortage in the general population, as mentioned earlier, coincided with the development of mercantilism. In short, to secure the development of an emerging capitalism, the labour of prisoners was to be exploited. Thus, in summary, the thesis put forward by Rusche and Kirchheimer proposes that the shift from prisons as places of custody to places of punishment and labour exploitation was based on economic rather than humanitarian motives: the principal objective was not the reformation of inmates, as argued by van der Slice, but the rational exploitation of their labour power.

Whilst, in theory, there remained a distinction between houses of correction (institutions for sentenced thieves, pickpockets and the like) and the workhouse (institutions for the detention of beggars and vagrants), Rusche and Kirchheimer contend that it was the conditions of the local labour market which frequently determined whether this separation actually took place. Valuable, able-bodied workers tended to be confined in the houses of correction for as long as possible, their term of confinement arbitrarily fixed by the houses' administrators:

> Of all the forces which were responsible for the new emphasis upon imprisonment as a punishment, the most important was the profit motive, both in the narrower sense of making the establishment pay and in the wider sense of making the whole penal system a part of the state's mercantilist program.

> (Rusche and Kirchheimer, 1939, p.67)

Despite the often-reported 'successes' of the system, the houses of correction had lost much of their distinctive identity by the end of the seventeenth century. In function and administration they largely became merged with the gaols. In the growing puritan moral climate of Stuart social policy, the able-bodied poor and minor offenders were increasingly treated as criminals, and their separation presented fewer and fewer conceptual problems for penal administration (McConville, 1981, p.46). Thus, by the eighteenth century, the prison had returned to its traditional roles of custody and coercion: that is, detaining the accused before trial and enforcing the payment of fines. Within a criminal justice system that extended the use of the death penalty to an ever-increasing range of offences, the prison and prison conditions were rarely a focus for attention. However squalid, disease-ridden, dangerous and expensive prisons were for their inmates, such conditions were tolerated because the primary response of policy-makers was to maintain the coercive function of imprisonment. Even by the end of the eighteenth century half of the average daily prison population comprised debtors (Morgan, 1977).

Penal reformer John Howard's description of prison regimes and prison conditions in the 1770s is indicative of the state of prisons at that time, as Extract 4.1 makes clear. As you will see, graphic descriptions, such as Howard's, provided part of the impetus for fundamental reform of the prison system in the late eighteenth century. Through these reforms, it is widely assumed, the modern prison was to emerge.

What were the main functions of the medieval prison?

Why have the houses of correction been described as the forerunners of modern systems of imprisonment?

In what ways can the houses of correction be viewed as both reformative and humanitarian (van der Slice) and punitive and exploitative (Rusche and Kirchheimer)?

## Extract 4.1  Howard: 'Distress in prisons'

There are prisons, into which whoever looks will, at first sight of the people confined, be convinced, that there is some great error in the management of them: their sallow meagre countenances declare, without words, that they are very miserable. Many who went in healthy, are in a few months changed to emaciated dejected objects. Some are seen pining under diseases, 'sick, and in prison'; expiring on the floors, in loathsome cells, of pestilential fevers, and the confluent smallpox; victims, I must not say to the cruelty, but I will say to the inattention, of sheriffs, and gentlemen in the commission of the peace.

The cause of this distress is, that many prisons are scantily supplied, and some almost totally destitute of the necessaries of life.

There are several bridewells (to begin with them) in which prisoners have no allowance of food at all. In some, the keeper farms what little is allowed them: and where he engages to supply each prisoner with one or two pennyworth of bread a day, I have known this shrunk to half, sometimes less than half the quantity, cut or broken from his own loaf.

It will perhaps be asked, does not their work maintain them? for every one knows that those offenders are committed to hard labour. The answer to that question, though true, will hardly be believed. There are few bridewells in which any work is done, or can be done. The prisoners have neither tools, nor materials of any kind: but spend their time in sloth, profaneness and debauchery, to a degree which, in some of those houses that I have seen, is extremely shocking.

Some keepers of these houses, who have represented to the magistrates the wants of their prisoners, and desired for them necessary food, have been silenced with these inconsiderate words, Let them work or starve. When those gentlemen know the former is impossible, do they not by that thoughtless sentence, inevitably doom poor creatures to the latter? …

Many prisons have no water. This defect is frequent in bridewells, and town gaols. In the felons' courts of some county gaols there is no water: in some places where there is water, prisoners are always locked up within doors, and have no more than the keeper or his servants think fit to bring them: in one place they were limited to three pints a day each: a scanty provision for drink and cleanliness!

And as to air, which is no less necessary than either of the two preceding articles, and given us by Providence quite gratis, without any care or labour of our own; yet, as if the bounteous goodness of Heaven excited our envy, methods are contrived to rob prisoners of this genuine cordial of life, as Dr. Hales very properly calls it: I mean by preventing that circulation and change of the salutiferous fluid, without which animals cannot live and thrive. It is well known that air which has performed its office in the lungs, is feculent and noxious. Writers upon the subject show, that a hogshead of air will last a man only an hour: but those who do not choose to consult philosophers; may judge from a notorious fact. In 1756, at Calcutta in Bengal, out of a hundred and seventy persons who were confined in a hole there one night, a hundred and fifty-four were taken out dead. The few survivors ascribed the mortality to their want of fresh air, and called the place Hell in miniature.

(Howard, 1929, pp.1, 3–4, originally published in 1777)

# **3**  Penal reform and the penitentiary

The bare bones of penal reform in the late eighteenth century are uncontroversial. Throughout much of the eighteenth century, prison conditions were such that there was no segregation of men from women, no classification of offenders, and no separation of the tried from the untried. The sale of alcohol to prisoners was freely permitted. Extortion by prison staff went unchecked. Prisons, as Howard (1929) recorded, were characterized by lack of light, air, sanitation, washing facilities and general cleanliness. Diseases, such as typhus, were rife. Many prisons were run as enterprises for private profit: tables of fees were drawn up, according to which the 'keeper' or 'gaoler' would provide such items as bedding, food and alcohol. Following his inspections, Howard recommended that secure, sanitary and cellular accommodation be provided; that prisoners be separated and classified according to offence; that useful labour be introduced; and the sale of liquor be prohibited. As a result, an Act of Parliament in 1784 provided for the establishment of separate cells in all new prisons, but was generally ignored – the principle of state management was virulently disputed (Forsythe, 1989). In 1774 the Discharged Prisoners Act had allowed for the payment of the fees of prisoners who were acquitted at their trials, and the Health of Prisoners Act required prisons to be ventilated, regularly cleaned and provided with baths and medical facilities; the use of underground cells (dungeons) was prohibited. In 1779 the Penitentiary Act detailed proposals for the building and management of two 'ideal penitentiary houses'. This initiative, which marked central government's first direct involvement in prison administration, was made not simply as a result of widespread dissatisfaction with existing forms of punishment, but because the American War of Independence of 1776 had left the government with nowhere to send those sentenced to transportation. With the loss of the American colonies, transportation had ceased in the same year and prisoners were housed instead on prison ships, known as hulks, and employed on public works, such as dredging rivers.

Influenced by the work of Howard, the Penitentiary Act promoted a new view of the purpose of imprisonment. The prisons proposed by the Act were to have both a punitive and a reformative function. The term 'penitentiary' was significant in its implication that prisoners were to undergo a process of expiation and penance. They were to be put to work 'of the hardest and most servile kind, in which drudgery is chiefly required ... such as treading in a wheel ... sawing stone, rasping logwood, chopping rags' (quoted in Harding *et al.*, 1985, p.117). Prisoners were also to be classified into groups within a reward/punishment hierarchy. Profits from work would pay for prison staff, uniforms were to be issued and prison governors appointed. From 1811, it became increasingly assumed that only the state was competent enough to prevent neglect and cruelty and to create reformatory systems of prison discipline (Forsythe, 1989). Because of the emphasis on hard (though unproductive) labour, the prison was envisaged not only as a morally and physically healthy place, but also as a positive means to reform the offender.

From 1785 there was a spate of local prison Acts which empowered local communities to build new prisons. Gloucester penitentiary was opened in 1789, 'a spacious and handsome' prison was opened in Manchester in 1790 and another at Ipswich in 1792 (Thomas, 1988, p.153). In 1816 the first

penitentiary

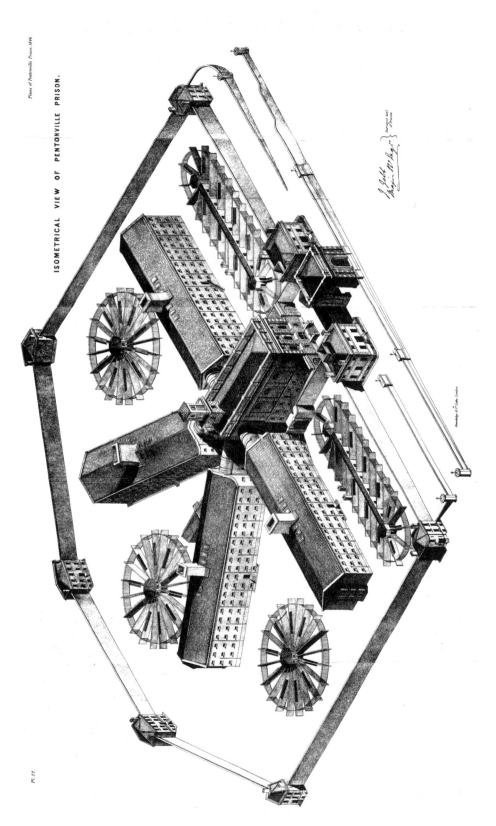

*Isometrical view of
Pentonville prison, 1844*

*national* penitentiary at Millbank was opened and with it the 'separate' system of solitary confinement was introduced. Meanwhile, the discovery and colonization of Australia resulted in – indeed, was founded upon – the restarting of transportation. However, by the late 1830s the Australian governments had become extremely reluctant to accept any more convicts and over the next 20 years central government in England was forced to build or reopen several new prisons, notably Pentonville in which convicts were to be subjected to a term of penal servitude; Dartmoor, which had originally served as a prison for French and American prisoners of war; Parkhurst, designed specifically for juveniles; and Brixton, the first purpose-built prison for women. The initial response of the early Victorians to their 'unwanted' populations was, it seems, the building of institutions for their confinement. By 1853 transportation had been abolished for the great majority of the criminally convicted.

The 1823 Gaol Act was the first comprehensive statement of principle from central government to be applied to local prisons and attempted to impose uniformity in penal practice at the same time as imposing Howard's recommendations for health requirements, abolition of the sale and the use of alcohol and the promotion of regular prison inspections. In 1835 government inspectors were introduced to visit prisons and report to the Secretary of State. Pentonville penitentiary was finally opened in London in 1842 and its regime of silence and solitude quickly became a model for prison architecture and discipline, not only in England, but throughout Europe. This was the culmination of over 60 years of attempts to devise a totally rational and reformative mode of imprisonment.

These legislative and institutional landmarks of prison reform are easy to establish. The precise reasons *why* such developments occurred, however, and with what effects, remain the subject of considerable debate. Cohen (1985) argues that, at the end of the eighteenth century, a major

**penal transformation**

transformation in modes of penal and social control was inaugurated, of which the emergence of the modern prison was but one reflection. By the mid nineteenth century a number of key shifts had taken place: from an arbitrary and decentralized state involvement in penal practice to a rationalized and centralized state-organized system; from little or no differentiation between deviant groups to their increasing classification and categorization into separate groups, each with their own particular problems and requiring specialized forms of intervention from accredited professionals or experts; from forms of punishment aimed at the 'body' (physical pain) to forms of punishment aimed at the 'mind' (isolation, penitence); and from a punitive rationale of neo-classicist general deterrence to one of neo-positivist individual reformation. Within these processes the prison emerged as 'the dominant instrument for changing undesirable behaviour and as the favoured form of punishment' (Cohen, 1985, p.13).

## ACTIVITY 4.1

Spend some time now studying the correctional changes listed by Cohen in Table 4.1. Note in particular his argument that, from the end of the eighteenth century, the prison emerges as a key site in which the principles of *centralization, rationalization, classification, professional dominance* and a *state monopoly over control* came to be realized. Make some notes of your own, summarizing the nature of these shifts.

| | | Phase one (pre-eighteenth century) | Phase two (from the nineteenth century) |
|---|---|---|---|
| Table 4.1 | Changes in deviancy control | | |
| 1 | State involvement | Weak, decentralized, arbitrary | Strong, centralized, rationalized |
| 2 | Place of control | 'Open': community, primary institutions | Closed, segregated institution: victory of the asylum, 'Great Incarcerations' |
| 3 | Focus of control | Undifferentiated | Concentrated |
| 4 | Visibility of control | Public, 'spectacular' | Boundaries clear, but invisible inside – 'discreet' |
| 5 | Categorization and differentiation of deviance | Hardly developed at all | Established and strengthened |
| 6 | Hegemony of law and criminal justice system | Not yet established; criminal law only one form of control | Monopoly of criminal justice system established, but then supplemented by new systems |
| 7 | Professional dominance | Not at all present | Established and strengthened |
| 8 | Object of intervention | External behaviour: 'body' | Internal states: 'mind' |
| 9 | Theories of punishment | Moralistic, traditional, then classical, 'just deserts' | Influenced by positivism and treatment ideal: 'neo-positivist' |
| 10 | Mode of control | Inclusive | Exclusive and stigmatizing |

Source: Cohen, 1985, pp.16–17, from Table 1

The remainder of section 3 will be devoted to examining competing theories and explanations of late eighteenth-century penal reform. Did the penitentiary symbolize the re-emergence of humanitarian ideals or did it trigger a more insidious and total regulation of 'deviant' populations? Did reform stem from the 'enlightened vision' of philanthropists or from the changing social and political needs of an emerging industrial capitalist economy? Or was it always a matter of the (often coincidental?) convergence of any number of determining factors? You will be invited to reflect on these issues through an analysis of competing explanations of this major correctional change.

## 3.1 The Whig tradition: humanitarian histories

The Whig tradition of historical research is characterized by Cohen (1985, p.18) as promoting an idealist view of history in which change occurs through advances in knowledge. The ideals and visions of key individuals are seen as providing the motor for social change. All change constitutes reform and is motivated by benevolence, altruism, philanthropy and humanitarianism. In addition, the accumulation of successive changes reveals an underlying progress in penal reform: the refinement of legislation indicates success.

humanitarianism

Writers in this tradition have dominated the field of social history research until quite recently. Historians have characteristically portrayed the origins, development and impact of prisons as humanitarian innovations that replaced more repressive forms of social control. As Pisciotta argues: 'writers in this tradition are readily identifiable because of their tendency to lionize the founders of the system and selectively emphasize their successes' (Pisciotta, 1981, p.111).

The principal starting-point in the study of the reform of the penal codes of Europe in the eighteenth century is usually taken to be the publication in 1764 of Cesare Beccaria's *On Crimes and Punishments* (**Beccaria, 1963**). This contained a wholesale condemnation of the use of the death penalty and its tendency to corrupt people rather than to prevent crime. Located within an emergent classicist and utilitarian philosophy, Beccaria argued that punishment should be predictable, rational and proportionate to the offence. In Britain such ideals were promoted by William Eden in his work *Principles of Penal Law*, published in 1771, but reached their most practical application in the utilitarian philosopher Jeremy Bentham's 1778 plan for a prison that he called the Panopticon. This architectural design would enable the constant surveillance of all prisoners from a central point while inmates were prevented from knowing when they were being watched. The prison was to be financed solely by the prisoners' labour and the best measurement of their reformation was to be the quantity of work they performed. This accorded with the principle of classicism that people behave in a rational fashion according to their calculation of the likely benefits or pains involved in their chosen course of action. Bentham's scheme was initially welcomed and certainly influenced later penitentiary designs, but, in consideration of questions of expense and commercialism, it was eventually to be abandoned in its pure form by the Holford Committee of 1810.

**panopticon**

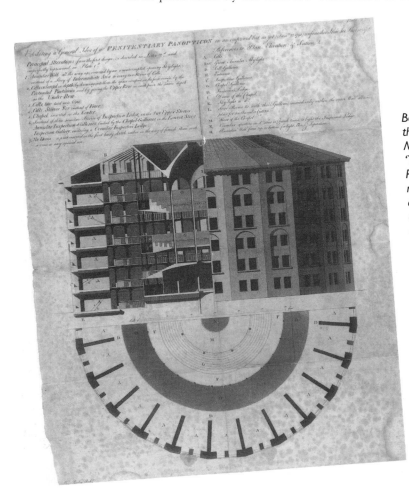

Bentham's design for a reformed prison: the Panopticon, 1791. As described in Melossi and Pavarini (1981, p.40): 'The formal principle upon which the Panopticon is based consisted of two multi-floored coaxial cylindrical containers, each having opposing and complementary functions: the circular crowns in correspondence to the floors of the outer cylinder, were placed between six radials in cellular units completely opened out towards the central space and lit by the outer perimeter; this section was allotted to those to be controlled. The inner coaxial cylinder, concealed by thin, opaque partitions placed along the length of the perimeter was for the warders — very few, it was specified — who, without any chance of being seen, could have exercised tight and constant control at every point of the outer cylinder by means of well placed peep-holes; nothing could have escaped their scrutiny'

Other figures who loom large in these traditional accounts are John Howard and Elizabeth Fry – not so much for their adherence to a classicist philosophy but because of their 'philanthropic vision'. As we have seen, philanthropy – the provision of practical benevolence – has a long history in alleviating the suffering of the poor and the incarcerated, dating back at least to the thirteenth-century Catholic practice of alms-giving.

*John Howard, 1726–1790*

Howard's own personal history lies in that of the wealthy country gentry. In 1775 he was appointed high sheriff for Bedfordshire, and from that time began to catalogue the conditions inside prisons and the abuses of power that the penal system appeared to encourage. In subsequent years he embarked on numerous self-financed travels in Britain and throughout Europe to witness and record prison conditions first-hand. His self-defined purpose was to 'attempt the relief of the miserable'. In this he was undoubtedly influenced by his own religious and spiritual enthusiasm: he 'confronted the horrors of the prison system as an angel of divine will grappling with evil' (Open University, 1987, p.52). Howard's work commanded attention not only for the shocking revelations it offered, but also for the novel conceptions of prison regimes that he developed on his travels. He was highly influential in designing an entirely new regime of punishment that eventually was given practical expression with the erection of the penitentiary. Howard believed that prisons should be quiet and clean, and based on a strict routine of prayer and work, and that prisoners should be excluded from the rest of society, uniformed, treated impersonally and

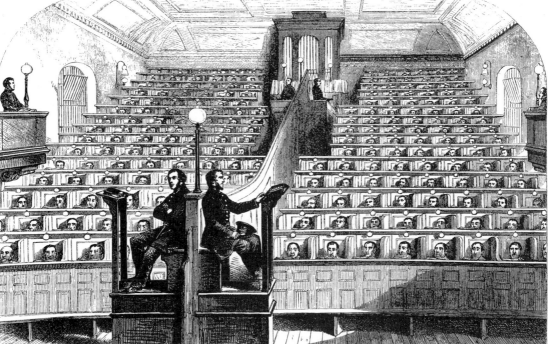

*The chapel at Pentonville where prisoners were screened from each other to prevent contact, c.1840*

segregated into classes in order to avoid moral contamination of the novice by the experienced offender. He did not question the right to punish, but was concerned that such punishment should not degenerate into cruelty, abuse and injustice. Above all, as Harding *et al.* record:

> Howard gave the developing bourgeoisie a perfect hero. He stressed the bourgeois values of authoritarianism, self reliance, frugality, the rejection of luxury and an obsession with inquiry and measurement and through his quasi-saintly character, he gave these values a rightness and a righteousness … for the bourgeoisie, the corrupt prison was a symbol of the corrupt nature of the old ruling class, and Howard a symbol of a new, caring, frugal, disciplined society of the bourgeois.

(Harding *et al.*, 1985, p.113)

However, by the time of his death in 1790, few of Howard's recommendations for penal reform had been implemented. Two Acts of Parliament had been passed as a result of his work – abolishing gaolers' fees and improving prison conditions – but even by the early nineteenth century little improvement in prisons had been achieved.

Elizabeth Fry was another English philanthropist who, like Howard, became involved in issues of penal reform. Born to a Quaker family in 1780,

she first visited Newgate Gaol in London in 1813 in order to distribute clothing, where she found conditions little changed from Howard's day. Though domestic matters prevented her from returning to Newgate for a further three years, from 1817 onwards she devoted herself to improving the moral and physical welfare of the women prisoners by tackling overcrowding (she had found, for example, that 300 women and their children had to share just two rooms and two cells in which they stayed night and day, in appalling conditions of 'riot, licentiousness and filth'), providing education and ensuring the segregation of the women and children from the men.

In 1817 Fry, together with other women who under her leadership had also become interested in the provision of education in Newgate, established the Association for the Improvement of the Female Prisoners in Newgate. This was the first of many Ladies' Societies for Promoting the Reformation of Female Prisoners to be formed, initially in other parts of England from 1821, subsequently in Scotland in

*Elizabeth Fry, 1780–1845*

1828 and in Ireland in 1834. These Societies gradually drew public attention to the plight of women in prison. Their general aim was to:

> provide for the clothing, the instructions and the employment of these females, to introduce them to a knowledge of the holy scriptures and to form in them … those habits of order, sobriety and industry which may render them docile and peaceable whilst in prison, and respectable when they leave it.

(quoted in Dobash *et al.*, 1986, p.44)

As a result, a new daily routine for women was initiated in which Bible classes and employment (needlework, knitting) were central. Begging, swearing and gambling were prohibited, behaviour was monitored by orderlies and any infractions reported to an appointed matron. The approach was one of simultaneously improving conditions and promoting moral reform through a combination of discipline and compassion. Above all, as

*Female convicts at work during the silent hour, Brixton prison, c.1850*

Zedner records, Elizabeth Fry's 'insistence on the need for individualisation became widely accepted as the most distinctive feature of the treatment of women' (Zedner, 1991, p.120). Indeed, the work of the Ladies' Societies was widely credited with improving not only conditions at Newgate and elsewhere, but also the 'manner and habits' of female prisoners, and with preventing recidivism.

The impact of people like Howard and Fry on penal reform has been lauded by many historians (for example, Gibson, 1971; Ramsay, 1977; Krebs, 1978; Radzinowicz, 1978) and their names are constantly evoked in any standard textbook on prison histories (for example, Fox, 1952; McConville, 1981; Harding *et al.*, 1985; Radzinowicz and Hood, 1990). As a consequence, the impression given is that the work of enlightened individuals was paramount in promoting the view that prisons were positive institutions and humane alternatives to the death penalty, corporal punishment and transportation. The tendency, as Cohen (1985, p.18) argues, is to view individual vision as the principal motor for change from a system of barbarity to one of humanitarianism.

## ACTIVITY 4.2

To consolidate your study so far, consider the following questions:

1  What are the key characteristics of a Whig interpretation of history?
2  Was humanitarianism the only principle underlying penal reform?

Making notes on your reponses will help you to compare the Whig interpretation of history with that of the revisionists, which is discussed in section 3.2 below.

Some recent historians have argued that the humanitarianism of the late eighteenth century was more rhetoric than reality. Good intentions are seen as capable of being frustrated and overturned by subsequent events. Cohen (1985, p.19) characterizes such analysis as disillusioned liberalism. In Rothman's (1971) account of the asylum and penitentiary institutions in Jacksonian America, for example, we are warned that the harbingers of benevolence must themselves be distrusted:

disillusioned liberalism

> the most popular historiographical response to the invention of the asylum is to call it a 'reform' but the volumes that follow this tradition do not ask why the society adopted this particular measure, rather than another. By describing the innovation as a reform, they assume that the asylum was an inevitable and sure step in the progress of humanity. Ostensibly it was an obvious improvement not only over existing conditions but over *other possible alternatives*. But such perspective is bad logic and bad history. There was nothing inevitable about the asylum form, no self-evident reason why philanthropists should have chosen it ... By what standard is it an improvement to relieve the poor within almshouses rather than in their own homes? By what criterion is a penitentiary an improvement over the stocks or a system of fines and whippings?

> (Rothman, 1971, pp.xiv–xv)

In this way Rothman questions the taken-for-granted meanings of reform, progress and philanthropy. Within the proliferation of institutions for the insane, the poor and the criminal, he witnesses not the dawning of a new humanitarianism, but an 'emphasis on authority, obedience and regularity turning all too predictably into a mechanical application of discipline. And by incarcerating the deviant and dependent and defending the step with hyperbolic rhetoric, they discouraged – really eliminated – the search for other solutions that might have been less susceptible to abuse' (Rothman, 1971, p.295).

Similarly, commenting on the development of prisons for women, Dobash *et al.* (1986) and Zedner (1991) note that Fry's faith in a policy of 'kind superintendence' was not universally shared. Opponents stressed that conditions should be deliberately made worse than those experienced outside; that prison should be made a hard and unpleasant place. With the creation of the penitentiaries (Millbank and Pentonville in London, Perth in Scotland) and the introduction of the 'separate system', the imposition of uniform regimes for men and women alike meant that Fry's vision of a network of reformative institutions for women was never realized. By the mid nineteenth century, women *were* separated from men in most prisons and women warders were appointed, but 'impersonal and more abstract approaches increasingly gained acceptance along with an emphasis on humiliation, degradation, human accounting, hard useful labour and religious exhortation' (Dobash *et al.*, 1986, p.61). Moreover, given their smaller numbers (a fifth of those convicted), the imprisonment of women frequently remained an afterthought to be fitted into a system designed for men with 'least effort and expense, with the result that they often suffered much worse conditions than men convicted of similar offences' (Zedner, 1991, p.136). Likewise, Dobash *et al.* conclude that, whilst regimes became similar, 'patriarchal and paternalist conceptions played a crucial role' such that the surveillance and regulation of women was 'always closer and more omnipresent than that usually directed at men' (Dobash *et al.*, 1986, p.61).

These latter accounts thus note how reformist ideals and attempts to humanize the prison were either barely implemented or were diluted by opposing political interests or unintended consequences. The paradoxes of humanitarian reform are such that improvements in conditions are set against increases in regimented control; that the desire to 'rescue' individuals rests uneasily against concurrent demands to establish the prison as punishment; and that the implementation of reform is far more complex than that implied by terms such as 'progress', 'benevolence' and 'philanthropy'.

## 3.2 The radical tradition: revisionist histories

The radical tradition within prison history research offers a different interpretation of that history and challenges almost every detail of Whig historiographies. Radical historians have contended that the prison and other correctional institutions were repressive forms of social control, born out of class conflict and designed to protect the vested interests of a wealthy and governing class. Below, we consider two variants of this radical tradition: first, that of an 'orthodox Marxism', which has argued that systems of punishment are manipulated by the powerful in order to maintain a cheap and reliable supply of labour; and, second, that of a more complex and critical persuasion, which places more emphasis on ideological, political and legal transformations in the process of re-establishing order on a new foundation. Both diverge from Rothman's (1971) stance by insisting that the new punitive element in penal regimes did not represent a *failure* of reform, but actually succeeded in its unstated purpose of establishing acceptance of the 'need' for 'disciplinary regimes' in all walks of life.

orthodox Marxism

### ACTIVITY 4.3

You should now read Extract 4.2 where Rusche and Kirchheimer evaluate the social and penal consequences of the Industrial Revolution for prison labour. As you do so, consider the following questions:

1    What in their view was the driving force behind penal reform?
2    How and why did the role of prison labour change?

## Extract 4.2   Rusche and Kirchheimer: 'Prison labour'

We have seen that the houses of correction used to spur the inmates to greater industry by paying them according to their work or by giving them a share of the profits. They were punished only if they failed to perform their task, whether from lack of skill or from laziness [Riedel, 1750, pp.78–9]. Now that it no longer paid to employ prisoners, however, they were frequently left with nothing to do. This raised the whole problem of the purpose of imprisonment, and brought its repressive, deterrent side to the fore. The way was open for the realization of the programs of reformers like Pearson and Mittelstädt, who sought to make the prisons rational and efficient means of deterring the lower classes from crime, means which would not allow the convict to perish, but which would impress him once and for all by fear and terror. England, with its large industrial reserve army, led the way. Work was introduced as a form of punishment, not as a source of profit, and moral arguments were brought forward as a justification. One experienced administrator explained in 1821 that work which was to produce profit would interfere with discipline and moral improvement, because, for purposes of manufacture, the taskmaster would seek to assemble prisoners who would otherwise not be permitted to associate with each other [Webb and Webb, 1922, p.85, quoting Holford].

Prison labor became a method of torture, and the authorities were expert enough in inventing new forms; occupations of a purely punitive character were made as fatiguing as possible and were dragged out for unbearable lengths of time [Koch, 1928, p.389]. Prisoners carried huge stones from one place to another and then back again, they worked pumps from which the water flowed back to its source, or trod mills which did no useful work. A simple form of treadwheel, easily applicable to all prisons, was devised by William Cubitt about 1818 for use in the Suffolk County Gaol at Bury, and it was from this example that the practice spread. The cheapness and simplicity of the 'stepping-mill' or 'everlasting staircase,' as it was called, the severe physical exertion required, and the hatred engendered by 'wheel-stepping' commended the new device to Quarter Sessions, and models were set up in every reformed prison, grinding corn or grinding nothing, raising water, supplying power for hemp-beating, cork-cutting, or other machines [Webb and Webb, 1922, p.97]. Not only was the treadwheel regarded as a success because it afforded a cheap and easy method of forcing prisoners to work, but also because it deterred persons who might use the gaol as a place of ultimate refuge [Webb and Webb, 1922, pp.98–9].

### References

Koch, C. (1928) 'Der soziale Gedanke im Strafvollzug', in Bummke, E. *Deutsches Gefängniswesen*, Berlin.

Riedel, A.C. (1750) *Beschreibung des im Fürstentum Bayreuth zu Sanct Georgen am See errichteten Zucht- und Arbeits-Hauses*, Bayreuth.

Webb, S. and Webb, B. (1922) *English Prisons under Local Government*, London.

(Rusche and Kirchheimer, 1939, p.112)

## COMMENT

Following their analysis of the house of correction, Rusche and Kirchheimer contend that the driving force for reform lay not in humanitarian principles, but in the economic necessities of the time. They argue that the shift from corporal and capital punishment to systems of incarceration was rendered necessary by the underlying aim of capitalism to socialize production and create a submissive and regulated workforce. The modern prison, it is argued, was designed to contain working-class unrest, teach habits of discipline and order, and return the criminal and deviant to the marketplace. The prison was rationalization    a part of a larger **rationalization** of social relations in nascent capitalism.

Within this development, although humanitarianism loomed large in its justificatory rhetoric, it had little or no place in practice. Prison conditions remained deplorable, and the new regimes of prison labour (for example, the use of the treadmill) were meaningless, degrading and unproductive. The new prison was intent not on teaching particular skills, but on inculcating the *disciplined* routine of work. As mentioned in section 2, Rusche and Kirchheimer's thesis maintains that there is a *direct relationship* between forms of punishment and wider labour-market conditions. So, for example, the origins of forced labour in the houses of correction lie in population decline and subsequent shortages of labour in the seventeenth century. Over-population in the eighteenth century coincided and combined with the emergence of industrial capitalism to create 'a roaming, landless, depressed class, competing for employment' (Piven and Cloward, 1972, p.33), together with the need for a compliant and disciplined labour force. The house of correction was the institutional result of the substitution of outdoor relief, as in poor law, by confinement and forced labour. The aim of the prison was to teach the discipline of labour and to make the poor accept any conditions imposed on them by an employer (Piven and Cloward, 1972, p.33).

*The treadmill at Brixton prison, 1821*

Conditions in all institutions, from the workhouse to the prison, had to be made worse than the life of even the poorest of free workers. As a result, prisons developed as systems of intensified punishment epitomized by unproductive hard labour. They formed one part of a wider strategy to impose ubiquitous control and regulation. A modern reading of this orthodox Marxist position makes much the same point:

> The bourgeoisie state assigns to all of them [segregated institutions] a directing role in the various moments of the formation, production and reproduction of the factory proletariat: for society they are essential instruments of social control, the aim of which is to secure for capital a workforce which by virtue of its moral attitude, physical health, intellectual capacity, orderliness, discipline, obedience, etc., will readily adapt to the whole regime of factory life and produce the maximum possible of surplus labour.

(Melossi, 1981, p.42)

According to this thesis, during the Industrial Revolution the rationale for imprisonment changed from being economic – and indirectly rehabilitative – to something more punitive and repressive. The creation of a reserve army of unemployed people throughout Europe made prison labour less of a sought-after commodity and the prison became more a means of inflicting control and intimidation. It is in these terms that Rusche and Kirchheimer (1939) talk of a decline and decay in prisons: as the rationale for prison in the old mercantilist social regime was to provide cheap forced labour, it became obsolete in the days of high unemployment and pauperism that accompanied the Industrial Revolution.

However, commentators on this Marxist theorization have criticized it for its reductionist and essentialist stance: that is, for developing in advance a one-dimensional theory of penal relations and then imposing this upon history. Indeed, it is notable that Rusche and Kirchheimer's analysis of penal institutions and labour-market conditions appears applicable to the mercantilist period of the sixteenth and seventeenth centuries, but in their consideration of the rise of capitalism, the primacy of the economic gives way to the significance of a bourgeois *ideology* of deterrence. The changing role of prison labour in itself suggests that a major transformation occurred in penal purpose in the late eighteenth century, and that histories of productive penal labour and deterrent labour are analytically separate and discontinuous. In other words, the correlation between imprisonment and production conditions is imposed by theory rather than explained empirically. Similarly, it can be argued that prisons were a logical concomitant of prevailing political philosophy rather than *consciously* devised as a tool to develop and sustain the social relations of capitalism. If the penal system is to be understood as a fundamentally ideological and political apparatus within capitalism, then any relationship it has with labour-market conditions cannot be posed as direct, unaffected by the superstructure in which it is located. As Hogg concludes: 'an analysis which postulates some *a priori* relationship between imprisonment and the capitalist mode of production relieves itself of the necessity to look at the contradictions, the discontinuities, the whole process of change in its specificity' (Hogg, 1979, p.69).

Similarly, Garland's review of Rusche and Kirchheimer's work finds that:

> As might be expected when such a single-minded interpretation is imposed upon a broad historical canvas, historians have been quick to show the many points at which the thesis needs to be qualified in the light of more detailed evidence … Historians of the house of correction have argued that although commercial motives played a part … few of them could in fact sustain any financial benefits … [Similarly] the building of penitentiaries and model prisons was often a massive financial expenditure undertaken with little prospect of reimbursement … prisoners' labour and its profitability was frequently subordinated to other considerations such as prison discipline, general deterrence or individual reformation.

(Garland, 1990, pp.106–7)

It was the task of refining the Rusche and Kirchheimer thesis (whilst acknowledging the whole new vista of understanding that it opened up) that was subsequently taken up by such writers as Michael Ignatieff (1978) in his attempt to realize the full complexity and contradictory nature of late eighteenth-century reform.

As Cohen (1985, p.23) notes, Ignatieff's history rejects 'economic determinism' and 'Marxist functionalism'. Instead, he developed a revisionist position which set out to explore what he refers to as the 'complex and autonomous structure of religious and philosophical beliefs' that informed the reformist vision of the penitentiary. In this respect he pays more attention to the stated intentions and complex motives of reformers. For Ignatieff, the new prison was not born from a functional necessity of the economic system, but from reformers' fears for social order, their political self-interest *and* their religious beliefs. Philanthropy, then, played a key role, but was mediated through the emergence of new sets of class relations brought about by the establishment of industrial capitalism. In Ignatieff's account the new control system succeeded because it convinced the offender and the rest of society of its humanity and justness, and was central to establishing the full legitimacy of the law and the legitimacy of the new class relations that it supported.

*revisionism*

His analysis of the development of the penitentiary dwells not on its purported new humanism, but on its role in replacing punishment of the body (for example, flogging) with punishment directed at the mind (such as solitary confinement). These new types of pain – the treadmill, the crank, the straitjacket, the solitude – represented not so much a failure of reform, but a success. To view reform as a cycle of good intentions (like Howard's) subsequently overturned by unintended consequences (as in Rothman's analysis), misses its wider ideological and symbolic functions and its ultimate success in 're-establishing order on a new foundation'. Thus while the penitentiary was continually criticized during the early nineteenth century for its functional shortcomings, it continued to 'command support because it was seen as an element of a larger vision of order that by the 1840s commanded the reflexive assent of the propertied and powerful' (Ignatieff, 1978, p.210).

Ignatieff explores the different strands that helped to form the 'ideology' of the new prison. In particular, he reveals how close parallels are drawn between the language of disease and the language of punishment. Reform was multifaceted: improving physical conditions, but also improving moral habits, instigating the ethos of discipline and founding a new social stability by popular consent. As Figure 4.1 reveals, the offences of prisoners were as much moral as legal in nature. In an increasingly unequal and divided society, the new prison was one means of providing an image of humanity whilst simultaneously fortifying consent 'without compromising security'. In conclusion, Ignatieff contends that lauding the process of reform obscures its function as a 'legitimation for an intensification of carceral power' (Ignatieff, 1978, p.212); humanitarianism was inextricably linked to the practice of domination and the establishment of disciplinary regimes throughout the social order.

*disciplinary regimes*

This approach is also shared by Foucault in his book *Discipline and Punish* (1977). However, Foucault differs from Ignatieff in his concentration not only on the materialist connection between prison and industrial capitalism, but also on the power of ideas, knowledge and discourses. Foucault is less concerned with exploring the origins of the prison *per se* and more with identifying a continuous disciplinary discourse (without giving privileged attention to any one source) that informed and was thoroughly intertwined with all forms of social control in the late eighteenth century. Thus the reform of prisoners, education of children, confinement of the insane and supervision of industrial workers all form part of an emerging

Figure 4.1 Crime in the early nineteenth century: a moral and legal problem. Prisoners confined at the Bridewell at Abingdon at the Easter Sessions, 4 April 1826

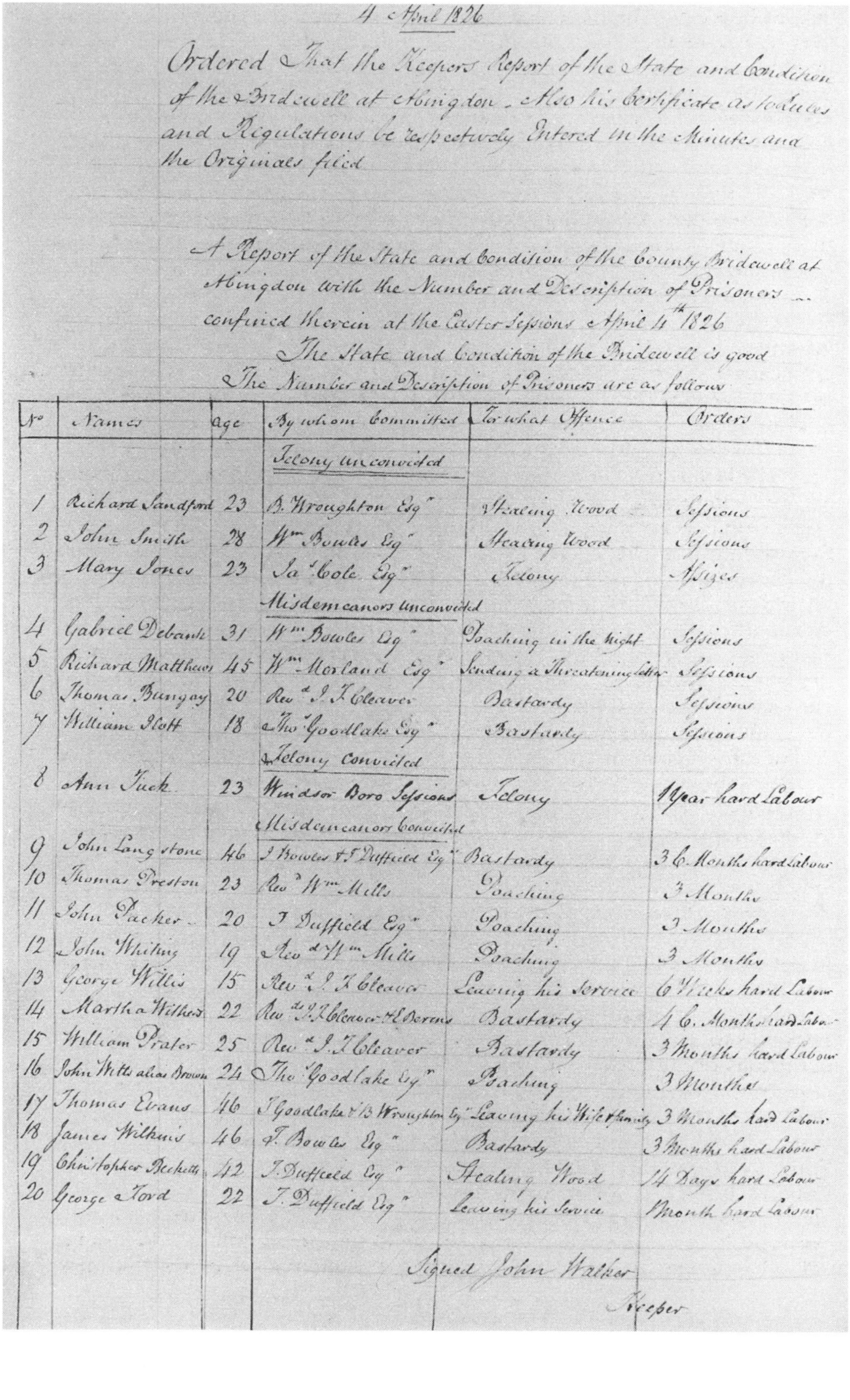

4 April 1826

Ordered That the Keepers Report of the State and Condition of the Bridewell at Abingdon. Also his Certificate as to Rules and Regulations be respectively Entered in the Minutes and the Originals filed

A Report of the State and Condition of the County Bridewell at Abingdon with the Number and Description of Prisoners confined therein at the Easter Sessions April 4th 1826

The State and Condition of the Bridewell is good

The Number and Description of Prisoners are as follows

| No | Names | age | By whom Committed | For what Offence | Orders |
|---|---|---|---|---|---|
| | | | Felony unconvicted | | |
| 1 | Richard Sandford | 23 | B. Wroughton Esqr | Stealing Wood | Sessions |
| 2 | John Smith | 28 | Wm Bowles Esqr | Stealing Wood | Sessions |
| 3 | Mary Jones | 23 | Jas Cole Esqr | Felony | Assizes |
| | | | Misdemeanors unconvicted | | |
| 4 | Gabriel Debank | 31 | Wm Bowles Esqr | Poaching in the Night | Sessions |
| 5 | Richard Matthews | 45 | Wm Morland Esqr | Sending a Threatening letter | Sessions |
| 6 | Thomas Bungay | 20 | Revd J. F. Cleaver | Bastardy | Sessions |
| 7 | William Ilott | 18 | Thos Goodlake Esqr | Bastardy | Sessions |
| | | | Felony Convicted | | |
| 8 | Ann Tuck | 23 | Windsor Boro Sessions | Felony | 1 Year hard Labour |
| | | | Misdemeanors Convicted | | |
| 9 | John Langstone | 46 | J Bowles & T Duffield Esqr | Bastardy | 3 C. Months hard Labour |
| 10 | Thomas Preston | 23 | Revd Wm Mills | Poaching | 3 Months |
| 11 | John Packer | 20 | T. Duffield Esqr | Poaching | 3 Months |
| 12 | John Whiting | 19 | Revd Wm Mills | Poaching | 3 Months |
| 13 | George Willis | 15 | Revd J. F. Cleaver | Leaving his Service | 6 Weeks hard Labour |
| 14 | Martha Wilkins | 22 | Revd J. F. Cleaver & E Berens | Bastardy | 4 C. Months hard Labour |
| 15 | William Prater | 25 | Revd J. F. Cleaver | Bastardy | 3 Months hard Labour |
| 16 | John Wills alias Brown | 24 | Thos Goodlake Esqr | Poaching | 3 Months |
| 17 | Thomas Evans | 46 | T Goodlake & B Wroughton Esqr | Leaving his Wife & family | 3 Months hard Labour |
| 18 | James Wilkins | 46 | T. Bowles Esqr | Bastardy | 3 Months hard Labour |
| 19 | Christopher Beckett | 42 | T. Duffield Esqr | Stealing Wood | 14 Days hard Labour |
| 20 | George Ford | 22 | T. Duffield Esqr | Leaving his Service | 1 Month hard Labour |

Signed John Walker

Keeper

'carceral society' The discourse is powerful enough ultimately to affect our very vision of the world: it enters the 'human soul'. All social relations become relations of domination. The power of the prison, then, is less explicable in terms of penal philosophy than it is in a 'power of normalization' that operates in such non-penal institutions as the school, the hospital and the factory. Power emanates not just from the state, or indeed from any particular institutions, but from *forms of knowledge* that inform all social relations at all levels in the social hierarchy. The emergence of prison is but one reflection of the diffusion of new forms of knowledge, grounded in the human sciences, which surfaced in the eighteenth century (for a discussion of Foucauldian analysis see, for example, Smart, 1989; Garland, 1990, Chapters 6 and 7). The aim is to produce a new kind of 'individual subjected to habits, rules, orders, an authority that is exercised continually around him and upon him, and which he must allow to function automatically in him' (**Foucault, 1977, pp.128–9**). Foucault's investigation of the prison in the early nineteenth century thus becomes a means of exploring the wider theme of how domination is achieved and how individuals are socially constructed in the modern world.

The key to Foucault's thesis is that, because the prison has always been a failure – in reducing crime and in preventing recidivism – the question of its continuing existence has to be addressed in different ways. He argues that the prison is useful in a strategy of political domination because it works to divorce crime from politics, enhances fear and divides the labouring classes against themselves: 'The prison does not control the criminal, so much as control the working class by creating the criminal' (Garland, 1990, p.150). The prison is retained because of its failures rather than in spite of them. In this process, the prison stands at one end of a continuum in which regulation and surveillance become normalized throughout the social body. Indeed, Foucault coins the phrase 'carceral archipelago' to describe the chain of institutions that stretches out from the prison, conjuring up images of a totalitarianism not usually ascribed to Western liberal democracies. Foucault's work remains influential because it allows a greater sensitivity to the nuances of the disciplinary and normalizing aspects of the penal system in the context of wider issues of power, knowledge and governance (Open University, 1992; Foucault, 1977).

Nevertheless, Foucauldian analysis in particular, and revisionist histories in general, have been taken to task for oversimplifying complex socio-historical processes. For example, Forsythe (1991, p.241) argues that a concentration on the social control aspects of reform tends to deny the genuine (rather than merely rhetorical) aspirations and achievements of the reformers to improve the lot of prisoners and to ameliorate the more barbaric conditions of imprisonment. Delacy's (1986) study of prisons in Lancashire reveals that the process of rationalization was not uniformly adopted throughout the country. In particular, she questions whether the 'separate system' did in fact operate in many prisons outside London, thus casting doubt both on Foucault's vision of a universal 'carceral archipelago' and Cohen's mapping of a general penal transformation (as in Table 4.1). Similarly, Spierenburg (1991) is sceptical of the idea that the modern prison dramatically emerged in a moment of rapid transformation in and around 1800. He prefers to see a more protracted evolution in which old and new

carceral society

practices co-existed for much of the period from 1770 to 1870. Ignatieff (1983), in a review of his earlier work, also acknowledges that the process of reform is never one-dimensional and cannot always be explained in terms of a disciplinary logic. Revisionism, he argues, was flawed by adopting a position which described all social relations in the language of domination and subordination. The challenge remains to:

> find a model of historical explanation which accounts for institutional change without imputing conspiratorial rationality to a ruling class, without reducing institutional development to a formless, ad hoc adjustment to contingent crisis and without assuming a hyper-idealist, all triumphant humanitarian crusade ... the problem is to develop a model that avoids these while actually providing explanation.

> (Ignatieff, 1983, pp.77–8)

Garland (1990) makes much the same point by arguing that the *specific* agencies, apparatuses, rules, procedures, strategies, rhetorics and representations that make up the penal complex each have their own *specific* histories and *specific* effects. Any broad theoretical model, whether Whiggish or revisionist, will tend to lose sight of such nuances through the application of predetermined structuring patterns:

> In the shaping of any penal event ... a large number of conflicting forces are at work. Broad ideological ambitions may run up against immediate financial constraints, political expediency may conflict with established sensibilities, the perceived requirements of security may differ from those of morality, the professional interests of one group may be in tension with those of another, and the pursuit of any one value will generally involve the violation of several others. These swarming circumstances are only ever resolved into particular outcomes by means of the struggles, negotiations, actions and decisions which are undertaken by those involved in the making and the implementation of policy, and can only be traced by detailed historical work. There is no settled hierarchy of purposes or causal priorities which prevails at every point allowing us to describe, once and for all, the sequence of forces and considerations which 'determine' the specific forms which penality displays ... Theory should be a set of interpretative tools for guiding and analysing empirical enquiry – not a substitute for it.

> (Garland, 1990, pp.285–6)

revision of
revisionism

In this form of analysis (sometimes referred to as a 'revision of revisionism') the insights of such theorists as Foucault, Rusche and Kirkhheimer are drawn on selectively as resources, rather than adopted wholesale. However, we can still assume that the process of historical interpretation can never simply rely on eclecticism. Some informed choices need to be made if we are to construct any integrated and meaningful picture of the trajectory of penal reform.

## ACTIVITY 4.4

Given opposite are six statements from various analysts of penal reform. You should be able to locate each of these in either a 'Whig', 'disillusioned liberal', 'orthodox Marxist' or 'revisionist' interpretation of the purpose of imprisonment in the late eighteenth and early nineteenth centuries.

### STATEMENT 1

Howard's work and abiding influence were not limited to the ascertainment and exposure of evil: he proposed remedies and influenced others to work for them ... he wished to bring back the forgotten notion that Houses of Correction should correct. Prisons should be sanitary and secure, moral improvement should be sought through the influence of religion and prisoners should be provided with useful work. [Through] the personal prestige of Howard with Parliament a well intentioned group of Acts was passed in which most of these ideas were embodied.

### STATEMENT 2

In the Victorian philanthropic tradition, prisoners were not the only ones whose right to be treated as human beings was made conditional on their submission to moral improvement. No attempt to raise the housing, educational, or sanitary standard of the poor was made without an accompanying attempt to colonize their minds. In this tradition, humanitarianism was inextricably linked to the practice of domination. The extension of the state's obligation to its citizens was invariably justified in terms of recasting their characters into that caricature of ascetic rectitude that the rich adopted as their self-image.

### STATEMENT 3

If there is an overall political issue around the prison, it is not whether it is to be corrective or not; whether the judges, the psychiatrists or the sociologists are to exercise more power in it than the administrators or supervisors; it is not even whether we should have prison or something other than prison. At present, the problem lies rather in the steep rise in the use of these mechanisms of normalization and the wide-ranging powers which, through the proliferation of new disciplines, they bring with them.

### STATEMENT 4

The luminaries who invented liberty also invented discipline.

### STATEMENT 5

The disciplinary moment of the work relation coincides with the institutional moment, that is with the entrance of the employee into the factory, namely into the place where the employer forcibly organizes the factors of production. It is the same in punitive relations: the condemned (free subject) becomes subordinated subject (prisoner) on entering the penitentiary ... For the worker the factory is like a prison (loss of liberty and subordination); for the inmate the prison is like a factory (work and discipline).

### STATEMENT 6

Proposals that promise the most grandiose consequences often legitimate the most unsatisfactory developments. One also grows wary about taking reform programs at face value; arrangements designed for the best of motives may have disastrous results. But the difficult problem is to review these events without falling into a deep cynicism.

## COMMENT

[Statement 1 is from Fox (1952); 2 from Ignatieff (1983); 3 and 4 from Foucault (1977); 5 from Melossi and Pavarini (1981) and 6 from Rothman (1971)].

The contrast between Whig and revisionist histories should now be clear. Of key importance is that, despite their internal differences, 'revisionist' histories stand against their 'Whig' counterparts in their argument that:

- The motives of philanthropic reformers were more complicated than a simple desire to 'do good' and to improve the conditions of imprisonment – they also, for example, were a reflection of religious zeal, Calvinist discipline and fear of the labouring poor.

- We should place the emergence of the prison in the social and historical context of the time.

- The emergence of the prison is related to the emergence of similar institutions of the same period.

- We need to move beyond stated intentions and reformist visions to theories that take cognizance of power, class relations and the state.

- Reform was a 'success' in terms of establishing a new social order functional to the requirements of industrial capital.

# 4  From reform to repression

During the nineteenth century the penal system was to undergo major reforms, but the rhetoric of prisoner reformation was to collapse. The death penalty diminished in importance as an imposed penalty, the use of corporal punishment declined, public whipping was abolished in 1862, transportation was abolished in 1868 and by the 1870s the prison was established as the normal punishment for both trivial and serious offences. For most of the century, prisons were controlled by local authorities, with subsequent wide variations in regimes, costs and conditions. The movement towards central government control of the whole prison system can be traced back to the early nineteenth century, and in particular to the appointment of inspectors

centralization   in 1835, but full centralization and nationalization did not occur until the passing of the Prison Act in 1877. The control of the prisons was then passed to a Prison Commission, whose main objective was to introduce a uniform and rational regime throughout the country, based firmly on the principle of deterrence by severity of punishment rigidly and efficiently applied. The most infrequently used prisons were closed down and those remaining were refurbished to conform to prescribed standards of architectural and sanitary design. Prison warders were appointed, trained and paid by central government, issued with uniforms and subject to disciplinary procedures. The general regime of local prisons was based on the 'separate system' in which prisoners worked, ate and slept in their cells, removed from any contact with their fellow inmates. Although different architectural designs were used, most prisons conformed to that of the cellular prison buildings in which each prisoner was held in a separate cell with standard dimensions and minimal furnishings, thus ensuring ease of surveillance and control. Prison work remained generally non-productive and of a harsh nature, designed to enforce obedience and discipline rather than to teach any particular industrial skills.

These developments, at one and the same time, marked a further rationalization of the prison system, and a shift in its justificatory rhetoric from one of prisoner reformation to one of deterrence and repression. As the prison evolved as the dominant form of punishment, the already existing debates between reformers and punishers, and between religious and secular approaches, focused on the specific form that prison discipline should take. Paramount was the felt need for *certainty* and *uniformity* in punishment. Discretion and individualization were successively removed from the system. As Weiner argues: 'power was now generally seen as most legitimate and most effective when least personal, most humane when least human' (Weiner, 1990, p.105). As a result, the prison became a highly regulated and impersonal instrument to contain and control. For example, a notice on the cell walls at Leicester County Gaol in the 1850s stated that the purpose of prison labour was to 'encourage habits of willing and steady industry and a cheerful obedience' (*Report of the Commissioners*, 1854, p.iv). The governor of Leicester Gaol was the first to use the crank for overtly punitive purposes, declaring that: 'if a man will not work, neither shall he eat' (*Report of the Commissioners*, 1854, p.v). The imposition of a regime of 1,800 revolutions of the crank before breakfast, 4,500 before dinner, 5,400 before supper and 2,700 after supper, clearly reflected the Victorian obsession with systematic regulation and classification. Throughout the penal system uniformity was imposed on all elements of prison life: in clothing, discipline, work and architectural design as well as in diet.

repression

*Penal servitude: a prisoner at the 'crank' in Surrey House of Correction, c.1860. As described by Hawkings (1992, p.24): 'Together with the treadmill the crank was used for prisoners sentenced to hard labour. It had the additional advantage from the prison authorities viewpoint that the prisoner was shut up in his cell. The crank was made up of a narrow iron drum mounted horizontally in a frame with a handle on one side which, when turned, caused a series of cups or scoops in the interior to revolve. At the lower part of the inside was a thick layer of sand or gravel which the cups scooped up and carried to the top of the wheel where they emptied themselves rather like a dredging machine. A dial plate fixed in front of the crank showed how many revolutions the machine had made. A man could make about 20 revolutions in a*

*minute moving a weight of up to 12 lbs per revolution, that is 1200 revolutions per hour. It was usual to stipulate that a prisoner completed 10,000 turns per day which would take him about 8 hours and 20 minutes. Some prisoners were able to turn the crank much faster than others and to retard their efforts the gaoler could turn a screw which tightened the mechanism and rendered the crank more difficult, and therefore slower, to rotate. Hence gaolers became known as "screws"'*

## DIETARIES.

The following are the amended Dietaries ordered at the Somerset Epiphany Session. 1850.

### Class 1.

Convicted Prisoners confined for any Term not exceeding Seven Days.

| Males. | | Females. | |
|---|---|---|---|
| Breakfast—Oatmeal Gruel | 1 pint. | Oatmeal Gruel | 1 pint. |
| Dinner——Bread | 1 lb. | Bread | 1 lb. |
| Supper——Oatmeal Gruel | 1 pint. | Oatmeal Gruel | 1 pint. |

### Class 2.

Convicted Prisoners for any Term exceeding Seven Days and not exceeding Twenty-one Days.

| Males. | | Females. | |
|---|---|---|---|
| Breakfast—Oatmeal Gruel | 1 pint. | Oatmeal Gruel | 1 pint. |
| „ Bread | 6 oz. | Bread | 6 oz. |
| Dinner——Bread | 12 oz. | Bread | 6 oz. |
| Supper——Oatmeal Gruel | 1 pint. | Oatmeal Gruel | 1 pint |
| „ Bread | 6 oz. | Bread | 6 oz. |

*Prisoners of this class employed at hard labour, to have, in addition, 1 pint of soup per week.*

### Class 3.

Convicted Prisoners employed at hard labour for Terms exceeding Twenty-one Days, but not more than Six Weeks; and convicted Prisoners not employed at hard labour for Terms exceeding Twenty-one days but not more than Four Months.

| Males. | | Females. | |
|---|---|---|---|
| Breakfast—Oatmeal Gruel | 1 pint. | Oatmeal Gruel | 1 pint. |
| „ Bread | 6 oz. | Bread | 6 oz. |
| SUNDAY AND THURSDAY. | | | |
| Dinner——Soup | 1 pint. | Soup | 1 pint. |
| „ Bread | 8 oz. | Bread | 6 oz. |
| TUESDAY AND SATURDAY. | | | |
| „ Cooked Meat without Bone | 3 oz. | Cooked Meat without Bone | 3 oz. |
| „ Bread | 8 oz. | Bread | 6 oz. |
| „ Potatoes | ½ lb. | Potatoes | ½ lb. |
| MONDAY, WEDNESDAY, AND FRIDAY. | | | |
| „ Bread | 8 oz. | Bread | 6 oz. |
| „ Potatoes | 1 lb. | Potatoes | 1 lb. |
| Supper——Same as Breakfast | | Same as Breakfast | |

### Class 4.

Convicted Prisoners employed at hard labour for Terms exceeding Six Weeks but not more than Four Months; and convicted Prisoners not employed at hard labour for Terms exceeding Four Months.

| Males. | | Females. | |
|---|---|---|---|
| Breakfast—Oatmeal Gruel | 1 pint. | Oatmeal Gruel | 1 pint. |
| „ Bread | 8 oz. | Bread | 6 oz. |
| SUNDAY, TUESDAY, THURSDAY, AND SATURDAY. | | | |
| Dinner——Cooked Meat without Bone | 3 oz. | Cooked Meat without Bone | 3 oz. |
| „ Potatoes | ½ lb. | Potatoes | ½ lb. |
| „ Bread | 8 oz. | Bread | 6 oz. |
| MONDAY, WEDNESDAY, AND FRIDAY. | | | |
| „ Soup | 1 pint. | Soup | 1 pint. |
| „ Bread | 8 oz. | Bread | 6 oz. |
| Supper——Same as Breakfast | | Same as Breakfast | |

*The Victorian obsession with classification: prison diet ordered at Somerset Quarter Sessions, 1850*

In such an environment, notions of reformation (through strict moral education) were collapsed into notions of deterrence: 'That pain was required for reformation was rarely questioned ... whether they inclined to stress deterrence or reformation, almost all early and mid-Victorians thought the latter should be as painful as the former' (Weiner, 1990, p.111). As the Earl of Chichester, appointed to superintend Pentonville, put it in 1856:

> Human nature is so constituted that when a man had been long addicted to a life of crime or sensual indulgence it requires a severe affliction to force him to reflect – he must be providentially deprived of those sources of animal pleasure and excitement which have hitherto enabled him to silence his conscience and to shut out from his mind all thoughts of the future – there must be something external to afflict, to break down his spirit, some bodily suffering or distress of mind, before the still small voice will be heard and the man brought to himself.

> (Earl of Chichester, quoted in Ignatieff, 1978, p.199)

## Class 5.

Convicted Prisoners employed at hard labour for Terms exceeding Four Months.

Males.      Females.

### SUNDAY, TUESDAY, THURSDAY, AND SATURDAY.

| Males | | Females | |
|---|---|---|---|
| Breakfast—Oatmeal Gruel | 1 pint. | Oatmeal Gruel | 1 pint. |
| „ Bread | 8 oz. | Bread | 6 oz. |
| Dinner——Cooked Meat without Bone | 4 oz. | Cooked Meat without Bone | 3 oz. |
| „ Potatoes | 1 lb. | Potatoes | ½ lb. |
| „ Bread | 6 oz. | Bread | 6 oz. |

### MONDAY, WEDNESDAY, AND FRIDAY.

| Males | | Females | |
|---|---|---|---|
| Breakfast—Cocoa | 1 pint. | Cocoa | 1 pint. |
| made of ¾ oz. of Flaked Cocoa or Cocoa Nibs, sweetened with ¾ oz. of Molasses or Sugar | | made of ¾ oz. of Flaked Cocoa or Cocoa Nibs, sweetened with ¾ oz. of Molasses or Sugar | |
| „ Bread | 8 oz. | Bread | 6 oz. |
| Dinner——Soup | 1 pint. | Soup | 1 pint. |
| „ Potatoes | 1 lb. | Potatoes | ½ lb. |
| „ Bread | 6 oz. | Bread | 6 oz. |
| Supper——Oatmeal Gruel | 1 pint. | Oatmeal Gruel | 1 pint. |
| „ Bread | 8 oz. | Bread | 6 oz. |

## Class 6.

Prisoners sentenced by Court to Solitary Confinement.

Males.    The ordinary Diet of their respective Classes.      Females.    The ordinary Diet of their respective Classes.

## Class 7.

Prisoners for examination, before Trial, and Misdemeanants of the first Division, who do not maintain themselves.

Males.    The same as Class 4.      Females.    The same as Class 4.

## Class 8.

Destitute Debtors.

Males.    The same as Class 4.      Females.    The same as Class 4.

## Class 9.

Prisoners under Punishment for Prison offences, for Terms not exceeding Three Days.

1 lb. of Bread per diem.

Prisoners in close confinement for Prison offences under the provision of the 42nd section of the Gaol Act.

| Males | | Females | |
|---|---|---|---|
| Breakfast—Gruel | 1 pint. | Gruel | 1 pint. |
| „ Bread | 8 oz. | Bread | 6 oz. |
| Dinner——Bread | 8 oz. | Bread | 6 oz. |
| Supper——Gruel | 1 pint. | Gruel | 1 pint. |
| „ Bread | 8 oz. | Bread | 6 oz. |

Note.—The Soup to contain, per pint, 3 ounces of cooked Meat without Bone, 3 ounces of Potatoes, 1 ounce of Barley, Rice, or Oatmeal, and 1 ounce of Onions or Leeks with pepper and salt. The Gruel to contain 2 ounces of Oatmeal per pint. The Gruel on alternate days to be sweetened with ¾ oz. of molasses or sugar, and seasoned with salt. In seasons when the potato crop has failed, 4 ounces of split peas made into a pudding, may be occasionally substituted : but the change must not be made more than *twice* in each week.—Boys under 14 years of age to be placed on the same diet as females.

The foregoing Dietary having been submitted to me, I hereby certify the same as proper to be adopted in the Gaols for the County of Somerset.

(Signed)

G. GREY.

Whitehall, 31st January, 1850.

From Wason's Albion Printing Office, Shepton-Mallet.

The issue came to a head in the 1860s with the ending of transportation to Australia. For the first time the authorities were faced with the task of administering long-term sentences in the rapidly growing number of convict prisons. At the end of their sentence, convicts were released on a ticket of leave or parole. In 1853 the first of such prisoners were released amidst much public panic.

With the outbreak of a spate of robberies in London in 1862, in which a garrotte was used to immobilize the victim, it was the parole system in particular, and philosophies of reformation in general, that were subject to sustained critique (Davis, 1980; **Sharpe, 1996**). In 1863 the Carnarvon Committee, set up to consider the relative merits of deterrence and reformation, came down firmly in favour of the former, reporting that severe labour 'is the chief means of exercising a deterrent effect' and that this was to be achieved through increased use of the crank and treadmill rather than by 'industrial occupation' (Forsythe, 1987, p.158). Indeed, the Committee heard that the Leicester system of 'no work, no food' based on crank labour in separate cells was a powerful deterrent and ought to be widely followed, despite the fact that prison inspectors in 1854 had condemned the practice as 'unwarranted by the Law of England' (*Report of the Commissioners*, 1854, p.v). The Earl of Carnarvon himself had argued in the House of Lords that: 'in a large proportion of the gaols and houses of correction in the kingdom there was an insufficiency of penal discipline' and that:

> it was perfectly idle to put into operation all the elaborate machinery provided in gaols for the instruction and reformation of prisoners, ideas which were fanciful theories likely to invite the criminal to commit crimes in the sure knowledge that there merely awaited him a good diet, warm bed and light, often voluntary, labour.

> (Earl of Carnarvon, quoted in Forsythe, 1987, p.145)

Instead, Carnarvon was impressed by the view that:

> the large majority of criminals were low and brutish 'mainly swayed by self gratification and animal appetite'. It followed that such brutes must be managed physically: 'the enforcement of continuous labour, which the true criminal abhors, and ... an uninviting diet, which is unquestionably the most odious penalty in his eyes'. Self gratifying instincts should be foiled by withholding all indulgences and diversions such as secular books, slates, hammocks and the like 'which are frequently awarded with too prodigal and indiscriminate a hand'. By taking a supposedly middle course between leniency and severity – 'a discipline which a low and sensual nature understands and dreads' – it would be possible to achieve individual deterrence of some kind by imparting 'a lively impression of the irksome and even painful discomfort which is an inseparable part of prison life'.

> (quoted phrases from Earl of Carnarvon, 1864, in McConville, 1995, p.55)

These views were subsequently embodied in the 1865 Prison Act which implemented by law the principles of deterrence and retribution throughout the penal system. The Act formally abolished the distinction between gaols and houses of correction and reinforced the 'separate system' in all prisons, stating that:

> In a prison where criminal prisoners are confined, such prisoners shall be prevented from holding any communication with each other, either by ... being kept in a separate cell by day and by night except when at chapel or exercise, or by every prisoner being confined by night in his cell and being subjected to such superintendence during the day as will prevent his communicating with any other prisoner.

> (Prison Act, 1865: 28 & 29 Vict., c.126)

The uniform application of Carnarvon's principles of deterrence and austerity was also not confined to the prisons of England and Wales. Lowe and McLaughlin (1993) suggest that mid nineteenth-century colonial administrators came to believe that they could and should control, guide and determine colonial prison regimes – from the Far East to the West Indies – through the adoption of the same rules and regulations that now operated in England.

For the next 30 years penal regimes were made as austere as possible, based on the twin practices of separate confinement and hard (unproductive) labour. Significantly, and in stark contrast to the 1830s, religion and the 'benefits' of moral instruction were conspicuous absences in the new penal discourse. In order to increase the punitive possibilities of prison, the Carnarvon Committee also recommended that dietary scales be lowered, that hammocks be replaced by hard wooden planks and that the daily time allowed for sleep be reduced to 8 hours. Although these measures were not given the force of law, McConville (1981, p.360) notes that, in all likelihood, they were widely practised given that local magistrates now had a mandatory duty to ensure that centrally determined modes of discipline were maintained. As Sim (1990, p.39) records, breaches of discipline were met with a 'further round of disciplinary activity' involving the use of shackles, manacles, chains, flogging, straitjackets and, in some cases, further reductions in diet. Thus he argues that prison doctors and surgeons were also drawn into the disciplinary network, with one doctor quoted as arguing that low diet:

> though it always seemed to me a more or less barbarous and senseless proceeding to apply to human beings, was nevertheless very necessary with unruly prisoners. I know of nothing approaching a scientific excuse for its use, except the principle on which a horse has his oats reduced in order to tame his spirit.
>
> (quoted in Sim, 1990, p.42)

The decline of reformation as a primary penal purpose was underlined by the appointment of Edmund Du Cane as chairman of the Prison Commission from 1877 to 1895. Du Cane argued that the purpose of imprisonment was to provide a *general* deterrence, rather than the deterrence or reformation of particular individuals. Thus: 'A sentence of penal servitude is ... applied on exactly the same system to every person subjected to it. The previous career and character of the prisoner makes no difference in the punishment to which he is subjected' (Du Cane, 1885, p.155). With this absence of individualization, the possibility of prisoner reformation was given a low, or no, priority. By the 1870s the reformatory vision and zeal of evangelists and philanthropists had been effectively excluded from the penal system (see Forsythe, 1987). As Fox laments: 'for death itself, the system had substituted a living death' (Fox, 1952, p.51). The Victorian prison did not entertain notions of treatment; it operated on pure classicist principles. Whilst prisoners were classified and categorized according to sex, age, conviction and sentence length, their individuality was not recognized:

> Based upon puritan assumptions about human motivation and personal responsibility, Victorian prison policy was inspired by a famous House of Lords Committee of 1863 which concluded that they, the members of the committee, did *not* consider: that the moral reformation of the offenders holds the primary place in the prison system; that mere industrial employment without wages is a sufficient punishment for many crimes; that punishment in itself is morally prejudicial to the criminal and useless to society, or that it is desirable to abolish both the crank and treadwheel as soon as possible.
>
> (Thomas and Pooley, 1980, pp.22–3)

Austin Bidwell, sentenced to life imprisonment for fraud, described his experience at Chatham Convict Prison:

An English prison is a vast machine in which a man counts for just nothing at all. He is to the establishment what a bale of merchandise is to a merchant's warehouse. The prison does not look on him as a man at all. He is merely an object which must move in a certain rut and occupy a certain niche provided for it. There is no room for the smallest sentiment. The vast machine of which he is an item keeps undisturbed on its course. Move with it and all is well. Resist and you will be crushed as inevitably as the man who plants himself on the railroad track when the express is coming. Without passion, without prejudice, but also without pity and without remorse the machine crushes and passes on. The dead man is carried to his grave and in ten minutes is as much forgotten as though he never existed.

(Bidwell, 1895, quoted in Priestley, 1985, p.229)

Were prisoner reformation and deterrence mutually exclusive modes of penal practice in the Victorian prison? Or was the latter a logical development of the former?

Why had the faith in reformation withered and how was a commitment to deterrence established and maintained?

How far can the discipline of the penitentiary and the post-1860 repressive practices throughout the prison system be considered a success or a failure?

# 5 From repression to rehabilitation

Between 1877 (when prison administration was centralized) and 1895 (the retirement of Du Cane as chairman of the Prison Commission) the Victorian obsession with certainty, severity and systematic uniformity reached its fullest expression. Yet even in these years it was becoming apparent that the aim of subjecting *all* prisoners to the same uniform discipline was self-defeating. Weiner argues that: 'the utilitarian drive toward rationalization ultimately worked against its own universalist principles' (Weiner, 1990, pp.308–9). This was particularly the case when the commitment to classifying prisoners continually threw up new and exceptional categories which did not seem to fit the criminal stereotype for which the regime of punitive deterrence had been designed.

Most notable was the case of the juvenile prisoner. As early as the 1820s prison inspectors were beginning to conclude that it was impractical to subject juveniles to the same penal regimes as those designed for adults. Uppermost in their minds was the belief that imprisonment with adults only served to strengthen the criminal habits of the young. As a result, a separate juvenile prison was established at Parkhurst in 1838 and by 1854 reformatory schools (previously developed on an *ad hoc* voluntary basis) were given legal recognition. As May (1973, p.12) argues, it was through such refinements in prisoner classification that the categories of *juvenile delinquent* and *young offender* were first established. An influential body of opinion from lawyers, magistrates, ministers of religion and prison administrators argued that children could not be held fully responsible for their misconduct and that their criminality could be accounted for more by a lack of moral and religious education than by any innate evil or self-volition –

they needed reformation rather than punishment. Mary Carpenter, the daughter of a Unitarian minister, was pivotal in the reformatory movement in which she sought to replace penal incarceration for the young with detention in educational schools and home-like reformatories. She was a staunch critic of the Parkhurst regime, arguing that its punitive control 'attempted to fashion children into machines through iron discipline instead of self acting beings' (Carpenter, 1851, p.321). The use of leg-irons, distinctive prison dress and inadequate diet were all condemned. Delinquent children, she claimed, needed to be returned to a family environment in which they could be 'gradually restored to the true position of childhood' (Carpenter, 1853, p.298). By 1858 over 50 reformatory schools had been established, mainly through voluntary effort, and Parkhurst was closed for juveniles in 1863.

reformation

However, state support for the schools was not won without opposition. A strong lobby persisted in arguing that all individuals, regardless of age, should be held responsible for their actions and that all should remain equal in the eyes of the law. Carpenter's vision was thus subject to legislative compromise. Before entering a reformatory, a prison sentence of at least 14 days had to be served. Moreover, the Youthful Offenders Act 1854 was only permissive and magistrates could continue to send juveniles to prison if they so decided. The reformatory system (which was to evolve first into the system of approved schools and subsequently into childrens homes in the twentieth century) was grafted on to existing penal institutions and did not replace them. For much of the century the presence of the reformatories did not preclude the committal of children to prison for the most petty of offences including stealing apples, trespassing in fields and vagrancy (Priestley, 1985, pp.55–6). In addition, the regimes in the reformatories were far from standardized on any domestic model. Whilst some schoolwork and religious instruction was usually present, the child's day consisted, in the main, of gruelling work: digging the land to convert the criminal through 'the sweat of his brow' (Radzinowicz and Hood, 1990, p.191). Court records from the 1880s show that reformatories were also used for the most trivial of offences:

> Patrick McGuiness, age 12, stealing one bottle of beer, no previous convictions, committed to one calendar month imprisonment and five years Reformatory.

> John Jones, age 12, stealing three pairs of boots, no previous convictions, committed to 21 days hard labour and four years Reformatory.

> William Folly, age 12, stealing 9d from the person, one previous conviction, committed to 14 days imprisonment and five years Reformatory.

> (quoted in Radzinowicz and Hood, 1990, pp.184–5)

Thus, whilst it would be misleading to view the reformatories as progressive institutions with liberal regimes, they nevertheless began the process of providing for 'exceptional' categories and in establishing alternative institutions to those of the 'Victorian orthodoxy'.

For most of the nineteenth century penal regimes for men and women were similar, even though women were gradually to be allocated to separate wings or to separate prisons (the first being Brixton in 1853). However, at the same time scores of reformatories and refuges were created expressly for the purpose of 'saving' girls and young women. Their work in these institutions was chiefly designed to train them to fill the 'enormous demand for household servants' (Dobash *et al.*, 1986, p.74). Women continued to be committed to prison at the same rate per conviction as men, but, due to reductions in their length of sentence, the female proportion of the local prison population fell from 22 per cent in 1870 to 16.5 per cent in 1895; in convict prisons from 14 per cent to 6.75 per cent (Weiner, 1990, p.309). Prison populations were thus also becoming more markedly male. Other groups which began to demand specific consideration were political prisoners (notably the Irish Nationalists), middle-class or 'gentleman' prisoners (usually imprisoned for embezzlement) and those with learning disabilities. All of these 'exceptions' put the case that they be considered as unfit for (and in some cases undeserving of) the full rigours of penal discipline.

By 1890 the efficacy of Du Cane's repressive regime was being increasingly called into question. Debate centred on two issues: the question of short sentences and the problem of recidivism (Garland, 1985, p.61). In England the average duration of all prison sentences was 28 days; in Scotland it was 15 days. This practice of using prison as a first resort and for minor offences became increasingly criticized for its high financial costs, its overcrowding and the fear of 'needless' contamination of young offenders by older prisoners. Recidivism – reported as high as 78 per cent for simple larceny – pointed to the failure of imprisonment itself, in particular its much toted ability to deter offenders: 'Prison was seen to produce that which it should prevent, to manufacture delinquents instead of mending them' (Garland, 1985, p.62). These practical issues merged with a growing reassessment of the state's role in the disciplining and regulation of the working classes to stimulate the appointment of a Departmental Committee of Inquiry to review the principles of the whole penal realm.

The resulting recommendations contained in the 1895 Gladstone Report mark another key transformation in British penal policy. Criticizing existing regimes for 'crushing self-respect' and 'starving all moral instinct', the report argued that reformation should coexist with deterrence and that rehabilitation should be given priority (see Extract 4.3).

rehabilitation

In place of inflexible and punitive methods of control, Gladstone proposed more scientific methods of *treatment*. First offenders, juveniles, habitual criminals, drunkards, the 'weak-minded', female prisoners with children and the unconvicted, it was argued, should be classified separately and treated according to their individual natures and needs. In 1898 the prison commissioners for the first time defined the purpose of imprisonment as 'the humanisation of the individual' (Weiner, 1990, p.378). Such a policy clearly marked a radical break with the past. Sir Evelyn Ruggles-Brise, chairman of the Prison Commission from 1895 to 1921, put the position clearly enough when he insisted that: 'each man convicted of crime is to be regarded as an individual, as a separate entity of morality, who by the application of influences, of discipline, labour, education, moral and religious, backed up on discharge by a well-organized system of patronage is capable of reinstatement in civic life' (Ruggles-Brise, 1911, quoted in Garland, 1985, p.26). Similarly, the editor of the *Journal of Mental Science* argued that: 'it is now recognized that primitive measures alone are not corrective, and effective reformation of criminals can only be attained by making our prisons true schools and moral hospitals' (quoted in Weiner, 1990, p.378). The contrast with Du Cane's objective, some 25 years earlier, could not have been more stark. It resurrected the notion that confinement should do more than punish and once more set in train a series of debates concerning the proper purpose of

## Extract 4.3 Departmental Committee on Prisons: 'The Gladstone Report'

*Character of Necessary Changes.*

**11,482.**

25. The next consideration is the general direction of any changes which the course of our examination into the facts make us think necessary or advisable. Sir Godfrey Lushington thus impressively summed up the influences under the present system unfavourable to reformation : " I regard as unfavourable to reformation the status " of a prisoner throughout his whole career ; the crushing of self-respect, the starving " of all moral instinct he may possess, the absence of all opportunity to do or receive a " kindness, the continual association with none but criminals, and that only as a separate " item amongst other items also separate ; the forced labour, and the denial of all " liberty. I believe the true mode of reforming a man or restoring him to society is " exactly in the opposite direction of all these ; but, of course, this is a mere idea. It " is quite impracticable in a prison. In fact the unfavourable features I have men- " tioned are inseparable from prison life." As a broad description of prison life we think this description is accurate ; we do not agree that all of these unfavourable features are irremovable. Already in many respects and in individual cases they have been modified, and we believe that this modification can be carried much further in the direction of the treatment adopted and practised by the best of the existing reformatories. We think that the system should be made more elastic, more capable of being adopted to the special cases of individual prisoners ; that prison discipline and treatment should be more effectually designed to maintain, stimulate, or awaken the higher susceptibilities of prisoners, to develop their moral instincts, to train them in orderly and industrial habits, and whenever possible to turn them out of prison better men and women, both physically and morally, than when they came in. Crime, its causes and treatment, has been the subject of much profound and scientific inquiry. Many of the problems it presents are practically at the present time insoluble. It may be true that some criminals are irreclaimable, just as some diseases are incurable, and in such cases it is not unreasonable to acquiesce in the theory that criminality is a disease, and the result of physical imperfection. But criminal anthropology as a science is in an embryo stage, and while scientific and more particularly medical observation and experience are of the most essential value in guiding opinion on the whole subject, it would be a loss of time to search for a perfect system in learned but conflicting theories, when so much can be done by the recognition of the plain fact that the great majority of prisoners are ordinary men and women amenable, more or less, to all those influences which affect persons outside.

**116, 8687, 9438.**

**Report, par. 72.**

26. From this point of view it is interesting to notice that the Royal Commission of 1879 acquiesced in the objection to the penal servitude system made on the ground that " it not only fails to reform offenders, but in the case of the less " hardened criminals, and especially of first offenders, produces a deteriorating effect " from the indiscriminate association of all classes of convicts in the public works." It is true that this referred to convict prisons only, and that in 1882 the star class of first offenders was instituted to meet the views of the Royal Commission. But we think for reasons which we shall subsequently proceed to state that the general prison system is still open to this reproach. Our inquiry has led us to think that the evils attributed to contamination have been exaggerated so far as male criminals are concerned. But grave evils are liable to occur from surreptitious communications among the women prisoners, and every care should be taken to keep them from being crowded together in chapel. Leaving this point aside for the present, we call attention to the finding of the Royal Commission in 1879, that the convict system not only failed to reform offenders, but on the less hardened, and especially the first offenders, it produced a deteriorating effect. The failure is yet to be found in local as well as convict prisons, but we are not inclined to attribute it to direct contamination by association as a primary cause of mischief.

(Departmental Committee on Prisons, 1895, p.8)

imprisonment. The issue remains, though, of how far such policy was put into practice. Forsythe, for example, argues that often the new projects fell short of the claims made for them. In particular, the local and convict prisons 'clung tenaciously to the concepts of measured punishment, moral culpability, limited deterrence and uniformly administered discipline' (Forsythe, 1991, p.239). The process of reform was thus often slow and imperceptible.

Nevertheless, from 1900 onwards a number of radical changes were made to the standard prison regime. Unproductive labour was officially abandoned, to be replaced by prison industries and work considered 'useful'. The 'separate system' was gradually eroded, so that prisoners could work in association. Educational facilities were increased and improved. Internal discipline was maintained through a reward/punishment system related to the introduction of remission. 'Specialists', such as psychologists, were appointed and prisoner categorization was extended. For juveniles, the Borstal system, largely derived from American experience, was introduced. A commitment to reformation became enshrined in the Prison Rule that stipulated that the purpose of imprisonment was to encourage prisoners to 'lead a good and useful life' (this became Prison Rule 6 in 1949 and was elevated to Prison Rule 1 in 1964).

However, as Garland (1985) notes, the most radical reforms of this period took place outside the prison system. It is in the introduction of a probation service, alternatives to imprisonment and the construction of specialist institutions (such as the Borstal where principles of rehabilitation were initiated) where Garland sees the major transformations that mark the beginning of current practice. As a result, rather than limit discussion to penality prison reform, he refers to wider developments in a whole realm of penality Thus he is able to claim that:

> the prison was decentred, shifted from its position as the central and predominant sanction to become one institution among many in an extended grid of penal sanctions. Of course it continued to be of major importance, but it was now deployed in a different manner, for a narrower section of the criminal population and often as a back up sanction for other institutions, rather than the place of first resort.

(Garland, 1985, p.23)

These external changes led to corresponding changes in the internal prison population. The numbers of the inebriate, the 'weak-minded', first offenders and juveniles were reduced, whilst the number of routine recidivists and more serious offenders increased. From a daily average of 17,000 prisoners in 1900, the prison and Borstal population fell to 11,000 by 1936.

In this sense the task of reforming the prison population grew more difficult, but it was a task that was addressed by a proliferation of welfare, treatment and rehabilitative programmes. Garland (1985) accounts for this shift with reference to the impact of a fundamental change in official discourses of penality which came to reflect a developing *positivist* notion of behaviour and social order. No longer were all inmates to be treated equally – they were to be differentiated according to the judgements of such non-judicial professionals as probation officers, welfare workers, doctors, psychiatrists and psychologists. They were to be pitied, cared for and reclaimed, rather than reviled. Their criminality was no longer considered a matter of self-volition, but thought to be instigated by a number of psychological, physiological and environmental conditions that were effectively out of each individual's control. Within this new discourse it made no sense merely to punish; the offender should also be treated.

Developments up to the outbreak of war in 1914 and in the subsequent inter-war years were to alter radically, not only penal policy, but also the place of prison within the wider framework of penal sanctions.

As a result of such developments, Garland (1985, p.31) has argued that the precise origins of the modern prison lie in the turn of this century and not with Howard's reforms of the late eighteenth century. How far would you agree?

# 6 Conclusion: questions of interpretation

Whilst it might be tempting to 'read' this history as one of a developing (albeit faltering and gradual) humanitarian approach to those imprisoned, the logic of a continual progressive improvement is far from easy to sustain. The new prisons of the early nineteenth century may be viewed as preferential to the Bloody Code, but the solitary confinement and regimes of hard unproductive labour may also be viewed as less 'humanitarian' than the productive labour regimes of the houses of correction. Is punishment that is aimed at the mind any more rational or beneficial than punishment that is aimed at the body? Similarly, the repressive regimes of the mid nineteenth century can be viewed not as some historical anomaly, but as a logical extension of the earlier ideas of reformation. The treatment programmes of the early twentieth century appear to be a more clear-cut example of humanitarianism, but if we are to follow the arguments of Foucault, they *penetrated* rather than overturned the primary rationale of deterrence. They were simply added on to a system whose purpose remained primarily punitive. Notions of rehabilitation thus expanded the 'carceral archipelago', extending the logic of disciplinary control out of the prisons and into the cities and communities.

From Cohen (1985, pp.15–30) we can caricature the literature of penal reform as offering four competing versions of history:

1  *Uneven progress* – reform is generated by benevolence and philanthropy. Mistakes may be made, but in the course of time, with goodwill and sufficient resources, the system is capable of being improved through good intentions (the Whig version).

2  *Good (but complicated) intentions but with disastrous consequences* – reform is not a matter of good intentions occasionally going wrong, but of continual failure. None of the reformist visions turned out as intended; the rhetoric of benevolence served to support a long discredited system by deflecting criticism and justifying 'more of the same' (the disillusioned liberal version).

3  *Discipline* – the rhetoric of reform always masks its real intentions of constructing a repressed and compliant labour force for capitalist exploitation (the orthodox Marxist version).

4  *Mystification* – reform was not a failure for its true rationale of subjugating populations to coercive discipline was never formally stated. In this sense reform was and continues to be a success. More and more people are drawn into a carceral network, both within and outside of the prison walls (the revisionist version).

These four 'visions' invite us to deconstruct the history of the prison in completely different ways. But, arguably, it is not a matter of which, if any, are 'correct'. Each allows us to see different aspects of the movement for reform. Arguably again, we need all four to appreciate fully the inconsistencies and complexities of the development of systems of punishment that are today so often taken for granted (but whose rationale remains far from clear: see Chapter 5). Above all, as our summary of this history has shown, the prison (and other forms of punishment) can be made to do different things at different times. Its role shifts between coercion, custody, punishment, deterrence, repression, reformation, therapeutic welfare and rehabilitation, depending on socio-political circumstance and historical contingency. The greatest anomaly of the late twentieth century is perhaps that the prison is asked – albeit with different emphases – to perform all of these roles at one and the same time.

## Further reading

The three most thorough empirical accounts of Victorian penal reform can be found in Radzinowicz and Hood (1990) and McConville (1981, 1995). A reformist understanding of this history is provided by Forsythe (1987, 1991), while Ignatieff (1978) and **Foucault (1977)** offer (differing) revisionist interpretations. Weiner (1990) attempts some synthesis of the two positions, whilst Garland (1990) gives the debate a much needed theoretical underpinning, at the same time arguing for 'integrated and pluralistic interpretations'. Meanwhile, Priestley's (1985) 'collective biography' is invaluable in revealing how Victorian 'total institutions' were experienced by prisoners themselves.

This chapter draws unashamedly on the framework first developed by Cohen (1985, Chapter 1). Students coming afresh to this area will be well served by beginning their study here.

## References

**Beccaria, C. (1963) *On Crimes and Punishments*, New York, Bobbs-Merrill. (First published in 1764.) (Extract reprinted in Muncie *et al.*, 1996.)**

Carpenter, M. (1851) *Reformatory Schools for the Children of the Perishing and Dangerous Classes and for Juvenile Offenders*, London, Gilpin.

Carpenter, M. (1853) *Juvenile Delinquents: Their Condition and Treatment*, London, Cash.

Cohen, S. (1985) *Visions of Social Control: Crime, Punishment and Classification*, Cambridge, Polity.

Davis, J. (1980) 'The London garotting panic of 1862', in Gatrell, V., Lenman, B. and Parker, G. (eds) *Crime and the Law*, London, Europa.

Delacy, M. (1986) *Prison Reform in Lancashire 1700–1850*, Manchester, Manchester University Press.

Departmental Committee on Prisons (1895) *Report from the Departmental Committee on Prisons* (The Gladstone Report), in *Reports from the Commissioner, Inspectors and Others: 1895*, House of Commons Parliamentary Papers.

Dobash, R.P., Dobash, R.E. and Gutteridge, S. (1986) *The Imprisonment of Women*, Oxford, Blackwell.

Du Cane, E.F. (1885) *The Punishment and Prevention of Crime*, London, Macmillan.

Forsythe, W.J. (1987) *The Reform of Prisoners 1830–1900*, London, Croom Helm.

Forsythe, W.J. (1989) 'Privatisation and British prisons – past and future', *Prison Service Journal*, January, pp.35–7.

Forsythe, W.J. (1991) *Penal Discipline, Reformatory Projects and the English Prison Commission 1895–1939*, Exeter, University of Exeter.

**Foucault, M. (1977) *Discipline and Punish: The Birth of the Prison* (trans. Alan Sheridan), London, Allen Lane. (Extract reprinted as 'The carceral' in Muncie *et al.*, 1996.)**

Fox, L. (1952) *The English Prison and Borstal Systems*, London, Routledge.

Garland, D. (1985) *Punishment and Welfare: A History of Penal Strategies*, Aldershot, Gower.

Garland, D. (1990) *Punishment and Modern Society: A Study in Social Theory*, Oxford, Oxford University Press.

Gibson, J. (1971) *John Howard and Elisabeth Fry*, London, Methuen.

Harding, C., Hines, B., Ireland, R. and Rawlings, P. (1985) *Imprisonment in England and Wales: A Concise History*, London, Croom Helm.

Hawkings, D.T. (1992) *Criminal Ancestors: A Guide to Historical Criminal Records in England and Wales*, Stroud, Alan Sutton.

Hogg, R. (1979) 'Imprisonment and society under early British capitalism', *Crime and Social Justice*, no.12, pp.4–17.

Howard, J. (1929) *The State of the Prisons*, London, Dent. (First published in 1777.)

Ignatieff, M. (1978) *A Just Measure of Pain: The Penitentiary in the Industrial Revolution*, London, Macmillan.

Ignatieff, M. (1983) 'State, civil society and total institutions: a critique of recent social histories of punishment', in Cohen, S. and Scull, A. (eds) *Social Control and the State*, London, Martin Robertson.

Krebs, A. (1978) 'John Howard's influence on the prison system in Europe', in Freeman, J. (ed.) *Prisons: Past and Future*, London, Heinemann.

Lowe, K. and McLaughlin, E. (1993) 'An Eldorado of riches and a place of unpunished crime: the politics of penal reform in Hong Kong 1877–1882', *Criminal Justice History: An International Annual Review*, vol.14, pp.57–91.

McConville, S. (1981) *A History of Prison Administration, Vol.1, 1750–1877*, London, Routledge.

McConville, S. (1995) *English Local Prisons 1860–1900: Next Only to Death*, London, Routledge.

Mannheim, H. (1939) *The Dilemma of Penal Reform*, London, Allen and Unwin.

May, M. (1973) 'Innocence and experience: the evolution of the concept of juvenile delinquency in the mid-nineteenth century', *Victorian Studies*, vol.17, no.1, pp.7–29.

Melossi, D. (1981) 'Creation of the modern prison in England and Europe (1550–1850)', in Melossi and Pavarini (1981).

Melossi, D. and Pavarini, M. (1981) *The Prison and the Factory: Origins of the Penitentiary System*, London, Macmillan.

Morgan, R. (1977) 'Divine philanthropy: John Howard reconsidered', *History*, vol.62, pp.388–410.

**Muncie, J., McLaughlin, E. and Langan, M. (eds) (1996) *Criminological Perspectives: A Reader*, London, Sage in association with The Open University.**

Open University (1987) *Law and Disorder: Histories of Crime and Justice*, in D310 *Crime, Justice and Society*, Block 2, Milton Keynes, The Open University.

Open University (1992) *Prisons and Penal Systems*, in D803 *Doing Prison Research*, Part 1, Milton Keynes, The Open University.

Pisciotta, A.W. (1981) 'Corrections, society and social control in America', in *Criminal Justice History*, vol.2, pp.109–30.

Piven, F. and Cloward, R. (1972) *Regulating the Poor: The Functions of Public Welfare*, London, Tavistock.

Priestley, P. (1985) *Victorian Prison Lives*, London, Methuen.

Pugh, R.B. (1968) *Imprisonment in Mediaeval England*, Cambridge, Cambridge University Press.

Radzinowicz, L. (1978) 'John Howard', in Freeman, J. (ed.) *Prisons: Past and Future*, London, Heinemann.

Radzinowicz, L. and Hood, R. (1990) *The Emergence of Penal Policy*, vol.5 of *A History of English Criminal Law*, Oxford, Clarendon.

Ramsay, M. (1977) 'John Howard and the discovery of the prison', *Howard Journal*, vol.16, pp.1–16.

*Report of the Commissioners into the Condition and Treatment of Prisoners in Leicester County Gaol and House of Correction* (1854), P.P.xxxiv, 197.

Rothman, D.J. (1971) *Discovery of the Asylum*, Boston, MA, Little Brown.

Rusche, G. and Kirchheimer, O. (1939) *Punishment and Social Structure*, New York, Columbia University Press. (Reissued in 1968 by Russell and Russell.)

**Sharpe, J. (1996) 'Crime, order and historical change' in Muncie, J. and McLaughlin, E. (eds) *The Problem of Crime*, London, Sage in association with The Open University.**

Sim, J. (1990) *Medical Power in Prisons*, Buckingham, Open University Press.

Smart, B. (1989) 'On discipline and social regulation', in Garland, D. and Young, P. (eds) *The Power to Punish: Contemporary Penality and Social Analysis*, Aldershot, Gower.

Spierenburg, P.C. (1991) *The Prison Experience: Disiplinary Institutions and Their Inmates in Early Modern Europe*, New Brunswick, NJ, Rutgers University Press.

Thomas, J.E. (1988) *House of Care: Prison and Prisoners in England 1500–1800,* Nottingham, Department of Adult Education, Nottingham University.

Thomas, J.E. and Pooley, D. (1980) *Exploding Prison: Prison Riots and the Case of Hull,* London, Junction Books.

van der Slice, A. (1937) 'Elizabethan houses of correction', *Journal of Criminal Law and Criminology*, vol.27, pp.45–67.

Weiner, M.J. (1990) *Reconstructing the Criminal*, Cambridge, Cambridge University Press.

Zedner, L. (1991) *Women, Crime and Custody in Victorian England*, Oxford, Clarendon.

# Chapter 5
# Prisons, Punishment and Penality

*by Richard Sparks*

## Contents

# 1 Introduction

*T*his chapter offers a critical introduction to the nature, purposes and scope of penal institutions in contemporary industrial societies. The discussion focuses principally on problems of imprisonment, but tries to place these in the context of other available forms of punishment. Prisons are the most controversial and politically sensitive institutions within modern penal systems. When questions of punishment arise in media coverage or political campaigns and speeches they often centre on imprisonment to the exclusion of other penalties or kinds of intervention: Are prison conditions too 'cushy' or too degrading? Should this or that individual have been sent to prison or not? Was this or that sentence too short (or, more rarely, too long) for the purposes of protecting the public or expressing their outrage? This position of centrality in public and political vocabularies of punishment persists despite the fact that in no modern penal system (including the most apparently 'punitive' such as that in the USA) are the majority of convicted offenders sent to prison. This chapter explores the practice of imprisonment, and the many debates and controversies that surround it, directly and in some detail. The use of imprisonment is an important question of public policy in its own right. Moreover, the passions that imprisonment evokes also crystallize a wider range of concerns about social responses to crime in modern societies. With this in view this chapter:

- Discusses some of the many objectives which prisons may be called upon to achieve. What does it mean to say that prisons do or do not 'work'? Can we envisage a prisons policy that would be rational, effective and orderly – and in these senses *legitimate* – or are the disputes intrinsic and permanent?

- Considers the notion of a 'crisis' in penal policy and looks at some of the efforts that have been undertaken towards reorganization and reform (especially the intervention of Lord Justice Woolf in England in 1991), exploring some of the dilemmas they pose for the future.

- Offers a comparative overview of prison populations in the UK, Europe and the USA and asks how the variations between these can best be explained. If different countries use imprisonment in different ways, can we say which, if any, of these is preferable to the others?

- Highlights one area of special controversy, namely the question of prison privatization, and queries what it can tell us about trends in the nature and scope of penal practice. Is privatization just another tactical means of reorganization, or does it betoken a more historically significant development in our conceptions of punishment?

The concluding section of the chapter returns to some of the issues of interpretation and principle raised throughout, in order to review what we can learn about our own and other societies from the ways in which each deploys its power to punish. In summary terms we hope that you will gain from this chapter:

- A sense of the variety of both the *practical* and *symbolic* functions that prisons and other forms of punishment may be called upon to accomplish.

- An understanding that modern penal systems are complex organizations, and that attempts to manage and change them confront difficult issues of both *effectiveness* and *legitimacy*.

- Through comparative analysis, an awareness that no one form or level of prison use is natural or inevitable, but that each raises its own problems of both *justification* and *explanation*.

- A number of important questions (though fewer answers) about what the future of Western penal systems might hold.

# **2** Prisons and the contested nature of punishment

Methods of punishment or correction have long been amongst the more vexed and contested aspects of public life. At different moments in their historical development modern Western societies have conceived of the causes of crime and disorder in distinct ways and have formulated their philosophies and practices of punishment variably, according to the dominant explanatory models, religious and other value systems and crime control priorities of the times. (If we were to extend this discussion to include non-Western or 'traditional' societies, the range of customs, practices and beliefs that could be termed 'punishments' would be seen to be even more bewilderingly wide.) Even within particular moments or periods, the historical record suggests sharp disagreement on matters of justification and of method, as the disputes between deterrence and reformation as aims of imprisonment in Victorian England indicate (see Chapter 4). Thus, although particular criteria for deciding on questions of appropriate punishment and particular institutional arrangements for delivering it may predominate at any given time, we cannot assume that they ever achieve a consensus of support nor that they will not be subject to change. On one level this is because real institutions of punishment have never been 'perfected' in the way that their more visionary advocates (such as John Howard's ideal images of penitentiary imprisonment) imagined they could be. On quite another level, it is because matters of penal policy always broach some of the most basic questions of justice, order and social control that any society confronts, and on which settled agreement always seems elusive. This is why Garland comments that:

> The punishment of offenders is a peculiarly unsettling and dismaying aspect of social life. As a social policy it is a continual disappointment, seeming always to fail in its ambitions and to be undercut by crises and contradictions of one sort or another. As a moral or political issue it provokes intemperate emotions, deeply conflicting interests, and intractable disagreements.

> (Garland, 1990, p.1)

It would appear that whenever we discuss questions of penal policy we find ourselves in the presence of uncertainty and controversy. Even defining punishment (given the range of practices and penalties which have claimed justification in its name) is no easy matter (as we shall see in section 2.1). Perhaps, then, we must give up the idea that we will one day discover a form of punishment which is undeniably just and self-evidently effective. Rather, we may have to accept that any social practice that is so much caught up with issues of authority, legitimacy and compulsion is inevitably subject to what philosophers call 'the conflict of interpretations'. The morality of punishment is, as Lacey (1988, p.14), puts it, 'incurably relative'.

## 2.1  Punishment as an 'essentially contested concept'

There is, of course, one overriding reason why punishment poses these sorts of problems in an especially acute way. By definition, punishing offenders is generally taken to imply the imposition of some form of 'hard treatment' (von Hirsch, 1993). It involves 'what are usually regarded as unpleasant consequences' (Lacey, 1988, p.9). Justifications for punishing may be offered on a number of grounds. Let us briefly outline some of the fundamental positions. For many philosophers, and perhaps most ordinary people, the justification for punishing resides simply in the view that the penalty is seen as *deserved* for the offence (in which case the punishment is described as *retributive*). For others the key question lies in a *practical* or *instrumental* benefit that is intended to follow. Thus it may be held that the principal aim of imposing a penalty for an offence is in order to *deter* its repetition, or to

incapacitation *incapacitate* the offender (that is, in some way to prevent them from repeating an action either by locking them up, placing them under supervision or removing their means of doing it). Still others propose that we

denunciation punish mainly in order to express social disapproval ('denunciation').

rehabilitation The most ambiguous case is where the penalty is held also to do the offender good (to *rehabilitate* them through participation in a programme of counselling, education or training). Yet even in the mildest forms of rehabilitation offenders will be placed under a degree of compulsion. They can be required to do things that may inconvenience them and which they would not do voluntarily (attend appointments with a probation officer, spend Saturday afternoons at an attendance centre), usually with the threat of more severe penalties if they do not comply. The tensions which inevitably arise within such mixtures of helping and compelling may be even more acute where attempts to bring about rehabilitation occur *within* prisons. In liberal democratic societies like our own, punishment generally equates to some form of *deprivation*, whether of liberty, time or money (and, we might add, social standing or reputation).

It is because punishment usually implies compulsion, and often deliberately imposed hardship, that decisions to punish always pose problems of moral justification and call for the provision of reasons. When we punish we are using the legal authority of the state to do things which would otherwise (if we did them privately, or if they were done without a sufficient reason) be '*prima facie* morally wrongful' (Lacey, 1988, p.14). Yet it is very often unclear whether punishment does achieve the effects that are claimed for it. Moreover, the major justifications that are used do not always go easily together. Retribution looks back towards the original offence, and seeks to

retribution punish proportionately (it is generally *intuitionist* with regard to what is deserved). Deterrence looks forward to the prevention of future crimes (it is

deterrence *consequentialist*; if it does not work it cannot claim justification). As one commentator puts it, these two principal justifications for punishing 'stand in open and flagrant contradiction' (Bean, 1981, p.1). The primary point is that we should never be complacent about our grounds for punishing. It is often far from self-evident in any given case just which objectives are being pursued, still less whether they will be successful, and debate is often further clouded by political contingencies (Prison Reform Trust, 1993).

In most criminal justice systems (and certainly in the famously 'eclectic' English case) the different rationales for punishing have often co-existed in various, more or less uneasy, combinations. Criminal sentencing is a complex intellectual and cultural phenomenon, capable of answering to a range of institutional and political demands. It tends, therefore, to resist codification, however many academic theorists of different stripes (be they pure retributivists or advocates of classical deterrence) insist that they have discovered the one true rationale for state punishment. Punishment is *overdetermined*: its aims may be simultaneously *instrumental* (concerned with the suppression of crime and the control of behaviour) and *symbolic* or *ideological* (concerned with the vindication of the law and its claims to exercise justice in the defence of the authority and legitimacy of the state). Historically, it is more common than not for retributive and deterrent principles to stand side by side in the armoury of possible sentences, even when purist advocates of each insist that they are logically incompatible.

## 2.2 The penal range and the choice of punishments

With the notable exception of the USA (see Zimring and Hawkins, 1986), the Western liberal democracies have abandoned the use of capital punishment. Even in the USA, where it is a highly politically charged issue, the death penalty is actually carried out only in a relative handful of cases each year (there were 14 executions in 1991), although the numbers executed have increased (31 in 1994); the number of persons under sentence of death, however, is very much larger (2,500 in 1991; 2,870 in 1994) (figures for 1991 from United States Department of Justice, 1992; for 1994 from Amnesty International, 1995, p.302). In other respects the 'penal range' (the variety of available penalties) in all such societies is broadly comparable, albeit organized and applied in very different ways. It extends from various forms of token penalty or admonition (in the UK, absolute and conditional discharges, binding over) through financial penalties (fines, compensation orders) and varieties of non-custodial or 'community' supervision (probation, community service, in some cases 'curfew orders') to imprisonment. In most systems, and certainly in the UK, financial penalties are by some margin the most commonly used. This has led some commentators (notably Young, 1989; see also Bottoms, 1983) to argue that in fact it is the 'cash nexus' of the fine that is the most characteristic form of contemporary punishment rather than the more drastic but more rarely used sanction of imprisonment.

Nevertheless, it is imprisonment which has probably received the lion's share of media debate, academic attention and political controversy. The reasons for this preoccupation are perhaps not too difficult to detect. The scale of punishment is organized hierarchically in the form of a 'tariff'. In most contemporary systems the prison is at the apex of this ordinal series of values. Although it is by no means the case that everyone who goes to prison has been convicted of grave offences, ordinary language (and judicial reasoning) generally sees a powerful connection between the severity of an offence and the likelihood or appropriateness of imprisonment. (This expectation was formalized in England and Wales in the sentencing structure of the 1991 Criminal Justice Act – see Chapter 3.) Moreover, imprisonment involves the deprivation of something on which most societies, and certainly ones in which liberalism is a dominant ideology, set a special value – liberty, freedom of movement and association. For this reason the general problems of justifying punishments are seen to apply in especially acute ways to imprisonment (witness the widespread public concern over 'miscarriage of justice' cases in England – most famously those of the Guildford Four and Birmingham Six; to be wrongfully imprisoned is acknowledged to be a very severe injustice: it is the wrongful application of the state's most draconian power over its citizens).

Plainly, other sanctions (such as community service orders and probation) also restrict liberty, but not in so obvious or readily understood a fashion. This leads to a number of ambiguities in the interpretation of such penalties. In much 'common-sense' discussion and in popular press imagery, non-custodial penalties are not regarded as 'proper' punishments at all. The equation between punishment and imprisonment for many people is so strong that for the offender to remain 'in the community' is for them to be 'let off'. Moreover, it is common for such measures to be described as 'alternatives to' imprisonment, implying that incarceration remains the central, perhaps the only 'real', sort of punishment.

We can therefore only really understand the uses of imprisonment within any particular criminal justice system in the context of the range of other measures that that system also applies. In recent times most Western
bifurcation penal systems have moved increasingly towards a stance of bifurcation (or 'twin tracking') in an explicit attempt to reserve imprisonment for the more serious offences, whilst providing an 'adequate' range of 'community penalties' for the rest. Certainly this philosophy underlay the British government's thinking in the formulation of the 1991 Criminal Justice Act which introduced the concept of a specific 'threshold' between custody and other penalties (see Wasik and Taylor, 1991, p.17). Whilst this strategy has an obvious plausibility, its actual effects can be uncertain or even counter-
diversion productive. It presents itself as a *diversionary* measure. Yet sentence lengths for the 'hard core' who continue to receive imprisonment may increase, as average prison terms in the UK did incrementally throughout the 1980s (Home Office, 1993; Morgan, 1994). At the same time, non-custodial penalties may also be made consciously more severe in order to be made 'credible' to sentencers. In addition, such penalties may not always be strictly or appropriately applied: that is, they may move *down-tariff*, supplanting other 'lesser' penalties. This is now widely held to have been the fate of the suspended sentence in the UK since its introduction in 1967 (Bottoms, 1987). It may also be reflected in the increasing popularity amongst sentencers in the UK of community service orders which have tended to displace the longer established penalty of probation since about 1980 (Cavadino and Dignan, 1992, p.171). Such measures can serve to increase prison populations, either because imprisonment may follow when their conditions are breached (and the more demanding those conditions become the more likely this seems to be), or because courts treat subsequent offences in a more serious light. In either case the result is not so much 'twin tracking' as *punitive bifurcation*, in which both 'tracks' become more stringent (Cavadino and Dignan, 1992, pp.108–9). The relation between imprisonment and its 'alternatives' is thus a complicated one. The history of attempts to introduce additional sentencing options, especially where these are meant to divert offenders from prison, is littered with unintended (and sometimes actively 'perverse') consequences.

Two considerations may be paramount in explaining why non-custodial sanctions have not had a profound effect in displacing the use of imprisonment. The first concerns, once again, the prison's symbolic position at the summit of the ascending scale of penalties. There would appear to be a widely held view amongst some sentencers, in press discourse and, perhaps by extension, in 'public opinion', that no other penalty adequately conveys the degree of reproof or censure necessary in responding to offences regarded as highly morally culpable (Bishop, 1988; Zimring and Hawkins, 1991). (One alternative conception is that espoused by Braithwaite who argues that sanctions should embody the ritual expression of both 'shaming' and 'reintegration' (**Braithwaite, 1989**; Braithwaite and Mugford, 1994; see also Cragg, 1992).

The second obstacle to decarceration includes a more practical dimension. A sanction is only likely to displace imprisonment to any marked degree if it is consistently used in cases where the offender *actually would otherwise* go to prison. But such cases do include a high proportion of offences involving demonstrable harm to others. Meanwhile, sentencers and members of the public tend to focus on one of the most obvious and salient features of imprisonment: self-evidently it does confine people and set them apart from the general community for the duration of their sentence. Despite many efforts and no little evidence to the contrary, it seems inherently difficult to persuade people *either* that prisons do not have a crime-preventive function through incapacitation to anything like the extent that is sometimes claimed for them (Greenberg, 1991; Zimring and Hawkins, 1991; Mathiesen, 1990), *or*, conversely, that other means of supervision, support or remedial assistance 'in the community' can do so.

As we have seen in Chapter 4, the activity of punishment is deeply involved in processes of social regulation and social change. It reflects changes in the distribution of power, in conceptions of individuals and their motivation, and in ideas of what is permissible or desirable in the defence of social order and legality. The reasons given by a judge when passing sentence are a 'vocabulary of motive' (Melossi, 1985). But as social scientists we may also wish to ask: Why does one such vocabulary, say deterrence or 'just deserts', come to predominate in one country or at one time rather than another? So, for instance, we might want to know why two neighbouring countries with very similar rates of recorded crime, such as England and Wales and The Netherlands, can come to differ markedly in their use of imprisonment (a real example, explored below in section 4.3). What might this reveal about differences in their political climates or intellectual culture? When we pose such questions we move from the traditional concerns of penology (Whom should we punish? How much? By what means?) towards what Garland and Young (1983b) have termed the 'social analysis of penality'. penality When we do this we will tend no longer to talk of 'punishment' in the singular (as an 'it'), but to think instead about the varied ideologies, knowledges, professional specialisms and decisions involved in the field of penal practices and about the relations between that 'penal realm' and other spheres of economic and political life. The resulting differences in the 'scale of imprisonment' (Zimring and Hawkins, 1991) may tell us something of importance about the 'sensibilities' towards punishment (Garland, 1990) that prevail in each country. More specifically, they may reveal both constant and variable aspects of the ways in which prisons are used. Such comparative knowledge can be useful in helping us to decide what level of imprisonment we are prepared to accept as necessary or legitimate.

## 2.3  Prisons and the problem of legitimacy

Prisons have a number of features that mark them out as unique amongst contemporary social institutions. Some of these are obvious but their implications are nonetheless important. Prisons confine people under conditions not of their own choosing, in close proximity with others whose company they may not desire, attended by custodians who are formally empowered to regulate their lives in intimate detail. It is true that prisons share some of these characteristics with other 'total institutions', if by 'total' we mean institutions that 'tend to encompass the whole of the lives of their inmates' (Goffman, 1961). Examples often cited of total institutions include barracks, boarding schools, children's homes and hospitals (see Cohen and Taylor, 1981); but the only really close analogy is probably with compulsory psychiatric confinement under mental health legislation. It is largely because of their 'total' character that prisons pose issues of *legitimacy* that are in some degree special. Why is this so? And why is it important? What is legitimacy anyway?

*Wakefield Prison, 1995: a 'total institution'*

It has long been argued that prison administrators hold 'a grant of power without equal' (Sykes, 1958, p.42) in liberal democratic societies. Many political theorists argue that questions of legitimacy arise whenever states claim the right to exercise power over their citizens, especially when they support these claims with reference to the necessity of upholding the law or other aspects of the 'general good' (such as the maintenance of public safety through the suppression of crime). Legitimacy can thus be defined as a claim to justified authority in the use of power. It would seem to follow that the greater the power in question the more urgently it stands in need of legitimation. Consider the following definition, taken from David Beetham's book *The Legitimation of Power* (1991):

legitimacy

> Power can be said to be legitimate to the extent that:
>
> (i)    it conforms to established rules
>
> (ii)   the rules can be justified by reference to beliefs shared by both dominant and subordinate
>
> (iii)  there is evidence of consent by the subordinate to the particular power relation.
>
> (Beetham, 1991, p.16)

Beetham argues that all systems of power relations seek legitimation. Such criteria are almost never perfectly fulfilled and each dimension of legitimacy has a corresponding form of non-legitimate power. Where power fails to conform to its own rules of legal validity it is illegitimate. Where it lacks justification in shared beliefs it experiences a legitimacy deficit. Where it fails to find legitimation through expressed consent it may finally experience a crisis of delegitimation (withdrawal of consent) (Beetham, 1991, p.20). Most pointedly for the present discussion of prisons: 'the form of power which is distinctive to [the political domain] – organized physical coercion – is one that both supremely stands in need of legitimation, yet is also uniquely able to breach all legitimacy. The legitimation of the state's power is thus both specially urgent and fateful in its consequences' (Beetham, 1991, p.40).

Prisons, like other forms of punishment but in a particularly acute way, confront questions of legitimacy because they assume an especially high degree of power over the lives of their inmates, and that power is in the last instance buttressed by the right to use sanctions, including physical force, to secure prisoners' compliance. The question of legitimacy is also complicated by two further considerations.

First, to confine an individual is also to place them in a position of dependency. As Mathiesen (1965) puts it, prisoners are reliant on prison staff for the 'distribution of benefits and burdens' in both formal and discretionary ways. In this respect, in claiming the authority to imprison one of its citizens, a state is undertaking a responsibility for the prisoner's health, safety and physical and psychological well-being which is qualitatively greater than that which it owes to the free citizen. Questions thus arise concerning the scope of prisoners' rights or entitlements (Richardson, 1985; Livingstone and Owen, 1993) and of the mechanisms of legal accountability (Gearty, 1991), inspection (Morgan and Evans, 1994) and standards (Woolf, 1991) that govern the operation of prisons in complex modern societies (see section 3.3 and section 5).

Second, the question of legitimacy also arises in relation to the internal order and organization of the prison. It is notoriously true that prisons sometimes erupt in violent upheavals, protest and riots (most famously in the USA at Attica in 1971 and in England at Strangeways in 1990 – see Adams, 1992). Some would argue that this is a risk inherent in the process of confinement. King puts the matter succinctly:

> It is best to acknowledge at the outset that there is no solution to the control problem in prisons, nor can there be. The control problem – of how to maintain 'good order and discipline' – is inherent and endemic. For as long as we have prisons – and an institution that has become so entrenched in our thinking shows no sign whatever of becoming disestablished – then we will continue to hold prisoners against their will. At bottom that is what it is about.

(King, 1985, p.187)

Yet, we also know that such endemic problems do not always and everywhere result in riots and major crises. It is intriguing and important to ask what marks the transition between a chronic background issue (in Beetham's terms a 'legitimacy deficit') and a serious breakdown of order (a 'crisis of delegitimation'). Answers to this question encompass a complex range of factors including levels of material provision in prison regimes (crowding, sanitation, food, work, education and so on – see King and McDermott, 1989) and procedural fairness (such as disciplinary and grievance procedures – see Woolf, 1991), as well as less readily quantifiable issues concerning the nature of social relationships between staff and prisoners (Sparks and Bottoms, 1995).

Since at least the late 1970s it has become commonplace to find references to the prison systems of a number of countries (the UK and the USA perhaps in particular, but latterly also countries such as Italy – see Pavarini, 1994) as being 'in crisis'. Increasingly, commentators on penal affairs have begun to think about such 'crises' – especially where they include serious problems of order or control – as being in the first instance problems of legitimation (Woolf, 1991; Sim, 1992; Cavadino and Dignan, 1992; Sparks, 1994; Sparks and Bottoms, 1995). We can thus regard legitimacy as a linking idea which runs throughout the apparently disparate questions of penal politics discussed in this chapter. Let us for the time being pose these issues as a series of open questions:

- Is the allocation of punishments in any given society justified by coherent principles? Is it consistent and procedurally fair? Do sentences in the main achieve their stated objectives? Is punishment legitimate in Beetham's first sense (conformity with established rules)?

- Do the system's present practices find widespread acceptance and support in the wider society or are they the subject of disagreement and ideological dispute? Are they therefore legitimate in Beetham's second and more 'external' sense (justification in terms of shared belief)?

- Can the system sustain itself over time in a relatively stable and orderly way or is it subject to repeated challenge and resistance? Can it secure the consent (or even simply compliance) of its own subordinate members – in this case prisoners and to some extent lower level staff? Or has it embarked upon a 'crisis of delegitimation' (withdrawal of consent)?

In our view these questions provide the framework for understanding what is meant by the term 'penal crisis' and for evaluating policy changes introduced with the aim of resolving or averting the most pressing problems. We turn now to a consideration of how these issues have been experienced in England and Wales in recent times. We then go on to ask more generally (in section 4): What can differences between countries in rates of imprisonment tell us about the extent to which each has elected to emphasize prisons or other options in addressing their crime problems, and why?

# 3 Crises, change and modernization in penal policy

It has become commonplace to use the term 'crisis' to describe the state of the prisons. It is the standard term of journalism. But just what is this 'crisis'? What *are* the main problems of the English and Welsh and Scottish prison systems? And why have they proved so resistant to change? Is 'crisis' perhaps an inappropriate term? Why might this be so? In common parlance the term 'crisis' denotes something severe but usually of short duration: Sterling crisis, Suez crisis and so forth. At the same time it includes an implication of change – if an illness reaches its crisis the patient either dies or begins to recover. It is a term that in its ordinary usage now refers us to the visible symptoms of a problem (in this case overcrowding, insanitary conditions, brutality, riots) rather than the structural properties of the system that generates them. When the word is used in this way a government can announce certain measures (end 'slopping out', improve visiting arrangements, install some telephones, build some more prisons) and claim, for all relevant purposes, to have averted the crisis, at least for the time being. Yet, as King and McDermott (1989) document, the English penal 'crisis', in particular, is not of this short-lived kind; rather, it is a durable state of affairs but one which reached a deepening severity throughout the 1970s and 1980s. It seems necessary, therefore, to try to get behind this 'headline' language in order to explore just what the principal problems of the system have been. It may be helpful to think of the 'crisis' as the conjunction of four main sets of issues, namely:

1   the rising prison population;
2   costs, crowding and conditions;
3   purpose;
4   order.

## 3.1  The prison population

In the 40 years between the end of the Second World War and the mid 1980s the prison population in England and Wales trebled from around 15,000 in 1946 to 45,000 in 1986. Much of this increase results from demographic factors and the six-fold increase in recorded crime during those post-war decades. Indeed, although the absolute numbers in prison rose inexorably, the use of imprisonment *as a proportion* of all sentences actually declined markedly for much of this period (Bottoms, 1983). The prison population began to rise particularly steeply from 1974 onwards, rising every year from 1974 to 1988. Moreover, after 1974 the earlier proportionate trend away from imprisonment was reversed. Whereas in 1974 imprisonment accounted for 15 per cent of all sentences imposed, by 1986 it represented 21 per cent (Hale, 1989, pp.334–5). Towards the end of the 1980s this proportionate usage again declined towards earlier levels and the prison population fell back somewhat for a time (Home Office, 1993), only to reach new record levels in 1995 (see *The Guardian*, 17 March 1995, reproduced below).

# Howard under fire as jail total hits record 51,243

**Alan Travis**
**Home Affairs Editor**

THE prison population yesterday broke the record for England and Wales when it reached 51,243 two years after Michael Howard, the Home Secretary, adopted his 'prison works' policy.

The figure was recorded as Mr Howard's proposed reforms of community sentences faced criticism from the National Probation Conference. He was told by chief probation officers and by employers that the reform package had caused grave concern and he needed to rise above 'simplistic solutions'.

The Prison Governors' Association warned that the jail system could not cope with the pressure, and that inmates were being allocated to jails where there were beds, regardless of the type of prison.

Prison numbers are rising by more than 200 a week and are up by 26 per cent on the 40,606 recorded in December 1992. Jails are holding 2,234 more inmates than they officially have

room for. The 51,243 figure includes 324 prisoners held in police cells – at a cost of more than £400 a night each – because of the overcrowding, and a record 2,012 women.

The prison population last reached these levels in July 1987, when the Government's reaction was to increase sharply the use of alternative penalties for minor offenders.

It is only the second time that the number has breached 50,000 in English history.

The Prison Service said yesterday it expected the number to continue to rise, since six new private prisons are in the pipeline and a further 2,000 places are to be provided in existing jails.

David Roddan, spokesman for the Prison Governors' Association, said the system could not cope with this kind of pressure.

'If we do not have the space to hold people in suitable conditions we will be back to the bad old days of 1987, when the adult prison system had become a dumping ground,' he said.

The Howard League for Penal Reform said the country could

no longer afford a Home Secretary obsessed with incarceration at the expense of preventing crime.

The Penal Affairs Consortium said the 'shameful figure' was the inevitable result of Mr Howard's criminal policy U-turn.

Mr Howard had to face his critics in the probation world after he published radical plans to shake up the training of probation officers and reform community sentences.

He told the conference in London that he rejected an approach which equated punishment in the community with social work with offenders.

Conference chairman Martin Bryant, of the Association of Chief Officers of Probation, told him tackling crime was complex and a home secretary had to rise above 'the clamour for simplistic solutions'.

Other senior probation figures told him his training proposals had demoralised qualified staff and caused grave concern.

(*The Guardian*, 17 March 1995)

The long-term trend in the prison population of England and Wales has thus been to increase in absolute numbers, but to fluctuate in proportionate terms. But it is also important to remember that such trends can contain (indeed conceal) some very abrupt changes in sentencing and 'surges' in prison numbers. Consider the strange case of 1993. By the end of 1993 the prison population of England and Wales stood at 47,200. This represented a rise of 4,600 in that year alone – an increase of some 16 per cent over the previous year's end. In the second half of the year the numbers in prison rose at the rate of 600 per month (Home Office, 1994). For many commentators this increase was regarded as particularly disappointing in that it followed some sharp falls (in the second half of 1992 the prison population fell by around 6,000, largely as result of changes to sentencing and parole decisions introduced in the Criminal Justice Act 1991) (Ashworth, 1993). These increases were particularly marked amongst young prisoners (those under 21) whose numbers rose by 22 per cent, despite the fact that this was one group whose representation within the prison population had fallen consistently during the 1980s. The numbers of prisoners on remand rose by an especially sharp 44 per cent during 1993. The number of women in prison also rose abruptly in this period, by around 16 per cent in 1993–94. There are some curious features to note here which have a bearing on how we are to explain changes in prison numbers. Whilst it is clear that the long-term structural trend in the prison population cannot be wholly divorced from the volume of recorded crime, it is also readily apparent that they have a degree of independence from one another. Indeed, the number of notifiable offences recorded by the police in 1993 *fell* by one per cent.

## 3.2  Costs, crowding and conditions

It is not easy to see how the rates of increase in the prison population experienced throughout the 1980s and again in 1993–95 could be indefinitely sustained. The prison estate enlarged substantially (indeed by a total of some 20,000 places) after the inception of the government's building programme in the early 1980s (McLaughlin and Muncie, 1994). By 1995 there were more than 130 Prison Service establishments in England and Wales, a further 22 in Scotland and six in Northern Ireland (see Figure 5.1).

Overall capacity and population came more or less into balance in the early 1990s for the first time in many years, although overcrowding remained an obdurate problem in the city centre local prisons. In England and Wales in March 1994 these were more than 20 per cent overcrowded: the worst – Leicester, Shrewsbury and Chelmsford – being of the order of 70 per cent overcrowded. At that point 15 prisons were overcrowded by more than 30 per cent and 8,500 prisoners were sleeping two to a cell designed for one (NACRO, 1994b), yet the rate of increase in population recorded in the second half of 1993 and first months of 1994 would necessitate opening a new prison every month.

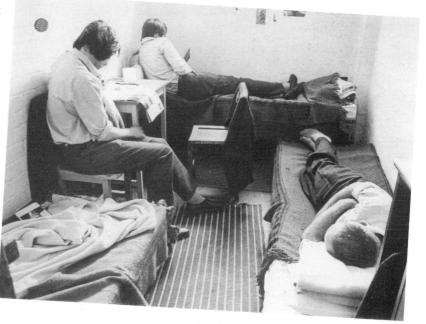

*A cell housing three people*

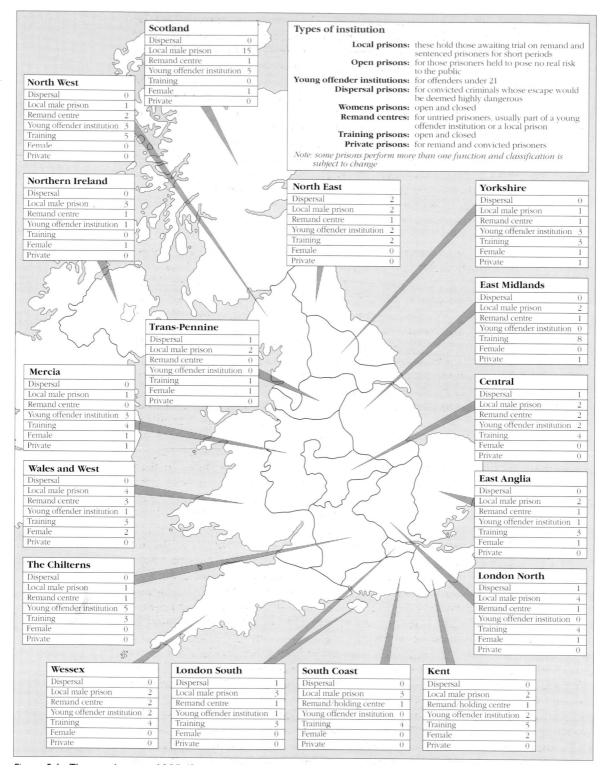

**Scotland**

| | |
|---|---|
| Dispersal | 0 |
| Local male prison | 15 |
| Remand centre | 1 |
| Young offender institution | 5 |
| Training | 0 |
| Female | 1 |
| Private | 0 |

**North West**

| | |
|---|---|
| Dispersal | 0 |
| Local male prison | 1 |
| Remand centre | 2 |
| Young offender institution | 3 |
| Training | 5 |
| Female | 0 |
| Private | 0 |

**Northern Ireland**

| | |
|---|---|
| Dispersal | 0 |
| Local male prison | 3 |
| Remand centre | 1 |
| Young offender institution | 1 |
| Training | 0 |
| Female | 1 |
| Private | 0 |

**Mercia**

| | |
|---|---|
| Dispersal | 0 |
| Local male prison | 1 |
| Remand centre | 0 |
| Young offender institution | 3 |
| Training | 4 |
| Female | 1 |
| Private | 1 |

**Wales and West**

| | |
|---|---|
| Dispersal | 0 |
| Local male prison | 4 |
| Remand centre | 3 |
| Young offender institution | 1 |
| Training | 3 |
| Female | 2 |
| Private | 0 |

**The Chilterns**

| | |
|---|---|
| Dispersal | 0 |
| Local male prison | 1 |
| Remand centre | 1 |
| Young offender institution | 5 |
| Training | 3 |
| Female | 0 |
| Private | 0 |

**Trans-Pennine**

| | |
|---|---|
| Dispersal | 1 |
| Local male prison | 2 |
| Remand centre | 0 |
| Young offender institution | 0 |
| Training | 1 |
| Female | 1 |
| Private | 0 |

**North East**

| | |
|---|---|
| Dispersal | 2 |
| Local male prison | 2 |
| Remand centre | 1 |
| Young offender institution | 2 |
| Training | 2 |
| Female | 0 |
| Private | 0 |

**Yorkshire**

| | |
|---|---|
| Dispersal | 0 |
| Local male prison | 1 |
| Remand centre | 1 |
| Young offender institution | 3 |
| Training | 3 |
| Female | 1 |
| Private | 1 |

**East Midlands**

| | |
|---|---|
| Dispersal | 0 |
| Local male prison | 2 |
| Remand centre | 1 |
| Young offender institution | 0 |
| Training | 8 |
| Female | 0 |
| Private | 1 |

**Central**

| | |
|---|---|
| Dispersal | 1 |
| Local male prison | 2 |
| Remand centre | 2 |
| Young offender institution | 2 |
| Training | 4 |
| Female | 0 |
| Private | 0 |

**East Anglia**

| | |
|---|---|
| Dispersal | 0 |
| Local male prison | 2 |
| Remand centre | 1 |
| Young offender institution | 1 |
| Training | 3 |
| Female | 1 |
| Private | 0 |

**London North**

| | |
|---|---|
| Dispersal | 1 |
| Local male prison | 4 |
| Remand centre | 1 |
| Young offender institution | 0 |
| Training | 4 |
| Female | 1 |
| Private | 0 |

**Wessex**

| | |
|---|---|
| Dispersal | 0 |
| Local male prison | 2 |
| Remand centre | 2 |
| Young offender institution | 2 |
| Training | 4 |
| Female | 0 |
| Private | 0 |

**London South**

| | |
|---|---|
| Dispersal | 1 |
| Local male prison | 3 |
| Remand centre | 1 |
| Young offender institution | 1 |
| Training | 3 |
| Female | 0 |
| Private | 0 |

**South Coast**

| | |
|---|---|
| Dispersal | 0 |
| Local male prison | 3 |
| Remand/holding centre | 1 |
| Young offender institution | 0 |
| Training | 4 |
| Female | 0 |
| Private | 0 |

**Kent**

| | |
|---|---|
| Dispersal | 0 |
| Local male prison | 2 |
| Remand/holding centre | 1 |
| Young offender institution | 2 |
| Training | 5 |
| Female | 2 |
| Private | 0 |

**Types of institution**

**Local prisons:** these hold those awaiting trial on remand and sentenced prisoners for short periods
**Open prisons:** for those prisoners held to pose no real risk to the public
**Young offender institutions:** for offenders under 21
**Dispersal prisons:** for convicted criminals whose escape would be deemed highly dangerous
**Womens prisons:** open and closed
**Remand centres:** for untried prisoners, usually part of a young offender institution or a local prison
**Training prisons:** open and closed
**Private prisons:** for remand and convicted prisoners

*Note: some prisons perform more than one function and classification is subject to change*

*Figure 5.1 The penal estate, 1995 (Source: based on* The Guardian, *8 October 1991; HM Prison Service, n.d.; Scottish Prison Service, 1995; Northern Ireland Prison Service, personal communication, November 1995)*

Home Office projections suggested a continued increase – to some 56,000 by the year 2002 (Home Office, 1995a) – but, as Zimring and Hawkins (1994) have suggested for California, such projections are least useful when they are most anxiously sought, namely during sudden upsurges in population. On 1993 trends the prison population would have exceeded this projection within two years (in fact, it reached 53,000 by the beginning of 1996). The prospect of routinely resorting to the use of police cells, old army camps and prison ships (all of which arose during the 1980s) recurred.

Imprisonment is very costly. The average cost of a prison sentence in 1991–92 was about £2,000 per month (substantially more in maximum security 'dispersal' prisons). This is of the order of 20 times more than for the same period of a probation or community service order (NACRO, 1994b). In that year the prisons cost the taxpayer over £1.5 billion (plus the capital costs of prison building: £1.1 billion since 1985 or £130,000 for every new place) (Home Office, 1993).

The persistence of overcrowding (partly engendered, albeit temporarily, by the system's very effort of modernization given the need to take accommodation out of use during refurbishment) has been routinely regretted by senior managers and condemned by a variety of interested commentators, such as the Chief Inspector of Prisons, representatives of the Prison Governors' Association and Prison Officers' Association and Lord Woolf. These factors have a major effect on conditions for prisoners and staff. Imagine the practical difficulties which arise in such workaday matters as bathing, clothing, visiting, education, ferrying prisoners to court, and so on (see King and McDermott, 1989). The Prison Officers' Association (1990) has argued strongly that such material strain on space and human resources has severely inhibited efforts to engender greater professionalism and creativity in working practices (see Hay and Sparks, 1991).

In addition to these obvious strains, the Prison Service is a complex organization in many less readily apparent respects. Prisons differ in their functions. For adult men (the largest group) these range from 'dispersal prisons' (highly secure long-term 'training' prisons for sentenced prisoners) through somewhat less secure training prisons and open prisons to local prisons and remand centres. Because of these distinctions prison space is a relatively inflexible resource and has long been unevenly distributed regionally. The very much smaller number of women in prison encounter the special problem that the dozen or so women's establishments are especially geographically far-flung, imposing uniquely serious difficulties in sustaining familial and other social relationships, though the pivot of the women's system in England remains one large multi-purpose institution at Holloway in north London and in Scotland at Cornton Vale near Stirling. Young Offender Institutions are similarly scattered, a fact that has been widely taken as exacerbating the problems of suicide, self-injury and bullying that historically afflict custodial institutions for young people (Liebling, 1992). Imprisonment remains numerically dominated by young adult men (though for various reasons, principally a trend towards greater average sentence lengths, the modal age of the prison population has tended to increase) and many would argue that the organization and culture of the prison system reflects this predominance. In general terms prisoners in the UK (in common with those elsewhere) are disproportionately likely to be poor, to be members of minority ethnic groups, to have few occupational skills or academic attainments, to have been in local authority care, to have no permanent address and to have received (or be reckoned eligible for) a psychiatric diagnosis of some kind (Prison Reform Trust, 1991; Gunn *et al.*, 1991; Morgan, 1994). Figures 5.2 and 5.3 respectively provide information on the offences for which prisoners in England have been convicted and on the gender and ethnic origin of prisoners.

*Figure 5.2 Population under sentence in Prison Service establishments on 30 June by offence group, 1989–94 (percentage was calculated excluding those with offence not recorded) (Source: Home Office, 1995b, p.9, Figure 6)*

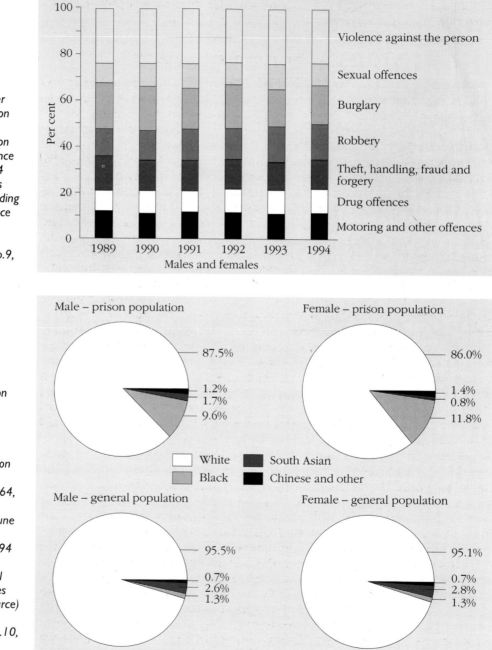

*Figure 5.3 Prison Service establishment population (UK nationals) and general population (UK nationals, males aged 15–64, females aged 15–54) on 30 June by gender and ethnic origin, 1994 (discrepancies in totals for general population figures as in original source) (Source: Home Office, 1995b, p.10, Figure 7)*

It is, moreover, important to consider how the dimensions of the 'crisis' that we have identified interact. The often strained and overburdened nature of the prison system has at times adversely affected both industrial relations and staff–prisoner relations. It has thereby inhibited the developments of attempts to move beyond reactive 'crisis management' postures towards any more proactive redefinition of the *aims and purposes* of imprisonment. Taken together, these matters have rather drastically undermined the *legitimacy* of the system, certainly in the eyes of many amongst its captive population. This in turn is intimately connected with the problem of *order.*

## 3.3 The problem of penal purpose

As we saw in Chapter 4, section 5, since 1895 an officially espoused aim of the English prison system has been to 'encourage and assist [prisoners] to lead a good and useful life'. Whilst doubt and scepticism has always attended this formulation, it was elevated in 1964 to the symbolically central position of Prison Rule 1. By the late 1970s, however, the combination of theoretical and practical doubts over the efficacy and coherence of such rehabilitative ideals (Martinson, 1974; Brody, 1976; Allen, 1981), with endemic industrial relations problems and the pressures of a rising population, meant that for many Rule 1 was considered a dead letter. In 1979 the May Committee concluded that: 'the rhetoric of treatment and training has had its day and should be replaced' (Home Office, 1979, para 4.9). On the other hand, the Committee were anxious (perhaps presciently) that to abandon such ambitions altogether would 'lead to the cynicism of human warehousing' (Home Office, 1979, para 4.24). They therefore proposed a notion of 'positive custody', which they hoped would provide an acceptably realistic compromise formulation. The May Committee spoke hopefully of custody as 'severe and yet positive' and envisaged that it could 'preserve and promote prisoners' self-respect' and 'prepare them for and assist them on discharge' (Home Office, 1979, para 4.26). 'Positive custody' has found few defenders. Its most articulate critics (King and Morgan, 1980) regarded it as a hybrid notion, lacking in content, yet still giving too much ground to the notion that people might be sent to prison in their own best interests, hence failing to inhibit the growth of the prison population. (In 1968 Wheeler had discovered that in the USA 'progressive' judges – that is, those most convinced of rehabilitative ideals – had in fact been passing longer sentences than their more classicist colleagues, presumably on precisely this premise.) King and Morgan proposed the alternative objective of 'humane containment' on the grounds that the expectations placed upon imprisonment should be scaled down to those which it could reasonably be called upon to achieve (the minimum necessary use of custody, the minimum necessary level of security, humane conditions of confinement under circumstances of as great a 'normalization' as compatible with the fact of custody). Of course, such 'minimum' levels beg the question of defining 'necessity' within a given set of rationales for imprisonment. Implicitly, 'humane containment' allies itself with a 'just deserts' position, perhaps in conjunction with a degree of 'selective incapacitation' for those adjudged most dangerous. (This was almost precisely the position subsequently adopted by the 1991 Criminal Justice Act – see Chapter 3.)

positive custody

humane
containment

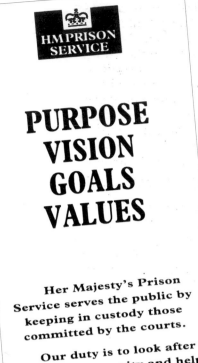

**HM PRISON SERVICE**

# PURPOSE
# VISION
# GOALS
# VALUES

Her Majesty's Prison Service serves the public by keeping in custody those committed by the courts.

Our duty is to look after them with humanity and help them lead law-abiding and useful lives in custody and after release.

*HM Prison Service
mission statement*

Neither 'positive custody' nor 'humane containment' have been regarded as wholly satisfactory by prison administrators. Ever since 1979 there has been a succession of attempts to revise and reformulate a coherent set of aims of imprisonment in the face of the demise of rehabilitation, 'treatment and training'. The less ambitious of these – for example, that of the Control Review Committee (Home Office, 1984) – accords closely with King and Morgan in emphasizing the prevention of 'further avoidable hardship' and the importance of respecting 'prisoners' lawful rights'. Yet such a 'humane containment plus' position (Bottoms, 1990) never looked likely to succeed in its primary purposes of providing *any* substantive principle which would legitimate the practice of imprisonment and which would offer prison staff 'something to believe in and some hope' (Dunbar, 1985) which might help motivate and co-ordinate their activity. Eventually in 1988 the Home Office issued a 'mission statement', a notice of which is now prominently displayed on entry to every prison in England and Wales.

Bottoms comments that this statement 'must be considered something of a disappointment' (Bottoms, 1990, p.15). He continues: 'It is difficult to quarrel with anything that is actually contained in the statement, except to doubt quite strongly the extent to which the last phrase is effectively translatable into practice'. Lord Justice Woolf is rather more critical, pointing out that the notion of 'humanity' commits one to rather less than other more stringent possible principles such as 'justice' (Woolf, 1991, para 10.20). Nonetheless this remains the official position. The greater part of subsequent activity has gone instead into formulating rather more managerially concrete 'tasks' and 'performance indicators', including identifiable targets for particular features of regimes (such as time spent in work or education and time out of cells). Such activity received a further stimulus from Woolf, whose intervention in 1991 was widely heralded by penal professionals as lending weight to efforts at modernization. The signal preoccupation of the prison system in England and Wales since the 1980s, therefore, has been with the efficiency of management practices, the distribution of resources and the cost-effective delivery of services. This trend in policy has produced reviews of management structure both within prisons themselves (under the Fresh Start initiative of 1987) and of more senior levels of decision-making. In 1993 the Prison Service, formerly a Department of State within the Home Office, became a semi-autonomous Executive Agency under a new Director General recruited from industry and with no civil service (let alone prison) background. In 1994 it published its first Business Plan and Corporate Plan, each with a strong emphasis on quantifiable measures of improvement in performance, backed for the first time by a published code of 'operating standards' for prison establishments.

The period of the later 1980s and early 1990s must thus be viewed as a rather paradoxical one within the contentious history of the English prison. It was marked on the one hand by sharp fluctuations in population (latterly by effectively uncontrolled and probably unassimilable expansion), and by great disparities in levels of crowding and regime provision; and punctuated by increasingly frequent, widespread and destructive disorders. At the same time the period saw some of the first genuinely strategic, modernizing official thinking on imprisonment in modern times. One can interpret these developments as being in part a pragmatic response to some demonstrably great problems of poor and uneven provision and conditions, in part the outcome of externally imposed demands for change (notably from Lord Woolf), and in part as resulting from a very general governmental pressure for 'value for money' that has affected all public services since the early 1980s (McLaughlin and Muncie, 1994). The latter point may itself merely express a longer-term development towards 'managerialism' in criminal justice throughout the advanced industrial societies at the end of the twentieth century (we take up this issue below in section 5 in discussion of one of its principal manifestations, namely privatization). Whether any of this is sufficient to fend away the underlying legitimacy deficit (Beetham, 1991), left by the decline of the rehabilitative ideal, the renewed politicization of penal issues of the 1990s and the resumption of expansionism, is altogether another question.

## 3.4   The problem of order

Almost since the very inception of penitentiary imprisonment riots and disturbances have occurred (Adams, 1992). It is more or less self-evident that prisoners do not necessarily respond compliantly either to the fact or to the conditions of their confinement. Between the end of the Second World War and the early 1980s serious collective disorder in English prisons remained largely confined to the long-term adult male 'training' prisons, and in particular the maximum security 'dispersal' system (Woolf, 1991, paras 9.8–9.18; Home Office, 1984, Annex D). In Scotland, similarly, the main focus of unrest remained the lonely fortress of Peterhead (Scraton et al., 1991). Official responses (commonly unpublished) concentrated in large measure on improvements in the hardware and technique of riot control and on the identification of ringleaders. The long-term prisons proved amenable to being depicted as congregations of dangerous and violent men with nothing to lose.

However, the 1980s saw a marked widening of the incidence and extent of prison disorders. In 1986 there was a series of disturbances in prisons affected by prison officers' industrial action. In 1988 there were riots in lower security Category C prisons. In 1989 *unconvicted* prisoners occupied the roof at Risley Remand Centre. In April 1990 the single most significant event in modern English penal history, the 25-day rebellion and siege at Strangeways prison in Manchester, took place, followed by a wave of disturbances across England and Wales. The allegation that participation in active protest was the prerogative of the desperate few could no longer be sustained. Lord Justice Woolf was invited by the Home Office to conduct an inquiry.

Disturbances at Risley Remand Centre in 1989: at any one time about 25 per cent of the total prison population is made up of those unconvicted or untried

Disturbances at Strangeways Prison in 1990: the single most significant event in modern English penal history

Woolf concluded that the scale and intensity of the 1990 protests at Manchester, Dartmoor, Bristol, Cardiff and elsewhere could only be attributed to a widely shared sense of injustice:

> A recurring theme in the evidence from prisoners who may have instigated, and who were involved in, the riots was that their actions were a response to the manner in which they were treated by the prison system. Although they did not always use these terms, they felt a lack of justice. If what they say is true, the failure of the Prison Service to fulfil its responsibilities to act with justice created in April 1990 serious difficulties in maintaining security and control in prisons.

> (Woolf, 1991, para 9.24)

Elsewhere Woolf went on to argue against the historically received view that prisoners' goods and services should be regarded as 'privileges', awarded or removed by discretion (for example, Woolf, 1991, para 14.32 ff.). He referred instead to the 'threshold quality of life' of all prisoners and to the 'legitimate expectations' that prisoners have of their treatment (for example, para 12.129). For him, serious attention to justice in prisons required the Prison Service to make available to prisoners at least (i) a humane regime (for example, 'a dry cell, integral sanitation, ... exercise, activities, association and food': para 10.20); and (ii) a reasoned explanation for all decisions adversely affecting individual prisoners, and fair procedures for dealing with prisoners' grievances and alleged indiscipline (para 10.20). Throughout his report, including the final paragraphs of the main text, Woolf emphasized his belief that such issues are fundamental to the stability of the system (see Extract 5.1).

What Woolf is outlining here (albeit at times only implicitly) is something akin to a theory of *legitimacy*, of a kind that sociologists and political theorists would recognize. He believes, that is to say, that there are variable conditions which render it more or less likely that prisoners will accept, however conditionally, the authority of their custodians. What is novel here is not so much the insight itself (which, in a more or less developed form, is frequently affirmed on prison wings and landings by prisoners and prison staff), but rather the insistence that official discourse should articulate and act upon it (for fuller accounts of the relationship between order and legitimacy in prisons see Cavadino and Dignan, 1992; Sparks and Bottoms, 1995).

Just how radically innovative or successful Woolf's diagnosis will be remains disputed. For example, Sim (1994) draws attention to the fact that the Home Office response was ambivalent. Formally, much of Woolf's reform agenda was accepted, albeit over a very lengthy timescale of implementation. Yet simultaneously a new criminal offence of 'prison mutiny' was created, carrying a maximum sentence of 10 years. Moreover, some of the most controversial aspects of penal control methods, namely governors' discretionary powers to segregate prisoners either for their own protection or 'in the interests of good order and discipline' (under Prison Rule 43) and to transfer them under the terms of Circular Instruction 37/1990 (subsequently Circular Instruction 29/1993), were left substantially unaltered by Woolf. Moreover, critics drew attention to those aspects of the 'institutional climates' of prisons which were much less determined by matters of procedure than by the informal cultures and working practices of prison staff (PROP, 1990; Sim, 1994; Sparks and Bottoms, 1995).

## Extract 5.1  Woolf: 'Justice in prisons'

9.19    The evidence from Part 1 of this Inquiry shows that there are three requirements which must be met if the prison system is to be stable: they are security, control and justice.

9.20    For present purposes, 'security' refers to the obligation of the Prison Service to prevent prisoners escaping. 'Control' deals with the obligation of the Prison Service to prevent prisoners being disruptive. 'Justice' refers to the obligation of the Prison Service to treat prisoners with humanity and fairness and to prepare them for their return to the community in a way which makes it less likely that they will reoffend. ...

9.37    The evidence of prisoners is that they will not join in disturbances in any numbers if they feel conditions are reasonable and relationships are satisfactory. These are matters of justice which the Prison Service must address more closely. They are fundamental to maintaining a stable prison system which is able to withstand and reject the depredations of disruptive and violent individuals. These are matters which must be resolved if we are to have peace in our prisons. ...

10.18    The Courts send prisoners to prison because in their judgement justice requires that the prisoner should receive a sentence of imprisonment. Imprisonment is the gravest punishment which it is open to the Courts to impose. The Courts do not, as they did at one time for some types of sentence, specify what form that punishment should take. They do not sentence someone to hard labour, or corrective training. They leave it to the Prison Service to decide how to provide the conditions of containment which are appropriate for that individual, having regard to all the relevant factors, including the length of sentence which he has to serve.

10.19    If the Prison Service contains that prisoner in conditions which are inhumane or degrading, or which are otherwise wholly inappropriate, then a punishment of imprisonment which was justly imposed, will result in injustice. It is no doubt for this reason, as well as because any other approach would offend the values of our society, that the Statement of Purpose acknowledges that it is the Prison Service's duty to look after prisoners with humanity. If it fulfils this duty, the Prison Service is partly achieving what the Court must be taken to have intended when it passed a sentence of imprisonment. This must be that, while the prisoner should be subjected to the stigma of imprisonment and should be confined in a prison, the prisoner is not to be subjected to inhumane or degrading treatment.

10.20    ... It is entirely acceptable to argue that the requirement to treat prisoners with humanity includes an obligation to treat them with justice. ...

14.437    Our suggestions are directed to one of the themes which has run through this report, the theme of justice in prisons secured through the exercise of responsibility and respect. The achievement of justice will itself enhance security and control. ...

14.438    ... Were these proposals to be followed, then we believe that they would substantially influence the way prisoners come to view the prison system. While not preventing all disruptions, they would marginalise those who claim they must resort to deeply damaging and costly disturbances on the grounds that there is no other way to have their voices heard.

(Woolf, 1991, pp.225–6; 228; 241; 431–2)

## ACTIVITY 5.1

To ensure that you have understood the discussion so far, make some notes that address the following questions:

1 What do you understand by the terms 'penal crisis' and 'legitimation crisis'?
2 Why is the British penal system so often seen as 'in crisis'?
3 How have the aims of imprisonment shifted in response to such 'crisis'?

## COMMENT

To differentiate the constituent elements within the 'crisis' of the penal system is to clarify the contribution made by each, not merely to an aggregation of discrete 'problems', but to its overall defensibility *as a system*. One somewhat optimistic aspect of this is the apparently greater preparedness not only of external critics, but also of some versions of official discourse (most particularly Woolf), to accept that the penal system confronts endemic problems of legitimacy, on the levels of its provision of appropriate conditions, its historical incapacity to provide a coherent statement of aims, and its long-standing inattention to problems of justice and procedural fairness in respect of discipline, grievances and other aspects of internal organization. However, by no means all the problems of the prison system are of its own creation. The numbers of people whom it must accommodate, and the adequacy of the reasons for which they are imprisoned in the first place, lie outside its control. In its responses to its entrenched legitimation problems the English system would appear to have adopted a dual strategy. First, under the promptings provided by Lord Woolf, it has moved to introduce an increased measure of procedural fairness and explicitness in its dealings with prisoners, particularly as regards disciplinary and grievance mechanisms and more generally in relation to the provision of reasons for decisions. Second, and in the longer term this is the more structurally significant outcome, it has in many respects rather decisively opted for the 'managerialist' road towards 'modernizing' its organization, its delivery of 'services' and its standards of 'performance'.

# 4 Contemporary penal systems in comparative perspective

The rising prison numbers in 1993 reinforced the long-standing position of the three UK prison systems (England and Wales, Scotland, Northern Ireland) as lying at or very near the top of any 'league table' of comparisons with their European neighbours. On figures provided by the Council of Europe, in 1991 the UK topped the list of Western European states, both in terms of absolute numbers and in proportion to its population, with an overall rate of detention of 92.1 per 100,000 inhabitants (see Table 5.1).

| Table 5.1 Imprisonment in Western Europe, 1991 | | |
|---|---|---|
| | Total prison population 1 September 1991 | Detention rate per 100,000 inhabitants |
| UK | 52,830 | 92.1 |
| Spain | 36,562 | 91.8 |
| Luxembourg | 348 | 90.3 |
| Austria | 6,655 | 87.5 |
| Switzerland | 5,6888 | 84.9 |
| France | 48,675 | 83.9 |
| Portugal | 8,092 | 82.0 |
| Germany | 49,658 | 78.8 |
| Denmark | 3,243 | 63.0 |
| Finland | 3,130 | 62.6 |
| Belgium | 6,035 | 60.5 |
| Ireland | 2,114 | 60.4 |
| Norway | 2,510 | 59.0 |
| Italy | 32,368 | 56.0 |
| Sweden | 4,731 | 55.0 |
| Greece | 5,008 | 49.5 |
| Netherlands | 6,662 | 44.4 |
| **The figures for the UK are as follows:** | | |
| England and Wales | 46,310 | 91.3 |
| Scotland | 4,860 | 95.2 |
| Northern Ireland | 1,660 | 105.7 |

Source: NACRO, 1994a, p.19

The most striking aspect of these figures is the very wide range which they record. Each of the top five countries listed had in 1991 a prison population in proportion to the number of its inhabitants approaching twice that of the smallest system, The Netherlands. Such comparisons raise many difficulties of interpretation. These 'headline' figures do not, for example, take any account of variations in recorded crime rates. When expressed as a rate per 100,000 recorded crimes then Italy, Austria, Germany and Greece all hold more prisoners proportionately than does England and Wales (Home Office, 1993). On the same comparison, however, England and Wales imprisons more than twice as many individuals as Finland, The Netherlands or Sweden.

There are a number of other aspects of the issue which this simple list tends to conceal. The 'rate of detention' as recorded in Table 5.1 is a measure of the 'stock' of prisoners on a given day. It gives no indication of the 'flow' of prisoners through the system. Such 'flow' data include the numbers of committals to prison. This is known as the 'rate of imprisonments' (that is, how many individuals are received into prison in the course of a year). We also need to consider the lengths of time spent in prison. It is only when we know all these things (rate of detention, rate of imprisonments, duration of

'stock' and 'flow' data

imprisonment) that we can really claim to describe how each system behaves. Such more detailed comparisons reveal some surprising discoveries. For example, Portugal has a moderately high rate of detention, yet its rate of imprisonments is traditionally very much lower than, say, England and Wales. This indicates that the average duration of imprisonment in Portugal is unusually long. The 'flow' is slow, so the 'stock' is high. In Norway the reverse is the case. Norway actually has a substantially greater rate of imprisonments than England and Wales. However, the average duration of imprisonment there is rather short. The 'flow' is quick, so the 'stock' remains comparatively low (see Muncie and Sparks, 1991a; Fitzmaurice and Pease, 1982; Young, 1986). In general terms a number of southern European countries (Portugal, Italy, Greece) have in common that they send fewer individuals to prison but for quite long periods. The Scandinavian countries (and to some extent The Netherlands) do quite otherwise. There, rather large numbers of individuals go to prison, but often quite briefly.

All of this complicates rather sharply our understanding of which countries are 'lenient' and which are 'punitive' (Pease, 1994), although it does suggest that restricting average sentence lengths is one of the most efficacious ways of keeping overall prison populations in check. The 'exceptional' nature of the British prison populations now appears in clearer relief. The high rate of detention in England and Wales, for example, results from the combination of a rather high (though not the highest) rate of imprisonments with a rather long (though not the longest) average duration (though this discovery still begs the question as to why the system in England and Wales acts in this particular fashion). Its 'flow' is both strong and slow, so its 'stock' is very high. Of these it is probably the duration of imprisonment in England and Wales that is the key factor. The lower prison population of The Netherlands partly reflects greater parsimony in the decision to prosecute in the first instance. The same holds for experience in Germany in the late 1980s (Graham, 1990; Feest, 1991) where it was the exercise of prosecutorial discretion rather than changes in legislation or sentencing that was credited with having reduced the prison population. Since additional restrictions were imposed on the use of cautioning as an alternative to prosecution in England and Wales in 1994, and since the average lengths of prison sentences increased from 8.1 months in 1981 to 14.7 months in 1991 (Home Office, 1993), the prospects for restraining the growth in the English and Welsh prison populations do not look very bright.

## 4.1 The prison population in the USA

There is, however, one Western society that makes the British prison populations look positively minute. In Europe only Hungary and Northern Ireland have in recent years exceeded 100 prisoners per 100,000 inhabitants. In the USA the numbers of persons confined in federal and state prisons has increased at an unprecedented rate since 1980 (from around 330,000 in 1980 to 950,000 in 1993 – see United States Department of Justice, 1994). When one includes the additional 450,000 persons held in local jails (usually for less than one year) the total number incarcerated in the USA exceeded 1.5 million in 1994: a number greater than 500 per 100,000 inhabitants. To calibrate these trends against European comparisons, as Figure 5.4 does for the years 1970–85, is to invite incredulity.

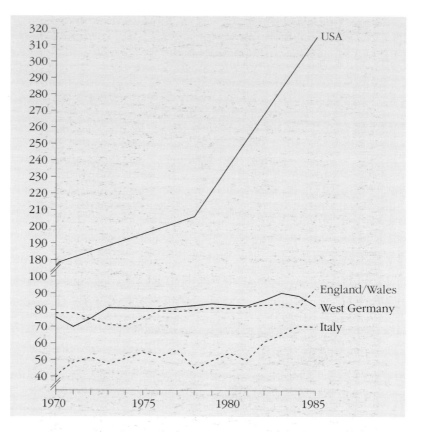

Figure 5.4 Average number of prisoners per 100,000 inhabitants for the USA, England and Wales, West Germany and Italy, 1970–85 (Source: Mathiesen, 1990, p.2, Figure 1.1)

This picture is by no means uniform within the USA. Some states (for example, Minnesota) continue to imprison on 'European' levels. But this merely underlines the fact that certain other states have behaved in an even more discrepant fashion. Of these the District of Columbia (an entirely urban area with a disproportionately poor black population) stands out as exceptional. There the imprisoned population in 1993 was 1,549 per 100,000 (that is, more than 1.5 per cent of the population were in prison at the same time) (Christie, 1993, p.84; United States Department of Justice, 1994).

Such figures have no parallel in the modern history of liberal democratic societies. They cry out for explanation. Yet some of the most temptingly obvious 'explanations' fail to hold water. Principal among these is that the USA must have an exceptionally high and ever-spiralling crime rate. This is certainly a commonly held view both within the USA itself and elsewhere. Many US citizens and policy-makers share the perception that the country's crime problem is out of control (witness, for example, *Newsweek's* cover story 'United States of Fear', 27 September 1993, reproduced opposite).

It is true that rates of many crimes in the USA (both officially recorded and as measured by victimization surveys) are high in international terms, but not to anything like the exceptional degree that is often asserted (United Nations, 1993). It is probably only in the crucially important but numerically quite small category of firearms-related violence that the USA is truly in a class of its own. Moreover, the USA is unusual amongst Western countries in that its recorded crime rates remained rather static during the 1980s. This confirms what we have already seen for England and Wales in 1993, namely that overall crime and imprisonment rates show no simple correspondence.

The same is true over longer time-scales for the USA in the 1960s (crime rose, imprisonment fell – Zimring and Hawkins, 1991, p.122) and for Australia in the 1970s (where also crime rose and imprisonment fell – Biles, 1983, p.168). As Zimring and Hawkins report for California (a state whose incarcerated population tripled during the 1980s):

> Most of the increased imprisonment in California was not directly related to either increases in crime or changes in population. Most crime levels in 1990 were close to their 1980 rates. And the kinds of crime associated with the largest share in California's prison expansion – drug offences, housebreaking and theft – are precisely the offences that flood the criminal justice systems of every major Western democracy. We think that the sorts of policy shifts observed in California could double the prison population of any country in Western Europe experiencing no change in the volume or character of crime.

> (Zimring and Hawkins, 1994, p.92)

The 'policy shifts' that Zimring and Hawkins have in mind here are changes in discretionary law enforcement and sentencing rather than being centrally directed or statutorily required. They are, as Zimring and Hawkins put it, 'more a matter of sentiment than legislation'. The shifts in question include a disproportionate increase in the numbers imprisoned for lesser property offences (they report a 565 per cent increase in the number of persons imprisoned for the various categories of theft – Zimring and Hawkins, 1994, p.88). Meanwhile, although there is some evidence from survey data of a *decline* in illicit drug use in the USA throughout the 1980s, the numbers of persons arrested for drugs offences increased sharply, as did the proportion of those imprisoned following conviction. In fact, the numbers of males in Californian prisons for drugs offences increased by *15 times* during the 1980s (Zimring and Hawkins, 1994, pp.88–90). This followed the national shift in the mid 1980s towards a widely publicized, symbolically powerful and punitively oriented 'War on Drugs' as a primary way in which the USA was to address its problems of addiction.

## 4.2 'Getting tough'

As Zimring and Hawkins comment, it would appear that, given sufficiently great changes in the 'penal climate' or political culture of a society, its prison population may have an 'open ended capacity for change' (Zimring and Hawkins, 1994, p.92). That is, marked changes in penal practice can occur without corresponding changes in crime rates, nor even radical changes in the statutory basis of sentencing. They seem to result rather from external pressures in the crime control culture more broadly conceived and the priorities that emerge there for the stringent suppression of certain kinds of activity in particular, in this case especially drugs offences. Thus, whilst it is true that recent US penal developments have no precedent *in peace time*, perhaps the USA is, strictly speaking, not 'at peace' but rather has 'declared war': the 'war on crime'.

### ACTIVITY 5.2

Read through Extract 5.2. As you do so, keep the following question in mind and make a note of your response: If Christie is correct to challenge the common-sense link between crime and punishment, what other sorts of explanations for levels of prison use do you think may be more plausible?

### COMMENT

Christie denies that there is *any* necessary connection between changes in crime rates and prison populations. He sees no 'natural limits' on either the upper or lower margins of possibility. For Christie, societies must be regarded as *choosing* to have a prison population of a certain size. What seems apparent from Zimring and Hawkins's (1994) discussion, and from Christie's, is that where changes in penal practice are sudden and drastic they are likely to stem from priorities that are political and ideological in origin rather than being simply pragmatic reactions to the demands of crime reduction. Moreover, the situation outlined by Zimring and Hawkins, in which very large numbers of people are indeed being arrested and imprisoned for certain offences, is itself likely to sustain a public perception of those crimes as a pressing problem, thereby reinforcing the pressure on elected politicians and public officials to show that something is being done. It is this sense of being seen to take firm measures that Mathiesen (1990, pp.138–9) calls the 'action function' of punishment.

It is for these reasons that Christie has consistently emphasized that the punishment levels that characterize different countries at particular times must be seen as *choices* (Christie, 1980, 1989, 1993). The volume of recorded and unrecorded crime in contemporary industrial societies is indeed very large – there is plenty of 'raw material' over which punishment choices may

## Extract 5.2  Christie: 'The crime explanation'

The conventional explanation of growth in prison rates is to see it as a reflection of growth in crime. The criminal starts it all, and society has to react. This is the re-active thinking ... [which does] not hold up for Europe. And it fares no better in the USA:

The prison population has doubled during the last ten years. But here is what the Bureau of Justice Statistics tells (*National Update January 1992*, p.5) about the number of victims in that period:

> Victimization rates continue a downward trend that began a decade ago.
>
> There were approximately 34.4 million personal and household crimes in 1990, compared with 41.4 million in 1981.
>
> From 1973 to 1990, the rate of personal crimes (rape, robbery, assault, personal theft) fell by 24.5% and the rate for household crimes (burglary, household theft, motor vehicle theft) fell by 26.1%.
>
> Because the NCVS (The National Crime Victimization Survey) counts only crimes for which the victim can be interviewed, homicides are not counted. Their exclusion does not substantially alter the overall estimates.

The number of victims has gone down. Furthermore, and again in sharp contrast to folk-beliefs on crime in the USA, the number of serious offences reported to the police also shows a slight decrease. The FBI [Federal Bureau of Investigation] statistics on serious offences started at 5.1 million in 1980 and ended at 4.8 million in 1989. But the severity of the sanctions for these crimes has increased. In 1980, 196 offenders were sentenced to prison for every 1,000 arrests for serious crimes. In 1990 the number of imprisonments for such crimes had increased to 332, according to the Bureau of Justice Statistics on Prisoners in 1990.

Mauer (1991, p.7) has these comments:

> While there is little question that the United States has a high rate of crime, there is much evidence that the increase in number of people behind bars in recent years is a consequence of harsher criminal justice policies of the past decade, rather than a direct consequence of rising crime.

Austin and Irvin (1990, p.1) say:

> National statistics show that the majority (65 per cent) of offenders are sentenced to prison for property, drug and public disorder crimes. A significant number (15 per cent) of all admissions have not been convicted of any crime but are returned to prison for violating their parole 'conditions' (e.g. curfew violations, failure to participate in a program, evidence of drug use, etc.)

From their own research – a study based on a random intake to prisons in three states – they also conclude that the vast majority of inmates are sentenced for petty crimes that involve little danger to public safety, or significant economic loss to victims.

The explosion in the number of prisoners in the USA cannot be explained as 'Caused by crime'. We have to look for other explanations.

### References

Austin, J. and Irvin, J. (1990) *Who Goes to Prison?*, The National Council on Crime and Delinquency, USA.

Mauer, M. (1991) *Americans Behind Bars: A Comparison of International Rates of Incarceration*, Washington, DC, The Sentencing Project.

(Christie, 1993, pp.90–2)

be exercised. Moreover, the scale of the problem, and especially its more shocking and dramatic aspects, is insistently emphasized in media coverage (Chibnall, 1977; Hall *et al.*, 1978; Ericson *et al.*, 1991; Schlesinger and Tumber, 1994; **Muncie, 1996**). It is therefore always possible for politicians to invoke 'public opinion' and social defence in the decision to 'get tough' (see *The Sunday Times*, 12 March 1995, reproduced below).

# Jails to become hell on earth

by Geordie Greig, New York

WHEN she thinks of the man who raped and murdered her seven-year-old daughter more than 21 years ago, Rosemarie d'Alessandro becomes angry. She pictures Joseph McGowan living a pampered life in prison, watching television, studying to become a lawyer and being kept warm, clothed and fed for free. She wants him to suffer.

Politicians across America could not agree more with this New Jersey woman: criminals have it too easy. But perhaps not for much longer. Legislation is being introduced in dozens of states to make punishments harsher.

Twenty years ago the central belief was that criminals should be rehabilitated and given the opportunity to start a new life. Prison was not simply punishment but a way to help offenders go straight.

This liberal approach has lost support from a public clamouring for swift and harsh retribution. Kirk Fordice, the Republican governor of Mississippi, wants life in prison to be so hellish that criminals will think twice before they offend. Already televisions and radios have been banned from the state's jails. Sports facilities have been dismantled and soon prisoners will be wearing striped uniforms.

Several jails in California are also doing away with weight-lifting equipment. In New Jersey there is a campaign to make prison life miserable, with almost no privileges. 'I don't think people would look forward to a life without television, basketball, weights, cigarettes and other amenities. It would make them think again,' said Gerald Cardinale, a state senator from New Jersey. There is even a move to charge prisoners rent.

Fed up with the rise in violent crime, Americans are in a dark mood. The biggest problem is young offenders: the number of children arrested for murder has doubled in 10 years. In the past fortnight three couples were killed by their children. Last week two seven-year-old twins were arrested in New Jersey for a string of burglaries. To public disgust they were released, too young to be charged.

But the get-tough agenda is spreading fast. Singapore, where Michael Fay, an American teenager, was caned last year for vandalism, is attracting admiration – and a school headmaster in Saint Louis, Missouri, has ordered unruly pupils to be handcuffed.

President Bill Clinton has tried to lead the get-tough campaign with his 'three strikes and you're out' law, which gives life sentences to criminals found guilty three times of certain federal offences. Some southern states want to replace this with execution.

Military-style boot camps are increasingly popular. Their method is to bash sense into criminals with a short, sharp shock. Inmates at Rikers Island jail in New York call their military unit the house of pain.

Some states have opted for even tougher sentences than those handed out by courts. Under Washington's 'predator law', officials can extend a rapist's sentence if they believe he is still a danger.

Special prisons known as 'maxi-maxis', where the tough nuts are kept away from the other inmates, are becoming more prevalent. Prisoners are kept in cells 23 hours a day.

In fact nothing is being ruled out in the renewed campaign. In Alabama 300 sets of leg irons will be clamped on convicts next month and they will be marched in a chain gang along public roads.

The death penalty, meanwhile, has never had stronger support from politicians despite statistical evidence that executions are not a deterrent. 'America is angry and wants blood,' said one criminal lawyer. 'It is as simple as that'.

Criminologists are alarmed, arguing that harsher punishment may win votes but will not eradicate crime. Worse conditions in prison, they say, will make inmates nastier, more violent and an even greater threat when they are released.

Todd Clear, professor at the department of criminal justice of Rutgers College, said: 'This get-tough attitude is laughably irrelevant to the crime problem. Just turning up the heat does not bring solutions.'

He may have a point. In California the 'three strikes' law has already run into trouble with far fewer guilty pleas because criminals, knowing they could face life for a third offence, refuse to plea bargain. As a result, courts are clogged up. The Los Angeles district attorney expects a 144 per cent increase in jury trials this year and believes more than half the increase is caused by the three strikes rule.

The new law has also produced disturbing anomalies. Earlier this month a man being judged for his third offence was sentenced to 25 years in prison. His crime was stealing a slice of pizza from some children.

(*The Sunday Times*, 12 March 1995)

The relationship between punishment and public opinion is no less complex than that between punishment and crime. As Zimring and Hawkins point out, evidence from US opinion polls since the early 1970s suggests that a substantial majority of those polled reliably express the view that the courts are too lenient. Moreover, this settled perception has shown no sign of responding to the actual increases in penal severity that took place during the 1980s (Zimring and Hawkins, 1991, p.129). Rather, a state of public dissatisfaction with the perceived leniency of the courts appears to be a 'chronic condition': it expresses public concern and anxiety rather than a detailed knowledge of real penal practice. If this strand in public sentiment really is a constant feature of contemporary social life it follows that *any* increase in penal severity could *always* be legitimated in terms of 'public opinion'. In this respect 'public opinion' is a sort of 'pool' – a resource that can be called upon in opportunist and episodic ways to legitimate political decisions: 'The *ad hoc* reference to punitive public attitudes when the prison population increases is analogous to the attribution of rainfall to the performance of a rain dance while conveniently overlooking all the occasions when the ceremony was not followed by rain but by prolonged periods of drought' (Zimring and Hawkins, 1991, p.130).

This is why both Christie and Zimring and Hawkins stress the open-ended nature of prison expansion. This is perhaps particularly evident when one possible function of imprisonment for crime control is touted with special vigour. In the USA that function has been incapacitation (**Wilson, 1983**; van den Haag, 1975; Zedlewski, 1987). It is a function especially suited to provide the motor of penal growth since:

> As long as levels of crime are high enough to generate substantial anxiety, those who view increased imprisonment as a solution will continue to demand more prisons and will do so in terms that do not change markedly at any level of incarceration. Indeed the more attenuated the relationship between the malady and the proposed remedy, the more insatiable will be the demand for more of the remedial measure.
>
> (Zimring and Hawkins, 1991, p.104)

### 4.2.1 The 'war on crime' and the question of 'race'

It seems true by definition that times characterized as 'wars' are exceptional. At least some of the conventions and proprieties that govern the normal conduct of affairs may be suspended in favour of a more forceful range of emergency measures. Wars also assume a definable 'enemy', in this case one 'within' one's own society. And the prevailing depictions of such enemies (as seen by 'us') will tend to emphasize their alien and threatening nature. Viewed from the perspective of those who experience such a sense of threat and who have something to protect (tradition, property, safety), the priority is that such 'dangerous others' should be vigorously controlled or removed. George Herbert Mead recognized something similar as long ago as 1917 in his essay on 'The psychology of punitive justice', when he observed that to see oneself as being in a battle is to call for 'the destruction, or defeat, or subjection, or reduction of the enemy' (Mead, 1968). This is also one possible inference from Hall *et al.*'s (1978) analysis of the 'mugging panic' in the UK during the 1970s; a sufficient level of social anxiety about crime, especially one focused against particular groups, can engender an 'exceptional moment' in the way that authority is organized and deployed (see **Muncie, 1996**).

CONTROLLING CRIME

One problematic feature of recent US (and to some extent British) crime control rhetoric is its concentration on the idea of a distinct and separate 'underclass', defined not just by poverty but also by deviant lifestyles and criminogenic sub-cultures (see Murray, 1985, on the USA; **Murray, 1990**, and Anderson, 1993, on the UK). In many such appraisals an equation is drawn between 'underclass', 'race', illegitimacy and crime. A possible outcome of such ways of thinking, therefore, is the polarization of much of social life, but especially of crime control, along 'racial' lines. There are diverse views on whether the disproportionate numbers of black and Hispanic prisoners in the USA actually result from discriminatory practices of policing and sentencing (Blumstein, 1988; Tonry, 1994). Nonetheless, in blunt empirical terms that disproportion is indeed stark. Tonry shows that by 1990 very nearly half of all prisoners and jail inmates in the USA were black, and their representation still increasing (at the end of the 1980s more black than white inmates were admitted annually to federal and state prisons) (Tonry, 1994, p.101). More alarmingly still, if one looks at these numbers as a rate of incarceration per 100,000 within each group, one discovers that black people were imprisoned at a rate of 1,860 to white people's 289 (Tonry, 1994, p.103), a ratio of 6.4:1. Tonry is careful to point out that most of this disproportion appears due to the over-representation of black people (especially young black men) in the kinds of crimes that most often come to the attention of law-enforcement agencies, rather than to overt racism at the point of sentence. He takes this over-representation to be a 'diagnostic marker of group social distress' (Tonry, 1994, p.112). However, he also argues that certain stances on crime control, most especially the US 'War on Drugs', have had 'foreseeably discriminatory effects' (Tonry, 1994, p.98) and that in social policy (as in criminal law itself) foreknowledge and intention should be regarded as morally equivalent: 'The decision heavily to favour law enforcement over prevention and treatment strategies in the American War on Drugs ... was preordained to affect young black males especially severely and for that reason alone (there are others) the "war" should never have been launched' (Tonry, 1994, p.112).

The implications of the frequency of imprisonment of young black men for their life chances and for the reproduction of disadvantage are indeed stark, even in the eyes of the most 'moderate' commentators:

if you focus on the highest risk group – black males in their twenties – the incarceration rate is about 4,200, or about 4.2 per cent of the group. That means that almost one in twenty black males in his twenties is in a state or federal prison today. Adding the local jails ... we are up to 6.3 per cent ... When you recognize that prison represents about one sixth of the number of people who are under the control of the criminal justice system (including probation and parole), you can then multiply the prior number by six and that comes to about twenty five per cent.

(Blumstein, 1991, p.53, quoted in Christie, 1993, p.120)

Tonry argues that this way of thinking about prison numbers can show that the level of 'racial' disproportion in US prisons is *more serious* even than the 'headline' figures of the overall prison population at first suggest. Yet the US situation is at the same time *less exceptional* in international terms than at first appears. For example, Tonry shows that the overall incarceration rate of 89 per 100,000 in England and Wales in 1990 (of whom about 14 per cent were black) conceals a rate of 547 per 100,000 black people (Tonry, 1994, p.98; see also Chapter 3 of this volume). This should certainly provide pause for thought. The particular combinations of racial inequality, urban social problems, high crime rates and 'get tough' political responses in the USA have produced a prison population which is exceptional on any measure. But this comparison offers no grounds for complacency. It should alert us to the unintended but 'foreseeably discriminatory' consequences that may follow in any country when politicians choose to speak to an anxious electorate in the language of 'going to war' against crime.

## 4.3 Explaining imprisonment

We have seen that broadly comparable societies differ markedly in their use of imprisonment and that amongst these the USA currently constitutes something of an exceptional case. Young (1986) identifies two major possible kinds of explanation for such differences. He terms these the 'deterministic' and the 'policy choice' models or schools of thought. By deterministic Young means those views which attribute the variations to social influences external to the criminal justice system itself, such as economic conditions. Policy choice explanations, on the other hand, emphasize the values, attitudes and beliefs of criminal justice decision-makers themselves.

The most influential style of 'deterministic' theory is probably that deriving from the work of Rusche and Kirchheimer (1939) (as outlined in Chapter 4). Rusche and Kirchheimer argued that the level of imprisonment was primarily a function of labour market conditions. In their view periods of economic hardship reduced the value of labour and hence the value placed on the life and capacities of the unemployed. Such periods also tended to give rise to fears of popular disturbance and crime amongst more affluent strata of society. Thus, they claimed, prisons would be used to deter members of the lower orders, whose temptations to resort to crime would be especially great during periods of economic upheaval (Melossi, 1985, 1993).

*deterministic model*

Few contemporary commentators argue for such a direct and apparently automatic relationship between economic conditions and punishment as Rusche and Kirchheimer did. However, their views have been revised and developed by a number of authors, notably Box and Hale (1982, 1985; Box, 1987; Hale, 1989). Box and Hale argue that there is indeed an association between increases in the prison population and recessionary periods in the economy, but that it is of a more complex and indirect nature than Rusche and Kirchheimer believed. Box and Hale use sophisticated statistical measures to argue that there is an independent relationship between unemployment and imprisonment. It is probably for this reason, they suggest, that the English prison population began its steep upward trend in 1974 with the onset of the oil crisis and the recession of the mid 1970s. But any such relationship is not automatic and direct; it is mediated by the beliefs and perceptions of sentencers. Box and Hale contend that judges and magistrates may well themselves believe that unemployment and idleness lead to crime, or at any rate to seeing the unemployed as potentially a problem population. Whether or not judges and magistrates are correct in this view, their anxieties may lead to an increasing severity in their sentencing decisions. Thus, Box and Hale contend, prison populations increase in times of recession, not simply because the criminal justice system

system. In particular, the 'Utrecht school' influentially advocated rehabilitative measures, and denied forcefully that prison was an appropriate environment in which to rehabilitate. This anti-penal emphasis was registered within the culture and training of the legal profession (from whom the judiciary are drawn) in ways never paralleled in British legal education. As Downes summarizes:

> Some of these trends can be accounted for by 'policy' considerations. The 'principle of opportunity', whereby the prosecutor may waive prosecutions for reasons of public interest, provides the constitutional imprimatur for considerable flexibility. The progressive waiving of prosecutions may thus be linked with the shortening of prison terms by judges. Explanations in terms of a generalised 'culture of tolerance' within the context of a 'politics of accommodation', help to explain how the elites concerned were enabled to carry their policies through without eliciting fierce opposition or public hostility. The context of an unusually generous welfare state which gave high priority to the assimilation of minority groups would also ease the task of justifying such measures. But the main burden of accounting for the trends seems to fall ultimately on variables closely connected with the actual accomplishment of sentencing by the prosecutors and judges themselves; and here the manner of judicial training and socialisation, and the character and timing of the brief ascendancy of rehabilitative policies, seem to be crucial.

> (Downes, 1982, pp.349–50)

Other examples of policy choice perspectives include the closure by Jerome Miller of the Massachussetts reform school system in 1970 (Rutherford, 1986) and the case of changes in the exercise of prosecutorial discretion which led to a reduction in the prison population in Germany in the mid 1980s (Feest, 1991). In each case the emphasis of such analyses falls on the innovative work of key criminal justice decision-makers themselves.

## ACTIVITY 5.4

In your view, how useful is the distinction that Young (1986) makes between 'deterministic' and 'policy choice' models of imprisonment levels? Making some notes on your response will enable you to summarize and clarify the discussion in this section.

## COMMENT

Young's differentiation appears to capture a difference of theoretical emphasis between those explanations which focus mainly on aspects of political economy (Box and Hale) and those which emphasize the differing nature of criminal justice systems themselves (Downes). However, the distinction cannot be a sharp one. Box and Hale's views stress that changes in sentencing practice are mediated by judicial attitudes; they do not just 'happen'. Conversely, Downes's more 'culturalist' interpretation of the Dutch case nevertheless places the 'culture of tolerance' within an understanding of its surrounding political and economic environment. And it has not been lost on a number of commentators that, as the Dutch economy has encountered its own problems of low growth and increased unemployment since 1980, so its prison population too has tended to rise (though not to anything approaching British, let alone US, levels) (Box, 1987; De Haan, 1990).

Perhaps the sharpest differences lie in the political implications that each approach supposes. Box and Hale's views tend to suggest that criminal justice is a 'second order' phenomenon; if you wish to change its operation, this may have to go hand in hand with other kinds of economic and social development. 'Policy choice' views (Downes, Rutherford, Christie) tend to be more optimistic. Education, political will and local innovation can all make significant impacts. In particular, it follows from Christie's claim that there are no 'natural limits' on the level of punishment (or 'pain delivery' as he terms it) and that: 'We are free to decide what level of pain we find acceptable' (Christie, 1989, p.9).

# 5 A case study of penal managerialism: the privatization debate

What do we mean when we speak of developments in criminal justice policy as having a 'managerialist' dimension? In essence, this term means that practices that have traditionally been thought of as being in the first instance about moral questions in the state's legitimate use of authority come to be reconsidered primarily in terms of the most efficient methods of organizing the functions and processes within the system. As an outlook, managerialism is less concerned with debating problems of purpose than with streamlining and modernizing systems that already exist. Amongst the numerous themes implicit in the 'managerialization' of public services (see Newman and Clarke, 1994), two stand out as having special relevance to prison systems. First, there is the prevalent view that in order to become efficient the organization must conform as fully as possible to 'good business practices' as these are held to exist in dynamic private companies. Second, there is the view that management itself is neutral with regard to the substantive goals of the system: these are defined elsewhere, in the political and judicial systems. The challenge of management is the effective superintendence of complex processes, in both their financial and their 'human resource' aspects. If these are indeed developmental tendencies of contemporary criminal justice management, one point at which they come together in a uniquely clear and important way is in the debate on the privatization (or contracting out) of prison management.

managerialism

Amongst the most striking features of the prison privatization debate in the UK is the rapidity with which the contracting out of prison management emerged as a favoured official stance. As late as 1987 it was possible for the then Home Secretary, Douglas Hurd, speaking in the House of Commons, to deny, in good faith as far as we know, that there was 'any prospect' of the delegation of prison management to private agencies on the horizon (quoted in Shaw, 1989, p.47). At that time serious intellectual advocacy of prison privatization in the UK was in its infancy (Young, 1987; House of Commons, 1987) and advocates were at pains to explain that they were calling only for 'experimental' initiatives and only in the context of the remand system (Fulton, 1989; Gardiner, 1989). Their hopes for a sympathetic hearing by the Home Office were to this extent realized in the publication in 1988 of the Green Paper *Private Sector Involvement in the Remand System* (Home Office, 1988).

privatization

In Mr Clarke's view this is the kernel of the argument – the prison which provides the better material conditions just *is* the better prison. It is argued strongly that the private sector is inherently better able to provide such conditions – indeed, the terms on which their contracts are awarded will ensure that they do so. In the unlikely event that they do not, then the mechanisms of competition will weed them out. The primary questions are costs and quantitative regime conditions.

## ACTIVITY 5.5

How persuasive do you find these arguments? Try to consider them dispassionately and on a 'best case' interpretation. Moreover, consider what your own position would be if you were Home Secretary, charged with overall responsibility for managing the prison system. In the face of rising prison populations, scarce resources, repeated scandalous revelations about decaying Victorian buildings and spartan regimes and many other problems, would you not wish to explore any innovation that might seem to offer possibilities of modernization? Does not privatization offer an opportunity to experiment and to develop new standards of accommodation and services? And might you not thereby change the way things are done in the state-run prisons too, by showing new examples of good practice and efficiency savings? You should seek to develop in your own mind the most convincing possible case for one side of the argument before going on to consider opposing views.

## 5.2 Objections to privatization

intuitionism   Many objections to privatization are *intuitionist*. They begin and end with the feeling that 'it is wrong to profit from punishment'. For those who hold this position strongly no further argument is possible or necessary. However, this leads at least one commentator (McConville, 1990) to observe (rather dismissively) that proponents and opponents of privatization are talking incommensurable languages, so that the argument between them can never be settled. It would seem that this intuition in itself is a rather slight basis for a critical perspective. Are there then further arguments which would rebut the weight of the privatization case more convincingly? Such a view might contend that the pro-privatization position may be correct in points of detail but still not touch the main concerns in the arguments about the nature of state punishment and the justifications for imprisonment. If this is correct, privatization misconceives what is really at stake politically, ideologically and economically in the operation of penal systems. Let us outline three specific sets of objections to privatization initiatives.

1   *Sentencing practices and prison populations:*

(a) Is privatization wedded to growth in the prison population? Privatization moves have to date primarily occurred in earnest in Western industrial states in those jurisdictions which have experienced the most prolonged and severe problems of high prison populations and high overcrowding – principally the USA and the UK. If privatization generally gains momentum and plausibility under the pressure of such contingencies, does this compromise its general claims to offer a preferable model for the future of prison systems as such? Thus privatization offers itself as a policy solution in those situations where prison populations are regarded as escaping willed political control.

This contrasts sharply with the lack of interest in privatization in most of those countries which have more deliberately and successfully chosen to limit penal expansion (Downes, 1988; McConville, 1990). For these reasons privatization makes sense only where one means to accept a prison estate at or above its present size. Or as the promotional literatures for the private prison contractors more eloquently have it: 'As a nation we have an unprecedented need to acquire new prisons and jails' (E.F. Hutton); 'The Fastest Way to Put Offenders Behind Bars' (Kellman Industries); 'Gelco Space Solves Overcrowding' (Gelco Space) (all quoted in Lilly and Knepper, 1992b, p.51; see also Christie, 1993; Shichor, 1993).

(b) Is privatization wedded to 'warehousing'? More speculatively, one might argue that there is an elective affinity between the provision of privately managed prisons and particular philosophies of sentencing. The sentencing principle most commonly espoused to date by private interests in the USA in their advertising is that of incapacitation. Its focus is on the provision of adequate space in which to contain humanely: 'We help separate the outside world from the inside world' (Electronic Control Security Inc., quoted in Lilly and Knepper, 1992b, p.51). Is it the case that privatization is intrinsically tied to what a number of radical critics have identified as a key function of contemporary penality: namely the containment of 'surplus' or dangerous populations (Box and Hale, 1985; Mathiesen, 1990)?

2   *The economics of private prisons and the problem of accountability:*

(a) Is there a 'corrections–commercial complex'? Lilly and Knepper (1992b) use this term by analogy with Eisenhower's prescient warning of the influence of the 'military–industrial complex'. Indeed, they point out that the similarity between the political economy of defence and of imprisonment is more than passing in that a number of the key corporate players in the private prisons industry are literally defence contractors looking to diversify in the aftermath of the end of the Cold War (Lilly and Knepper, 1992a, p.184). The two positions are strikingly comparable. In each territory there is only one domestic customer (the state – or in the USA the individual states and the federal government) and obvious export markets (other states). The state contracts for what it regards as a vital function. It thus develops close relations of mutual dependency with its contractors (see Shichor, 1993). Far from Logan's (1990) optimistic vision of a state free to hire and fire contractors at will in the event of unsatisfactory performance or a reduction in demand, the more likely outcome is one of a high level of dependency on a small number of near-monopoly providers.

(b) Is this a 'sub-governmental system'? What results in such market conditions is a routine exchange of expertise and personnel between government agencies and corporate contractors. In Lilly and Knepper's view this exchange can be characterized as constituting a 'sub-governmental system' (Lilly and Knepper, 1992b, p.45). Governmental and private experts interact regularly and in private, and identify the outcomes of the mutual deliberations as constituting the public interest. All of this raises issues of the most basic kind for accountability and political control (not to mention ethical propriety and financial management).

Simon's argument. The danger (and Feeley and Simon's argument can be read as much as prophecy or awful warning as analysis) would be that punishment comes to be seen increasingly as a set of spheres of expertise rather than as a focus for informed public deliberation and discussion. Such a consequence, Feeley and Simon suggest (1992, p.470), would be 'fatal to a democratic civil order'.

# 6  Conclusion

This chapter has consciously 'painted with a broad brush'. It has focused on questions of the scale of imprisonment in contemporary societies, the tenuous relationship between crime rates and imprisonment and the vulnerability of prison populations to political and economic circumstances. It has introduced the nature of penal 'crises'. Lastly, it has looked at some of the emergent trends towards managerialism and privatization which seem likely to characterize the penality of the first decades of the coming century. We have approached the topic in this way in the hope of providing as wide a context of understanding as is possible in the space available, so that you can use this as a basis for your own further exploration into more specific policy questions and as a platform for the evaluation of particular debates and political campaigns as they occur.

One such campaign was launched in October 1993 when the Home Secretary, Michael Howard, announced to the rapture of his audience at the Conservative Party conference that 'Prison Works'. This claim rested on an amalgam of deterrent and (to a degree previously unfamiliar in British penal politics) incapacitative principles. Howard thus shifted the ground of discussion to a position much closer to the American experience where 'truth in sentencing' (that is, hostility to early release mechanisms) and 'three strikes and you're out' (that is, indefinite detention for persistent offenders) provisions have provided much of the motor of growth behind sustained (indeed 'open-ended') prison expansion. How are we to understand this development? It may well be (see section 2) that there are grounds for thinking that incapacitation is a more dubious enterprise in strictly penological terms than Mr Howard's slogan admits: yet it is also an intrinsic dimension of imprisonment and its intuitive appeal is strong. On another level (that of securing electoral advantage) we might argue that Mr Howard was acting very much as Melossi (1985) or Box (1987) might have predicted (see section 4). During a period of marked public anxiety about crime, of economic stringency and of considerable unpopularity for the governing party, the appeal to severity in punishment speaks powerfully to popular 'sensibilities' (Garland, 1990) and discontents (Hall *et al.*, 1978). On a third level (the emergent 'new penality' which Feeley and Simon, 1992, claim to identify) Howard's comments might be seen as part of a longer-run development, namely the shift towards the incapacitative 'management' of a crime problem regarded as in all other respects intractable. The point of this brief vignette is not simply to dispute Howard's claim that 'Prison Works', though any such assertion is plainly a gross misrepresentation of penological knowledge. Rather, it is to show that any such rhetorical intervention is open to examination simultaneously on several levels – as a truth claim, as a political tactic and as part of an underlying systemic rationale. These are the forms of analysis which this chapter advocates and seeks to make available to you.

# Further reading

On theories of punishment see Walker (1991) or Bean (1981) for accessible overviews; for more sophisticated (but still readable) treatments see Lacey (1988) and Cragg (1992). Garland's (1990) informative overview of sociological accounts gives further insight into why the conflict of interpretations over the problem of punishment is unresolvable. On the British prison system generally see Morgan (1994) or Cavadino and Dignan (1992) for well-informed introductions, or Player and Jenkins (1994) for a survey of more particular issues. For the many questions regarding especially the imprisonment of women see Carlen (1983, 1990). For information on prisoners' families see Shaw (1992). On suicide and self-injury see Liebling (1992). On Scotland see Scraton *et al.* (1991) (with special reference to prison disorders) or (for an intelligent view by a thoughtful system 'insider') Coyle (1991). On prison rules, prisoners' rights and prison discipline see Maguire *et al.* (1985) and Livingstone and Owen (1993). On privatization see Ryan and Ward (1989) for a judicious overview, or Logan (1990) for some intelligent partisanship.

# References

Adams, R. (1992) *Prison Riots in Britain and the USA*, London, Macmillan.

Allen, F. (1981) *The Decline of the Rehabilitative Ideal*, New Haven, CT, Yale University Press.

Amnesty International (1995) *Amnesty International Report 1995*, London, Amnesty International.

Anderson, D. (ed.) (1993) *The Loss of Virtue*, London, Social Affairs Unit.

Ashworth, A. (1993) 'Sentencing by numbers', *Criminal Justice Matters*, no.14, pp.6–7.

Bean, P. (1981) *Punishment: A Philosophical and Criminological Inquiry*, Oxford, Martin Robertson.

Beetham, D. (1991) *The Legitimation of Power*, London, Macmillan.

Biles, D. (1983) 'Crime and imprisonment: a two decade comparison between England and Wales and Australia', *British Journal of Criminology*, vol.23, no.2, pp.166–72.

Bishop, N. (1988) *Non-custodial Alternatives in Europe*, Helsinki, Institute for Crime Prevention and Control.

Blumstein, A. (1988) 'Prison populations: a system out of control?', in Tonry, M. and Morris, N. (eds) *Crime and Justice: An Annual Review of Research*, Chicago, IL, University of Chicago Press.

Bottoms, A. (1983) 'Neglected features of contemporary penal systems', in Garland and Young (1983a).

Bottoms, A. (1987) 'Limiting prison use', *Howard Journal of Criminal Justice*, vol.26, no.3, pp.177–202.

Bottoms, A. (1990) 'The aims of imprisonment', in Garland, D. (ed.) *Justice, Guilt and Forgiveness in the Penal System,* Edinburgh, University of Edinburgh.

Box, S. (1987) *Recession, Crime and Punishment*, London, Macmillan.

Box, S. and Hale, C. (1982) 'Economic crisis and the rising prisoner population in England and Wales', *Crime and Social Justice*, vol.17, pp.20–35.

Box, S. and Hale, C. (1985) 'Unemployment, imprisonment and prison overcrowding', *Contemporary Crises*, vol.9, pp.208–29.

**Braithwaite, J. (1989) *Crime, Shame and Reintegration*, Cambridge and New York, Cambridge University Press. (Extract reprinted as 'Reintegrative shaming' in Muncie *et al*., 1996.)**

Braithwaite, J. and Mugford, S. (1994) 'Conditions of successful reintegration ceremonies', *British Journal of Criminology*, vol.34, no.2, pp.139–71.

Brody, S. (1976) *The Effectiveness of Sentencing*, London, HMSO.

Carlen, P. (1983) *Women's Imprisonment*, London, Routledge and Kegan Paul.

Carlen, P. (1990) *Alternatives to Women's Imprisonment*, Buckingham, Open University Press.

Cavadino, M. and Dignan, J. (1992) *The Penal System: An Introduction*, London, Sage.

Chibnall, S. (1977) *Law and Order News*, London, Tavistock.

Christie, N. (1980) *Limits to Pain*, Oxford, Martin Robertson.

Christie, N. (1989) Address to the conference on 'The Meaning of Imprisonment', Lincoln, July 1989.

Christie, N. (1993) *Crime Control as Industry: Towards GULAGS, Western Style?*, London, Routledge.

Clarke, J., Cochrane, A. and McLaughlin, E. (eds) (1994) *Managing Social Policy*, London, Sage.

Clarke, K. (1992) 'Prisoners with private means', *The Independent*, 22 December, p.17.

Cohen, S. and Taylor, L. (1981) *Psychological Survival* (2nd edn), Harmondsworth, Penguin.

Coyle, A. (1991) *Inside: Rethinking Scotland's Prisons*, Edinburgh, Scottish Child.

Cragg, W. (1992) *The Practice of Punishment*, London, Routledge.

Currie, E. (1990) 'Heavy with human tears', in Taylor, I. (ed.) *The Social Effects of Free Market Policies*, Hemel Hempstead, Harvester Wheatsheaf.

De Haan, W. (1990) *The Politics of Redress*, London, Unwin Hyman.

Downes, D. (1982) 'The origins and consequences of Dutch penal policy since 1945', *British Journal of Criminology*, vol.22, no.4, pp.325–50.

Downes, D. (1988) *Contrasts in Tolerance*, London, Macmillan.

Dunbar, I. (1985) *A Sense of Direction*, London, HM Prison Service.

Ericson, R.V., Baranek, P. and Chan, J. (1991) *Representing Order*, Buckingham, Open University Press.

Farrell, M. (ed.) (1989) *Punishment for Profit?*, London, Institute for the Study and Treatment of Delinquency.

**Feeley, S. and Simon, J. (1992) 'The new penology: notes on the emerging strategy of corrections and its implications', *Criminology*, vol.30, no.4, pp.452–74. (Extract reprinted as 'The new penology' in Muncie *et al.*, 1996.)**

Feest, J. (1991) 'Reducing the prison population: lessons from the West German experience', in Muncie and Sparks (1991b).

Fitzmaurice, C. and Pease, K. (1982) 'Prison sentences and populations: a comparison of some European countries', *Justice of the Peace*, vol.146, pp.575–9.

**Foucault, M. (1977) *Discipline and Punish: The Birth of the Prison* (trans. Alan Sheridan), London, Allen Lane. (Extract reprinted as 'The carceral' in Muncie *et al.*, 1996.)**

Fulton, R. (1989) 'Private sector involvement in the remand system' in Farrell (1989).

Gardiner, E. (1989) 'Prisons – an alternative approach', in Farrell (1989).

Garland, D. (1990) *Punishment and Modern Society*, Oxford, Oxford University Press.

Garland, D. and Young, P.J. (eds) (1983a) *The Power to Punish*, Aldershot, Gower.

Garland, D. and Young, P.J. (1983b) 'Towards a social analysis of penality', in Garland and Young (1983a).

Gearty, C. (1991) 'The prisons and the courts', in Muncie and Sparks (1991b).

Goffman, E. (1961) 'On the characteristics of total institutions', in Cressey, D. (ed.) *The Prison: Studies in Institutional Organization and Change*, New York, Holt, Rinehart and Winston.

Grabosky, P. (1979) 'Economic conditions and penal severity: testing a neo-marxian hypothesis' (unpublished MS).

Graham, J. (1990) 'Decarceration in the Federal Republic of Germany', *British Journal of Criminology*, vol.30, no.2, pp.150–70.

Greenberg, D. (1977) 'The dynamics of oscillatory punishment processes', *Journal of Criminal Law and Criminology*, vol.68, pp.643–51.

Greenberg, D. (1991) 'The cost–benefit analysis of imprisonment', *Social Justice*, vol.17, no.4, pp.49–75.

Gunn, J., Maden, A. and Swinton, M. (1991) *Mentally Disordered Prisoners*, London, HMSO.

Hale, C. (1989) 'Economy, punishment and imprisonment', *Contemporary Crises*, vol.13, pp.327–49.

Hall, S., Critcher, C., Jefferson, T., Clarke, J. and Roberts, B. (1978) *Policing the Crisis*, London, Macmillan.

Hay, W. and Sparks, R. (1991) 'What is a prison officer?', *Prison Service Journal*, no.83, pp.2–7.

HM Prison Service (n.d.) Map of 'Prison establishments in England and Wales', London, HMSO.

Home Office (1979) *Committee of Inquiry into the United Kingdom Prison Services* (May Committee), London, HMSO.

Home Office (1984) *Managing the Long-Term Prison System: The Report of the Control Review Committee*, London, HMSO.

Home Office (1988) *Private Sector Involvement in the Remand System*, London, HMSO.

Home Office (1993) *Digest 2: Information on the Criminal Justice System in England and Wales*, Home Office Research and Statistics Department, London, HMSO.

Home Office (1994) *The Prison Population in 1993*, Home Office Statistical Bulletin, Issue 16/94, London, Government Statistical Service.

Home Office (1995a) *Projections of Long-term Trends in the Prison Population to 2002*, Home Office Statistical Bulletin, Issue 4/95, London, Government Statistical Service.

Home Office (1995b) *The Prison Population in 1994*, Home Office Statistical Bulletin, Issue 8/95, London, Government Statistical Service.

House of Commons (1987) *Fourth Report from the Home Affairs Committee: Contract Provision of Prisons*, London, HMSO.

Jankovic, I. (1977) 'Labor market and imprisonment', *Crime and Social Justice*, 8, pp.17–31.

King, R.D. (1985) 'Control in prisons', in Maguire *et al.* (1985).

King, R.D. and McDermott, K. (1989) 'British prisons, 1970–1987: the ever-deepening crisis', *British Journal of Criminology*, vol.29, pp.107–28.

King, R.D. and Morgan, R. (1980) *The Future of the Prison System*, Farnborough, Gower.

Lacey, N. (1988) *State Punishment*, London, Routledge.

Liebling, A. (1992) *Suicides in Prison*, London, Routledge.

Lilly, J.R. and Knepper, P. (1992a) 'An international perspective on the privatization of corrections', *The Howard Journal*, vol.31, no.3, pp.174–91.

Lilly, J.R. and Knepper, P. (1992b) 'The corrections–commercial complex', *Prison Service Journal*, no.87, pp.43–52.

Livingstone, S. and Owen, T. (1993) *Prison Law*, Oxford, Oxford University Press.

Logan, C. (1990) *Private Prisons: Cons and Pros*, Oxford, Oxford University Press.

Maguire, M., Vagg, J. and Morgan, R. (eds) (1985) *Accountability and Prisons*, London, Tavistock.

Martinson, R. (1974) 'What works? Questions and answers about prison reform', *The Public Interest*, no.35, pp.22–54.

Mathiesen, T. (1965) *The Defences of the Weak*, London, Tavistock.

Mathiesen, T. (1990) *Prison on Trial*, London, Sage.

McConville, S. (1990) 'The privatization of penal services', in Council of Europe, *Privatization of Crime Control*, Strasbourg, Council of Europe.

McLaughlin, E. and Muncie, J. (1994) 'Managing the criminal justice system', in Clarke *et al.* (1994).

Mead, G.H. (1968) 'The psychology of punitive justice' (first published in 1917), in Petras, J.W. (ed.) *G.H. Mead: Essays in Social Philosophy*, New York, Teachers' College Press.

Melossi, D. (1985) 'Punishment and social action: changing vocabularies of motive within a political business cycle', *Current Perspectives in Social Theory*, vol.6, pp.169–97.

Melossi, D. (1993) 'Gazette of morality and social whip: punishment, hegemony and the case of the USA, 1970–92', *Social and Legal Studies*, vol.2, pp.259–79.

Morgan, R. (1994) 'Imprisonment', in Maguire, M., Morgan, R. and Reiner, R. (eds) *The Oxford Handbook of Criminology*, Oxford, Oxford University Press.

Morgan, R. and Evans, M. (1994) 'Inspecting prisons – the view from Strasbourg', *British Journal of Criminology*, vol.34, no.1, pp.144–59.

**Muncie, J. (1996) 'The construction and deconstruction of crime', in Muncie, J. and McLaughlin, E. (eds) *The Problem of Crime*, London, Sage in association with The Open University.**

Muncie, J. and Sparks, R. (1991a) 'Expansion and contraction in European penal systems', in Muncie and Sparks (1991b).

Muncie, J. and Sparks, R. (eds) (1991b) *Imprisonment: European Perspectives*, Hemel Hempstead, Harvester Wheatsheaf.

**Muncie, J., McLaughlin, E. and Langan, M. (eds) (1996) *Criminological Perspectives: A Reader*, London, Sage in association with The Open University.**

Murray, C. (1985) *Losing Ground,* New York, Basic Books.

**Murray, C. (1990) *The Emerging Underclass*, London, Institute of Economic Affairs. (Extract reprinted as 'The underclass' in Muncie *et al.*, 1996.)**

NACRO (1994a) *Criminal Justice Digest*, April, London, National Association for the Care and Resettlement of Offenders.

NACRO (1994b) *Prison Overcrowding – Recent Developments*, NACRO Briefing, 28, July, London, National Association for the Care and Resettlement of Offenders.

Newman, J. and Clarke, J. (1994) 'The managerialization of public services', in Clarke *et al.* (1994).

Pavarini, M. (1994) 'The new penology and politics in crisis: the Italian case', *British Journal of Criminology*, vol.34, no.1, pp.49–61.

Pease, K. (1990) 'Punishment demand and punishment numbers', in Gottfredson, D. and Clarke, R. (eds) *Policy and Theory in Criminal Justice*, Aldershot, Avebury.

Pease, K. (1994) 'Cross-national imprisonment rates: limitations of method and possible conclusions', *British Journal of Criminology,* vol.34, no.1, pp.116–30.

Peters, A. (1986) 'Main currents in criminal law theory', in van Dijk, J. *et al.* (eds) *Criminal Law in Action,* Arnhem, Gouda Quint.

Player, E. and Jenkins, M. (eds) (1994) *Prisons After Woolf*, London, Routledge.

Prison Officers' Association (1990) 'Evidence submitted to Lord Justice Woolf's Inquiry' (unpublished MS).

Prison Reform Trust (1991) *The Identikit Prisoner*, London, Prison Reform Trust.

Prison Reform Trust (1993) *Does Prison Work?*, London, Prison Reform Trust.

PROP (Preservation of the Rights of Prisoners) (1990) 'Evidence submitted to Lord Justice Woolf's Inquiry' (unpublished MS).

Richardson, G. (1985) 'The case for prisoners' rights', in Maguire *et al.* (1985).

Rusche, G. and Kirchheimer, O. (1939) *Punishment and Social Structure*, New York, Columbia University Press. (Reissued in 1968 by Russell and Russell.)

Rutherford, A. (1986) *Prisons and the Process of Justice*, Oxford, Oxford University Press.

Ryan, M. and Ward, T. (1989) *Privatization and the Penal System*, Buckingham, Open University Press.

Schlesinger, P. and Tumber, H. (1994) *Reporting Crime: The Media Politics of Criminal Justice*, Oxford, Clarendon Press.

Scottish Prison Service (1995) *Annual Report for 1994–95*, Edinburgh, HMSO.

Scraton, P., Sim, J. and Skidmore, P. (1991) *Prisons Under Protest*, Buckingham, Open University Press.

Shaw, R. (1992) *Prisoners' Children: What are the Issues?*, London, Routledge.

Shaw, S. (1989) 'Penal sanctions: private affluence or public squalor?', in Farrell (1989).

Shichor, D. (1993) 'The corporate context of private prisons', *Crime, Law and Social Change*, vol.20, pp.113–38.

Sim, J. (1992) '"When you ain't got nothing you got nothing to lose": the Peterhead rebellion, the state and the case for prison abolition', in Bottomley, A.K., Fowles, A.J. and Reiner, R. (eds) *Criminal Justice: Theory and Practice*, London, British Society of Criminology.

Sim, J. (1994) 'Reforming the penal wasteland: a critical reading of the Woolf report', in Player and Jenkins (1994).

Sparks, J.R. (1994) 'Can prisons be legitimate?', *British Journal of Criminology*, vol.34, no.1, pp.14–28.

Sparks, J.R. and Bottoms, A.E. (1995) 'Legitimacy and order in prisons', *British Journal of Sociology*, vol.46, no.1, pp.45–62.

Sykes, G. (1958) *The Society of Captives*, Princeton, NJ, Princeton University Press.

Tonry, M. (1994) 'Racial disproportion in US prisons', *British Journal of Criminology*, vol.34, no.1, pp.97–115.

United Nations (1993) *Understanding Crime: Experiences of Crime and Crime Control*, Rome, United Nations.

United States Department of Justice (1992) *Capital Punishment 1991*, Bureau of Justice Statistics Bulletin, Washington, DC, Department of Justice.

United States Department of Justice (1994) *Prisoners in 1993*, Bureau of Justice Statistics Bulletin, Washington, DC, Department of Justice.

van den Haag, E. (1975) *Punishing Criminals*, New York, Basic Books.

von Hirsch, A. (1993) *Censure and Sanction,* Oxford, Oxford University Press.

Walker, N. (1991) *Why Punish?,* Oxford, Oxford University Press.

Wasik, M. and Taylor, R. (1991) *Blackstone's Guide to the Criminal Justice Act 1991,* London, Blackstone Press.

Weiss, R.P. (1989) 'Private prisons and the state', in Matthews, R. (ed.) *Privatizing Criminal Justice,* London, Sage.

Wheeler, S. (1968) 'Agents of delinquency control: a comparative analysis', in Wheeler, S. (ed.) *Controlling Delinquents,* New York, Wiley.

Wilkins, L. (1984) *Consumerist Criminology,* Aldershot, Gower.

**Wilson, J.Q. (1983) *Thinking About Crime* (2nd revised edn), New York, Basic Books. (Extract reprinted as 'On deterrence' in Muncie *et al.,* 1996.)**

Woolf, Lord Justice (1991) *Prison Disturbances, April 1990,* London, HMSO.

Young, P. (1987) *The Prison Cell,* London, Adam Smith Institute Research.

Young, P.J. (1989) 'Punishment, money and a sense of justice', in Carlen, P. and Cook, D. (eds) *Paying for Crime,* Milton Keynes, Open University Press.

Young, W. (1986) 'Influences on the use of imprisonment', *The Howard Journal,* vol.25, no.2, pp.125–36.

Zedlewski, E. (1987) 'Making confinement decisions', *Research in Brief,* Washington, DC, National Institute of Justice.

Zimring, F. and Hawkins, G. (1986) *Capital Punishment and the American Agenda,* Cambridge, Cambridge University Press.

Zimring, F. and Hawkins, G. (1991) *The Scale of Imprisonment,* Chicago, Il., University of Chicago Press.

Zimring, F. and Hawkins, G. (1994) 'The growth of imprisonment in California', *British Journal of Criminology,* vol.34, no.1, pp.83–95.

# Chapter 6
# The Politics and Practice of Youth Justice

*by John Pitts*

## Contents

# 1 Introduction

*L*ike many other areas of government policy, youth justice is a political 'hot potato' and, because of this, the policies which emerge are often powered more by the need to gain political credibility than a desire to discover the origins and nature of the problem and an effective solution to it. This need becomes particularly urgent in periods when the capacity of the major socializing institutions – the family, the school and the workplace – to instil the appropriate values, attitudes and behaviours into our children is called into question.

Official statistics indicate that, by and large, young people under the age of 21 are responsible for around half of all crimes committed (Bottomley and Pease, 1986; Home Office, 1995, p.21). Certainly, those crimes which attract most publicity, and which the public most fears, tend to be committed by the young. As a result, at the heart of the political issue of 'crime' is a question about our society's capacity to transform its junior members into honest and productive citizens.

social reproduction

This is a concern about what sociologists have called 'social reproduction': the processes whereby, from generation to generation, the key economic, social and biological roles and tasks necessary to the continuation of a society are allocated. However, in modern economies, characterized by rapid technological and social change, the question of the type of society we should be striving to reproduce is politically contentious. Governments that turn their attention to what children and young people should learn or how they should behave are, therefore, seldom engaged in a politically neutral activity. On the contrary, they usually have firm, if contradictory, ideas about the type of social order that should be preserved or brought into being. They frequently attempt to advance these ideas through their educational and youth justice policies.

This chapter will, among other things, use youth justice as a case study of the ways in which changing economic imperatives and political ideologies filter down through social and criminal justice policies to influence the practices of the police officers, social workers, probation officers and magistrates who make the youth justice system work.

Historically, youth justice has oscillated between the goals of care and control. The late 1950s and the 1960s witnessed policies, supported by both Conservative and Labour governments, which aimed to respond to the social and psychological problems of which youth crime was believed to be a symptom. However, in England and Wales these attempts to 'decriminalize' youth crime – to take it out of the hands of magistrates, laywers and the police, and place it in the hands of psychologists, social workers and youth workers, and to replace 'punishment' with a concern for the 'welfare' needs of a young person – met with strong resistance from the legal establishment, the probation service and some politicians. The early and mid 1970s saw a reaction against such 'welfarism' and an increasingly strident demand that we should get 'back to justice' – back to the due process of law – and that punishment should, once again, occupy a central role in the English youth justice system.

The first Thatcher administration of 1979 entered parliament promising to 'restore the rule of law', to 'make the streets safe once more for ordinary citizens', and to give a 'short, sharp shock' to those young offenders who did not heed their warning (Pitts, 1988). The mid 1980s, however, saw the emergence of a pragmatic criminal justice strategy based on a policy of 'bifurcation' (see Chapter 5), which produced a 'corporatist' youth justice system in which the police and social welfare agencies co-operated to manage the system 'cost-effectively', and in which concern for the social and psychological needs of young offenders (welfarism) was marginalized. By the 1990s, economic recession and a new 'moral panic' ensured that youth crime and youth justice were, once again, on the political agenda.

Sections 2 to 5 trace these policy developments in England and Wales and look at the key characteristics of the Scottish system. Section 6 then turns to the question of whether, and to what extent, current youth justice policies can offer solutions to the problems of youth crime in the UK at the end of the twentieth century. After a brief consideration, in section 7, of recent developments in criminal justice and social policies in the USA, France and Germany, the chapter concludes with an exploration of alternative futures.

# 2   Competing interventions

## 2.1   The rise of the welfare model

The latter part of the nineteenth century witnessed the development of separate institutions for the care and containment of children and young people in trouble with the law (see Chapter 4). In 1908 a separate juvenile court was created and by the mid 1930s a national system of approved schools and Borstal institutions had been established. These developments were indicative of a widespread belief that juvenile offenders needed to be treated differently from adults because they were less culpable and, by dint of age and impressionability, more amenable to forms of rehabilitation which responded to their social, educational, vocational or emotional needs. While the practices within these institutions were frequently at odds with their stated intentions, the emergence of approved schools and Borstals was a product of a set of ideas which remained more or less unchallenged until the early 1970s. These ideas, known variously as 'welfarism' or the 'rehabilitative ideal', held that, through scientifically informed professional interventions with individuals, families and groups, in institutions and in the community, it would be possible to change both the behaviour and the attitudes of children and young people who broke the law (Garland, 1985). Arguably, these ideas found their fullest political expression in the youth justice policies of the 1960s.

welfarism

The late 1950s and early 1960s was a perplexing time. The widespread assumption that, because crime was a product of poverty, with the advent of prosperity it would simply wither away, had proved to be unfounded. By the late 1950s in the USA and the UK, the only thing growing faster than per capita incomes was the youth crime rate.

*The Teddy Boys, the first of many working-class youth sub-cultures to trigger moral panic and public condemnation*

Meanwhile, on the streets and in the coffee bars and fish and chip shops of the UK, Teddy Boys were provoking the ire of moral commentators who offered dire warnings about the direction in which our newly affluent society was headed. Believing that what happens in the USA 'today' happens in the UK 'tomorrow', they 'read' films like *Rebel Without a Cause* and *The Wild Ones* as portents of an anarchic future in which roving bands of amoral young people would hold the adult world to ransom (Hall and Jefferson, 1976).

The government was under pressure to do something about this apparent crisis of social reproduction. What they did reflected contemporary assumptions, held by politicians across the entire political spectrum, on both sides of the Atlantic, about how an enlightened modern state should respond to problems amongst its children and young people.

What policy options do you think were available to modern states in this situation? It might be worth keeping in mind that conceptualization of the 'problem' as being that of 'young thugs', 'boys being boys' or 'children in trouble' will have a considerable influence on the choice of policy.

## 2.2 Welfarism and crime control

The social and youth justice policies which grew out of the politics of the period immediately following the Second World War identified the state as the leader in the task of social reconstruction. This leadership involved the identification of gaps in the provision of education, training, housing, health and welfare, and the construction of appropriate state services to fill these gaps. Social problems, such as crime, were to be analysed by social scientists commissioned by the state and solved by state professionals, like social workers, who would intervene in families and communities.

Social scientists were commissioned and, in due course, reported. The Albermarle Report, *The Youth Service in England and Wales* (1960), took evidence from Jimmy Saville, a popular radio disc-jockey of the time, and many other people believed to have their 'fingers on the pulse' of modern youth. This report located the origins of the problem in the behaviour of working-class parents who, seduced by their newfound prosperity, were failing to offer guidance and leadership to their adolescent children. Albermarle's solution was the 'youth leader' – an adult who would offer this guidance and help re-orientate the young to their civic, social and political responsibilities. In education, the contemporary orthodoxy attributed the relatively poor academic performance, and in some cases the equally poor behaviour, of some working-class primary school children to their mothers' choice of lucrative employment over child-care responsibilities. The 1963

Children and Young Persons Act (Home Office, 1963) attempted to stem this alleged abdication of parental responsibility by establishing Family Advice Centres in high-crime neighbourhoods. The explanation of youth crime which emerged from these deliberations highlighted acquisitiveness, the failure of parents in general and the failure of mothers in particular (Clarke, 1980b).

But was parental failure at the root of the problem? Harold Wilson's Labour administration, elected in 1964, saw the problem not simply as a failure of parents to inculcate appropriate values and attitudes in their children, but as a consequence of 'modernization'. Indeed, the government, supported by modernizing social scientists, argued that, far from a failure to reproduce traditional attitudes, beliefs and behaviour, social reproduction was operating so well that it was acting as a brake on the economy. Working-class girls and boys, it was said, were simply following their parents into the same offices and factories rather than seizing the new opportunities offered by what Wilson had described as 'the white heat of the technological revolution'. The educational research of the 1950s and early 1960s bemoaned their 'low' expectations and their failure to take advantage of the opportunities generated by the expansion of education, training and the new technology. The problem was perceived as one of 'cultural lag', of young people constrained by working-class culture to reproduce traditional occupational patterns, thus limiting their potential social mobility. This 'progressive' view suggested that only by an upward revision of social expectations could the full potential of the 'technological revolution' be realized, the upward social and occupational mobility of working-class young people achieved and the status frustration which underlay most youth crime alleviated. This situation was to be achieved through the development of a more relevant educational experience and the provision of skilled helpers trained to enable young people to shrug off redundant and self-defeating deviant behaviour (Clarke, 1980b).

*Crime – A Challenge to Us All* (The Longford Report), the influential report of a Labour Party Study Group (1964), noted that working-class families lacked access to such skilled help. This meant that, rather than being diverted into 'treatment' as middle-class young people in similar difficulties might be, working-class young people were projected into the youth justice system where the stigma of a court appearance compounded their nascent criminal careers (see Extract 6.1).

The solution devised by the Labour administration was to provide more social workers, more community workers, more primary school teachers and more youth workers. They were to enter and work with those communities and families still blighted by cultural lag and enable their residents 'to catch up with the "fortunate majority"' (Clarke, 1980b, p.92).

One effect of such welfarist policies and strategies was to remove questions of poverty, social inequality, opportunity and crime from the place they occupied on the political and moral agenda and to relocate them on a list of social anomalies to be eradicated by a scientifically informed process of 'social engineering' (Habermas, 1976). The more radical version of 'welfarism' pursued by the Wilson administration was predicated on the premise that we were living in a society in which the gap between the 'haves' and the 'have nots' was narrowing and that rational planning and 'the appliance of science' would finally eliminate poverty.

## Extract 6.1  Longford: 'Crime – a challenge to us all'

Chronic or serious delinquency in a child is, in the main, we believe, evidence of lack of the care, the guidance and the opportunities to which every child is entitled. There are very few children who do not behave badly at times; but the children of parents with ample means rarely appear before juvenile courts. The machinery of the law is reserved mainly for working-class children who, more often than not, are also handicapped by being taught in too big classes in unsatisfactory school buildings with few amenities or opportunities for out-of-school activities. ...

We believe that in justice to our children, and for the health and well-being of society, no child in early adolescence should have to face criminal proceedings: these children should receive the kind of treatment they need, without any stigma or any association with the penal system.

Obviously the stage of development and the needs of children of any particular physical age vary widely, but there must be some dividing line. We believe that this line should be drawn at the statutory school-leaving age, and that no child under this age should be subjected to criminal proceedings. If society requires the child to remain at school, society may fairly be expected to ensure that he [sic] receives not only formal education but also training in social responsibility. ...

Opportunities for young people to develop and use to the full all their latent talents and frustrated energies – mental as well as physical – are not only their right but also the community's greatest safeguard against hooliganism, vandalism, and anti-social behaviour generally. Penal measures alone can never succeed. They must be supplemented (and eventually, we hope, made largely unnecessary) by the provision of a wide variety of things to do which will catch the imagination and engage the energies of boys and girls. ...

What is needed, therefore, is a mobilization of the whole community in a new drive for the *positive* prevention of crime, and an understanding by the whole community that the enlightened treatment of offenders is essential both for this limited but important end and for social progress in its widest sense.

(Labour Party Study Group, 1964, pp.21, 24–5, 29, 70)

However, beneath this wave of scientific optimism poverty was being rediscovered. Research published in the mid 1960s revealed that, far from being the classless and equal society to which the Wilson government was committed, the UK in the 1960s was characterized by discrepancies of wealth and opportunity at least as stark as they had been in the 1930s (Abel-Smith and Townsend, 1965). It may well have been the case that virtually everybody had a much higher income and a higher standard of living, but the gap between the rich and the poor had, if anything, widened. It also became evident that the proportion of working-class children entering university had not risen at all in the post-war period, underlining the fact that the 'open and equal society', to which all the major political parties were committed, remained a chimera. This 'rediscovery of poverty' had an important impact upon the youth justice and social policies which emanated from the Wilson administration in the mid to late 1960s.

## 2.3  The 1969 Children and Young Persons Act

In the run-up to what eventually became the 1969 Children and Young Persons Act (Home Office, 1969), politicians, radical social scientists, progressive Home Office civil servants and members of the social work profession attempted to transform the youth justice system in England and Wales. They tried, amongst other things, to raise the age of criminal responsibility from 10 to 17, to transfer the control of youth justice from central to local government and to abolish the imprisonment of children and young people. Three related beliefs informed their endeavours:

1   That social inequality, and the social disadvantages it engendered, were instrumental in propelling young people into delinquency.

2   That the stigma involved in a court appearance merely compounded such social disadvantage by confirming the young offender's delinquent identity.

3   That the state, through its social, economic and criminal justice policies, should play a central role in combating, and responding humanely to, both the causes and the consequences of social inequality.

The reformers wanted to replace a court-based system, founded upon the principle of 'just deserts', with a system based upon a scientific understanding of social inequality and its consequences. In justification they pointed to the fact that the juvenile court was first and foremost a mechanism for processing the most deprived working-class children and young people. How, they asked, could such a system, which responded only to the offence and ignored its ultimate social and psychological causes, deliver 'just deserts' in an unjust society? They aimed to replace custody in Borstals and detention centres with community homes (these erstwhile approved schools, having been transferred to local authority control, were to become 'therapeutic communities') and 'intermediate treatment' (IT). IT was to replace both detention centres, in which young people aged between 15 and 17 spent short terms of imprisonment of up to three months, and attendance centres, where young people aged between 14 and 17 were sentenced to spend their Saturday afternoons up to a maximum of 48 hours.

intermediate treatment

While the Wilson government was clear about what intermediate treatment was not – namely, an attendance centre or a detention centre – since 1969, practitioners, politicians and lawyers have continued to debate what IT ought to be. Early IT emphasized voluntary participation in recreational and educational activities which were used as a means of building relationships with children and young people in trouble and offering them experiences which would 'compensate' for the bad experiences which had led them into crime. However, by the 1980s, IT had thrown off its welfarist trappings and emerged as a hard-headed, confrontational response to 'offending behaviour' (this will be considered in section 3.1.1).

The reforms of the 1960s aimed to recast the young offender as a victim of social deprivation and the psychological problems which such deprivation engendered. As such, young offenders required the scientifically informed interventions of 'trained experts' rather than punishment. This attempt to *decriminalize* and *depoliticize* the youth justice system of England and Wales encountered sustained resistance from the Conservative opposition and the legal and academic establishments (Pitts, 1988). In Scotland, however, things worked out rather differently.

## 2.4 Welfarism in Scotland

The Kilbrandon Report (Scottish Home and Health Department and Scottish Education Department, 1964) appeared in Scotland a few years earlier than *Children in Trouble*, the White Paper which announced the measures to be enacted in England and Wales in the 1969 Children and Young Persons Act (Home Office, 1968). Like *Children in Trouble*, Kilbrandon argued that social work intervention in youth crime was most likely to be effective if it concentrated upon the social and emotional problems of children and young people in trouble rather than on their offences: if it focused on needs rather than deeds. The subsequent Social Work (Scotland) Act (1968) brought into being a system of children's hearings which eventually came into operation in 1972. Children's hearings are presided over by a Reporter and peopled by professional experts and lay representatives of the local community. Anybody has the right to refer children and young people over the age of eight to a hearing if they are concerned about their social, emotional or moral development. However, in practice, the bulk of these referrals come from the police and, as Morris and McIssac (1978) have argued, because the police are more interested in clearing up crime than in the social, emotional or moral well-being of those who perpetrate it, the system's stated commitment to the welfare of the child tends to be subverted by the professional imperatives of the police. Morris and McIssac conclude: 'if we wish to create a system in which welfare values dominate, the role of the police requires re-consideration' (Morris and McIssac, 1978, p.193).

The Social Work (Scotland) Act marked the end of a separate probation service in Scotland and its replacement by an expanded local authority social work service. The local authorities became responsible for the supervision of both juvenile and adult offenders and this responsibility is handled by generic area social work teams. Arguably, this has eroded the quality of social work with offenders in Scotland because they have tended to assume a low priority beside mental health and child protection cases. Beyond this, committals to residential care and custody actually increased in the wake of the implementation of the Social Work (Scotland) Act and this raises the question of whether ideologies of Scottish welfarism made any significant difference to the day-to-day practice of youth justice on the ground, and whether they placed any barrier in the way of the drift towards punishment which occurred in other parts of the UK in the 1970s.

## 2.5 The 1970s and the renaissance of punishment

Those sections of the 1969 Children and Young Persons Act which threatened the power and supremacy of the bench and the judiciary, although they had been passed by parliament, were not implemented by Edward Heath's Conservative administration which came to power in 1970. The advent of the 1969 Children and Young Persons Act witnessed both the high watermark and the exhaustion of social democratic reform in the post-war period in the UK. According to Booker, these reforms had been based on 'the utopian belief that through drastic social and political reorganisation, aided by the greater use of state planning we should be able to create a new kind of just, fair and equal society' (Booker, 1980, p.9). It was an optimistic ideology, predicated on the belief that the intrinsic altruism and goodness of human beings could be realized if the fruits of a perpetually expanding economy could be scientifically targeted on social problems. When, in the late 1960s and early 1970s, the economy went into the kind of protracted recession which the dominant Keynesian explanations of economic life maintained were no longer possible, doubt was cast upon the entire reforming endeavour.

The 1970 Heath administration offered a new and harder version of conservatism to match the starker economic realities which followed the economic boom of the 1960s. Heath entered government promising to control inflation, the unions and crime and this pledge ensured that the abolition of the imprisonment of young offenders, which only months before had seemed a possibility, was scrubbed from the political agenda.

The Heath administration retained many of the measures ushered in by the 1969 Children and Young Persons Act but, crucially, failed to implement those which placed limitations on the power of magistrates. It did not raise the age of criminal responsibility, thus ensuring that the supply of delinquents to be dealt with by the police and the courts was not diminished. It did not phase out the attendance and detention centres in favour of the new community-based intermediate treatment schemes, as the Act had intended, though it placed no impediment in the way of the development of IT. It did not prevent young people under 17 being sentenced to Borstal training by the courts, but it gave social workers the power to place them in the revamped approved school – the community home (with education) (CHE). In doing so, it increased substantially the numbers of people who could decide whether or not a child should be removed from home.

The early 1970s saw the emergence of a youth justice system which was not, as the reformers of the 1960s had hoped, transformed, but substantially expanded. This was the period which witnessed a widening of the net of control as the elements of the new system brought into being by the 1969 Act were absorbed into a larger system which retained its traditional commitment to imprisonment as the ultimate disciplinary backstop (**Cohen, 1979**).

net widening

Social work and the courts and prisons constituted the two faces of the new youth justice system. The two elements grew out of very different assumptions about the nature of the young offender, the origins of his or her offending and desirable responses to it and so, perhaps inevitably, the scene was set for a struggle between the forces of 'welfare' and the forces of 'justice' for the body of the delinquent. This was a struggle which the forces of justice won hands down. Between 1965 and 1977, the numbers of young people aged 14 to 17 entering detention centres rose from 1,404 to 5,757. In the same period the Borstal population remained fairly static, but the proportion of 15- to 17-year-old inmates rose from 12.3 per cent to over 30 per cent. In 1965, 21 per cent of convicted young offenders aged 14 to 17 were dealt with in police-administered attendance centres and prison department-administered detention centres and Borstals. By 1977 this proportion had risen to 38 per cent. The period also saw a decline in the numbers of young people aged 14 to 17 entering approved schools/CHEs: from 8.3 per cent of those found guilty of indictable offences in 1965 to 4.2 per cent in 1977. Supervision in the community by social workers or probation officers also declined from 18.5 per cent of convicted young offenders in 1965 to 13.5 per cent in 1977. These developments occurred, moreover, in a period in which serious juvenile offending was fairly static and, in some instances, in decline (Pitts, 1988).

## ACTIVITY 6.1

As a means of summarizing the discussion so far, list the key elements of welfarist youth justice strategies. How were these compromised in England and Wales in the 1970s?

## 2.6 'Race', crime and justice

As the system expanded, it became apparent that a disproportionate number of black young people of Afro-Caribbean origin were entering both residential care and penal institutions. Until the mid 1980s, the Home Office was unwilling to give any information about the involvement of black and Asian young people in the justice system, but it was evident to anybody who stood in an inner-city juvenile court, or on a landing in a Borstal in the south of England, where most people of Afro-Caribbean origin in Britain live, that black young people were heavily represented.

Gradually, research and investigative journalism began to unearth the facts. In 1982, the journalist Martin Kettle revealed that:

> In April this year, according to the Home Office, 50 per cent of the population of Ashford remand centre was black. Brixton (another remand prison) and Aylesbury prisons were between 25 per cent and 35 per cent black. So were Rochester, Dover and Hewell Grange Borstals and Blantyre House detention centre. Others with more than 10 per cent black inmates were Wormwood Scrubs, Parkhurst, Albany, Wandsworth and Reading prisons and Wellingborough, Bulwood Hall and Feltham Borstals.

> (Kettle, 1982)

The black prison population, like the black population in general, is young. Thus, when the Home Office responded to this and similar reports by indicating that the black population in the penal system constituted only 8 per cent of male and 12 per cent of female prisoners, it failed to indicate that in the Borstals and detention centres of the south of England, black prisoners constituted around 37 per cent of the inmates (Pitts, 1988).

Initially, these facts were presented by most of the media as a vindication of the view that delinquency was more pervasive and more serious amongst black children and young people. However, as social scientists and political campaigners looked more closely at the processes which culminated in the over-representation of black youngsters in care and custody, other explanations began to suggest themselves.

Research undertaken by the Policy Studies Institute (Smith and Gray, 1985) indicated that black young people of Afro-Caribbean origin were four times more likely to be stopped and searched by the police than white young people. Landau's (1981) study of police cautioning, whereby the police are able to choose whether to formally warn a young person rather than prosecute them, showed that white young people were twice as likely to be cautioned, and that black first offenders were subject to 'immediate charge' decisions significantly more than their white counterparts. This meant that a larger proportion of black young people were entering youth courts than white young people. Once in court, for equivalent offences, black defendants were more likely to receive custodial sentences than white defendants and less likely to be offered a place in an 'alternative to custody' (Pitts, 1988). If

police cautioning

they were imprisoned, black young people were also likely to attract longer sentences (Taylor, 1981).

The public controversy generated by this research caused the Home Office Prison Department, the probation service and local authority social services departments to take stock of the ways in which they were dealing with black young people in trouble. As the 1980s progressed, anti-racist 'policies', 'statements' and 'training' were instituted in an attempt to eradicate the injustices occasioned by racism. Nonetheless, whereas in 1985 Home Office figures indicated that 'West Indian, Guyanese and African' prisoners constituted 8 per cent of the male prison population and 12.2 per cent of the female prison population, by 1992 these proportions had risen to 10.2 per cent and 20.1 per cent respectively (Home Office, 1994).

## 2.7 'It's different for girls'

The relative infrequency with which young women become involved with the law has been taken by some commentators as an indication that the youth justice system deals with them leniently (see Chapter 3). Self report studies indicate that girls are involved in far more offending than the official statistics suggest, although significantly less than their male counterparts (Graham and Bowling, 1996). However, when girls are apprehended, the responses of the police, courts and social workers are often far more intrusive and controlling. Hudson (1985), investigating official responses to children and young people in trouble under the welfare-oriented Children and Young Persons Act (1969), observes that:

> The common scenario for boys in court is that the act which is the subject of the charge is inveighed against by the magistrates, with the mother saying that 'he's a good boy at home'; whereas the girl in Care proceedings is a pathetic lonely figure, with the mother often the principal witness against her. Not only will the proceedings have been the culmination of a process of rejection by the girl's parents, but the outcome will mean a much more drastic intervention than with boys – a two or three-year supervision order or a long spell in a residential establishment, as opposed to a fine or a conditional discharge.
>
> (Hudson, 1985)

The severity of these responses is accounted for by a belief, held by generations of criminologists, and those who operate justice systems, that most female offending is 'unnatural': an expression of an overly masculine constitution, or a failure to adjust to the feminine role (Hudson, 1985; Heidensohn, 1987). There is, however, one category of female crime which is regarded as 'natural' and that is shoplifting:

> Assault, criminal damage, burglary, TDA [taking and driving away] and so on, are all taken more seriously in girls than boys because they are presumed to be so rare and so role-abnormal. Shoplifting is the only crime that is considered normal for girls, but precisely because it is a woman's crime, shoplifting attracts psychiatric explanations in a way that other everyday crimes do not. Our stereotyped images of the shoplifter are all female; the menopausal housewife, the confused foreign tourist, the mother unable to feed her family legitimately, the teenage girl unable to afford make-up, the magpie female of any age, tempted by bright jewellery or luxury underwear.
>
> (Hudson, 1985)

Female offenders cannot win – if they commit typical 'men's crimes' they are regarded as unnatural, but if they commit 'women's crimes' they are deemed irrational. The identification of female offending as symptomatic of a deeper disorder, concerned with a failure to achieve an 'appropriate' or 'adequate' 'femininity', or as an expression of vulnerability to biological or emotional impulses, has important consequences for rehabilitative responses to, and institutional regimes for, women (Carlen, 1985; see also Chapter 3 of this volume). The far higher profile of psychiatry and psychology in women's prisons and the fact that the programme of the only attendance centre for adolescent girls in the UK revolved around homecraft and child care, testify to the importance placed upon the successful social reproduction of an appropriate femininity. As Hudson (1985) observes, intervention with young women invariably focuses on their 'femaleness' while scant attention is paid to their youthfulness. Whereas offending by boys is often attributed to adolescent silliness, a normal, albeit misplaced, expression of their burgeoning masculinity and something which they will probably 'grow out of', offending by girls is taken far more seriously because it is seen to be a portent of future problems of gender adjustment which will only be arrested by prompt action.

The renaissance of imprisonment, the failure to effect significant social change through social work intervention, and social work's apparent tendency – particularly in the cases of girls and of black young people of Afro-Caribbean origin – to worsen the problems to which it was supposed to be a solution, along with cuts in the resources of local authority social services departments, caused many reformers, academic commentators and people working in social welfare during the 1970s to rethink the ideas which had informed their practices and their strategies for social change and penal reform. Gradually, a new theoretical and ideological orthodoxy began to emerge, the tenor of which contrasted starkly with the optimism of the 1960s.

# 3   The retreat from welfare

## 3.1   Welfarism under attack

The recession which began at the end of the 1960s quite literally marked the end of an era in the development of the welfare state. As the 1970s progressed, the optimism of the 1960s was supplanted by a mood of pessimism as successive governments struggled to come to grips with a steadily worsening economic crisis. This pessimism was reflected in social and criminal justice policies, in the theories developed by social scientists and in the practices of professional workers. At the heart of these changes was a rejection of the 'welfarist' criminal justice policies of the 1960s. This critique had four main components.

### 3.1.1   The liberal justice lobby

Emerging first in the USA in the mid 1960s, but gaining ground in England and Wales by the mid 1970s, the liberal justice lobby attacked the social work presence in the youth justice system for its capacity to make unwarranted incursions into the lives and liberties of children and young people in trouble. Pouring scorn upon professional social work's claims to any specialized knowledge or expertise, the argument was often long on rhetoric but short on evidence and analysis (Morris *et al.*, 1980). Social workers were to be barred from the courts, and solicitors and magistrates, armed only with their law books and good common sense, were to defend young offenders against the rampant professional entrepreneurism of social work which, they maintained, often led to young people in trouble, in general, and young women in particular, serving what were, in effect, *indeterminate* sentences in residential institutions for moral rather than legal infractions (Hudson, 1985).

For intermediate treatment this rush into the arms of the law ushered in the 'justice model', which changed profoundly the practice of social work with children and young people in trouble. IT projects developed 'programmes' or 'packages', often designed in consultation with magistrates, to serve as alternatives to custody for adjudicated 'high-tariff' offenders. These programmes, characteristically, included an element, variously described as 'offending workshops' or 'correctional curricula', in which the offender was required to 'address', with staff, and sometimes with other offenders, the criminal act(s) which had brought them to the project. Some *intensive* IT projects, in an effort to shore up their credibility with sentencers, also included specifically punitive programme elements, including manual labour and restriction of liberty. The 'justice model' was claimed to have a number of clear advantages over the 'welfare model', which it was said to have superseded:

justice model

- Everybody knew what it was. The magistrate, the worker and the young offender all knew that participation in an IT programme was a direct result of a penalty imposed by the court: 'young offenders' were getting their 'just deserts'.

- Everybody knew where they were. The magistrate knew that he or she must impose one of a number of specified penalties if the young offender failed to comply with the conditions of their order. The worker, the offender and the offender's parents knew the programme that the offender must be put through and the sanctions to be imposed if he or she failed to comply with it.

- Everybody was talking the same language. There was a shared culture in which the talk was of offending, punishment and reparation. The techniques adopted focused on offending. There was no talk of 'need' or 'deprivation' since, within the justice model, no link was made between the personal or social circumstances of young offenders and the crime(s) they had committed.

The justice model provided a means whereby the political objective of a rational, manageable and cost-effective penal system might be realized, not least because it left out a number of politically inconvenient realities:

> It is interesting to note that the 'Justice Model' ... has tended to absorb only those elements of social scientific theory which support time-limited, individualised interventions with an exclusive focus on offending. Those perspectives which address the personal, cultural, social, economic and racial factors which may increase the vulnerability of young people to involvement in crime or heightened surveillance by the police, are not admitted.

> (Pitts, 1992a, p.138)

### 3.1.2 Traditional conservatism

Traditional conservatism located the main victims of the economic recession as its cause, finding in the behaviour of young offenders the example, *par excellence,* of what was wrong with the country. Because this viewpoint conflates the 'laws of God', the 'laws of nature' and the 'law of the land', it has no trouble in transforming economic crises into moral ones (see Morgan, 1978). This account of the world was a major force in the creation of those criminal justice policies of the early 1980s which required workers to justify themselves in terms of their capacity to exert control over 'young offenders', rather than to offer help and support to 'children and young people in trouble'.

### 3.1.3 Radical criminology

The radical left-wing criminological critique tended to identify social work as the velvet glove disguising 'the iron fist of capitalist oppression'. In this account social workers were unwitting agents, who served only to blunt the edge, or blur the reality, of class domination. In its softer version, the left-wing critique located social workers as the 'zookeepers' of deviance who imposed deviant labels upon people who were engaged in relatively innocuous behaviour, perfectly acceptable in its own cultural milieu, but unfairly stigmatized by powerful agents of social control. Whether they were postponing the revolution by promoting false consciousness amongst their clients, or lurching clumsily through the social world saying 'bad things' about 'OK people', the left-wing criminological critique located social workers as part of the problem rather than as part of the solution (**Taylor *et al.*, 1973**).

### 3.1.4 Administrative criminology

The mid 1970s witnessed the abandonment by conventional criminology of its central project: the investigation of the causes of crime and the development of rehabilitative techniques with which to ameliorate or eradicate it (**Young, 1986**). In the light of all the available 'scientific' evidence, the criminological establishment came reluctantly to the view that, like the search for the philosopher's stone, the quest for an effective method of rehabilitating criminals was probably a lost cause:

> It does not seem to matter what form of treatment in the correctional system is attempted, whether vocational training or academic education; whether counselling inmates individually, in groups or not at all; whether therapy is administered by social workers or psychiatrists; whether the institutional context of the treatment is custodial or benign; whether the sentences are short or long; whether the person is placed on probation or released on parole or whether the treatment takes place in the community or an institution.

**(Wilson, 1975, p.169)**

This 'decline of the rehabilitative ideal' (Preston, 1980) signalled a profound change in the concerns of conventional criminology, away from the origins of crime and criminality to a preoccupation with the administration and effectiveness of the apparatus of justice and control (see **Clarke, 1980a**). One of the by-products of this change was to highlight the ineffectiveness of social work as a means of stopping people committing crimes. This effectively put an end to the relationship which had previously been assumed to exist between some criminologists and social workers. The assumption that criminology would develop a correctional technology, which the social work technicians would then operationalize, had to be abandoned. The 'decline of the rehabilitative ideal' removed an important theoretical prop from the practice of social work with offenders and threatened to leave social workers without a job to do in the criminal justice system.

## ACTIVITY 6.2

Identify and list those ideas which are *shared* by: the justice model, traditional conservatism, radical/left-wing criminology and administrative criminology. When you have done so, identify those ideas which *distinguish* these positions from each other.

Taken together, these four critiques left a gaping hole where welfarism and rehabilitation had once been, but this was filled soon enough with a new theory and a new practice.

## 3.2 Back to justice: the rise of neo-conservative criminology

The defining features of conservatism up to the mid 1970s were its espousal of: social and economic individualism; anti-intellectualism; an emphasis on authority, moral discipline and imperfect human nature; gut-level reactions on law and order and other emotive social issues; and political pragmatism on less emotive ones. Up to that point, conservatives were people who strove to maintain the status quo and radicals were the people who had visions of a 'better world' (Scruton, 1980).

From the mid 1970s, however, the UK and the USA witnessed the emergence of a radical neo-conservative (New Right) intelligentsia, with a vision of a better world and a commitment to fundamental social change. This highly influential group embarked on a political, economic and intellectual crusade which had an enormous impact on Anglo-American politics and criminal justice policy.

neo-conservatism

In his influential critique of the criminal justice policies and strategies of the 1960s, **James Q. Wilson (1975)** offered a pessimistic account of the way in which the world worked and what, if anything, could be changed. Wilson, a neo-conservative intellectual and Ronald Reagan's adviser on crime and justice, became a shaping force in Anglo-American crime control in the 1980s. At the core of his critique of the 'welfarist' criminal justice policies of the 1960s was a repudiation of the idea that by a process of 'social engineering' a better type of human being could be produced. Wilson is far more pessimistic about 'human nature' and the capacity of social intervention to change it. He writes:

> Wicked people exist. Nothing avails except to set them apart from innocent people. And many people, neither wicked nor innocent, but watchful, dissembling, and calculating of their opportunities, ponder our reaction to wickedness as a cue to what they might profitably do. We have trifled with the wicked, made sport of the innocent, and encouraged the calculators. Justice suffers and so do we all.

**(Wilson, 1975, p.209)**

This 'rediscovery' of wickedness was echoed by the English social commentator, Patricia Morgan, who, in 1978, produced *Delinquent Fantasies*, a critique of welfarist youth justice strategies. She writes of the spread of 'a delinquent syndrome, a conglomeration of behaviour, speech, appearance and attitudes, a frightening ugliness and hostility which pervades human interaction, a flaunting of contempt for other human beings, a delight in crudity, cruelty and violence, a desire to challenge and humiliate but never, but never to please' (Morgan, 1978, p.13).

But for neo-conservatives the impetus to commit crime is not simply an expression of individual wickedness, it also contains an implicit social element which can be stated as follows:

- Capitalist societies are most successful if the hidden hand of the market is given free reign and state intervention in the social and economic sphere is minimized.

- Because those who seize opportunities will become richer and those who do not, being unprotected by redistributive taxation and employment and social legislation, become relatively poorer, successful capitalist societies will also become progressively less equal.

- This inequality will serve as an incentive to many to seize the new opportunities generated by the free market and enrich themselves, but for a small minority who lack the ability or moral fibre to do so, they will serve as an incentive to cheat.

- Thus successful capitalist societies will also be societies in which there is pressure towards an increase in crime. The more successful they become, the more crime-prone they will be.

In this discourse we are apparently faced with a choice between a poorer, more equal and less crime-prone society or a richer, less equal and more crime-prone society. However, Wilson (1975) argues that this is not really a choice at all. Any US politician proposing to redistribute the wealth necessary to achieve even a semblance of social equality, he argues, would never be elected. Any discussion with the victims of crime, who are usually the poor themselves, he says, indicates that they do not want to be poorer and more equal; they want tougher action against crime.

punitive justice

Wilson notes that, despite the increases in crime levels, the numbers of people actually involved in serious crime remains small and that these people are different from other people. The solution, then, lies in punitive justice: to identify this hard core of serious offenders and take them out of circulation. As for the others, increasing the certainty of detection, the construction of more severe penalties and the reduction of opportunities for gain through illicit activity will suffice.

How do neo-conservatives understand criminal motivation? In what ways does this understanding differ from the account offered by 'welfarism'?

Why were the neo-conservative accounts of the causes of crime and its policy prescriptions so influential in England and Wales and the USA in the 1980s and early 1990s?

# 4   Thatcherism and young offenders

Although Margaret Thatcher entered government in 1979 promising to 'restore the rule of law', at that point her ideas about criminal justice policy owed more to the rhetoric of traditional conservatism than to the theories of Wilson (1975).

At a conference on youth justice in 1979, Patrick Mayhew, a Minister of State at the Home Office, borrowing a phrase from the Duke of Edinburgh, bemoaned 'the rising tide of anarchy and violence threatening to engulf our shores' (DHSS, 1979). In the same year, James Anderton, Chief Constable of the Greater Manchester Police, called for 'labour camps' for 'young thugs' and William Whitelaw, the Home Secretary, promised to provide them and, in doing so, give previously unprecedented numbers of 'hooligans' a 'short, sharp shock' (Pitts, 1988). Arguably, the rhetorical flourishes of early Thatcherism had three main functions. They aimed to placate the vocal right wing which had been swept into parliament by the Thatcher landslide; they served as a demonstration of toughness to an electorate which had been wooed with promises of safe streets; and they were an attempt to divert attention away from a faltering economy (Pitts, 1988).

## 4.1   Early Thatcherism, bifurcation and runaway incarceration

The 1982 Criminal Justice Act was heralded as the piece of legislation which would 'restore the rule of law', yet, paradoxically, it reduced the minimum period a child or young person could spend in a detention centre to three weeks. This apparent paradox was created by a legislative strategy which Bottoms (1977) describes as 'bifurcation'.

bifurcation

The attraction of 'bifurcated' youth justice strategies to 'law and order' governments is that they allow them to have their law and order cake while at the same time eating their public expenditure one. Bifurcated policies redescribe, and then redistribute, deviant populations. Some catagories of offenders are represented as more serious and menacing while others, who had previously been regarded as a threat, are represented as relatively unproblematic. The activity of a small number of offenders is 'dramatized' while that of others is 'normalized'. Bifurcated strategies increase the penalties imposed upon the dramatized group while reducing those imposed upon the normalized group. These policies often involve the development of community-based alternatives to residential care or custody for groups of newly normalized offenders who were previously incarcerated.

## 4.2   A short, sharp shock

The announcement of the shorter detention centre sentence was accompanied by a great deal of public relations activity on the part of the Home Office to demonstrate that if young offenders were subjected to the new, tougher regimes for shorter periods the deterrent effect would be greater (Pitts, 1988). It encouraged magistrates to make greater use of this 'new' sentencing option and, in anticipation of success, it warned the governors of the new detention centres to prepare themselves for a 40 per cent increase in throughput. The shorter detention centre sentence was accompanied in 1983 by an investment of £15 million in the Department of Health and Social Security (DHSS) (now the Department of Health) Intermediate Treatment Initiative which was to provide 4,500 'alternatives to custody' for persistent young offenders. The government was trying to persuade magistrates to sentence larger numbers of less problematic children and young people, whom they described as 'hooligans', to a very brief and relatively inexpensive spell 'inside'. They were also trying to persuade magistrates to divert simultaneously a similar number of more serious young offenders, who attracted much longer and much more expensive custodial sentences (and who, since the mid 1970s, had constituted an important element in the crisis of overcrowding in British prisons) to alternatives to custody, in the community.

However, the government had given magistrates a mixed message. The Home Secretary, as a politician, had said that we must 'get tough', but the Home Secretary as a penal administrator had said that we must limit the use of custody. The bench, by and large, had listened to the first message and ignored the second. Thus the youth custody centre (formally Borstal) population did not grow by the anticipated 15 per cent between 1983 and 1990, but by 65 per cent between May 1983 and May 1984 (Pitts, 1988). The new-style detention centres did not grow by the predicted 40 per cent; in fact the population declined (Muncie, 1990). Thus the 1982 Act, far from achieving its twin aims of 'getting tough' and easing pressure on the prison, had caused the most rapid growth in the custody of young people in British history. A strategy which aimed to incapacitate the minority of serious and persistent offenders, while 'managing' the rest, was still urgently needed.

*Detention centre inmates in 1983: part of the most dramatic expansion of youth custody in British history*

## 4.3 Late Thatcherism: corporatism and the cost-effective management of deviant populations

By the early to mid 1980s, the Home Office was more sympathetic to managerialist approaches to social problems and losing patience with juvenile court magistrates who appeared to be wedded to what was considered an outdated, unscientific 'eye-for-an-eye' *modus operandi*. It supported the development of a rational, cost-effective youth justice system and, in doing so, espoused a radical, 'scientific' managerial style of the type pioneered in the boroughs of Westminster and Wandsworth. Describing their 'mission' in terms of 'targets', 'minimum standards' and 'performance indicators' they were anti-union, anti-professional and pro-privatization. This was 'full-blown' Thatcherism and it set itself against restrictive practices in the police, the law and the Prison Service (see Chapters 2, 3 and 5). Indeed, within a very short space of time these professional groups, which had previously regarded Conservative governments as their ally, were talking of betrayal. It is therefore particularly ironic that, having alienated and enraged most of the other professional interest groups in the justice system, the government established what was, in effect, an alliance with a previously marginal group of radical youth justice professionals in the voluntary and statutory sectors (Pitts, 1988; Nellis, 1989).

managerialism

What were the main differences between early and late Thatcherism as evidenced by government youth justice policies?

Between 1983 and 1989 the numbers of juveniles imprisoned in England and Wales fell from 7,900 to 2,200. Although the period from 1979 to 1989 witnessed a 25 per cent decrease in the numbers of children and young people in the age range in the UK, there was a reduction in juvenile imprisonment of approximately 68 per cent (Allen, 1991). The projects developed within the DHSS Intermediate Treatment Initiative were a key factor in this reduction (see section 4.2).

What commended the Initiative to the government, and persuaded it to attempt a similar strategy for young adult offenders in the late 1980s and early 1990s, was the apparent ability of workers in Initiative projects to co-operate with and influence the decisions of the police and the magistrates. This was achieved, in practice, by the development of inter-agency juvenile panels which, by the end of the 1980s, existed in most local authorities in England and Wales. The panels, comprising representatives of welfare agencies, the youth service, the police and education departments, reviewed the cases of all apprehended children and young people entering the youth justice system and, wherever possible, diverted them away from court. This was achieved by using police cautions more extensively to divert first offenders from prosecution and by the development of a system known as 'cautioning plus', to deal with more persistent offenders. Cautioning plus offered these young people further cautions on the condition that they attended additional educational, recreational or therapeutic activities. As the number of offences rose, so offenders' involvement in these activities increased. Thus, on a fourth offence, for example, a young person might find themselves involved in their local youth club, an offending programme run by the youth justice section of the local authority social services department, and a course of family therapy with a local counselling agency. These developments led Pratt

inter-agency
juvenile panels

corporatist
model

(1989) to observe that the 'welfare' and 'justice' models had now been supplanted by a 'corporatist model' of youth justice in which a partnership of social workers, youth workers, police and magistrates co-operated to produce a cost-effective mechanism for the effective processing of adjudicated offenders. Youth justice workers also developed working relationships with local juvenile court magistrates in an attempt to encourage them to divert young offenders away from custody and into 'alternative to custody' programmes. As Bottoms *et al.* (1990) have demonstrated, the confidence of magistrates in the common-sense 'hard-headedness' of these programmes, and the competence of the workers who staffed them, were the most important factors in the success of the Intermediate Treatment Initiative.

What are the major differences between the 'corporatist', 'welfare' and 'justice' models of youth justice?

# 5 The contradictions of the 1980s and 1990s

## 5.1 Ideological commitments and political pragmatism

punishment in
the community

Until 1988, a strategy of 'punishment in the community' worked well enough. This was a period of boom and the government was content to give crime in general, and youth crime in particular, a relatively low profile. As the economy went into recession, however, the government resorted to blaming the attitudes and behaviour of young people, their parents and teachers for current economic ills. This is a strategy which works best for new governments, but by now the Conservatives had been in power for almost a decade. As a result, they encountered some serious 'presentational' problems. There were, for example, many traditional Tory voters who had not forgiven the Thatcher administration for its failed promised crusade against crime. Beyond the Conservative Party were many more who could not make the connection between a steadily rising crime rate and the government's purported victories in the 'fight against crime'. More damaging were those senior police officers who, as the decade wore on, felt obliged to speak out against what they perceived as the government's divisive and criminogenic social and economic policies.

The government responded to these difficulties by arguing that apparent policy failures were merely examples of the pressing need for such policies. It maintained that it was, in fact, taking tough action to contain a crime wave which was running out of control in all other advanced industrial societies. Thus ministers were particularly heartened when, in 1988, recorded crime dropped by 5 per cent, and they began to believe that their financial investment in law and order (a real increase of 87 per cent during the Conservatives' time in office) was at last paying off. It looked, for a moment, as if the rhetoric might at last be converging with the reality.

But the level of recorded crime rose sharply from the end of 1989, climbing by 17 per cent in 1990 and a further 16 per cent in 1991 (Home Office, 1992). Now the government went on to the offensive, placing the blame for its apparent failure to achieve policy objectives on the police, probation officers, social workers and even the people who were supposed to be the beneficiaries of those policies. In marked contrast with the utterances of his colleague Patrick Mayhew 12 years before, at the 1991 Conservative Party conference, Kenneth Baker, the then Home Secretary, responded to the unprecedented increase in recorded crime by suggesting that its victims were not taking proper care of their property. But the response from the audience suggested that the rhetoric had run its course.

The fact that these unprecedented increases coincided with the onset of the recession of the late 1980s was lost on nobody: friend or foe. In 1990 the Home Office published a study which offered clear evidence that property crime had grown more sharply when disposable income declined and that it slowed again when personal consumption increased (**Field, 1990**). The evidence was unequivocal: economic need precipitated crime on the social and economic margins. The study gave substance to what more and more people, across the entire political spectrum, had long suspected.

## 5.2  A neo-conservative criminology

In the early 1980s, neo-conservatives had invoked the 'trickle-down effect' (the process whereby the wealth amassed by the few is assumed to percolate down eventually to the many) to justify the apparent callousness of the free-market experiment. But it simply had not happened. Instead, the late 1980s and early 1990s witnessed accelerating social and economic polarization and growing crime and public disorder. As a result, neo-conservative politicians and intellectuals came under increasing pressure to account for the apparent failure of their criminal justice policies.

In *Thinking About Crime*, Wilson (1975) had presented a picture of a world in which rational individuals acted to maximize their pleasure and minimize their pain. In this scenario, as we have already noted, the job of the state was simply to ensure that wrongdoers would incur an appropriate penalty if they broke the law. By 1984 Charles Murray was arguing that the 'free market' in morality, described by Wilson, was being skewed by a welfare system which, by rewarding young women for having children out of wedlock, was creating an 'underclass' with wholly different moral values. Young women, Murray maintained, choose not to marry young men but to marry the state instead. The solution, he argued, was to cut welfare payments altogether, thus 'starving women back into marriage'. 'It is all horribly sexist I know', said Murray, 'but it happens to be true'. Of the putative fathers he subsequently wrote: 'Young men who don't work don't make good marriage material. Often they don't get married at all; when they do, they don't have the ability to fill their traditional role. In either case, too many of them remain barbarians' (**Murray, 1990, p.23**) (see Extract 6.2).

underclass

The political appeal of the 'underclass' thesis lies in the fact that it offers a scientific rationale for social inequality. It tells prosperous people that their success is deserved and that their social advantages have not been won at the expense of the poor. It affirms, in Bourdieu and Passeron's (1964) terms, that what is often, in fact, a 'social inheritance' is a product of personal gifts and talents. Although the 'underclass' thesis tends to collapse in the face of empirical evidence (Glennerster and Midgley, 1991; Dean and Taylor-Gooby, 1992), it is a crucial element in the ideological transformation of the problem to which government policy is the intended solution. The 'underclass' thesis also offers a rationale for governmental withdrawal from the public sphere and reductions in public expenditure.

## Extract 6.2  Murray: 'Underclass: the crisis deepens'

When I wrote about the nascent British underclass five years ago, I briefly referred to young males as 'essentially barbarians' who are civilised by marriage. Since then, that image has become all too literal in the American inner city, where male teenage behaviour is often a caricature of the barbarian male: retaliate against anyone who shows you the slightest disrespect ('disses' you). Sleep with and impregnate as many girls as possible. Violence is a sign of strength. To worry about tomorrow is weakness. To die young is glorious. What makes this trend so disturbing is not just that these principles describe behaviour, but that inner-city boys articulate them *as principles*. They are, explicitly, the code by which they live.

This comes as no surprise to observers who for many years have predicted what would become of a generation of fatherless boys. Adolescence and testosterone are a destructive combination, and the only antidote is a civilising process that begins in infancy and is completed by marriage. I am arguing that the civilising process *cannot* occur in communities where the two-parent family is not the norm, and this will turn out to be as true of England as America. The real problem with the 'alternative' of unmarried parenthood is that it offers no ethical alternative for socialising little boys. For males, the ethical code of the two-parent family is the only game in town.

(Murray, 1994, p.26)

In 1985, in *Crime and Human Nature*, Wilson and Herrnstein indicated their belief that the behaviour described by Murray (1984) was not only becoming 'normal' amongst certain populations, but that it may also have been 'natural': 'Crime cannot be understood without taking into account predispositions and their biological roots' (Wilson and Herrnstein, 1985, p.103). By 1994, Herrnstein and Murray were arguing that not only do members of the underclass appear to have a biological predisposition to crime, which is exacerbated by the misguided generosity of the state, but that they also have an intellectual proclivity because they are 'demonstrably' less intelligent. Thus, Herrnstein and Murray maintain, not only is the existing distribution of wealth and privilege normal, it is also natural. It is interesting that the IQ debate, which, in the hands of Murray is a reaffirmation of social Darwinism, often resurfaces at times of heightened social anxiety (Hall *et al.*, 1978). It serves to assuage the status anxieties of the prosperous by positing scientific confirmation of the link between measured intelligence, personal ability, wealth and social status.

## 5.3  Waiting for the barbarians

Over the period, the object of neo-conservative analysis changed from a 'sovereign individual', exercising 'free will' in the 'free market', to a morally, culturally and, by the mid 1990s, biologically and intellectually deficient adolescent male barbarian (Wilson and Herrnstein, 1985; Herrnstein and Murray, 1994). The fact that neo-conservative criminology was prepared to make these remarkable analytical leaps, from free will to determinism, in order to rescue its political project should not surprise us. That they were aided and abetted in this endeavour by commentators who might, in other contexts, be regarded as 'progressives', should. Melanie Phillips notes that:

> Peter Lilley and Sue Slipman, doughty defender of single parents, are suddenly singing in close harmony. In a speech last week, the Social Security Secretary blamed low pay and unemployment for turning young men into unmarriageable prospects. Ms Slipman talks about how the collapse of the male role through lack of work is manufacturing the kind of yob no self-respecting woman would choose as a spouse. Suddenly a government widely assumed to be hostile to single mothers seems to agree that the real problem is men ... The question being asked is, how can we civilise young men when family structures, employment and moral authority are so weakened?

> (*The Observer*, 26 June 1994, p.27)

Beatrix Campbell takes the argument a step further. For her, unemployment and the 'collapse of the male role' do not manufacture this barbarism in men, they simply reveal something which was always there. She writes:

> Among unemployed men – so the argument goes – poverty produces an identity crisis, their unemployment leaves them without a role. Is it a wonder, we sigh, that they turn to crime? However, ... these conversations about men and crime tell a different story, one that shows how unemployment reveals a mode of masculinity whereas the commonsense has been that it causes a crisis of masculinity.

> (Campbell, 1993, p.202)

## ACTIVITY 6.3

Note down what you perceive to be the similarities and differences between the views of Murray and Campbell on the question of unemployed working-class young men, fatherhood and crime.

## COMMENT

Campbell appears to accept the broad sweep of the revised neo-conservative's argument, merely castigating its proponents for laying the blame at the door of women. In this view of the world, the origins of the 'deviant' behaviour of some young men – crime, riot, domestic violence and child abuse – must be sought in a universal *masculine* proclivity whose excesses are sanctioned by the dominant patriarchal social order (Kelly, 1988; McLeod and Saraga, 1991). This idea is, as Wise (1990) has observed, far too 'grand, bland and abstract', not least because it leaves open the question of whether we can therefore hold individual perpetrators responsible for their actions and why, in reality, only a small minority of men express this proclivity in these ways.

Clearly, a consideration of how young, unemployed, working-class men experience and express their **masculinity** is central to any explanation of the rising recorded crime rate of the late 1980s and early 1990s. It is not at all clear, however, that those who engaged in this 'crime wave' were simply acting in conformity with a culturally determined, misogynistic and destructive 'mode of masculinity' (Campbell, 1993), or the alternative norms

masculinity

and practices of an anti-social underclass (Murray, 1990). Indeed, the available evidence points in quite a different direction from either of these possibilities (**Segal, 1990**; Hope, 1994).

While proceeding from the notion that crime is a gendered activity, these accounts, by misrepresenting the nature, and overstating the dimensions, of the problem, over-predict, massively, the amount of crime which will be generated (Miller, 1958; Matza, 1964). They explain neither why youth crime takes markedly different forms in different neighbourhoods, nor why different people in the same neighbourhood respond in markedly different ways to similar pressures towards criminality.

## 5.4   The rehabilitation of rehabilitation

The new neo-conservative orthodoxy was manna from heaven for a government forced back into an interventionist mode on the law and order front. The attempt to deter 'rational man' from crime by the threat of detection and the administration of a 'just measure of pain' had not been wholly successful. Now, this endeavour was to be supplemented by a neo-conservative rehabilitation which would restore offenders to rationality and disciplined conformity.

From the late 1980s, the behavioural and cognitive origins of crime, and techniques for modifying the thoughts and actions of law-breakers, were once again topics of enormous interest in the Home Office, the probation service and the academic community (Ross *et al.*, 1988; Raynor *et al.*, 1994). Whereas the rehabilitative techniques of the 1960s and early 1970s addressed the social and emotional deficits believed to propel individuals and groups into crime, neo-conservative rehabilitation was concerned to remedy the behavioural, cognitive or disciplinary deficiencies of individual offenders and restore them to total rationality. In the late 1980s, three cognitive psychologists, recognizing which way the political wind was blowing, produced a theory which, by asserting that many offenders display a lag in the acquisition of the cognitive skills necessary to a law-abiding life, gave scientific legitimacy to the right-wing discourse on crime. The programme which flowed from this analysis was classroom-based, highly prescriptive and very expensive. This was a free-market (utilitarian) rehabilitation which aimed to engender the cognitive skills necessary to calculate how one's pleasure might be maximized and one's pain minimized (Ross *et al.*, 1988). However, the idea at the core of this approach – that the majority of offenders are in some way intrinsically different from 'normal' people – is difficult to sustain (**Sykes and Matza, 1957**; Matza, 1969; Taylor *et al.*, 1973). That this difference consists in a failure to develop the capacity for moral choice is open to question.

Whereas a decade before, when everybody agreed that 'nothing worked', such matters were deemed to have nothing to contribute to crime reduction, now they emerged as crucial to 'the fight against crime'. Crucial and urgent, according to Christopher Nuttall, Director of Research and Statistics at the Home Office, who, at a meeting of chief probation officers in 1992, said: '"Nothing works" should be killed; not just because it's not right but because it has had a terrible effect. Let's not talk about it anymore. Let's talk about what does work' (quoted in Cohen and Durham, 1993). And criminologists who, 15 years before, had helped to bury the 'rehabilitative ideal', quickly set about exhuming it with a will (Blagg and Smith, 1989; Pitts, 1992a). This rehabilitation of rehabilitation was, in large part, precipitated by the need to 'flesh out' the idea of 'punishment in the community' which was embodied in the 1991 Criminal Justice Act (see Chapter 3, Extract 3.1).

## ACTIVITY 6.4

What, if anything, do you think can be done to stop individuals committing criminal offences? Make a note of your response. If your answer is 'nothing', list the reasons why you think this is so.

The 1991 Criminal Justice Act was to be the means whereby the lessons learned in the 1983 Intermediate Treatment Initiative would be generalized to young adult offenders aged 18 to 25. It was preceded by the *Punishment, Custody and the Community* Green Paper (Home Office, 1988) which, amongst other things, recommended that, in preparing what were now called 'pre-sentence reports', probation officers should assess the dangerousness of defendants, and the risks they posed to the public, in order to facilitate decision-making by magistrates and judges. Probation, which had once offered a 'social work service to the courts', was to be the means whereby the new 'community penalties' were to be imposed upon offenders. To ensure that probation officers were being 'tough' enough, the Home Office issued 'national standards' which detailed the nature, duration and frequency of contact between probation officers and offenders. It was clear that now the primary task of probation officers, irrespective of the client's social and emotional needs, was to confront 'offending behaviour' wherever it occurred. This was a fortunate turn of events for the vendors of neo-conservative rehabilitations.

Notwithstanding the political and media clamour surrounding 'punishment in the community', many probation officers and social workers were becoming increasingly frustrated by what they saw as a widening gap between the ideologically inspired correctional programmes they were required to pursue and their clients' real needs. David Brindle writes:

> Fewer than one in eight offenders serving probation is in full time work or training a survey by NAPO suggests today ... The survey was conducted in May among 1,331 offenders on probation in 19 areas of England and Wales. It found that 12 per cent had a full-time job or training place, with another 4 per cent receiving a mixture of income and benefits. ... More than 30 of the 75 probation officers in the survey reported that over 90 per cent of their clients were dependent upon benefits ... People on probation are twice as likely as other jobless to be long-term unemployed.

> (Brindle, 1993)

Ironically, the renaissance of the ideology of the rational, calculating and culpable offender coincides with what appears to be an increase in the numbers of people on probation officers' caseloads whose rationality is frequently or permanently impaired by their addiction to drugs or alcohol. A study in Northamptonshire in 1982 found that 47 per cent of clients had an alcohol-related problem (Harding, 1987). In a review undertaken by the Inner London Probation Service in 1989, it emerged that a minimum of 30 per cent of the clients of the service had a drink or drug problem which had a serious impact on their propensity to offend. In one area, 50 per cent of the clients had serious problems of addiction (Pitts, 1992a).

## 5.5   Repoliticization, crime waves and social disorder

As we have seen, until the late 1980s the government operated a criminal justice system in which practice was informed by ideological imperatives rather than evidence about what might work. This was a system in which cost-effective reductions in the prison population were achieved by stealth. It was a system of justice which appeared to be utterly unresponsive, indeed unrelated, to the crime and disorder happening out in the world. This is the more remarkable when we remember that the 1980s and early 1990s witnessed widespread social disorder amongst young people. It was the decade in which, with increasing frequency, working-class young people from 'areas of disrepute', took to the streets of British towns and cities, with bricks, home-made fire bombs and, latterly, firearms, to do battle with each other and the police (Campbell, 1993). It was also the decade which witnessed an unprecedented increase in the recorded crime rate.

As the recession deepened, crime in general, and the behaviour of young people in particular, was put back on to the agendas of the major political parties. As the political discourse on youth crime developed and tougher legislation was mooted, the courts anticipated future changes by reversing the downward trend of the 1980s and imposing more custodial sentences on juveniles. In 1991 there were riots in Cardiff, Oxford and Tyneside. Terms such as 'bail bandits', 'ram raiders' and 'twockers' entered the language, displacing the 'muggers', 'hooligans' and 'lager louts' of yesteryear.

By 1992 the promised economic recovery still had not materialized and the government became even more vitriolic in its condemnation of young offenders. At the end of 1992 a 14-year-old boy was shot dead in Manchester's Moss Side, the apparently innocent victim of the 'Crack Wars'. Also in Manchester, a 15-year-old girl was abducted, imprisoned and eventually tortured to death by her 'friends'. In south London, a 12-year-old boy was stabbed in his school playground. Alongside these events, the press was bemoaning the dramatic increase in the number of live births out of wedlock in the UK which had risen from 11 per cent to 17 per cent in the 1980s. The press reported record increases in the crime rate and in youth unemployment. And in February 1993 it reported the start of the trial of the two 10-year-old boys charged with killing two-year-old James Bulger. On the same day, *The Daily Telegraph*'s annual 'state of the nation' survey indicated that, for the first time since 1948, more British citizens wanted to emigrate than stay in this country: worse still, most of them were not particularly concerned about where they would go (*The Daily Telegraph*, 23 February 1993).

*Will social historians look back on the 'teenage crime wave' of the 1990s as a classic example of a moral panic?*

*In the 1980s and 1990s public disorder and clashes between young men and the police became a feature of life in many UK towns and cities*

The then Home Secretary, Kenneth Clarke's reaction to these events was to announce, in March 1993, the introduction of a secure training order aimed at 'that comparatively small group of very persistent juvenile offenders whose repeated offending makes them a menace to the community' (see Hagell and Newburn, 1994). Not to be outdone, Tony Blair, then Labour Party shadow Home Secretary, demanded a regime of 'tough love', a phrase he had borrowed from US President Bill Clinton, in which containment and confrontation in secure units would be tempered by responsiveness to the offender's needs. The Labour MP Ken Livingstone advocated longer prison sentences, and David Blunkett, then shadow Health Secretary, called for the return of National Service. Although National Service is routinely invoked by politicians as a panacea for moral decline amongst the young, the fact that military service might have initiated more criminal careers than it thwarted is seldom considered (Howell *et al.*, 1995).

It suddenly appeared as if politicians across the entire political spectrum had felt for the last 10 years that things, particularly juvenile things, were 'getting out of hand'. The repoliticization and remoralization of youth crime and youth justice was underway and this time the political Left and Centre were determined to wrest the political issue of 'law and order' from the grasp of the Tories if they possibly could.

As in the late 1950s, the early 1960s, the late 1960s and the late 1970s, the abdication of responsibility for moral leadership by parents, teachers and public figures, was identified as a key causal factor. Beyond this, a lack of vigilance about the videos and television programmes children watched was cited as pivotal in the failure to give them the 'quality time' that they needed in an increasingly violent and morally perplexing world. The problem was an indication of where the parents and the teachers had gone wrong. The behaviour of the young was a portent of what was happening to our society and the even bleaker future which lay in store. Like Albermarle (1960), and the 1963 Children and Young Persons Act, 'experts' bemoaned the demise of a 'golden age' of caring communities and concerned parents. Whether from Left or Right, they all called for a radical reversal of current 'permissive' policies. It was time to 'get a grip'.

It is worth reminding ourselves, as Cohen (1972) points out, that moral panics emerge during periods of rapid social change in which social, economic and class relations are undergoing a realignment. Their function, he argues, is to attach the heightened concerns and anxieties generated by such change on to a concrete subject who then becomes a 'folk devil'. In such a climate an act or an incident may serve as a catalyst to spark off the panic, after which discrete and unrelated phenomena are woven together in order to prove that things are, in fact, on the slide and that 'something' must be done (see **Muncie, 1996**).

## 5.6  Doing 'something'

As we have noted, the Home Secretary, Kenneth Clarke, responded to the death of James Bulger with the secure training order and a new type of secure training centre which was designed to house the 200 most serious and persistent young offenders in England and Wales aged between 12 and 15, who were deemed to be responsible for 60 per cent of the youth crime in the country. He also abandoned the unit fine system and the new regulations concerning the ways in which the bench should handle previous offences (see Chapter 3). This had the effect of rendering once 'irrelevant' previous

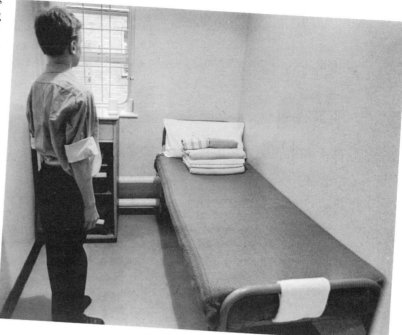

offences relevant again, thus undermining years of painstaking work by civil servants and justice system professionals to insert some rationality into the sentencing process. Predictions about the consequences of Kenneth Clarke's panic reaction for the prison population vary between a rise of some 5,000 and 10,000 per annum (see Chapter 5).

Taken together these changes threaten to usher in a massive renaissance of youth imprisonment in the mid and late 1990s. Yet, as Hagell and Newburn (1994) have observed, it is by no means evident that persistent offenders are also serious offenders and it is simply untrue that 200 persistent and serious young offenders are responsible for 60 per cent of all youth crime. However, the notion of a hard core of persistent and serious offenders who are known to the authorities, and whose apprehension would usher in a low-crime future, is at the core of the policies which flow from the account of the world offered by neo-conservatism. Beyond this, of course, such a 'heavy duty' hard core is the stuff from which bifurcated criminal justice policies, which appear to offer governments the opportunity to 'get tough' and save money at the same time, are constructed. If this is the intention, the Home Secretary might do well to reflect on the fate of such bifurcated policies in the 1980s.

*Doing something: youth custody for the intractable hard core?*

## 5.7 The renaissance of imprisonment

Within weeks of becoming Home Secretary in July 1993, Michael Howard set about putting his personal stamp upon youth justice policy. The secure training centres were, it seemed, to be rethought. On the basis of 'leaked' information from a 'senior insider', the *Daily Mail* reported that:

> Home Secretary Michael Howard ordered a drastic rethink when it became clear that the scheme would be enormously expensive and too limited to deal with the explosion of youth crime.
>
> Ministers believe that hundreds more young thugs need to be locked-up. ... 'The pressure is for a scheme involving rather less sophisticated centres, putting the emphasis on discipline and punishment rather than the expensive rehabilitation and training programmes which require highly specialised staff'.

> (*Daily Mail*, 9 August 1993)

Even though, by 1996, the government had been unable to secure planning permission for any of its proposed secure training centres, Howard remained committed to tougher regimes. In *The Times* of 6 February 1995, under the headline 'Howard plans "house of pain" regimes for youth offenders', we read that: 'The Government is to introduce American-style "boot camps" in Britain to provide tougher and more physically demanding regimes aimed at knocking criminal tendencies out of young offenders'. Howard's definitive statement on imprisonment was made to the 1993 Conservative Party conference when he told his audience that:

> Prison Works, it ensures that we are protected from murderers, muggers and rapists – and it makes many who are tempted to commit crime think twice … This may mean that many more people will go to prison. I do not flinch from that. We shall no longer judge the success of our system of justice by a fall in our prison population.

> (Howard, 1993, p.12)

This statement suggested that the government was prepared to do everything necessary to seize the political initiative on law and order.

## ACTIVITY 6.5

What do you believe motivated the Conservative government to reintroduce tougher prison regimes for young offenders in the mid 1990s:

- A concern for the victims of crime?
- A concern for the perpetrators of crime?
- A concern for the moral health of society?
- A concern for the electoral fortunes of the Conservative Party?
- All of these?

## COMMENT

As Downes (1994) has observed, by the mid 1990s Conservative explanations of, and solutions to, crime bore a remarkable resemblance to those of the former Soviet Union. Social and economic causes are deemed irrelevant since, in the new, classless 'Opportunity Britain' brought into being by the 'free market revolution', citizens are 'at ease with themselves'. Crime is therefore attributable either to the biological, psychological and intellectual deficiencies of individual offenders or to indiscipline. In this perspective, this indiscipline is encouraged by the counter-revolutionary elements within the teaching profession, social work and the probation service, deviationists (Tory wets), lone mothers and 'degenerate' parents who grew up in the 1960s, and, of course, the Labour Party and the trade unions. The solution is to elaborate a justice system which offers the correct mixture of rehabilitative treatment and punishment.

In 1979, in a speech to youth justice workers in Sheffield, Patrick Mayhew had invoked the 'rising tide' metaphor to describe an alleged phenomenon out in the 'real world', with which the government planned to deal. In 1993, Michael Howard was referring to a 'tidal wave' of concern about crime in the UK. It was all too clear, however, that now it was the 'concern about crime' rather than crime itself which concerned the government. In the sphere of criminal justice policy in the mid 1990s the question: Will it work? had long since been replaced with the question: Will it 'play' in the marginals?

Beyond the world of political symbols *is* a 'real world', inhabited by real young people. What was happening there?

# 6 Social reproduction in the 1990s

## 6.1 Farewell to the working class

In the 1960s it was not uncommon for young people in trouble to avoid a custodial sentence by joining the armed forces. Many magistrates would refrain from sending boys to Borstal because they believed that, like Borstal, the army would teach them a 'trade' and 'make a man of them'. Apprentices, trainees and students were unlikely to receive custodial sentences for similar reasons. For their part, probation officers would often cite the rehabilitative powers of 'going steady', which usually involved getting a 'steady' job in order to 'to save up to get married' and 'put a few things away in the bottom drawer'. These magistrates and probation officers were 'putting their money' on 'social reproduction'.

As we have noted, in the 1960s social scientists observed that social reproduction was operating so well that it was acting as a brake on the economy. This 'progressive' view suggested that only by an upward revision of social expectations could the full potential of the 'technological revolution' be realized, and a classless society brought into being. In reality, the problem of social mobility was far more complex. As Hargreaves (1967) and Willis (1977) revealed, the processes whereby 'working-class kids' in secondary school were propelled into 'working-class jobs' had a lot to do with real social and economic divisions which found expression in the low-key 'class struggle' being fought out in the back rows of 3C where the virtues of hard manual labour were celebrated and core 'working-class' values rehearsed as an antidote to the 'middle class' values of the school.

Yet, even as these young men and women affirmed, in a variety of sub-cultural forms, their loyalty to the working class, the dramatic economic changes of the 1960s onwards meant that the 'working class' whose core values they celebrated was slipping away into the past. Martin Jacques writes:

> The most dramatic single change in our society, as in similar societies elsewhere, has been the decline in the size and cohesion of the traditional working class. For well over a century the presence of the working class left an enormously powerful imprint on culture and politics. It provided many social disciplines and acted as an organising principle and a central divide in our political system ... That society is now of fond memory. We are no longer organised in slabs that condition social behaviour and aspiration. The underlying reason for the change is the decline of the industrial working class.
>
> (Jacques, 1993)

In place of the steadily increasing prosperity of the 1960s, working-class young people from the 1970s onwards were confronted with the prospect of social discontinuity and downward social mobility in a changing and shrinking post-industrial labour market. A set of cultural values and assumptions, a particular sexual division of labour and clearly demarcated gender roles – a whole way of life in fact – was cut adrift from its economic *raison d'être*. This was a particularly fateful development for those working-class young men whose identities were shaped by the attitudes and values of the industrial workplace. What these attitudes and values added up to was a clear social injunction about what it was to be a man or a woman, the roles they should discharge and the social space they should occupy.

The problem was not simply that these young men could not follow their fathers and uncles into the factories but that, as a result, all their other roles and relationships – indeed, the very shape of their future lives and identities – were called into question:

> Once identities were frozen in aspic. If you were a male car worker you wore certain things, spent your weekends in set ways, drove a particular kind of car and went on holiday in a particular kind of place … Our world has turned full circle and what you do and what you buy increasingly determine who you are.

(Jacques, 1993)

But what they did and what they bought were increasingly circumscribed by bourgeoning youth unemployment which demolished the apprenticeship system, eradicated skilled and semi-skilled male jobs in industry and drove many working-class people still in employment out of the inner cities. At the same time, the creation of new 'women's' jobs in the service sector led to a new distribution of economic power in many working-class households.

## 6.2 Maverick masculinities

Campbell (1993), in her account of the 1991 riots, argues that one of the consequences of these economic changes was to drive young men in chronically disadvantaged neighbourhoods back into the social spaces which, in daylight hours at least, had previously been the exclusive domain of women, namely the home and the neighbourhood. Once there, they were faced with the problem of reconstructing a plausible male identity and they did this through, usually violent, attempts to wrest that terrain from women through domestic violence, riot and displays of machismo at the wheels of stolen cars.

As we have seen in section 5.3, for Campbell these crimes are a product of a 'mode of masculinity' which is revealed in circumstances of local economic crisis. There is a disjunction in the social reproduction of gender roles which, in turn, is a product of the dramatic economic changes of the 1970s and 1980s. Yet, while this may well be true, the resolution of male status frustration through symbolic criminal acts is not a new phenomenon (Cohen, 1955). For working-class young men, who, like other men, are evaluated by their peers on the basis of their power to make an impact upon the world 'out there', adolescence is, characteristically, a period of heightened status frustration.

Prior to the mid 1960s this frustration and the stresses it generated was a largely chronological affair, the point of greatest strain being the point at which the adolescent most desired the trappings of adult power but was constrained by school or earning power from acquiring them. This was a problem which was resolved by a process of growing up and therefore 'growing out of crime'.

## 6.3 Social immobility and protracted adolescence

Adolescence is a period of transition, but how long it lasts and when it ends depends upon whether a young person has the social and economic wherewithal to proceed to the next stage in the life-cycle.

In his study, undertaken in the USA during the great depression of the 1930s, Whyte (1943) 'hung out' with a group of 'corner boys' in an Italian neighbourhood. As the book proceeds, we realize that Doc and the Nortons are not teenagers but men, some of them in their mid to late twenties, and that they have been hanging out on the same corner for over 10 years. They have been doing this because, having no steady jobs, they have no money to pay rent, buy furniture and do all the other things one would need to do to become a 'family man' in Cornerville. They are, as a result, frozen in a state of perpetual adolescence.

In east London in the early 1990s, black youth justice workers observed, in conversation with the author, that the upper age of members in one local Afro-Caribbean 'posse' had risen to over 30. One of the consequences of this has been that the older members have introduced some of the younger ones to more serious crime. Like Doc and the Nortons, these men could not make the transition from adolescence to higher status adult roles because they simply did not have the means to do so.

Enforced adolescence means that young people on the social and economic margins are, quite literally, prevented from growing up. This has important implications for their involvement in crime because all the evidence we have suggests that 'growing up' – the assumption of adult roles, rights and responsibilities – also means growing out of crime (Rutherford, 1986).

It is against the backdrop of this expanding pool of economically marginal, reluctant adolescents that the violent public disorder which is coming to characterize 'areas of disrepute' throughout England, and for which Brixton in 1981 was the 'prototype', must be understood. These young

*A question of 'teenage kicks', crime, aggressive masculinity, poverty or social deprivation? Youths entering empty property in Tower Hamlets, London*

men are condemned by poverty and unemployment to inhabit overcrowded, under-resourced, high-crime neighbourhoods. They are compelled by social structure and culture to be less than whole people, trapped in a limbo world somewhere between childhood and adulthood long after the 'developmental tasks' of adolescence have been completed (Graham and Bowling, 1996). Moreover, they are fixed ideologically, destined to serve as folk devils, to provide the screen upon which the fears and fantasies of those near the social centre are projected.

If this is so, what kind of criminal justice strategies can governments develop?

# **7** American and European options

## **7.1** American nightmares

The Thatcher administration explained rising crime in the UK in the 1980s in terms of universal trends in advanced industrial societies. As we shall see, this alleged universality is questionable, but it is the case that in the USA in the 1970s and 1980s, where neo-conservative free-market principles found their fullest expression, crime rates, like the other indices of poverty and inequality, rose and rose (**Currie, 1991**). There is little doubt that the social divisions created by a redistribution of wealth away from the 'have nots' and the demolition of welfare systems in the USA have effectively led to the abandonment of low-income, high-crime neighbourhoods to their own devices.

This impoverishment of the social sphere has been accompanied by the type of neo-conservative criminal justice policies which, according to Wilson (1975), would contain the pressures that lead to a higher crime rate. Between 1979 and 1989 there was a 103.5 per cent increase in the numbers of juveniles in public and private correctional facilities, with Nevada and California topping the league table with a juvenile incarceration rate of 700 and 600 per 100,000 respectively, and Hawaii occupying the bottom slot with 103 per 100,000. Incarceration rates were highest in neighbourhoods and amongst social and ethnic groups where poverty and social inequality were most marked. An analysis of the ethnic origins of the inmates of juvenile custodial facilities in California in 1989 illustrates this point (Krisberg and Austin, 1993) (see Table 6.1).

### Table 6.1  Juveniles in custody by ethnicity, California, 1989

|  | Percentage of total juvenile population of California | Percentage in custodial institutions |
|---|---|---|
| Anglo-American | 46.6 | 26.8 |
| Afro-American | 8.7 | 37.0 |
| Hispanic American | 34.4 | 32.4 |
| Asian American | 10.3 | 3.7 |

Source: based on Krisberg and Austin, 1993, p.124, Table 4.8

These increases in custodial populations were accompanied by the incapacitation of persistent offenders through exemplary sentences and the reintroduction of the death penalty in all but 17 states. Neo-conservative policies reached their fullest expression in the late 1980s when the US Supreme Court ruled that juveniles and people with learning disabilities were fit subjects for capital punishment. Meanwhile, property crime and crimes of violence in poor and low-income neighbourhoods in the USA have rocketed.

## 7.2 The European experience

In the USA, with its radical neo-conservative social, economic and criminal justice policies, juvenile imprisonment and recorded crime appeared to follow one another inexorably upwards. In England and Wales, France and Germany, however, reductions in juvenile imprisonment did not appear to be related to variations in the crime rate. In England and Wales the crime rate rose steadily until the late 1980s and then steepened sharply, rising fastest in the poorest neighbourhoods (Hope, 1994). In West Germany recorded youth crime rose slightly (Graham, 1990) and in France, after a rise in the early 1980s, it fell again from 1985 (de Liege, 1991). Nor were these changes related in any obvious way to population shifts. England and Wales, in common with most other Western European states, witnessed a decline in its 10- to 18-year-old population over the period. However, a 25 per cent decrease in the juvenile population was paralleled by a 150 per cent increase in recorded youth crime (Hagell and Newburn, 1994).

Yet, in England and Wales in the 1980s, the numbers of juveniles imprisoned by the courts fell by 75 per cent. In France there was a 50 per cent reduction and in West Germany a fall of around 40 per cent (Pitts, 1992b; de Liege, 1991; Graham, 1990). This said, it was also the case that, throughout Western Europe, the 1980s witnessed an increase in the proportion of black, Asian, North African, African, Turkish, South Moluccan and other 'non-indigenous' European young people in European juvenile custodial institutions (Albrecht, 1991). Nor can these trends be inferred, in any straightforward way, from the political complexion of governments. While in England and Wales, for example, the law and order rhetoric sounded 'American', the reduction in the use of custody for juveniles was congruent with trends in most other Western European countries.

What are the factors which might account for differences in youth crime and imprisonment rates in Germany, France, England and Wales and the USA during the 1980s?

## 7.3 The marginality of criminal justice policy

As Table 6.2 indicates, the key distinguishing feature of Anglo-American neo-conservative governments was their failure to introduce or develop significant social programmes in high-crime neighbourhoods. This suggests two things: first, that criminal justice policies alone may not make much impact on crime; and, second, that social and economic policies may. Indeed, research undertaken by the Netherlands Ministry of Justice and the University of Constanz in Germany suggest that the style of rehabilitative programme selected by the probation officer or social worker appears to have no significant bearing upon a young person's re-offending (van der Laan, 1993; Spiess, 1994). Spiess indicates that, in fact, in the case of persistent young offenders, probation is most effective when it ignores rehabilitative programmes for at least the first 12 weeks of a probation order, and instead helps the probationer find decent accommodation, sort out their finances, stabilize their addictions and develop or sustain a relatively secure emotional relationship with another person.

# Chapter 7
# Community and Crime Prevention

*by Sandra Walklate*

## Contents

# 1 Introduction

Historically, crime prevention in Britain was always considered to be the responsibility of the police (see Chapter 1). Indeed, this historical legacy is still keenly felt in the form of the dedicated Crime Prevention Officer and in police involvement in many crime prevention initiatives. However, the role of crime prevention in policework has always been accorded a somewhat lower status than other kinds of policework. There is evidence for this in the acceptance by many police forces that effective crime prevention can only be achieved through co-operation between the police and the community. Recognition of this fact raises important theoretical and practical questions: What, for example, do we understand by the concept of 'community'? What do we understand as constituting the central features of the policing task? How might we understand the relationship between the citizen and the state? What is meant by democratic participation in such processes? Questions such as these underpin the discussion in this chapter concerning the relationship between crime prevention and the community.

A community-based understanding of crime prevention was given a definitive focus by the Conservative Party in the early 1980s. This reflected a change of emphasis not only in the nature of crime prevention, but also in the way in which the Conservative government perceived its role as a deliverer of public services. Home Office circular 8/84 stated that crime prevention was no longer, only or simply, an issue to be addressed by police forces. It argued that effective crime prevention could only be put into place on the basis of inter-agency co-operation. As the Scottish circular on the same issue states, 'Just as the incidence of crime can affect the whole community, so too its prevention is a task for the community' (quoted by Bottoms, 1990, p.4).

This change of emphasis – from police to community – in crime prevention policy reflects at least two different assumptions. The first concerns an understanding of the causes of crime and subsequently how it might be prevented (an issue which threads its way through this chapter). The second concerns an understanding of the nature of communities and parallels the political assertion by the Conservative Party of a role for the community in a range of policy activities, from health care through to education and crime, which de-emphasize the role of the government in these matters. However, there are a number of more particular reasons why the role of the community in crime prevention should have been put to the fore in this way in the early 1980s. It will be useful for us to explore some of them.

First, the report by Lord Justice Scarman on the civil disturbances in inner-city areas in 1981 made a number of recommendations concerning police–community relations – such as the need for community consultative committees and lay visitors to police stations – which were intended to improve police–community contacts, lessen conflict between the police and the community, and harness support for police activity. In this way, the need for consensual community support for policing was reiterated. Second, the use of the British Crime Survey for the first time in 1982 suggested that law-breaking was about four times as high as that recorded by the police. While much of this was less serious crime, it clearly indicated that the police alone could not combat such a level of crime (see **Muncie, 1996**). Third, the Home

Office Crime Prevention Unit, established in 1983, provided the opportunity for the development of a critical perspective on crime prevention policy. This perspective pointed to the ineffectiveness of using the criminal justice system alone as a deterrent to crime. Fourth, the government committed itself to looking for more cost-effective ways of delivering public services, including those services, such as the police, which have traditionally been regarded as being operationally free from government interference.

All of these factors pointed to the difficulties inherent in expecting the police to respond to the crime problem proactively, reactively and in a preventive capacity all at the same time, and to re-examining the role of the police in crime prevention especially. In this respect the case was strongly made for a wider sharing of the crime prevention role. It is useful to remember, however, that this assertion of a role for the community in crime prevention was as much a part of a wider political strategy permeating a whole range of policy areas in the early 1980s as it was rooted in any evidence that community-based responses to crime prevention might prove to be more effective. This community rhetoric constituted, in part, a search for a politically defensible policy while simultaneously demanding cutbacks in public expenditure. In other words, it represented one way of ensuring that aspects of the criminal justice system could be seen to work, if only in economic terms.

This chapter takes as its starting point the idea that communities have a role to play in crime prevention. It is important to note, however, that while such a role has been identified as desirable, its actual form and recommended content varies considerably. We shall therefore be concerned here to document such policy variations and to examine the different presumptions they make concerning both the nature of crime and the communities in which crime is seen to be a problem. It is also important to note that crime prevention policy has been active in a number of different contexts – from situational to social – since the early 1980s. This chapter will be concerned to locate community-based crime prevention policies within a broader spectrum of crime prevention activity.

## 2 Initiatives in crime prevention

Home Office circular 8/84, issued in 1984, constituted a significant moment in the development of crime prevention initiatives. This circular, with its emphasis on a multi-agency approach to crime prevention (or what is perhaps more commonly referred to in the 1990s as the 'partnership' approach) sparked a number of subsequent government-led initiatives.

In 1986 the Home Office Crime Prevention Unit established the Five Towns Initiative. This was intended to act as a demonstration of how the 1984 circular might work. The towns included in this project were Bolton, North Tyneside, Croydon, Swansea and Wellingborough. The project ran for 18 months, with some of the crime prevention projects it generated continuing beyond this initial period. After this, in 1988, the government launched the Safer Cities Programme. This was a bigger and more ambitious version of the Five Towns Initiative, with 16 cities chosen initially to participate in the scheme. This programme, again overseen by the Home Office, sponsored crime prevention projects in these cities for an initial three-year period, by which time it was expected that the schemes would have secured independent funding in order to continue their work. For example, Salford Safer Cities became Safer Salford in April 1994, sponsored by Marks and Spencer. Finally, in 1989 an organization called Crime Concern was established, again with Home Office money initially. This organization is now a registered charity whose main function is to disseminate good practice in the crime prevention field.

This summary of developments clearly locates the responsibility for the development of crime prevention policy centrally within the Home Office. However, government departments other than the Home Office also support a range of crime prevention activity, for example the Department of the Environment through Priority Housing Estates and the Urban Aid Programme. Moreover, police forces, voluntary agencies and academics have all been involved in a variety of ways in developing and implementing crime prevention initiatives of different kinds. Many of these initiatives have taken as read the premise of the 1984 Home Office circular that the community has a key role to play in crime prevention. While this might be a common thread between such initiatives, they can vary considerably in content and style of implementation. Since such differences can sometimes feed into the potential effectiveness of a particular initiative, it will be useful to consider for a moment the different ways in which it is possible to think about, and implement, crime prevention policy.

## 2.1  Ways of thinking about crime prevention policy

Responses to crime and criminal victimization can vary widely. We have seen already, for example, that responses can be led by the police, government or more locally, perhaps involving voluntary organizations. The key questions are: What characterizes these responses? How are they formulated? How does this set the tone for their subsequent development? There are a number of different ways of thinking about responses to crime prevention. For example, Smith (1986), in discussing public responses to criminal victimization, distinguishes 'individual reactive protective' responses from 'collective reactive protective' responses. In this way she is attempting to alert us to the difference between individual prevention strategies and community ones, a distinction we shall build on below. Lewis and Salem (1986), on the other hand, draw our attention to different dimensions of crime prevention activity. In discussing responses to the fear of crime in particular, they identify policies characterized by either coercion or co-operation and/or empowerment, all of which may have a 'top-down' or a 'bottom-up' implementation style. The central role of the Home Office, as we have already seen, sets the general tone of policy and can thus be characterized as a top-down style. This distinction between top-down or bottom-up can sometimes be more apparent than real, but can play a crucial part in ensuring the support of a particular community in the implementation of an initiative.

Identifying the nature of policies in this way is useful. However, what is also important is to appreciate what kind of crime is being targeted by such policies. If we add to the distinctions identified above the usual distinctions made between 'crime of the streets', 'crime of the suites', and 'crime behind closed doors', it is perhaps easy to understand why it is difficult to adopt too simplistic an approach to analysing crime prevention. It is also perhaps easier to understand why, when faced with the question of 'what works?', the answer may inevitably be 'it depends!' Successful crime prevention policy will depend on how a policy is implemented, its style of implementation, its crime focus, and so on. In the context of community crime prevention policy, it may also depend on the nature of the community infrastructure, how far policy-makers and practitioners are sensitive to that infrastructure, and how a particular community or neighbourhood may be responding to crime independent of any formal policy process. In the following discussion we shall see that all of these questions have a bearing on the nature and extent of the success of community crime prevention policy. It will be useful therefore to ask what kind of crime is being targeted by the kind of policy under discussion, whether the policy has been implemented in a top-down or bottom-up style, whether it has been police-led, government-led or locally led, and whether it is targeted at individuals or the community in general.

Though the relationship between the community and crime prevention is the key focus of this chapter, there are other ways of responding to crime preventatively. In order to contextualize community-based responses to crime prevention, we shall consider briefly three other themes in crime prevention policy: offender-centred strategies, victim-centred strategies, and environment-centred strategies. We shall examine each of these in turn, but it is important to remember that these headings are really only a heuristic device to encourage critical thinking about the different policy themes it is possible to identify in this area. It may be that some of the initiatives discussed could fit under more than one heading. You should keep this in mind as you work through the rest of this chapter. But first a comment about the concept of prevention.

## 2.2 Prevention: what does it mean?

Little theoretical work in the social sciences has examined the concept of prevention. Overall it is possible to observe that prevention is seen to be a 'good' thing because social problems are 'bad' things (Freeman, 1992). As a concept it has been borrowed from debates on public health, yet even in that arena, what the notion of prevention involves and how it might be differently explored are rarely examined. It is clear, however, that most understandings of prevention entail the possibility of both predicting an outcome and intervening in that process to change the predicted outcome. This implies two separate processes if the ultimate aim of preventive policy is to make a difference to human behaviour or experience or both. In the context of crime prevention, it presumes that in the first instance we know, can agree upon and can identify the causes of crime. In the second instance it presumes that we know, can agree upon and can identify the appropriate policy responses that will inhibit crime. These, of course, reflect a long-standing debate which precedes the more current concern with the role of the community. As the remainder of this chapter illustrates, these are neither simple nor straightforward issues.

prevention

# 3 Offender-centred strategies

Offender-centred strategies for crime prevention can be found in a number of different guises. In October 1993, for example, the Home Secretary, Michael Howard, made an impassioned statement to the Conservative Party conference. This was reported by *The Guardian* under the headline 'Prison

Works!' In his speech Howard argued that prison works as a deterrent to crime, because it incapacitates offenders from further offending and because it also serves the purpose of retribution (see also Chapter 5). Emphasizing the role of the prison system as a preventive strategy proved to be very popular at the conference. The strategy is an expensive option, and it is not particularly novel. Similar strategies historically have either taken the form of the prevention of recidivism (through, at best, rehabilitation or, at worst, incapacitation), or the mobilization of support for what Elias (1986) has called 'enforcement crackdowns'. The notion that 'prison works' fits easily under this latter heading.

Enforcement crackdowns can enjoy the support of a broad spectrum of political viewpoints. These can be divided primarily into two broad camps: those who adopt a tough stance on law and order, and those who favour a softer approach. Those arguing for a tough stance on crime are really invoking the use of the criminal justice system as a deterrent, and the constituencies sharing this viewpoint can be very varied. Elias (1986) names the Victims Committee of the International Association of Chiefs of Police, and Victim Advocates for Law and Order (VALOR) in the USA as examples of victim groups who espouse the view that more prosecutions, convictions and punishments will prevent crime. Victim groups expressing such views are also to be found in the United Kingdom. For example, Victims of Violence, started on Merseyside and led by Joan Jonkers, is an organization known for expressing similar views. Such views also find frequent support in different police organizations, such as the Police Federation. Moreover, feminists in both the UK and the USA have been known to adopt a tough stance on crimes of sexual violence. Many of these organizations invoke the image of the victim in support of their views. Such an image has been used frequently in the UK by politicians advocating a strong stance on law and order.

Enforcement crackdowns can, however, encapsulate a 'softer' edge. At this 'softer' end of offender-centred strategies lies the view that prisons are about rehabilitation, not punishment. Initiatives such as Intermediate Treatment for potential juvenile offenders (see Chapter 6), and latterly mediation and reparation projects, are designed with a preventive/ rehabilitative goal in mind. This softer approach takes the view that offenders are educable, trainable and supervisable, and through these processes those known to be criminal, or thought to be at risk of offending, can be targeted and redirected in their behaviour.

Whether 'hard' or 'soft', both of these approaches assume that the cause of offending behaviour lies within the individual, who, once having learned the 'error of their ways' will cease to offend in the future. Indeed, there is some evidence to suggest that factors such as personality, attitudes and moral sense predispose some individuals to commit crime. As a consequence, offender-centred strategies have been shown to be more or less effective with particular offenders at particular times. As crime prevention strategies, however, their effectiveness is significantly limited by the presumption that the cause of crime lies within individual pathology. Moreover, there is considerable evidence to suggest that the causes of crime are more social in origin, and, of course, it is those social dimensions which offender-centred strategies are not designed to address.

# 4   Victim-centred strategies

As has already been suggested, the victim of crime became a symbolically important feature of law and order rhetoric during the 1980s. The emergence of the image of the victim to some extent coincided with the emergence of Victim Support, established nationally in 1979, as *the* organization speaking for, and offering support to, victims of crime. It is possible to argue that this imagery has become so powerful that crime prevention literature and strategies have become deeply embedded in a discourse of victimization avoidance – a discourse that has proceeded in the absence of little critical comment.

*victimization avoidance*

However, victim-centred strategies, rather like offender-centred strategies, can take a number of different forms. The victim of crime may, of course, be an individual human being, an animal, or an individual property or business. However, victimization avoidance as a way of thinking about crime and crime prevention has permeated a range of different organizational responses to crime. For example, insurance companies can now lay down fairly strict crime prevention criteria before offering household insurance in some postcode areas. They are thus able to dictate what kinds of locks should be fitted and where. Should the householder fail to put the relevant hardware in place, the insurance company does not have to pay out on a claim. This clearly places the responsibility for the prevention of burglary on the householder and implies that failure to do so is tantamount to inviting the crime to happen. Such a 'target hardening' approach to crime prevention is one feature of what has been referred to as situational crime prevention (discussed more fully in section 5 below) but shares the underlying presumption of a victim-centred approach. As a crime prevention strategy it clearly implies that the *precipitative* behaviour or lack of action on the part of the victim is the clue to understanding why crime occurs.

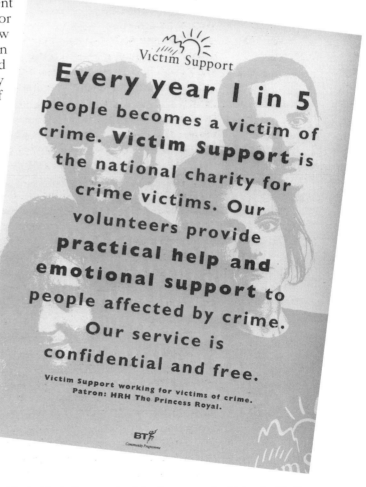

Victim Support

**Every year 1 in 5** people becomes a victim of crime. **Victim Support** is the national charity for crime victims. Our volunteers provide **practical help and emotional support** to people affected by crime. Our service is confidential and free.

Victim Support working for victims of crime. Patron: HRH The Princess Royal.

BT
Community Programme

*Since its establishment in 1979, Victim Support, together with similar organizations, has ensured a higher profile for the interests of victims in criminal justice and criminological matters*

victim
precipitation

Focusing on the precipitative behaviour of the victim has been used as a way of explaining homicide and rape by victimologists. The concept of victim precipitation was originally formulated by Wolfgang in the 1940s. As a lawyer-cum-criminologist, he was concerned to understand the nature of the culpability for a crime. The connections between culpability and victim precipitation have been made explicit by the courts on more than one occasion, especially in the context of rape, and have been translated as 'contributory negligence' (Jeffreys and Radford, 1984). However, in more general terms, focusing on the precipitative behaviour of the victim is a way of thinking about crime and criminal victimization which has very deep roots. With respect to crime prevention advice to women in particular, the translation of this precipitative view into a victimization avoidance policy strategy, and the victim-blaming connotations that this subsequently implies, are worthy of further consideration.

## 4.1  Avoiding sexual danger

Crime prevention advice to women can range from taking self-defence classes to avoiding 'risky' places after dark. Much of this advice locates the responsibility for taking precautions with the potential victim of crime. So, for example, women are advised not to walk in poorly lit areas, to avoid walking on their own late at night, or, if drivers, to lock themselves in their car when driving alone. The basic message is: be prepared and know how you would deal with an attack. Of course, the irony in all of this advice is, as Stanko (1990) has cogently argued (but see also Crawford *et al.*, 1990), women do not need to be told about taking such precautions. They have devised many of their own. Moreover, as Stanko goes on to observe,

> Crime prevention advice revolves around public crime. And while the police and criminal justice system are slowly becoming involved, private violence is still seen as something different than public violence. Crime prevention advice, including much of the advice about avoiding sexual assault, focuses on the public domain. It is easier to give advice about checking the back seat of your car for intruders, or advising against standing at dimly lit bus stops, than finding ways of advising women not to trust so-called 'trustworthy' men.
>
> (Stanko, 1990, p.4)

This brief discussion draws our attention to a number of important issues concerning crime prevention activity and its targets. Thinking about the advice offered to women on avoiding sexual danger, as Stanko rightly points out, encourages us to think about what kind of criminal victimization is being privileged in the crime prevention literature. In other words, it draws our attention to the presumption that the key source of danger to women is strangers – that is, men they do not know as opposed to men they do know. Yet there is a wealth of evidence from feminist research and other sources that women are in greatest danger from men they know (see **Saraga, 1996**). From this experience women are well practised, indeed expert, at devising strategies for their personal safety. This highlights the way in which 'top-down' strategies can miss the mark by telling people to do what they are already well practised at! Such remedies encourage us to think that the cause of crime lies with the victim's own behaviour, rather than with that of the perpetrators. In this particular instance it places the responsibility for women's experiences of sexual violence with women rather than with men.

With this question in mind, you might like to consider the contents of the two crime prevention leaflets shown below, issued by the Greater Manchester Police Authority.

## ON SEXUAL VIOLENCE

Greater Manchester Police Authority
Telephone : 061 793 3127

THERE ARE LOTS OF PAMPHLETS, BOOKS AND OTHER INFORMATION ABOUT HOW WOMEN CAN AVOID OR DEAL WITH RAPE, SEXUAL ATTACKS OR HARASSMENT.

THE PURPOSE OF THIS LEAFLET IS SIMPLY TO REASSURE WOMEN ABOUT THEMSELVES AND SET OUT WHERE YOU CAN GET ADVICE AND ASSISTANCE IF YOU NEED IT.

### FEELING OF GUILT

If you are raped or sexually attacked, assaulted or harassed, you should not feel guilty about it or believe that you are to blame. The rapist or sexual attacker is always to blame. You are entitled to the full support of the law and society if you call upon their assistance.

### YOUR BEHAVIOUR

How you dress, and how you act is your own business. No man is entitled to draw any conclusions from it about your willingness to have sex or your worth as a person. Once you say "no", at any stage of the activity or association, a man must accept his advances are not acceptable and stop.

### MAKE YOUR ASSUMPTIONS

Some men are different from others. There are often no tell tale signs in a man's behaviour to show if he is one of the nice ones that won't try to attack you sexually or otherwise or one of the dangerous ones that will. If you are not sure, do not place yourself in potentially dangerous situations.

### WHAT IF IT'S SOMEONE I KNOW

The previous points hold true in your home. Many rapes are carried out by men known to women and in their own home - even close relatives. You must make no assumptions about them and you should not feel guilty or responsible for anything that happens. The fault lies with them if you are assaulted or raped.

### THE POLICE ARE THERE TO PROTECT YOU

Every woman is entitled to demand that anyone who rapes or attacks her is prosecuted. You are entitled to call on the police for protection if you are attacked or if you reasonably fear an attack. If, after you have called the police, you want to withdraw an accusation, you can do so, but you should not do this because of threats from anyone.
There are a large number of women officers in the Greater Manchester Police and you can ask to speak to a woman officer if you feel easier doing so.

### WHAT YOU CAN DO

The Greater Manchester Police Authority have produced this leaflet and its counterpart "Simple Advice to Men to avoid Sexual Violence to Women" in an attempt to curb violent crimes against women. The Authority hope that the leaflets will reach all the public of Greater Manchester via Police/Community Liaison Panels, colleges, schools and places of work. You can make your contribution to the Authority's campaign by encouraging the men and boys whom you come into contact with to discuss this leaflet and the mens leaflet with their workmates and school mates in a sensible and supportive way. By doing so, you could be saving yourself or your mother, sister or daughter from a vicious and humiliating attack.
Although this leaflet makes it clear that men are always to blame for any rape or sexual attack or other violence, it is advisable to take reasonable precautions to avoid attacks and there are a number of leaflets available giving advice about this.

## VIOLENCE AGAINST WOMEN IS A CRIME

### VIOLENCE AGAINST WOMEN IS A CRIME

WHEN THE SUBJECT OF SEXUAL VIOLENCE TO WOMEN IS RAISED, A LOT OF MEN TREAT IT AS A JOKE. IT IS NO JOKE — IT IS DEADLY SERIOUS. RAPE AND SEXUAL ATTACKS RUIN THE QUALITY OF LIFE FOR MANY WOMEN — AND MANY MEN TOO, WHO ARE THE HUSBANDS, FATHERS, BOY FRIENDS, SONS OR FRIENDS OF WOMEN VICTIMS.

THIS LEAFLET SETS OUT GUIDELINES TO BE FOLLOWED WHEN YOU ARE IN THE COMPANY OF A WOMEN OR GIRL OR WITH OTHER MEN.

### YOU ARE RESPONSIBLE IN LAW

**Remember, "no" means "no".**
Any sexual contact which you have with a woman or girl without her clear consent given freely without any threat or pressure is a serious criminal offence. No matter how much you may have or may think you have been encouraged or provoked, if she says "stop" or "no" you alone are fully responsible for any further sexual contact which is criminal and you could be sent to jail for it.

If you try to get a woman's "consent" because of the threat of your greater physical strength, position of power at work, or by intimidation, threats, or harassment, you are still wholly, morally and legally responsible for your behaviour.

### DON'T DRAW CONCLUSIONS

A woman is entitled to dress or behave in any way she likes. You cannot assume that because she may look provocative or sexy that she wants sex with you or anyone else. You should not draw conclusions that she wants or consents to any sexual contact from what she says. A woman may speak to you on any topic. You should not assume that this means she wants to have sex with you.

### WATCH YOUR LANGUAGE

How you behave when other men talk about sexual violence could affect the life of your mother, sister, girl friend or daughter. If you talk in such a way as to give the impression that men are entitled to sex and women are required to provide it, you could be beginning a chain reaction which results in someone being raped or murdered. This is equally true if you appear to support or agree with other men talking in that way.

### YOUR BIGGEST RESPONSIBILITY IS AT HOME

The previous advice holds good in relation to women or girls whom you live with — your wife, girl-friend, daughter, step-daughter or sister. You have a special responsibility to women and girls whom you can easily dominate because of family circumstances. The fact that violence against women in the home is a crime is now generally accepted by both society and the police.

### TAKE ALL COMPLAINTS SERIOUSLY

In every society people depend on each other. You can help by taking action if a woman is being raped, attacked, or assaulted, whether inside or outside the home.

You should always call the police, or arrange for them to be called. If a woman comes to you in fear of attack, all you need to do is take her seriously, stay with her, and call the police.

### ALL WOMEN AND GIRLS DESERVE RESPECT ....

One of the most basic human rights is the right to freedom from fear of violence. One of the most basic human responsibilities is to respect one another equally and not make women feel anxious or afraid because of your behaviour. Any conduct in the company of women which they find frightening, threatening or unpleasant is a breach of that responsibility; so is "touching up" or unwanted attention.

*Greater Manchester Police Authority crime prevention leaflets*

## ACTIVITY 7.1

Visit your local police station and ask for a sample of their crime prevention literature. Consider what advice, if any, is given regarding personal safety. If such advice is given, compare and contrast the literature you have gathered with the advice leaflets offered to both women and men in Greater Manchester. Ask yourself the following questions:

1   Who is presumed to be responsible for violence towards women in this literature?

2   What specific advice is offered to women?

3   Does the advice offered make sense to you?

4   How does the advice compare or contrast with your own precautionary strategies?

5   If you are a woman, what ways have you adopted of keeping yourself safe?

6   How, and under what circumstances, do you think such advice might work – how might it prevent criminal behaviour?

This discussion is not intended to deny the 'good sense' offered in crime prevention literature for women, nor is it intended to deny that the public domain is not a significant arena for crime prevention activity as far as women are concerned. Indeed, the public domain is also an important arena of crime prevention advice for men, but one wonders what would happen if men were told to stay off the streets at night. Moreover, some local authorities have attempted to take gender issues seriously in respect of crime prevention in the public domain. So, for example, improved street lighting (Painter, 1988), the introduction of women-only taxi services, late-night bus services for women, and all-female sessions at leisure centres (all examples cited by the research organization Comedia, 1991) may have improved the quality of life for those women who have used them. Perhaps the most significant point of this discussion is that it reminds us that communities are *gendered*. Communities are, at a minimum, spaces occupied by men and women (also adults *and* children, young *and* old, and people from ethnic minorities). In this sense it is important to consider such questions as 'whose crime?' and 'whose community?'. Answers to these questions may vary, of course, according to whose interests are being privileged by the policy-making process.

Victim-centred strategies can be about empowerment – enabling people to engage in activities or go to places which they otherwise would not; or they can be about blaming – looking for a way of reducing crime by encouraging individuals to change their behaviour in less positive ways, for example staying in rather than going out. In each case, it could be argued that they share a concern to reduce the opportunities for crime to occur. Reducing the opportunities for crime was the objective of one of the major crime prevention strategies of the early 1980s, namely situational crime prevention – here referred to more generally as environment-centred strategies.

# 5 Environment-centred strategies

Environment-centred strategies include both the specific targeting associated with situational crime prevention and the more general approach of 'designing out crime'. Clarke and Mayhew (1980) define situational crime prevention measures as:

**situational crime prevention**

- being directed at specific crimes;
- managing, designing or manipulating the immediate environment in which such crime occurs;
- ensuring that these measures are systematic and permanent;
- reducing overall opportunities for crime.

Bottoms (1990) suggests that such opportunity-reducing measures could include target hardening (for example more secure doors and windows), removing the means for criminal activity (for example screening devices at airports), or increasing surveillance (for example closed-circuit television (CCTV) cameras in shopping malls and high streets).

**target hardening**

*A surveillance camera maintains a watchful eye in Liverpool*

Targeting specific offences in this way has met with some success. Hough and Mo (1986) suggest, on the basis of British Crime Survey data, that attempted burglaries are prevented from being completed burglaries by the presence of crime prevention hardware. Obviously such findings need to be compared with what burglars themselves say will deter them: some research has shown that they rate the chance of being seen much more highly than the presence of hardware as an effective deterrent (Bennett and Wright, 1984). However, the work of Allatt (1984a and 1984b) on 'target hardening' on a 'hard to let' housing estate seems to point to some success with these kinds of initiative.

Manipulating the environment in order to prevent and/or reduce crime has also been explored as a more general strategy. These approaches stem largely from the work of Newman (1972), and have been taken up most extensively in the UK by Coleman (1985). This view of crime prevention implies a form of architectural determinism; in other words, the built environment provides the precipitative framework in which crime can be made more or less easy. The aim of these crime prevention programmes is to restructure the environment in order to reduce the opportunities for crime to occur. This may involve, for example, the disassembling of concrete walkways, which often permit numerous routes of unsurveyed access and egress on some housing estates, so as to make it harder for criminals to move around an estate unseen and unhindered. However, whether we define situational crime prevention narrowly as in specific target hardening, or whether we define it more generally as in environmental design, these strategies share a common problem. They raise the question of what happens to the potential criminal behaviour. This is referred to as the problem of displacement.

displacement       Theoretically, displacement can take a number of different forms. Barr and Pease (1992), citing Hakim and Rengert (1981), list four possible displacement effects:

- temporal – committing the intended crime at a different time;
- spatial – committing the intended crime at a different place;
- tactical – committing the same crime in a different way;
- target – committing a different crime from that originally intended.

How and under what circumstances these different types of displacement occur is not a clear-cut issue. Barr and Pease (1992) point out that the basic premise underlying situational crime prevention initiatives was derived from evidence relating to suicide. The change from toxic to non-toxic domestic usage of gas appeared to lead to a reduction in the suicide rate! However, the extent to which such opportunity reduction has an effect in the context of crime means identifying what kind of displacement occurs, how much, and when. Understanding whether an offender chooses to offend at a different place, a different time, or chooses to commit a different crime, is quite a complex process. It cannot merely be assumed that target hardening pushes one kind of offending somewhere else. Indeed, for the more 'professional' burglars, for example, target hardening a business may mean that they simply become more adept at negotiating those harder targets! In effect few situational crime prevention strategies have been seriously evaluated to take on board these possibilities. As a consequence Barr and Pease (1992) prefer to talk of crime *deflection* rather than displacement. In other words, situational measures may move crime from a chosen target rather than reduce crime overall.

As was stated earlier, any preventive strategy makes certain presumptions about the possible explanations for, and the possibility of, predicting crime. In the case of offender-centred strategies and victim-centred strategies the locus of the cause of crime is clearly self-evident: it lies either with the individual offender or with the individual victim. In environment-centred strategies the locus of the cause of crime lies within a certain kind of 'architectural determinism' (Kinsey *et al.*, 1986). Environmental strategies view behaviour in general, and criminal behaviour in particular, as a product of the opportunities presented by physical structures. This view of crime causation implies that offenders engage in a rational decision-making process prior to offending and clearly connects with a neo-classical, conservative approach to criminology. In other words, it is assumed that offenders weigh up the relative risks and advantages of committing a certain offence under certain circumstances and decide on a course of action in the light of this: that is, they choose to offend or not on the basis of their rational assessment of the opportunities presented to them (see **Clarke, 1980**). To what extent this view can account for different kinds of law-breaking behaviour is highly problematic.

There is no doubt that the presence of opportunities can make crime easier. For example, a significant proportion of burglaries are facilitated by doors and windows being left open when property is unoccupied. The operative word here, however, is facilitated. As Bright (1991) points out, the fact remains that most people do not burgle houses or steal cars. He goes on to comment: 'While situational crime prevention, theoretically, can reduce the estimated 70 per cent of recorded crime that is thought to be opportunistic, it is unable to prevent many violent crimes such as some categories of assault, domestic violence, child abuse and racially motivated crime' (Bright, 1991, p.66). In other words, at best it is a very limited crime prevention strategy addressing a limited range of crimes with potentially limited impact.

Facilitation, then, does not equate with causation. However, the effect, in policy terms, of making things harder for the criminal has led to very particular ways of thinking about crime prevention. First, it encourages us to think of crime prevention in terms of technical expertise: fit the infra-red burglar alarm, install a CCTV camera, or remove the walkways from a housing estate and the crime problem is solved. Second, target hardening can have disastrous repercussions when individuals, or individual housing estates, develop a 'fortress mentality' in dealing with their routine day-to-day lives (Davis, 1990). In other words, many environment-centred crime prevention strategies also have wider social and community consequences.

# 6 Community-centred strategies

To argue that certain crimes occur in some areas with greater frequency than in others is not new. Police statistics, while problematic in their structure and interpretation, have always shown this. What is relatively new perhaps is the impetus that has been given to this phenomenon through the use of the criminal victimization survey (Reiss, 1986). Such surveys, whether sponsored by the Home Office or by local authorities (and therefore by definition geographically focused), have consistently revealed that people living in certain areas, especially inner-city areas and poorer council housing estates, suffer disproportionately from both street crime and household crime. Recognition of this phenomenon, in crime prevention terms, has taken the form of an emphasis on and development of community crime prevention strategies. Hope and Shaw (1988a) offer two reasons for this emphasis: first, an increasing awareness of the impact of the fear of crime and an increasing belief that such fear is having a deleterious effect on 'community life'; and second, an increasing awareness that many people are affected by crime either as victims or as friends of victims. However, while the idea of the potential effectiveness of community strategies has been invoked since the early 1980s, we need to be clear about what is meant by 'community' in this context.

# 6.1  What is a community?

In some ways this is the sociological question *par excellence*. As with the concept of prevention, there is a presumption that communities are a 'good thing'. This is deeply embedded not only in popular consciousness, but also in much sociological thinking. That thinking, which has attempted to map the changing trajectories of modernizing societies, commonly assumes that traditional communities, together with extended family ties, neighbourliness, a sense of belonging and a personal sense of place and identity, have been destroyed by the processes of modernization. Indeed, so great was the sociological concern about the impact of the processes of modernization on community life that during the 1950s a whole generation of sociological work had 'the community' as its central focus (see, for example, Willmott and Young, 1962). Though this work produced a wealth of information about the nature of modern communities, their local networks and the kind of family ties that were being constructed, the concept of 'community' itself has remained relatively underdeveloped. Yet it is clear that as a concept it is used in different ways with different meanings. As Crawford (1995, p.98) points out, while the concept of community does not have a fixed meaning, especially in the crime prevention debate, it is certainly 'both a signifier and referent around which complex and contradictory effects, meanings and definitional struggles coalesce'.

disorganized community

Hope and Shaw (1988a) identify two main ways in which the concept of 'community' has been invoked in criminological thought: the disorganized community and the disadvantaged community. The notion of the disorganized community emanates from the work of Shaw and McKay, who were influential in the Chicago School. Portraying the city in ecological terms emanated from a concern with the 'zone of transition', a 'community' which is continuously inhabited by new immigrants and characterized by the absence of shared norms (see **Graham and Clarke, 1996**, and **Bottoms and Wiles, 1992**). In this view the absence of shared norms was seen to be the key to understanding offending behaviour. Moreover, securing and fostering social organization through the socialization process was seen to be the crime prevention solution. In other words, it was the failure of community life that fostered crime. The second concept of community identified by Hope and Shaw (1988a), the disadvantaged community, emerged much later from the work of writers such as Cloward and Ohlin (1960). These writers argued that juveniles turned to delinquency as a result of frustration: that is, as a result of their desire to aspire to economic advance being met with the reality that this was not achievable.

disadvantaged community

Both of these images of the community were derived from criminological thought that originated in North America. In empirical terms they found little validity in the UK at the time they were proposed. However, it is clear that given some of the consistent patterns of unemployment and social deprivation in some communities, there is some mileage, for example, in resurrecting a notion of the disadvantaged community. Indeed, a version of this can be found in the writing of Young and others who espouse a left realist agenda for criminology (see **Lea and Young, 1984** and **Young, 1986**). Using the term 'relative deprivation' rather than 'disadvantage', and focusing on 'lived realities', Young (1992, p.38) states: 'Crime is one form of sub-cultural adaptation which occurs when material circumstances block cultural aspirations and where non-cultural alternatives are absent or less attractive.' In many housing estates and inner-city areas, these are the kinds of conditions that exist and in which certain kinds of crime thrive. It is also these kinds of communities that have been differently targeted with varying degrees of success by the community crime prevention industry, in which, Willmott (1987) has observed, community is a 'seductive word'.

Willmott suggests that it is useful to distinguish between the 'territorial community' (those people who live in a particular area), the 'interest community' (those people who have something in common over and above the geographical area in which they live), and the 'attachment community' (people who have a sense of belonging to a place). Of course, the way in which we experience living in our 'communities' may comprise any one or a mixture of these categorizations at any moment, or they may change over time. Moreover, these experiences may not be coterminous with one another. Viewing 'communities' experientially, however, is not necessarily the focus of policy initiatives, though policies too may be differently informed by each of the categories identified above. Such policies may differ in other respects, as we shall see.

## ACTIVITY 7.2

At this juncture it would be useful to think about your own 'community'. What do you understand by that term? Is this a concept that has relevance for you? Are you thinking about where you live, your neighbourhood, your locality, or some other, perhaps larger, unit? Is your thinking informed by your feelings about where you live, or have you constructed some geographical boundary in your head? How do these thoughts interconnect? How might a crime prevention policy-maker think about your community, and how far might such thinking match with your own understanding of your community?

Given the central importance of the appeal to the concept of community in recent crime prevention policy rhetoric and practice, the following discussion, implicitly and explicitly, addresses these questions:

- What do we understand by the concept of community, and how might different definitions of community lead in different directions with respect to crime prevention?

- What do we understand by crime prevention, and to what extent have crime prevention initiatives been subjected to fashionable policy and political influences?

- Are there different kinds of community crime prevention initiatives; if so, what do they comprise?

- What kind of community crime prevention initiatives are likely to succeed, for whom, where, and under what circumstances?

- What might communities of the future look like, given current crime prevention trends?

It is possible to identify the emergence of two main crime prevention strategies during the 1980s, and these invoke the image of the community in differing ways. The first, Neighbourhood Watch, invokes the *citizen* as a member of the community and invites greater citizen participation in crime prevention. The second, multi-agency co-operation, invokes the community through the greater co-operation of the various agencies who work in an area.

## 6.2  Neighbourhood Watch: the eyes and ears of the police?

Neighbourhood
Watch

Neighbourhood Watch schemes take their lead from the USA. The first Neighbourhood Watch scheme in the UK was established in 1982, and by 1994 there were reported to be 115,000 schemes (*The Guardian*, 6 April 1994). They have been defined as the 'mobilization of informal community controls' directed 'in the defence of communities against a perceived predatory threat from outside' (Hope and Shaw, 1988a, p.12). In crime prevention terms there are two arguments which commend them as possible policy strategies. First, they propose an opportunity reduction view of crime – they presume that increased surveillance will deter criminals by encouraging citizens to be the eyes and ears of the police on the street. Second, they propose to reduce the 'incivilities' of urban life through creating and harnessing social cohesion by increasing contact between neighbours, in the hope that this will lead to a greater trust between citizens and a consequent reduction in the fear of crime.

It is clear that the growth and development of Neighbourhood Watch schemes across the UK has been remarkable; what is less certain is what such schemes actually achieve. The 1984 British Crime Survey afforded an opportunity to examine the development of these schemes a little more closely. Having analysed the data, Hope (1988, p.159) states: 'Where the strongest spontaneous support for Neighbourhood Watch resides is in those communities where people are sufficiently worried about crime, where they feel the need to do something about it, and where they feel positively towards their neighbours and to the community in general.' He goes on to add that those people who appear to be willing to involve themselves in these schemes are white, middle-aged, and lower-middle/middle-class. These findings seem to concur with other research which has been concerned to measure the overall effectiveness of the schemes. Collectively, these findings point to the fact that Neighbourhood Watch schemes are most likely to achieve some of their objectives (primarily fear reduction) among white, middle-class homeowner (Bennion *et al.*, 1985; Donnison *et al.*, 1986; Bennett, 1987).

Neighbourhood Watch seems to be popular in areas where worry about crime is likely to be high, but where the risk from residential crime is relatively low: that is, in areas where crime is likely to be perceived as being a threat external to the community. On the other hand, in areas where the recorded crime rate is higher, that is in areas of poorer public sector housing, poorer older terraced housing and multi-racial areas, Neighbourhood Watch is less popular. In these areas it is likely that the crime problem is not seen or experienced as a threat from outside the community, but one with which members of the community routinely live. One study suggests that up to 60 per cent of offenders live less than a mile away from the scene of their crime (Cooper, 1989). People may see and hear what is going on, but do not necessarily possess the local trust and support from their neighbours should they report such incidents. Indeed, some may be positively intimidated from doing so.

There are, of course, a number of problems in assuming that all the registered Neighbourhood Watch schemes work effectively and in line with their objectives. There is a suspicion that many are inactive or exist only on paper. Moreover, a significant input of police time is required for them to work effectively, and this can be a key variable in the overall achievement of objectives (Bennett, 1987). Why they have proved to be so popular in the leafy suburbs tells us more about the willingness of people living in such areas to participate generally than it does about the success of the schemes themselves.

Of course, none of these issues necessarily means that the idea of Neighbourhood Watch is in itself misplaced. As Bright (1991, p.78) suggests, difficulties such as these raise a number of important questions:

- What can be done to sustain the interest and involvement of scheme members?

- How should schemes be managed and supported (given the demands it places on the police)?

- How can their potential be developed in high crime areas?

None of these questions necessarily presumes, for Bright, that Neighbourhood Watch can effectively reduce crime. However, as Bright points out, its popularity could be capitalized upon through, for example, the development of a national network of organizations in which good practice could be shared, and by expanding the remit of schemes to include strategies designed to enhance the quality of life (refuse, dog nuisance, play facilities, and so on). Bright's analysis suggests that many schemes have already begun

*A private street-patrol officer on duty in Sedgefield, County Durham; the force is funded and operated by the local council*

to diversify in this way, and consequently have the potential to keep the membership active as well as improve the quality of life. This view highlights the constructive potential for locally based schemes. But Bright is not the only one to have highlighted their potential.

At a Neighbourhood Watch conference in 1994 the idea was mooted that the remit of Watch schemes could be expanded to include crime prevention patrols. This was met with some criticism and resistance by those committed to the basic Watch principles. Yet community patrols of various kinds are clearly on the increase.

## ACTIVITY 7.3

Read the articles from *The Guardian* reproduced overleaf and then answer the following questions:

1   What do you think are the key similarities and differences between the proposal for patrol watch schemes and the development of community police forces?

2   What questions do both developments raise concerning the idea of community? What are the dangers inherent in this idea?

3   In what ways, if any, could either of these developments be identified as vigilantism? Do you think this is a potential problem? If so, why? What mechanisms would need to be put into place in order to prevent vigilantism?

4   What relationship between citizen and state is envisaged by developments such as these? What are their respective responsibilities in crime prevention?

# Pounding to a brand new beat

## by Peter Hetherington and Alan Travis

AS DARKNESS falls, Officer David Corrigan slowly drives his Ford Escort, with its familiar police-style Day-Glo stripe, towards a group of 25 youths standing menacingly around the railway museum in Shildon, County Durham.

A few bricks and insults are hurled. The officer, in regulation dark uniform and peaked cap, backs away. The crowd disappears into the night. And 34-year-old Corrigan, a former Para with lengthy service in Northern Ireland, congratulates himself on another crime-stopping job well done.

'As soon as I showed up, they disappeared,' he recalls the following morning in the roster room of force headquarters, brimming with the latest technology to service the modern beat officer. 'If I wasn't there, the place could have been wrecked. They seemed intent on breaking in.'

David Corrigan could easily pass for a modern bobby. Yet he is no policeman. In his smart, white shirt with the 'Community Force' emblem stitched to the front, he represents the new breed of private street-patrol officer increasingly seen by local councils as an effective way to fight crime. The councils accept that they will never replace the police force itself – not least because of their strictly limited legal powers.

But they see that the 'real' police are overworked and understaffed, and are prepared to fund and operate their own streetwise forces.

This is not simply the use of private security firms to re-assure well-to-do neighbour-hoods. Sedgefield District Council in Durham, whose streets David Corrigan patrols, claims proudly to be Britain's first council-run community-style policing force. Next week, the London Borough of Wandsworth plans to follow by establishing its own network of 'uniformed watchers' – trained volunteers, backed up by professional help. And according to organisers in Sedgefield, visitors from other councils throughout the country have been showing keen interest in establishing their own community forces. In an age of increasing concern about crime, the private council-run street patrol has evidently found its role.

Yet in Shildon, last Wednesday night, Patrol Officer Corrigan had to defer to higher authority outside the museum. He is one of 18 patrol officers and back-up staff on the recently formed 'community force' (motto: 'Serve with Honour') who provide round-the-clock cover for 90,000 people in south Durham with beat patrols and from six white Pandas. He has powers only of persuasion and, as a last resort, citizen's arrest – although a high-powered radio, linked to HQ in a council depot, plus a mobile phone, can summon police when necessary. He did so on Wednesday: officers arrived within minutes and some youths took flight.

Sedgefield's force became fully operational in January after an initiative by the leader of the Labour council, Brian Stephens. Canvassing voters, he found that crime and the police's apparent inability to curb lawlessness was an over-riding concern. There was also a wider concern, which few councillors will publicly articulate. 'People just weren't happy with the police,' volunteers one. 'You phoned up about a burglary and they arrived two hours later. The people just weren't happy so we decided to act.'

Sedgefield set aside £185,000 to launch its force last autumn, and recruited staff aged 28 to 45. The officer in charge, John Reed, who retired last year from Durham Constabulary as a chief inspector, is under no illusions about the reaction of his former boss, Chief Constable Frank Taylor. 'Last October he said he was wary, then later gave it a cautious welcome, and I can understand that. This is something completely new. We are somewhere between a security service and the police. We are a crime-prevention force. The police investigate crime, although I accept they have a prevention role as well. But if we come across criminal behaviour we report it. We are the eyes and ears.' Over the past few months, he insists his officers have curbed attempted burglaries, car thefts and vandalism simply by 'being seen'.

Already, he says, the force has established a good relationship with council-tax payers. 'People are coming and telling us about nuisances. We are not working in competition with the police and our terms of reference are obviously different.'

But Eric Anderson, deputy head of the force, acknowledges that the dividing line seems academic to many residents. He detects resentment among former colleagues in the local police force, where he was a sergeant. The official reaction last year hardly helped. 'People should be aware they are only getting a few extra eyes and ears,' a Durham police spokesman said. 'We would be happier if the money spent on this went to employing more officers.' Resentment, perhaps? 'There had to be, hadn't there?' Anderson responds. 'What the police cannot do these days is provide some visible reassurance.'

In the community-force headquarters, an illuminated operations board charts the movement of each patrol car while Kath McNulty, a clerical officer, logs each incident on a computer. After a month or so, incidents are compared to detect crime patterns. Nothing is left to chance. In the hard world outside, caution remains the key. Patrol officers receive extensive training in personal skills, as well as in first aid. They are preparing for a National Vocational Qualification (NVQ) in security. Most accept that, sooner or later, a patrolman will make a citizen's arrest. 'We've come close to it, but nothing yet,' says the chief.

Michael Howard, the Home Secretary, has perhaps unsurprisingly failed to make any public endorsement of the Sedgefield scheme, nor for that matter a similar project in Stockton-on-Tees. But it will be a strange local-election campaign if he does not take time in the next three weeks to plug the latest 'innovation' from Wandsworth, the Conservatives' flagship London borough.

Wandsworth's leaders have promised to spend £275,000 improving neighbourhood security. Plans include setting up a network of patrols made up of walkie-talkie-equipped volunteers – 'preferably with a military or police background' – to act as the police's 'eyes and ears'.

The council claims it will be the 'most organised move of its kind yet seen in Britain,' with four professional team-leaders training volunteers and co-ordinating their efforts to help banish drug dealing, burglary, mugging and graffiti. The Wandsworth scheme will first go to consultation and probably not begin before Christmas. But all this local-authority activity throws into sharp relief a problem with which the Home Secretary has been grappling for the past year.

Next week, the annual national crime figures will be published. For the first time in five year, the figures are expected to show a slight fall in the overall volume of recorded crime. Burglary is likely to be singled out as the area showing the largest fall, as police campaigns around the country (such as the Met's Operation Bumblebee), involving a large concentration of officers and intelligence, begin to bite. Michael Howard will no doubt trumpet these successes as his own – although senior officers believe they have little to do with his 27-point law-and-order package and everything to do with the police developing their approach to community policing.

Howard's problem has been that he has spent nearly a year calling for a new partnership between public and police. Yet when the public has responded by backing 'have-a-go vigilantes', he has drawn the line.

Among his first decisions when he became Home Secretary last year was to raise the national recruitment target for the force of special constables – the unpaid part-timers who are under police control – from 25,000 to 30,000. It was a well-intentioned way of trying to increase police numbers in the face of the continuing Treasury freeze on the recruitment of full-time constables. Unfortunately the public has failed to respond. The number of specials has been stuck at around 19,000.

Howard then took to the idea of neighbourhood patrols, after a trip to Washington DC last summer. But during the summer some British citizens, frustrated at what they saw as the inability of the police to deliver an effective service, started to mete out their own version of justice to suspected local criminals. The reported wave of 'vigilantism' reached its peak when Duncan Bond and Mark Chapman (the 'Norfolk Two') were sentenced to five years' imprisonment, later reduced to six months after a public outcry.

The Lord Chief Justice, Lord Taylor, warned that if individuals took the law into their own hands, law and order would break down. The event also prompted Michael Howard to refine his 'partnership with the public' message. Government advice became: 'Be vigilant, not a vigilante'.

In December he urged Britain's 115,000 Neighbourhood Watch schemes to mount their own civilian patrols. This, he said, would mark a 'major advance' in the partnership of police and community in the war against crime. But ask the Home Office now what has happened to that scheme and you are met with a deafening silence, beyond the statement that 'we are in consultation with the Association of Chief Police Officers on the whole issue of voluntary patrols'.

The ACPO president, Sir John Smith, explained the police view back in December: 'We will have to ensure that people who go out patrolling, if that's what happens, are appropriately managed and linked in to the police to ensure they don't become a self-motivated set of vigilantes, which would be a serious concern to us.'

Police suspicions of the official encouragement of such civilian patrols have been fuelled by the current Home Office review of their functions. Police leaders have expressed particular contempt for the growth in commercial security patrols. Unlike the community force at Sedgefield, these private companies – increasingly being brought in to patrol housing estates and individual roads – are funded by a small weekly levy per household.

Earlier this month the Chief Constable of Avon and Somerset, David Shattock, warned that the growth of some firms' untrained employees would result in a serious injury or death. 'In Bristol there's a proliferation of private security firms patrolling the streets. I don't welcome it,' he said recently, adding that one company advised its 'security guards' that baseball caps were a sure sign that young men were criminals. The police are also sceptical about whether such patrols actually cut crime. The recently retired Chief Inspector of Constabulary, Sir John Woodcock, said in his last annual report that their use in upmarket housing estates only shifted crime to poorer areas.

Nor is it just the police who are concerned at the growth of private street security. Pressure groups have been warning about the dangers of 'privatised' city streets: even yesterday, uniformed security guards began to protect a new barrier that limits public access to a public road at the Chelsea Harbour development in London. This follows the recent closure of roads at Canary Wharf, in Docklands, to public traffic on security grounds.

'What began in the countryside with the enclosure movement is now being seen in cities,' says Simon Fairlie of the Ecologist magazine. 'The harrying of travellers, the criminalisation of trespass, it's all part of the same phenomenon.' Rodney Legg, of the Open Spaces Society, also sees a worrying trend that, for all its aims of barring the guilty, nonetheless accuses the innocent. 'People are defining space as their own and then limiting access to it,' he says. 'We are losing the public ethos and reaching the point where people are regarded as threats unless they are known'.

Back in Durham, John Reed has no doubt that the ethos of Sedgefield's community force is the way forward. 'Where we lead, others will follow,' he says. 'We've had deputations from lots of councils.'

Yet some of his officers have a warning for any community going too far down the road of private security. 'Our great virtue is that we are accountable to local people through the council,' says one. 'We're not in this for profit, like a private firm. Just imagine ... a group of residents clubs together for security. One house refused to pay. Think about it. They could become the prime target.'

(*The Guardian Outlook*, 16–17 April 1994, p.23)

# Scorned patrol

## Laurence Pollock

IMAGINE your street is plagued with burglaries, car theft is an everyday occurrence and the police appear to have given up. The offer of a private patrol, visible, regular, concerned and reasonably priced might seem the ideal solution. But then you learn that the operator has a criminal record.

Last week David Shattock, chief constable of Avon and Somerset, said this had already happened in his area, and he was powerless to stop such schemes operating. Despite the dangers of abuse, street patrols are clearly on the agenda at the Home Office, whether paid for or mounted by local volunteers. The Home Secretary gave enthusiastic encouragement for this at the last annual Neighbourhood Watch conference just before Christmas. His announcement brought swift reaction from many sources, but no comment from a national spokesperson for Neighbourhood Watch.

Despite the phenomenal growth of this self-help movement, it still does not have the apparatus to speak for itself. There are 115,000 local groups covering more than five million homes, but there is no national HQ, elected committee, president, general secretary or chief executive.

The annual conference has no policy-making or representative function but in the afternoon, after the Home Secretary and the media had gone, it got to work with a vengeance. Speaker after speaker denounced the patrol plan and on an informal show of hands it was overwhelmingly rejected. Among the concerns was: who is suitable to run a patrol? After Mr Shattock's statement that is a serious question.

Colleen Atkins of North Bedfordshire Homewatch was incensed at the idea. She has a formidable record in co-ordinating local crime prevention measures and helped found one of the first Home/Neighbourhood Watch schemes in the country 10 years ago. Her group was voted national best in 1990. Representatives of North Bedfordshire groups, which she co-ordinates, voted unanimously to reject street patrols. So she wrote to Sir John Smith, President of the Association of Chief Police Officers (ACPO) raising a string of vital questions: who would the patrols be answerable to, who would select the members, what thought had been given to racial confrontations, and how would members be covered for insurance?

Sir John in his reply acknowledged the 'concern' felt by the conference and the validity of the questions. The Home Office and ACPO are drawing up guidelines to cover the operation of patrols. But Neighbourhood Watch as an organisation has no formal input into the making of policy. That is why Colleen Atkins has been writing to all the delegates at the conference and the police forces to build up a national network of co-ordinators and members. Only this way, she believes, will the movement be able to speak authoritatively on vital issues. There are already reports of a number of federations emerging.

Nevertheless, Michael Howard in his speech laid some claim to popular support for patrolling. He cited a Gallup poll commissioned by Crime Concern, the crime prevention charity, and the General Accident insurance company: 46 per cent of the 1,000 interviewees said schemes should be allowed to organise and run crime prevention patrols – a third were opposed. On another question, which the Home Office did not cite, the sample was split 44 per cent for and against squads patrolling streets to prevent crime and arrest those committing criminal acts.

It is clear that moves are afoot to shift Neighbourhood Watch up a gear as the Government wrestles with crime statistics and tries to hold down the cost of policing. The most recent unconfirmed reports suggest that overall recorded crime totals for England and Wales showed a fall of just under one per cent between 1992 and 1993. But a survey carried out by the Guardian in January revealed that in many areas, clear-up rates were also still falling. And the British Crime Survey for 1992 suggests the total number of offences is about three times the reported level.

Mr Howard himself wants existing Neighbourhood Watch schemes 'moving in some new direction'. If that happens it will involve Crime Concern, the Home Office funded charity. It is one of the few significant links between Whitehall and the mean streets. It acts as an umbrella for Neighbourhood Watch activity. Chief executive, Nigel Whiskin, is also thinking strategically: 'It is more than just curtain twitching. It's about making a community work ... For that to happen, the concept needs firmer and stronger leadership and a bigger vision.'

He regards 'patrol' as an emotive, loaded word. It could involve nothing more than escorting someone who is nervous about going out or 'laying something on' for kids who are a 'bit of a problem'.

'If we want to see Neighbourhood Watch developed and expanded, we can't expect the police, working with finite cash limits, to spend more time on it.' The message that comes from Mr Howard or his representatives is that the proposals for street patrols are permissive, not prescriptive. But this is unlikely to reassure activists who are convinced street patrols will split their movement.

When a number of co-ordinators met in Colleen Atkins's flat there was mounting concern. The area – large Victorian and Edwardian villas near the centre of Bedford – has its peaks and troughs of criminality but there is commitment to and belief in the basic approach. But there is already a private security company in Bedfordshire doing presentations to parish councils and offering to patrol for a fee.

A broad church, Neighbourhood Watch has not so far needed a structure with paid officials, policymaking committees and national premises. It is a lean burn movement. But Mr Howard has thrown down a challenge which some activists say can only be met by becoming an organisation that can speak for itself.

*(The Guardian, 6 April 1994, p.12)*

## COMMENT

The discussion of Neighbourhood Watch, and the exercise you have just completed, have alerted us to a number of issues. First, it is clear that harnessing citizen support for community crime prevention strategies of this kind is fraught with difficulties. In terms of implementation, ensuring active participation across a full range of communities has yet to be achieved. Second, in terms of effectiveness, Neighbourhood Watch appears to have achieved some success in making people feel better about the crime problem in their local area. However, there appears to be little evidence to support a view that such initiatives have resulted in a reduction in crime. Finally, there are differing views as to how the potential of Neighbourhood Watch popularity might be developed. The dividing line between some of these suggestions and vigilantism serves to remind us that community-based initiatives are not always, by definition, a 'good thing'.

Taken together, the issues outlined above raise an underlying problem for community-based initiatives of this kind. That problem relates to their central purpose: is it to reduce crime or to reduce the fear of crime? If it is the former, then as a policy initiative it shares many of the same assumptions about the causes of crime as the environmentally based initiatives discussed earlier: they both articulate an opportunistic view of crime. Not only does this raise the question of displacement but, perhaps more importantly in this particular context, it raises questions about the assumptions being made concerning the communities themselves. It has already been stated that Neighbourhood Watch schemes fit most readily with a view of crime which is seen as a threat from outside the community. In addition, however, they assume a very static image of the community, although we know that communities change, people grow up, new people move in, others move out, and so on. All of these processes can have an impact on crime independently of any crime prevention strategy. Finally, Neighbourhood Watch schemes take as their central focus 'public' crime – that which occurs on the streets or against property. Yet, for many people, especially women, most of the crime they experience directly takes place in the private domain and involves victims and offenders who are typically known to each other. In taking account of the gendered nature of communities, it is a matter of political preference in times of resource shortage in understanding what kind of crime is targeted with what kind of initiative.

## 6.3 Multi-agency co-operation

The second strand to community crime prevention that emerged in the 1980s took the form of multi-agency co-operation. Hope and Shaw define the purpose of multi-agency co-operation as follows:

multi-agency co-operation

> In as much as crime within local communities is likely to be sustained by a broad range of factors – in housing, education, recreation, etc. – the agencies and organisations who are in some way responsible for, or capable of, affecting those factors, ought to join in common cause so that they are not working at cross purposes or sustaining crime inadvertently.

(Hope and Shaw, 1988a, p.13)

This approach to crime prevention endeavours to take Home Office circular 8/84 to heart. However, as an approach to crime prevention it has been researched relatively little. The most important piece of work in this area was sponsored by the Economic and Social Research Council (ESRC) in the mid 1980s and conducted by a research team based at the University of Lancaster and Middlesex Polytechnic (Sampson *et al.*, 1988).

Sampson *et al.* identified two traditional ways of thinking about multi-agency co-operation at a theoretical level: the *benevolent* and the *conspiratorial.* The benevolent sees the idea of forming a consensus between different organizations with different goals as unproblematic. The conspiratorial view, usually associated with those on the political left, sees such developments as an extension of the coercive role of the state. Sampson *et al.*'s own research on the process of implementing multi-agency strategies points to the inadequacy of both of these positions and to the importance of developing a 'more socially nuanced understanding which is alive to the complexities of locally based crime prevention initiatives and of power differentials running between state agencies, as well as to the competing sectional interests within existing communities' (Sampson *et al.*, 1988, p.482).

This does not mean, of course, that multi-agency work is non-problematic. On the contrary, there are dilemmas to be faced by agencies participating in such initiatives. As a policy process they may be less than democratic – that is, dominated by the expert status of the police (Kinsey *et al.*, 1986). They may also compromise the role of other agencies, for example by determining the nature of social work with young people or probation work with ex-offenders (Blagg *et al.*, 1988). Issues such as these led Bottoms (1990, p.16) to ask a number of important questions about the multi-agency approach:

- Do different agencies have different amounts of power in inter-agency crime prevention forums, and does it matter?

- How much autonomy is it necessary for each agency to lose for the sake of the collective good, and are they willing to lose it?

- To what extent is it right to recognize that different agencies (such as the police and social work departments) have different assigned functions, and that these functions will necessarily limit the extent to which co-operation between agencies may properly (and ethically) occur?

The question remains, of course, as to what multi-agency co-operation might achieve with respect to crime prevention and the community. Sampson *et al.*'s research cited above offers us two possibilities. The first constitutes a broadening of the focus of what had been traditionally conceived of as crime prevention business. For example, Blagg *et al.* state:

> What is most striking is the contrast between the neglect of domestic violence as a site upon which to enact measures of crime prevention (in other words to regard such violence as crime) or to invoke the concept of inter-agency co-operation when set against the elaborate liaison apparatus which is arranged around child protection.

> (Blagg *et al.*, 1988, p.217)

Viewed from the 1990s this is a particularly astute observation, as we shall see in section 6.8 below. Suffice it to say at this stage that multi-agency co-operation has indeed become one of the by-words of responses to 'domestic' violence, especially in the wake of Home Office circular 60/1990. That circular reminded all chief constables of the potential power of arrest in domestic situations, made it clear that 'domestic' violence was to be taken as seriously as violence occurring in the street, encouraged the use of arrest for the perpetrators of 'domestic' violence, and advised police forces of the need to support the victim. However, Blagg *et al.* were rightly drawing attention to the way in which the crime prevention agenda had, until this time, assumed a vision of the crime problem as being located solely in the public domain.

The second possibility exposed by Blagg *et al.* lay in the view that communities were not necessarily being consulted about their concerns with respect to crime. This points to the tensions that exist between statutory agencies (who have the power to define the local problem and allocate resources to it) and the local communities in which they are working. This tension may sometimes result in decisions being taken in the face of local opposition and/or demands for a different problem to be addressed with a different resource allocation. Such a top-down implementation style can also result in the further stereotyping of a community (Sampson *et al.*, 1988) and/or the overlooking of problems genuinely felt by people living in a particular locality. These tensions point to the need for closer and more effective consultation with communities for such implementation styles to work.

## ACTIVITY 7.4

Make a list of the main limitations of Neighbourhood Watch and community-centred strategies as you now understand them.

## COMMENT

Neighbourhood Watch and multi-agency co-operation, as conventionally understood, are limited by the fact that they tend to be police-led and they tend to operate with a focus on property crime, street crime, or 'nuisances'. They are also initiatives which primarily reflect a territorial definition of the community where crime is seen as an external threat or is recognized as a problem internal to the community and may result in the further stereotyping of that community. In addition, both tend to operate with a top-down implementation style, often neglecting less formal groups and glossing over the problems of trying to create 'social cohesion' as a crime prevention strategy. Moreover, there is a sense in which the kinds of communities successfully targeted by both of these policy initiatives are those communities in which some semblance of social cohesion already exists: the leafy suburbs, or those areas in which the statutory agencies still find some basis of co-operation. However, there is a third strand to community-centred crime prevention which runs somewhat contrary to these first two. This strand is informed by the concept of community safety rather than crime prevention *per se*, and can be identified in the work of the National Association for the Care and Resettlement of Offenders (NACRO) and the Safer Cities Programme. The work of NACRO in particular focuses on a very different kind of community to that discussed so far.

# 6.4  Community safety

### 6.4.1  The NACRO framework

social crime prevention

Bottoms (1990) suggests that the most ambitious social crime prevention programmes in the UK to date have been established by NACRO, a voluntary organization which set up a Crime Prevention Unit in 1979 and a Safe Neighbourhood Unit in 1980. The initiatives emanating from this organization frequently include elements of both situational and social crime prevention. Social crime prevention, as opposed to situational crime prevention, endeavours to address the root causes of crime. The initiatives are focused primarily on multiply deprived housing estates in high crime-rate areas. These projects involve active consultation with the local community 'to tease out possible solutions to the problems from their knowledge of the area' (Whiskin, 1987). They are based on a concept of community safety whose origins can be located not only in the work of NACRO but also in the work of the police monitoring groups that emerged in some police authority areas following the Scarman Report in 1981.

community safety

Bright (1987, pp.49–50) outlines the NACRO framework as including:

- strategies for the involvement of local councils
- services for victims of crime
- strategies for protecting those most at risk (women, ethnic minorities, children)
- schemes for involving the police
- schemes tailored to different residential areas

Although, as Whiskin (1987) states, a framework of this kind is not strikingly original, it does draw attention to a number of critical features of the community crime prevention industry which are, arguably, neglected by both multi-agency approaches and Neighbourhood Watch schemes.

First, the framework starts from the premise that tackling criminal victimization and the fear of such victimization is the responsibility of a broad base within the community: formal agencies, informal agencies, and community networks. This implies that it is necessary not only to ensure community participation, but also to establish mechanisms to ensure that participation is both facilitated and representative. Second, it is a framework within which the definition of the crime problem incorporates an understanding of criminal victimization that takes into account the structural variables of age, ethnicity and sex – facets of community crime prevention which are not commented on explicitly in the initiatives discussed above. Third, it proposes a genuinely co-operative approach to community crime prevention. This moves close to the idea of empowerment. Taken together, the features of the NACRO framework for crime prevention come closest to resonating with all three definitions of community identified by Willmott (1987) and discussed earlier.

empowerment

The NACRO framework requires the formulation of a locally based action plan, and an implementation process usually involving a complex mixture of situational/environmental measures and social strategies. Because of the complexity of these initiatives it has proved difficult to evaluate their effectiveness. As Rock (1988) comments, while it may be clear that NACRO interventions have an effect, the reason why is uncertain. Indeed, there is some controversy concerning the overall effectiveness of the NACRO approach to crime prevention and reduction (see, for example, Poyner *et al.*,

1986). Nevertheless, NACRO projects present a view of crime prevention which has had a considerable impact on policy thinking and from which, Bright (1991) argues, a number of lessons have been learned.

First, NACRO initiatives illustrate that the best projects are multi-focused in housing estates with multiple problems. This often means that evaluation has to be long-term before any effects can be noted. It also means that issues like estate design, play provision, employment opportunities, policing and estate management need as much attention as crime prevention itself. Second, NACRO schemes show that residents will only become involved in such initiatives if the local council and local police are both seen to be using their resources and their power to address local problems. Third, the schemes clearly suggest that resources are needed to improve the environment (to tackle vandalism and poor street lighting, for example) alongside the need for community participation and multi-agency co-operation. Bright (1991) argues that the variable availability of resources during the 1980s was frequently a factor in what was achievable or not within these projects.

However, the rhetoric of community safety has not been solely confined to NACRO projects: the Safer Cities initiative launched by the government in the 1980s shares in the use of this terminology.

### 6.4.2 Safer Cities

The Safer Cities Programme was the Home Office contribution to the Action for Cities initiative introduced by the government in 1988. Building on the knowledge acquired from the earlier Five Towns Initiative and the associated demonstration projects, Safer Cities aims to: reduce crime, lessen the fear of crime, and 'create safer cities where economic and community life can flourish' (Tilley, 1993). Having established a locally based programme designed to achieve these aims, each Safer Cities initiative is expected to do one of two things: either to end community involvement having met the original aims, or to have established an alternative source of funding to that provided by the Home Office in order to continue working. As a programme, then, it shares the partnership approach to crime prevention. In this case, partnership however, the partnership is between central government in the main and local projects. The brief of local projects is to forge multi-agency contacts, especially in the formation of their steering committees. The realization of such a partnership is obviously a key variable for projects not guaranteed permanent status. It is of interest to our discussion to explore what is meant by 'community safety' in this context, since this has not always been made clear (see Extract 7.1).

In his evaluation of the Safer Cities initiative Tilley (1992) comments that the terms 'community safety' and 'crime prevention' appear to be used interchangeably. He suggests that, in practice, schemes have concerned themselves with issues beyond the usual target hardening or Neighbourhood Watch approach to crime prevention but have perhaps not gone so far as to include issues like noise or pollution which might be associated with community safety. So the aims of Safer Cities are broad, and it is interesting to note in particular the emphasis on the role of crime prevention in relation to the business community within each scheme area. Moreover, Safer Cities schemes have funded projects in schools, in relation to domestic violence, as well as the more usual target hardening work. Given these broad aims, it is relevant to examine how the Safer Cities Programme has fared since its inception.

## Extract 7.1  The Morgan Report: 'Crime prevention and community safety'

3.1  Early on, the Working Group noted the absence of a definition of crime prevention in Circulars 8/84, 44/90 and the accompanying booklet, *Partnership in Crime Prevention*. Although none of the responses submitted by Chief Constables or local authority Chief Executives attempted a definition, the Association of Chief Police Officers (ACPO), in a separate document entitled *The Role of the Force Crime Prevention Officer*, defined crime prevention as: 'the anticipation, recognition and appraisal of a crime risk and the initiation of the pre-emptive action to remove or reduce it'.

3.2  A somewhat different perspective informs the Association of District Councils' report *Promoting Safer Communities*. This comments: 'More and more the phrase crime prevention is understood to be about promoting community safety and examining wider social issues'.

3.3  Responses from local authorities and police forces made use of such terms as '*crime reduction strategies and policies*', '*situational crime prevention*', '*social crime prevention policy*' and '*community safety*', which covered a wide variety of activities and perspectives. However, for the most part, crime prevention was perceived in terms of schemes for reducing the opportunities for crime.

3.4  It is the view of the Working Group that the social aspects of crime prevention, which seek to reduce those influences which lead to offending behaviour, and the fear of crime, need to receive attention at least equal to that given to the situational aspects of crime prevention, in which efforts are made to reduce opportunities and '*harden*' potential targets for crime.

3.5  We have been impressed by the need identified by the leading organizations for a broad spectrum of activities, ranging from the prevention of opportunity through deterrence to more social aspects of crime prevention. These include diversion of existing and potential offenders, dealing with offenders after sentence, and more general attention to youth activity. We have also been impressed by the stress placed by both Ministers and officials of the Home Office and other government Departments on the need for crime prevention measures which address the causes of offending.

3.6  The term '*crime prevention*' is often narrowly interpreted and this reinforces the view that it is solely the responsibility of the police. On the other hand, the term '*community safety*' is open to wider interpretation and could encourage greater participation from all sections of the community in the fight against crime.

3.7  We see community safety as having both social and situational aspects, as being concerned with people, communities and organizations including families, victims and at risk groups, as well as with attempting to reduce particular types of crime and the fear of crime. Community safety should be seen as the legitimate concern of all in the local community.

(Home Office, 1991, p.13)

Evaluation is built into the Safer Cities Programme, but it is important to consider what is being evaluated: the programme as a whole, individual projects, or individual schemes within projects? Each of these different levels of evaluation suggests a rather complex evaluative model. Tilley's (1992) work offers some comments on the implementation process of the programme as a whole. His analysis draws attention to a number of issues for the schemes, including the difficulties of:

- placing crime prevention as a central issue on local authority agendas, where lack of recognition at worst, or lack of a coherent response at best, are key problems to address;

- being faced with a lack of credibility, especially from other agencies well established in local communities;

- the absence of an expected 'blueprint for action' from central government;
- the danger of the police or some other powerful local agency taking the lead in setting the local agenda.

Tilley (1992) highlights the crucial role played by the co-ordinators and their assistants, who by definition are required to be members of the local community, in steering a constructive course through these difficulties, and their role in ultimately establishing an exit strategy – that is, a plan of action for disengaging from the community. Tilley also provides a useful overview of the kinds of strategies that have been put in place under the auspices of Safer Cities (see Table 7.1).

Commenting on this range of interventions, Tilley suggests that, all other things being equal and providing that funds are available, difficulties increase going from left to right and from top to bottom. The bottom right-hand corner constitutes the most threatening strategy to existing agency practices.

## ACTIVITY 7.5

Table 7.1 presents some useful concrete examples of the kinds of crime prevention work conducted by Safer Cities. Using this chart, make notes on the following questions:

1   How do you think this view of community crime prevention compares with that proposed by the NACRO model?
2   What kind of definition of the 'community' is assumed by Safer Cities and NACRO? How do these definitions compare? Who is included and who is excluded by these definitions?
3   Compare and contrast the implementation styles of each version of community safety. Which do you think is most likely to succeed?

Tilley goes on to state:

> Even though in a fully fleshed-out Community Safety Strategy it may not be appropriate that the police and local authority have the dominant voices, it is clear that their co-operation is a *sine qua non* of any longer term community safety/crime prevention strategy. If the agreement of either of these to participate is not forthcoming, no workable strategy can develop.

(Tilley, 1992, p.18)

Thus within the Safer Cities Programme we are faced with a similar organizational dilemma to that found in other initiatives that have a different emphasis. There is a clear strain within any crime prevention programme towards a top-down style stemming from the necessary involvement of both the police and the local authority. This observation, of course, does not necessarily imply that such initiatives are doomed to failure or by definition will only ever have limited success. It does, though, beg a number of questions concerning how the needs of people living in those communities that have been targeted for action are identified, taken account of, and/or indeed met. How these processes are or are not achieved is more often than not a matter of political vision, and in the context of crime prevention, as elsewhere, criminologists differ both theoretically and politically as to how best to achieve success in the crime prevention arena (see section 6.6).

| Table 7.1   Examples of interventions by scope and level of penetration | | |
| --- | --- | --- |
| **Level of intervention** | **Physical intervention** | **Social intervention** |
| First level: conduct of new dedicated initiatives | Examples:<br>• installation/provision of door locks<br>• window locks<br>• fencing<br>• blocking or creating alleyways<br>• lighting<br>• creation of curtilage parking<br>• personal alarms<br>• burglar alarms<br>• CCTV<br>• aspects of risk management in schools and hospitals | Examples:<br>• schemes for those at risk of offending such as youth facilities or parent support groups<br>• victim or potential victim schemes such as advice centres<br>• offender-based programmes such as motor projects or careers advice<br>• training for staff in public houses in dealing with violence<br>• aspects of risk management in schools and hospitals<br>• Neighbourhood Watch, Pub Watch, etc. |
| Second level: incorporation into new, potentially relevant initiatives | Examples:<br>• design of new housing estates<br>• shopping complexes<br>• public buildings such as schools, colleges and hospitals<br>• siting of banks and post offices | Examples:<br>• new school curriculum contents<br>• management of new commercial concerns |
| Third level: re-examination of existing patterns of practice | Examples:<br>• council repair practices for burgled properties<br>• council policies for removal of graffiti<br>• rubbish collection practices<br>• provision of screechers to female employees and students | Examples:<br>• school culture and management<br>• methods of running children's homes<br>• patterns of service delivery in health visiting<br>• housing allocation policies<br>• styles of policing high-crime areas<br>• service delivery by police to crime victims<br>• victim support for offender victims<br>• recruitment policies for victim support<br>• employment services to ex-offenders<br>• policies relating to race and gender relations in public and private sector institutions |

Source: Tilley, 1992, p.29

## 6.5   Mixed-policy community strategies

Implicitly and explicitly, community-centred crime prevention programmes frequently advocate a mixture of both situational and social crime prevention initiatives. Two projects in particular point to the potential for success of such mixed strategies: the Kirkholt Burglary Prevention Project in Rochdale and the Hilldrop Project in Islington, north London.

The Kirkholt Burglary Project, influenced by Canadian research, was predicated on evidence of repeat or multiple victimization. In other words, built into the prevention programme was the knowledge that the chances of a house being burgled within six weeks of an initial incident were very high. The main preventive activity was therefore focused on the recently victimized. The measures introduced included: the removal of pre-payment meters, more rapid repairs after a burglary, the target hardening of property, a property-marking scheme, a security survey, and the establishment of so-called 'cocoon' Neighbourhood Watch schemes involving the victimized house and immediate neighbours. The results of this programme were impressive, with a large reduction in burglary and only minimal evidence of displacement (Forrester *et al.*, 1988). It is, of course, difficult to say which, if any, of the measures produced this effect. However, it is clear that the considerable resource investment of different kinds that took place in this community certainly had an impact.

The Hilldrop Project also deployed a mixture of crime prevention measures, but adopted a different way of gauging the crime prevention needs of the community. Following a local crime survey of the people living in the area, a team of researchers and policy-makers devised a list of crime prevention priorities for the area. These included target hardening, women's self-defence classes, increased beat policing, curriculum activity in schools, and the development of a form of Neighbourhood Watch scheme (Lea *et al.*, 1988).

It is interesting that both of these projects incorporated a version of Neighbourhood Watch into their programmes, perhaps validating the need to rethink what such schemes can achieve and how they might best deliver some form of success. It is also interesting to note that as projects they were differently sponsored (the first by the Home Office, the second by a local authority) and that they bear the hallmarks of different political flavours to the crime prevention policy process.

## 6.6   Community crime prevention: look left or right?

The community crime prevention initiatives we have so far discussed target different factors as the cause of criminal behaviour. One of the key differences between these initiatives is the extent to which social factors such as social deprivation, poor housing and unemployment are highlighted as factors which need to be taken into account in crime prevention policy. The NACRO initiatives have come closest to constituting *social* crime prevention programmes in this sense (see also Chapter 6 for a discussion of French social crime prevention initiatives). The extent to which such social factors are seen to contribute to crime is clearly connected to political visions of the crime problem. The denial that unemployment is a contributory factor to crime, for example, has been a characteristic of the response to crime of those on the right. It comes as no surprise, then, to observe that those communities in which crime is seen as an internal rather than an external threat are also those in which there are other social problems; they consequently demand more resources as well as the political will to devise and introduce policies that take those factors on board.

Since the early 1980s, government policy has put much effort into supporting community responses to crime prevention. These responses, primarily Neighbourhood Watch and Safer Cities, have relied on communities that comprise citizens with the personal and economic resources, free of intimidation, to put such policies to good effect. The available evidence clearly illustrates how, where and when success has been achieved by these policies. The question remains as to whether left-wing strategies would look any different.

In many respects those on the left invoke the same rhetoric as those on the right concerning the need for a role for the community in crime prevention. How that community is to be approached, harnessed and encouraged in its organization of crime prevention is clearly different, as perhaps the NACRO definition of community safety illustrates. Left realism makes much of putting the victim of crime at the centre of any policy agenda, but in the context of a democratic process. As Lea (1987, p.369) states, 'The maximization of democratic participation is ultimately the solution both to the problem of what is crime and to the problem of how to deal with it'. Lea further argues that an important feature of a realist approach to crime prevention would involve a real plurality of agencies, both formal and informal, centrally and locally organized. Crawford *et al.* (1990) describe such an agenda in more detail. They identify five crime prevention strategies:

*   individual crime prevention
*   crime reduction
*   crime detection
*   crime deterrence
*   victim support

All of these need to take account of specific local problems, types of crime, the environment (including the quality of life), multi-agency approaches, consultation, political will and the evaluation of effectiveness. This vision of crime prevention espouses a view of policy-making as a *process* (as negotiated between bottom-up and top-down styles). It is also concerned to empower communities through co-operation. This is in contrast to the more right-wing stance which is more top-down in style and makes consultation less of a feature. The extent to which empowerment is realizable is practically very different. Jefferson *et al.* (1988) point out the difficulties of implementing policies that are sensitive to the questions of participation, representation and the community. While these practical problems need to be acknowledged, such an ideal endeavours to take the interests of various groups into account. This raises the question: which groups?

Many of the initiatives we have discussed so far have adopted either situational or social crime prevention as their main focus (or indeed have devised strategies that combine the two). Currie (1988) neatly sidesteps this bifurcation in his analysis of crime prevention activity. He identifies two 'phases' in community crime prevention activity, and argues that:

> Their views of what it means to strengthen a community in order to fight crime differ sharply. Moreover, they differ in their view (and even more in their practice) on what kinds of communities should receive most attention, and

similarly, on what kind of crime should be most heavily targeted by community prevention – or indeed whether reducing crime is the main priority at all. By the same token, the two 'phases' differ in the degree to which they are concerned with the offender, or potential offender, as a focus of intervention. Finally, they differ on the balance to be struck between public and private responsibility for crime prevention and more generally for the enhancement of community life.

(Currie, 1988, p.280)

Currie goes on to state:

> There is no sense, for example, that the people you are dealing with might include a neighbour's kid who has a learning problem and hangs about on the corner because he is afraid to go to school, or your sister's abusive husband – hardly a stranger – but an intimate member of a local household.

(Currie, 1988, p.281–2)

Currie refers to these contradictions as showing a 'lack of structural awareness' (see also **Currie, 1991**). In some respects the concerns he identifies can be redefined as reflecting a need to emphasize a *public* sense of well-being (Taylor, 1991) over and above a private one. This raises a crucial question concerning the way in which communities targeted by the crime prevention policy discussed here can be understood as *gendered* communities.

## 6.7  Whose crime? Whose community?

Currie's (1988) analysis makes explicit a number of assumptions concerning community crime prevention in particular, and crime prevention in general. The explication of those assumptions not only draws our attention to what kind of communities are targeted for crime prevention work, but also to who is targeted within those communities. The general rhetoric concerning citizen involvement in community crime prevention presumes, of course, that we can identify and agree upon who the citizens are who make up a community and what the crime concerns are for such citizens. Such presumptions can render certain groups and their needs more or less visible. In the context of crime prevention directed at women, as we have seen already, this has frequently meant regarding their personal crime prevention behaviour as a focus for concern. If, however, we were to examine more closely the kinds of crime that affect women and the kind of crime prevention activity that is increasingly being adopted to address such crime, the question of the role of the community in the context of crime prevention might be framed somewhat differently. We shall examine these issues in the particular context of 'domestic' violence (the use of inverted commas here indicates the highly problematic nature of the meaning of 'domestic' violence – see Edwards, 1989).

## 6.8  Responding to 'domestic' violence

Home Office circular 60/1990, which was issued to all chief constables (and other chief executives of various service delivery agencies), urged police forces to treat 'domestic' violence as seriously as violence occurring between strangers in the street. The circular reminded chief constables in particular of

323

the range of statutory and common law powers they have available to them to arrest perpetrators of violence, and encouraged them to consider the establishment of dedicated 'domestic' violence units as part of their policy response to support the victims. This circular offered a twofold approach to 'domestic' violence: a 'presumption to arrest' policy, backed by a policy framework supportive of the 'victim'.

In some respects this circular has been very influential. As Radford and Stanko (1991) have commented, police forces appear to have been competing with one another to see who can put the most imaginative policy response into practice. This is not the place, however, to discuss the document's strengths and weaknesses. Suffice it to say that this policy constitutes a partial translation to the UK of an essentially North American response to 'domestic' violence (Morley and Mullender, 1991). This in itself poses some difficulties without addressing whether or not as a policy it constitutes an adequate or effective way of responding to the complex needs of women. The central concern here is: what does such a policy response represent in relation to the question of crime prevention?

In many ways, as a preventive response, the strategies recommended and adopted following circular 60/1990 represent an 'enforcement crackdown' policy (Elias, 1986). It rests on the assumption that treating 'domestic' violence like other incidents of violence will have a preventive effect. In other words, by treating such behaviour as an offence and using the available legal framework to arrest the perpetrator, two consequences will emerge: it will convey the general message that such behaviour is no longer acceptable, while the act of arresting the perpetrator will have a deterrent effect on that individual engaging in similar behaviour in the future. A number of questions arise from this kind of policy stance.

First, as a policy it rests on the presumption that arrest does have a deterrent effect in these circumstances. The evidence for this is partial and inconclusive, and in some circumstances may actually make the situation worse for the victim (Berk and Sherman, 1984; Sherman, 1992). Second, this policy also presumes that the normative response of police officers is to arrest the offender in non-domestic incidents of violence. As Chatterton (1983) and others have shown, the decision to arrest is a far more complex process. These presumptions are particularly interesting given the patent failure of arrest to deter persistent offenders from committing other kinds of crime. Why, then, should it be presumed that arrest is a 'reasonable deterrent strategy' in 'domestic' incidents?

Asking this question does not imply that such a strategy should either be abandoned or not taken seriously. Any strategy which affords some protection for a woman in a violent relationship, for however short a period, has to be acknowledged as offering something and, perhaps more important, conveying the message that her needs are being taken seriously. What emerges, however, is the individualistic offender-centred nature of this policy – a policy in which the rhetoric of the community is notable by its absence. Such an absence is all the more remarkable given the sheer weight of its presence in policy responses across a broad spectrum of issues since the early 1980s. In addition, the North American evidence (on which policies in this area appear to draw so heavily) indicates that a 'presumption to arrest' policy is at its most effective when put in place alongside a range of community-based initiatives such as refuge facilities for women and children, counselling initiatives for men, and so on (Jaffe et al., 1986).

As this policy initiative has unfolded in practice, what has not been absent has been a focus on a multi-agency approach to co-ordinate common local practices. Characterized in some areas by the establishment of Domestic Violence Forums, in which both statutory and voluntary agencies meet to co-ordinate policy, this is the kind of approach heralded as possible by the work of Blagg *et al.* (1988) (see section 6.3).

The foregoing discussion presumes that one of the goals of this policy initiative on 'domestic' violence was crime prevention, which may, of course, not necessarily be the case. Indeed, there is some evidence to suggest otherwise. It may make some sense, for example, to view this particular policy direction as constituting one element in a range of processes occurring within policing to do with 'value for money', efficiency and the securing of consent, rather than as necessarily being a crime prevention policy. Yet this policy does convey a preventive message: arrest the offender and support the victim. Such a message raises some fundamentally contradictory questions for crime prevention policy for women in general. Why, for example, does so much crime prevention literature focus on the threat to women from strangers, when women know that those most likely to be troublesome to them are so-called 'trustworthy' men? (Stanko, 1992). And why do so many community crime prevention initiatives presume that the community in which they are working is a coherent one in which all individuals share the same or similar concerns about the same or similar law-breaking activity? The issue of 'domestic' violence clearly encourages us to think much more carefully about what is both visible and invisible in the community crime prevention industry. It also encourages us to think about communities as a gendered experience in relation to crime and how that might be best addressed (see **Saraga, 1996**).

It is important to note the extent to which this multi-agency approach to crime prevention has permeated responses to 'crime behind closed doors' as well as 'crime of the streets'. Moreover, it is pertinent to examine some of the underpinning characteristics of that multi-agency work across the spectrum of crime prevention activity. Indeed, it is valuable to reflect on the extent to which the acceptance of multi-agency strategies has also implicitly involved an acceptance of the need to disrupt the traditional barriers between those services considered to be under the auspices of public provision and those considered to be more appropriately provided from within the private sphere. As Crawford (1994) observes, local agency forums on crime prevention frequently bring together people from a diversity of agencies and groups not easily categorized as public or private. Moreover, as Loveday (1994) comments, such activities have also frequently ensured the further marginalization and sometimes exclusion of local authorities. As Crawford

A poster issued by the Edinburgh Zero Tolerance Campaign against 'domestic' violence

(1994) goes on to argue, these characteristics, often couched in terms of partnership, herald the development of corporatism at the local level. Such a development makes it very difficult to draw any lines between the responsibilities of the state and those of civil society as boundaries between organizations become increasingly blurred in the search for co-ordinated policy and action. Moreover, questions concerning who is actually setting the local policy agenda are becoming increasingly difficult to resolve.

Processes such as these can have a number of effects. They can result in the construction of a crime prevention policy agenda for a particular community, on which all the agencies can agree but which may gloss over the needs of that local community, including the needs of the various 'publics' within it (for example women, minority ethnic groups, children, the elderly). Indeed, and perhaps more important, such policy constructions may gloss over the conflicts that exist within a particular community and between neighbouring communities. As Crawford (1995, p.105)) has commented, an assumption is frequently made in appealing to the community that 'more community equals less crime' – a view which implicitly denies that the community itself may be criminogenic. Yet it is important to recognize that, as Campbell (1993) has observed, some of Britain's 'dangerous places' are also among some of Britain's most economically deprived areas. These areas are also assessed to be the most crime-ridden, and some of that crime is produced and sustained within those areas themselves (see **Graham and Clarke, 1996**). Corporatist multi-agency strategies may achieve little for people living in these areas if they fail to recognize the conflicts and tensions that exist within the infrastructure of these communities, where intimidation or the normative requirement of 'no grassing' may undermine any involvement in anything that remotely hints of 'official' practice.

# 7 Conclusion: crime prevention and communities of the future?

Raising the questions of 'whose crime?' and 'whose community?' draws attention to the need to challenge the presumed separation of the public from the private in crime prevention policy. Challenging this separation has a number of consequences.

First, it constitutes a challenge to understanding who or what counts as 'the public' in a particular community. In this respect it may require a critical examination of the gendered dimensions of crime prevention policy. This may mean that it is necessary to consider how, and in what ways, gender (or ethnicity or age) acts as a mediating variable, enhancing or inhibiting the success of any initiative. As an illustration of the potential value in doing this, a survey conducted in Tayside relating to women and safety identified the potentially complex interrelationship between where you live and how safe you feel (Tayside Women's Forum, 1988). Thus a person's sense of well-being in public may be mediated not only by their 'private' experiences, but also by their interconnectedness with their local community.

Second, with respect to community crime prevention initiatives *per se*, this challenge suggests that we do not know, and as yet do not take enough account of, the infrastructure of communities and what may or may not work within them. The consensus view that the multi-agency approach is a 'good thing' may in fact add to the routine daily problems being faced by people in some economically deprived areas, whether that be in peripheral council estates or in inner-city areas. In some of these areas, as our discussion has demonstrated, some people may feel more protected by the power that the local gang asserts on their streets (in keeping hard drugs out of their area, for example) than by any multi-agency initiative. Raising these fundamental questions about the infrastructure of communities may lead us to the conclusion that if we are to take the crime problem seriously, in all its forms but especially as a gendered experience, it may be necessary to target the behaviour of men in general and young men in particular (Campbell, 1993).

Third, understanding communities as gendered communities with their own infrastructure and conflicts may also mean that we have to reconsider what it means to feel safe in a community and for whom. For example, how do we begin to understand the more recent developments in the technology of crime prevention, such as the increased deployment of CCTV and other styles of surveillance in city centres, and their impact? One interesting feature of this move has been the extent to which women in particular have supported the introduction of such surveillance techniques in spite of the civil liberties issues that they raise.

While such situational strategies might be attracting some 'public' support in city centres, it has to be said that the continued and persistent emphasis overall on situational crime prevention at the expense of paying more attention to what might be achieved by social crime prevention may have unintended and deleterious effects on the quality of life for everyone. For example, Davis states that:

> The dire predictions of Richard Nixon's 1969 National Commission on the Causes and Prevention of Violence have been tragically fulfilled: we live in 'fortress cities' brutally divided between 'fortified cells' of affluent society and 'places of terror' where the police battle the criminalised poor ... In many instances the semiotics of so-called 'defensible space' are just about as subtle as the swaggering white cop.

> (Davis, 1990, pp.225–6)

Davis is commenting here on the changing urban landscape of Los Angeles, where the privately policed shopping mall and the privately policed suburban developments ensure that the wealthy move safely and unthreatened from one secure environment to another. Thus we are beginning to see, in the USA at least, real physical as well as economic and social boundaries between the wealthy and the poor. The combining together of situational and environmental strategies to produce this effect in the UK is clearly possible, as the social and economic gap grows between those communities which have (and are relatively crime-free) and those communities which have not (and are relatively crime-soaked) (Hutton, 1994). Understanding the effects of these processes, their relationship with law-breaking behaviour, and the subsequent effects that crime has on communities unprotected by private police and technological hardware is the real challenge of community crime prevention policy.

# Further reading

A solid overview of the development of community crime prevention is given in the collection of essays edited by Hope and Shaw (1988b), while Bottoms (1990) is another useful reference. Campbell (1993) offers an interesting insight into understanding some of the processes at play in some economically deprived communities and the provocative questions that these processes raise for crime prevention. Looking to the future, one challenging image of the community is presented by Davis (1990). For an introduction to situational crime prevention see **Clarke (1980)**. **Currie (1991)** provides a more radical vision of what should be involved in effective social crime prevention strategies in market societies.

# References

Allatt, P. (1984a) 'Residential security: containment and displacement of burglary', *Howard Journal of Criminal Justice,* vol.23, no.2, pp.99–116.

Allatt, P. (1984b) 'Fear of crime: the effect of improved residential security on a difficult to let estate', *Howard Journal of Criminal Justice*, vol.23, no.3, pp.170–182.

Barr, R. and Pease, K. (1992) 'The problem of displacement', in Evans, D.J., Fyfe, N.R. and Herbert, D.T. (eds) *Crime, Policing and Place: Essays in Environmental Criminology*, London, Routledge and Kegan Paul.

Bennett, T. (1987) *An Evaluation of Two Neighbourhood Watch Schemes in London: Executive Summary. Final Report to the Home Office Research and Planning Unit*, Cambridge, Institute of Criminology.

Bennett, T. and Wright, R. (1984) *Burglars on Burglary*, Aldershot, Gower.

Bennion, C., Davies, A., Hesse, B., Joshua, L., McGloin, P., Munn, C. and Tester, S. (1985) 'Neighbourhood Watch: the eyes and ears of urban policing?', *Occasional Papers in Sociology and Social Policy,* no.6, Guildford, University of Surrey.

Berk, R.A. and Sherman, L.W. (1984) 'The specific deterrent effects of arrest for domestic assault', *American Sociological Review*, vol.49, pp.261–72.

Blagg, H., Pearson, G., Sampson, A., Smith, D. and Stubbs, P. (1988) 'Inter-agency co-ordination: rhetoric and reality', in Hope and Shaw (1988b).

Bottoms, A.E. (1990) 'Crime prevention facing the 1990s', *Policing and Society,* vol.1, no.1, pp.3–22.

**Bottoms, A.E. and Wiles, P. (1992) 'Explanations of crime and place', in Evans, D.J., Fyle, N.R. and Herbert, D.T., *Crime, Policing and Place*, London, Routledge and Kegan Paul. (Extract reprinted in Muncie *et al.*, 1996.)**

Bright, J. (1987) 'Community safety, crime prevention and the local authority', in Willmott, P. (ed.) *Policing in the Community*, London, Policy Studies Institute.

Bright, J. (1991) 'Crime prevention: the British experience', in Stenson and Cowell (1991).

Campbell, B. (1993) *Goliath: Britain's Dangerous Places*, London, Virago.

Chatterton, M. (1983) 'Police work and assault charges', in Punch, M. (ed.) *Control in the Police Organisation*, Cambridge, Mass., MIT Press.

**Clarke, R.V.G. (1980) '"Situational" crime prevention: theory and practice', *British Journal of Criminology*, vol.20, no.2, pp.136–47. (Reprinted in Muncie *et al.*, 1996.)**

Clarke, R.V. and Mayhew, P. (eds) (1980) *Designing Out Crime*, London, HMSO.

Cloward, R.A., and Ohlin, L.C. (1960) *Delinquency and Opportunity*, Glencoe, Ill., Free Press.

Coleman, A. (1985) *Utopia on Trial*, London, Hilary Shipman.

Comedia (1991) *Out of Hours: Summary Report*, London, Calouste Gulbenkian Foundation.

Cooper, B. (1989) *Management and Prevention of Juvenile Crime Problems*, Home Office Police Research Group Crime Prevention Unit paper, no.20, London, HMSO.

Crawford, A. (1994) 'The partnership approach to community crime prevention: corporatism at the local level?', *Social and Legal Studies*, vol.3, pp.497–519.

Crawford, A. (1995) 'Appeals to community and crime prevention', *Crime, Law and Social Change*, vol.22, pp.97–126.

Crawford, A., Jones, T., Woodhouse, T. and Young, J. (1990) *The Second Islington Crime Survey*, Middlesex University, Centre for Criminology.

Currie, E. (1988) 'Two visions of crime prevention', in Hope and Shaw (1988b).

**Currie, E. (1991) 'Social crime prevention strategies in a market society', in *International Developments in Crime and Social Policy*, London, NACRO. (Extract reprinted in Muncie *et al.*, 1996.)**

Davis, M. (1990) *City of Quartz: Excavating the Future in Los Angeles*, London, Verso.

Donnison, H., Skola, J. and Thomas, P. (1986) *Neighbourhood Watch: Policing the People*, London, The Libertarian Research and Education Trust.

Edwards, S. (1989) *Policing 'Domestic' Violence*, London, Sage.

Elias, R. (1986) *The Politics of Victimization*, Oxford, Oxford University Press.

Forrester, D., Chatterton, M., and Pease, K. (1988) *The Kirkholt Burglary Prevention Project*, Crime Prevention Unit Paper 13, London, HMSO.

Freeman, R. (1992) 'The idea of prevention: a critical review', in Scott, S., Williams, G., Platt, S. and Thomas, H. (eds) *Private Risks and Public Dangers*, Aldershot, Avebury.

**Graham, P. and Clarke, J. (1996) 'Dangerous places: crime and the city', in Muncie and McLaughlin (1996).**

Hakim, S. and Rengert, G.F. (1981) *The Crime Spill Over*, Beverly Hills, Sage.

Home Office (1991) *Safer Communities: The Local Delivery of Crime Prevention Through the Partnership Approach*, Report of the Standing Conference on Crime Prevention (the Morgan Report), London, HMSO.

Hope, T. (1988) 'Support for Neighbourhood Watch: a British Crime Survey analysis', in Hope and Shaw (1988b).

Hope, T. and Shaw, M. (1988a) 'Community approaches to reducing crime', in Hope and Shaw (1988b).

Hope, T. and Shaw, M. (eds) (1988b) *Communities and Crime Reduction*, London, HMSO.

Hough, M. and Mo, P. (1986) 'If at first you don't succeed', *Home Office Research Bulletin*, no.21, pp.10–13.

Hutton, W. (1994) 'A question of relativity', *Search*, no.20, summer.

Jaffe, P., Wolfe, D.A., Telford, A. and Austin, G. (1986) 'The impact of police laying charges in incidents of wife abuse', *Journal of Family Violence*, vol.1, pp.37–49.

Jefferson, T., McLaughlin, E. and Robertson, L. (1988) 'Monitoring the monitors: accountability, democracy and policewatching in Britain', *Contemporary Crises*, vol.12, no.2, pp.91–106.

Jeffreys, S. and Radford, J. (1984) 'Contributory negligence or being a woman? The car rapist case', in Scraton, P. and Gordon, P. (eds) *Causes for Concern*, Harmondsworth, Penguin.

Kinsey, R., Lea, J., and Young, J. (1986) *Losing the Fight Against Crime*, Oxford, Blackwell.

Lea, J. (1987) 'Left realism: a defence', *Contemporary Crises*, vol.11, pp.357–70.

**Lea, J. and Young, J. (1984) *What Is To Be Done About Law and Order?*, Harmondsworth, Penguin. (Extract reprinted as 'Relative deprivation' in Muncie *et al.*, 1996.)**

Lea, J., Jones, T., Woodhouse, T., and Young, J. (1988) *Preventing Crime: The Hilldrop Environmental Improvement Survey: First Report*, Middlesex University, Centre for Criminology.

Lewis, D.A. and Salem, G. (1986) *Fear of Crime: Incivility and the Production of a Social Problem*, New Brunswick, NJ, Transaction.

Loveday, B. (1994) 'Government strategies for community crime prevention programmes in England and Wales: a study in failure?', *International Journal of the Sociology of Law*, vol.22, pp.181–202.

Morley, R., and Mullender, A. (1991) 'Preventing violence against women in the home: feminist dilemmas concerning recent British developments', paper presented to the British Criminology Conference, July.

**Muncie, J. (1996) 'The construction and deconstruction of crime', in Muncie and McLaughlin (1996).**

**Muncie, J. and McLaughlin, E. (eds) (1996) *The Problem of Crime*, London, Sage in association with The Open University.**

**Muncie, J., McLaughlin, E. and Langan, M. (eds) (1996) *Criminological Perspectives: A Reader*, London, Sage in association with The Open University.**

Newman, O. (1972) *Defensible Space*, New York, Macmillan.

Painter, K. (1988) *Lighting and Crime Prevention: The Edmonton Project*, Middlesex Polytechnic, Centre for Criminology.

Poyner, B., Webb, B. and Woodall, R. (1986) *Crime Reduction on Housing Estates: An Evaluation of NACRO's Crime Prevention Programme*, London, Tavistock Institute of Human Relations.

Radford, J. and Stanko, E.A. (1991) 'Violence against women and children: the contradictions of crime control under patriarchy', in Stenson and Cowell (1991).

Reiss, A. (1986) 'Official statistics and survey statistics', in Fattah, E.A. (ed.) *From Crime Policy to Victim Policy*, London, Macmillan.

Rock, P. (1988) 'Crime reduction initiatives on problem estates', in Hope and Shaw (1988b).

Sampson, A., Stubbs, P., Smith, D., Pearson, G. and Blagg, H. (1988) 'Crime, localities and the multi-agency approach', *British Journal of Criminology*, vol.28, pp.478–93.

**Saraga, E. (1996) 'Dangerous places: the family as a site of crime', in Muncie and McLaughlin (1996).**

Sherman, L.W. (1992) *Policing Domestic Violence: Experiments and Dilemmas*, New York, Free Press.

Smith, S. (1986) *Crime, Space and Society*, Cambridge, Cambridge University Press.

Stanko, E.A. (1990) 'When precaution is normal: a feminist critique of crime prevention', in Gelsthorpe, L. and Morris, A. (eds) *Feminist Perspectives in Criminology*, Buckingham, Open University Press.

Stanko, E.A. (1992) Plenary address, Violence Against Women Conference, Manchester, May.

Stenson, K. and Cowell, D. (eds) *The Politics of Crime Control*, London, Sage.

Taylor, I. (1991) *Not Places in Which You'd Linger: Public Transport and Well-Being in Manchester*, University of Salford, Department of Sociology.

Tayside Women's Forum (1988) *Women and Safety: Survey Report,* Dundee, Tayside Regional Council.

Tilley, N. (1992) *Safer Cities and Community Safety Strategies*, Crime Prevention Unit Series, Paper 38, Home Office Police Research Group, London, HMSO.

Tilley, N. (1993) 'Crime prevention and the Safer Cities story', *Howard Journal of Criminal Justice*, vol.32, no.1.

Whiskin, N. (1987) 'Crime prevention: an inter-agency approach at neighbourhood level', in Junger-Tas, J., Rutting, A. and Wilzing, J. (eds) *Crime Control in Local Communities in Europe*, Lochem, J.B. van den Brink.

Willmott, P. (1987) 'Introduction', in Willmott, P. (ed.) *Policing and the Community*, London, Policy Studies Institute.

Willmott, P. and Young, M. (1962) *Family and Kinship in East London*, Harmondsworth, Penguin.

**Young, J. (1986) 'The failure of criminology', in Matthews, R. and Young, J. (eds) *Confronting Crime*, London, Sage. (Extract reprinted in Muncie *et al.*, 1996.)**

Young, J. (1992) 'Ten points of realism', in Young, J. and Matthews, R. (eds) *Rethinking Criminology: The Realist Debate*, London, Sage.

# Acknowledgements

We have made every attempt to obtain permission to reproduce material in this book. Copyright holders of material which has not been acknowledged should contact the Rights Department at The Open University.

Grateful acknowledgement is made to the following sources for permission to reproduce material in this volume:

## Text

**Chapter 2:** Erlichman, J. (1995) 'Riot police thwart animal welfare protest', *The Guardian*, 19 January 1995; Waddington, P. (1993) 'Guns won't protect the police', *The Independent*, 24 October 1993; McGhie, J. (1989) 'Lonely cop who blew the whistle', *The Observer*, 24 September 1989; Campbell, D. (1992) 'Wrongful conviction due to "human error"', *The Guardian*, 17 December 1992; **Chapter 3:** Doran, A. (1993) 'New silks from same top drawer', *Daily Mail*, 10 April 1993; Griffiths, J.A.G. (1991) *The Politics of the Judiciary*, pp.272–3, 327–8, HarperCollins *Publishers* Limited; Brown, C. and Bennetto, J. (1994) 'Howard wants to curtail right to elect trial by jury', *The Independent*, 8 October 1994; Dyer, C. (1992) 'Blacks' jail risk "increased by biased judges"', *The Guardian*, 10 December 1992; Dyer, C. (1994) 'Judges take course in how to remove race bias in court', *The Guardian*, 31 January 1994; Dyer, C. (1994) 'Judges "are resisting race training"', *The Guardian*, 18 February 1994; Travis, A. (1994) 'Courts "lenient toward women"', *The Guardian*, 20 May 1994, pie charts: 'Sentencing adults: percentage males and females sentenced for offences', Home Office, 1992; Lightfoot, L. and Anderson, A. (1995) 'Courts condemn women to tougher sentences than men', *The Sunday Times*, 9 April 1995, © Times Newspapers Ltd, 1995; **Chapter 4:** *Punishment and Social Structure* by Georg Rusche and Otto Kirchheimer. Copyright © 1939 by Columbia University Press. Reprinted with permission of the publisher; **Chapter 5:** Travis, A. (1995) 'Howard under fire as jail total hits record 51,243', *The Guardian*, 17 March 1995; The Rt Hon Justice Woolf and His Honour Judge Stephen Tumim (1991) *Prison Disturbances April 1990*, © Crown Copyright. Reproduced with the permission of the Controller of Her Majesty's Stationery Office; Greig, G. (1995) 'Jails to become hell on earth', *The Sunday Times*, 12 March 1995, © Times Newspapers Limited, 1995; **Chapter 7:** Hetherington, P. and Travis, A. (1994) 'Pounding to a brand new beat', *The Guardian Outlook*, 16–17 April 1994; Pollock, L. (1994) 'Scorned patrol', *The Guardian*, 6 April 1994; Independent Working Group under the Chairmanship of James Morgan (1991) *Safer Communities: The Local Delivery of Crime Prevention Through the Partnership Approach*, August 1991, © Crown Copyright. Reproduced with the permission of the Controller of Her Majesty's Stationery Office.

## Figures

*Figure 2.1: Your Police: The Facts*, May 1993, Association of Chief Police Officers; *Figures 2.2 and 2.3: Helping with Enquiries: Tackling Crime Effectively*, Audit Commission, © 1993 Crown Copyright. Reproduced with the permission of the Controller of Her Majesty's Stationery Office; *Figures 2.4 and 2.6: Report of Her Majesty's Chief Inspector of Constabulary for the Year 1993*, © Crown Copyright. Reproduced with the permission of the Controller of Her Majesty's Stationery Office; *Figure 2.5:* Jones, S. (1986) *Policewomen and Equality: Formal Policy versus Informal Practice*, figure 6.1, Macmillan; *Figure 2.7: Home Office Statistical Bulletin*, 21 June 1995, figure 3, Home Office Research and Statistics Department © Crown Copyright. Reproduced with the permission of the Controller of Her Majesty's Stationery Office; *Figure 2.8:* Finbarr Sheehy, *Guardian Education,* 12 October 1993, p.11; *Figure 4.1:* courtesy of Berkshire Record Office; *Figure 5.1:* adapted from 'The penal estate', *The Guardian*, 8 October 1991; *Figures 5.2 and 5.3: Home Office Statistical Bulletin*, Issue 8/95, 27 April 1995, a publication of the Government Statistical Service, © Crown Copyright. Reproduced with the permission of the Controller of Her Majesty's Stationery Office; *Figure 5.4:* Mathiesen, T. (1990) *Prison on Trial: A Critical Assessment,* figure 1.1, Sage Publications Limited, © Thomas Mathiesen 1990; *Figure 5.5:* Box, S. (1987) *Recession, Crime and Punishment,* figure 5.1, Macmillan Press Ltd.

## Tables

*Tables 1.1 and 1.2:* Palmer, S.H. (1988) *Police and Protest in England and Ireland 1780–1850,* Cambridge University Press; *Table 2.2:* Kirby, T. (1993) 'Five hours of paperwork after a simple arrest', *The Independent,* 25 September 1993; *Table 3.2:* Farrington, D.P. and Morris, A. (1983) 'Sex, sentencing and reconviction', *British Journal of Criminology,* vol.23, no.3, July 1983, Oxford University Press; *Table 4.1:* Cohen, Professor S. (1985) *Visions of Social Control: Crime, Punishment and Classification,* pp.16–17, Polity Press; *Table 5.1: Criminal Justice Digest,* p.19, April 1994, National Association for the Care and Resettlement of Offenders; *Table 7.1:* Tilley, N. (1992) *Safer Cities and Community Safety Strategies,* Police Research Group Crime Prevention Unit Series: Paper No. 38, London, Home Office Police Department, © Crown Copyright. Reproduced with the permission of the Controller of Her Majesty's Stationery Office.

## Photographs / illustrations

*p.11:* courtesy of the Metropolitan Police Museum; *p.13:* by courtesy of the National Portrait Gallery, London; *p.14:* reproduced by permission of the Public Record Office, HO 61/9 June–July 1833 PRO London; *p.15:* Greater Manchester Police Museum; *p.31:* photograph from the January 1991 issue of *Special Beat,* source unknown; *p.32:* courtesy of Cambridge University Library; *p.36:* Hulton-Deutsch/Fox; *p.38 (left):* Bildarchiv Preussischer Kulturbesitz; *p.38 (centre):* Roger-Viollet; *p.38 (right):* courtesy of the Metropolitan Police Museum; *p.55:* reproduced by kind permission of Mrs Warner and of the Estate of Jack Warner. Photograph: BBC Photo Library; *p.57:* courtesy of John Thaw/copyright Central Broadcasting Limited; *p.59:* Pam Isherwood/Format; *p.67:* David Hoffman; *p.68:* Alex MacNaughton; *p.71:* Eamonn McCabe/*The Guardian; p.78:* courtesy of the Press Office, Lancashire Constabulary; *p.84:* David Hoffman; *p.109:* Press Association/Martin Keene; *p.115:* David Hoffman; *p.124:* Press Association; *p.126:* Popperfoto/Reuter; *p.129:* David Hoffman; *p.165:* Plan 22, pages 452–3 in: Report of the Surveyor-General of Prisons ... Pentonville Prison, 1844. British Parliamentary Papers 1844 [594] XXVIII; *p.168:* from the Bentham Papers, University College, London; *p.169 (top):* Mansell Collection; *p.169 (bottom), p.171 and p.183:* from Mayhew, H. and Binney, J. (1862) *The Criminal Prisons of London and Scenes of Prison Life,* London, Griffin Bohn and Company; *p.170:* by courtesy of the National Portrait Gallery, London; *p.175:* Guildhall Library, Corporation of London/photograph by Geremy Butler; *p.178:* courtesy of Berkshire Record Office; *pp.184–5:* courtesy of Somerset Archive and Record Service; *p.204:* Yorkshire Post Newspapers Ltd; *p.209:* Central Office of Information; *p.214:* courtesy of the Press Office, The Prison Service; *p.216 (top):* Mercury Press Agency; *p.216 (bottom):* Denis Thorpe/*The Guardian; p.223:* copyright 1995 Newsweek Inc. All rights reserved. Reprinted by permission. Photograph: Ken Schles/Onyx; *p.234:* Press Association; *p.252:* Chris Steele-Perkins/Magnum; *p.266 and p.277:* Katalin Arkell; *p.274 and p.281:* David Hoffman; *p.275 (top):* copyright 1996 North News and Pictures; *p.275 (bottom):* Press Association; *p.299:* Victim Support; *p.303 and p.309:* Don McPhee/*The Guardian; p.325:* Edinburgh District Council Women's Unit, Zero Tolerance Division/copyright the Estate of Franki Raffles; *p.301:* extracts from leaflets on sexual violence towards women: courtesy of the Greater Manchester Police Authority.

## Cover

Photograph by Nigel Francis. Robert Harding Picture Library.

# Index

Home Office 4
*Crime, Justice and Protecting the Public* (White Paper) 116–18
and the police 22, 40, 42
and the privatization of prisons 233, 234
Home Office Crime Prevention Unit 294–5
Home Secretary
and the judiciary 123
and the police 19, 21, 91, 95, 98–9
and Prison Service accountability 235–6
Hood, R. 133, 135
Hope, T. 308, 313
houses of correction 160–2, 174, 175, 193
Howard, John 162, 163, 164, 166, 169–70, 171–2, 177, 193, 199
Howard, Michael 240, 277–8, 297–8
Hudson, B. 259
hulks (prison ships) 164
humane containment, imprisonment as 213–14
humane containment plus 214
humanitarianism, and penal reform 167, 172–3, 175, 177, 181, 193

Ignatieff, Michael 176–7, 180, 182
impartiality, and the criminal justice system 120–5
incapacitation, punishment as 200, 240
industrial disputes, and the police 22, 23
infanticide, women imprisoned for 146
informalism, and criminal justice 150
institutions, for young offenders 251
instrumental aims of punishment 201
inter-agency juvenile panels 267
interest community 307
intermediate treatment *see* IT
interrogation in the police station 82, 86–91
intuitionism, as objection to privatization 236–8
Ireland, police force 17, 18, 25, 40, 45, 72
Irish immigrants, and the police 27
IT (intermediate treatment) 255, 257, 261, 266
Initiative 267, 268, 273

Jacques, Martin 279, 280
Jefferson, T. 67, 68, 69, 95
judiciary
neutrality of 120–5
and 'race' bias 135, 136
juries 125–8
selection of jurors 125, 127

just deserts principle
in sentencing 140, 213
and youth justice 255
justice
delivery of justice and injustices 114–28
'feminist' concept of 147
formal and substantive 113
group justice model 129
individual justice model 129
'miscarriage of justice' cases 108, 202
'paper' and 'real' 147
and penal policy 199, 218
procedural 123, 125, 129
punitive 264
questions of 108–11
criminal justice 111–14
relational 150
substantive 129
*see also* criminal justice system
justice model of youth justice 261, 268
juvenile prisoners 188–9, 190, 192
*see also* youth justice

Kant, Immanuel 109
Kettle, Martin 258
Kilbrandon Report (1964) 256
King, Michael 285
King, R.D. 206, 213, 214
Kirchheimer, O. 161, 162, 173, 174, 175, 176, 180, 229
Kirkholt Burglary Project 321
Klockars, C.B. 60
Knepper, P. 237

Labour governments
and the 1970s 1–2
and IT (intermediate treatment) 255
and youth crime control 253–4
Labour Party Study Group, *Crime – A Challenge to Us All* (Longford Report) 253, 254
labour in prisons
houses of correction 193
and the Industrial Revolution 173–4, 175, 176
in the nineteenth century 182, 183, 185–6, 187, 192, 193
Lacey, N. 200
law, substantially and formally rational 113
law enforcement
and the discretion of police officers 73
*see also* local law enforcement
law formulation, and the police 82–3
Lea, J. 306
left realist approach to crime 322
legal accountability, of the police 92

legal aid 114
legal reforms, in the 1820s 13
legitimacy
of the police 33, 66
and prison privatization 238–9
of prisons 198, 199, 204–7, 215, 217, 219
Lesbian and Gay Police Association 81
liberal justice lobby, critique of welfarism 260–1
liberalism
disillusioned, and penal reform 172, 180, 181, 193
and imprisonment as punishment 201–2
liberty, and justice 110–11
Lilly, J.R. 237
Livingstone, Ken 276
local law enforcement
and the creation of professional constables 14–15
and the police 14–15, 20–1, 22, 23–4
in the United States 46
and prisons 182
Logan, Charles 234–5, 237
London
Bow Street Runners 12, 41
and the origins of the police 9, 11–13, 12, 18
police organization 40–1
targeting of criminal areas in 27
*see also* Metropolitan Police
London County Council, and the police 20–1
Longford Report, *Crime – A Challenge to Us All* 253, 254

McAdoo, William 46
McConville, M. 88, 133, 187, 236
McIsaac, M. 256
magistrates
and chief constables 211
and the creation of professional constables 15
eighteenth century 10, 11
English 17
increased power of 3
Irish 17
social background 120
and youth justice 257, 265–6, 268
magistrates' courts 5, 120, 124, 125
and minority ethnic groups 131, 133
and women 137, 138, 140, 144
male barbarianism 270–1
male prison population 211, 212
in the United States 224
young black men 228
managerial accountability, and the police 97–100